DEDICATION

*To firemen past and present,
for a century of
dedicated community service*

© The Board of Fire Commissioners of NSW 1984.
This book is copyright under the Berne
Convention. No reproduction without permission.
All rights reserved.

First published in 1984 by
George Allen & Unwin Australia Pty Ltd
8 Napier Street, North Sydney, NSW 2060 Australia

George Allen & Unwin (Publishers) Ltd
Park Lane, Hemel Hempstead, Herts HP2 4TE,
England

Allen & Unwin Inc.
Fifty Cross Street, Winchester, Mass 01890 USA

National Library of Australia
Cataloguing-in-Publication entry:

Adrian, C J (Colin John).
  Fighting fire.

  Bibliography.
  Includes index.
  ISBN 0 86861 569 2.

  1. Fire departments—New
  South Wales—Sydney—History.
  2. Fire Fighters—New South Wales
  —Sydney—History. 3. Sydney
  (NSW)—Fires and fire
  prevention. I. Title.
  363.3′78′099441

Library of Congress Catalog Card
    Number: 84-71331

Designed by Martin Hendry
Set in Palatino by Graphicraft Typesetters Ltd,
    Hong Kong
Printed by Globe Press Pty Ltd, Melbourne

Endpapers: Spectacular action shots of the fire
which completed the demolition of Buckinghams
Department Store, Oxford Street in 1968 (front).
Photographer Ron Berg's split-second timing
produced Australia's most famous fire photograph
(back).
Page 1: Crossed hatchets—symbols of bravery and
courage—adorn the tiled Headquarters fire station
walls
Page 2: Solid brass helmets protected Sydney
firemen for over 80 years until replaced by the
safer, but less inspiring, fibreglass helmets in 1964
This page: General Post Office volunteers pose
proudly at the christening of their engine 'Gazette'

CONTENTS

Foreword 7
Preface 8
Abbreviations 9

1
WE STRIVE TO SAVE
Founding Sydney Fire Services 11

2
STATUTORY AUTHORITY
Constitution, Function and Personality 35

3
WHAT BURNS NEVER RETURNS
Prevention and Protection 57

4
A HOME AWAY FROM HOME
Fire Stations 75

5
A CENTURY OF SERVICE
Firemen From Past to Present 109

6
THE FOURTH ARM OF DEFENCE
Firemen at War 143

7
NEDDIES, COFFEE POTS & FLYING PIGS
Firefighting Equipment 157

8
RED ALERT
Fires and Rescues 191

9
A MILLION DOLLAR SERVICE
The Fire Brigade Today 223

Notes 234
Appendices 237
Bibliography 265
Other Sources 266
Acknowledgements 266
Index 268

FOREWORD

ONE HUNDRED YEARS AGO, THE CITY OF Sydney saw the beginnings of what is today one of the most modern and efficient fire services in the world. During the past century many things have changed, but what has remained constant is the dedication and unswerving commitment to the protection of life and property by the men and women of the NSW Fire Brigades. The Service, from its humble beginnings, has evolved to meet the ever-increasing demand created by our technological advancement, our striving to build structures to accommodate more people and more materials, to make them higher and to fill them with materials more combustible than one might have dreamed of only a few years ago. This, together with the need to sustain our society by the movement of all manner of things by many means of transport, have all combined to make the firefighter's job more perilous, more exacting and more demanding. The Fire Service has met the challenge and enjoys one of the best safety records in the world.

The firefighter's task does not end with simply confronting a blaze and attempting to quell the ferocity of what has often been called man's best friend and worst enemy. Indeed, the proud safety record enjoyed not only in NSW but throughout the country can be attributed in part to the close consultation which takes place between officers of the Fire Service, architects, designers and builders. Such consultation is essential to the process of providing the community with homes, factories, warehouses and office blocks which incorporate the most modern of safety features in their design.

Nonetheless, firefighters daily venture into situations which involve great personal risk. Never has a firefighter been distracted from his duty to save lives and property by the knowledge that he or she might well fall victim to the ravages of this dangerous and demanding occupation. Constantly we hear of the term 'above and beyond the call of duty' being applied to acts performed by men and women who make up the various organisations which daily protect the community. Rarely, however, can we appreciate the stresses and strains encountered by our firefighters.

More recently, our Fire Service has been able to extend its expertise into the area of rescue, working closely with other rescue agencies, a task which requires special skills, a sense of duty to fellow man and little thought of personal safety.

The Fire Service has for the past 100 years rightly enjoyed the admiration and respect of all sections of our community. This recognition is fully justified and has been hard won. But, while our firefighters recognise their duty to us in protecting our friends, our families and our fellow citizens, let us not forget our duty to them. The cornerstone of fire safety lies in prevention, and it behoves each and every citizen of our community to ensure that the risks confronted by our firefighters are minimised by our responsible and careful attitudes in the use of fire.

It is my privilege to be the Minister responsible for the Fire Service in this centenary year. It is a service of which the Government of NSW, I, as Minister, and the people who comprise this great State, are justly proud. On behalf of all who rely so heavily on the protection given by the Fire Brigade, let me congratulate all involved in the firefighting service for 100 years of proud achievement. We can be confident that the next 100 years will see a continuation of the dedication and skills which allow us all to go about our daily business in the comfort of the knowledge that as far as protection from the ravages of fire is concerned, we have the best there is.

PETER ANDERSON
Minister for Police and Emergency Services

Arthur Streeton's *Fireman's Funeral*, 1894. A crowd of over 10 000 lined George Street outside the Town Hall and the Queen Victoria markets site, to witness the funeral procession of Fireman Brown

PREFACE

FROM A HUMBLE BEGINNING LAST CENtury Sydney fire services now embrace 73 fire stations, staffed by more than 2000 firefighters. Prior to the 1884 Act which formally constituted a State government-organised fire service, Sydney's fire protection was provided from the mid–1800s by volunteer and insurance company brigades. In April 1884 the Metropolitan Fire Brigades Board held their first meeting and in July the Brigades became operational, initially with one central fire station supported by 22 volunteer fire companies.

In 1910 the Metropolitan Fire Brigades was replaced by a new statutory body, the Board of Fire Commissioners of NSW, responsible under the Fire Brigades Act for fire service provision in Sydney and all other 'urban' areas of NSW. On the centenary of officially organised fire brigades in Sydney the Board of Fire Commissioners remains the responsible statutory authority, the largest autonomous fire service in the western world, with a yearly expenditure in excess of $100 million.

The size of both Sydney's population (in excess of 3.5 million) and of the authority responsible for fire protection has made the task of documenting the development of the Fire Service a challenging one. It has been impossible to document a personalised history of each and every brigade (although a summary is included in Appendix 4.1). Many personalities and events of local significance have been passed over because of space limitations and the need to focus on Sydney. Nevertheless, examples have been adopted throughout to exemplify the nature of changes in different eras and their expression at the level of the individual/brigade. Similarly, five brigade activities in country centres of NSW have only been included when relevant to Sydney or to the service as a whole.

Partly because of the organisational size of the Board of Fire Commissioners and also because of an assumed interest of most readers in specific aspects of the service, the chapters are organised on a thematic basis. To appreciate the development of the service however, each chapter is organised chronologically with subsections distinguishing significant eras.

To assist readers a list of abbreviations is provided. A detailed list of acknowledgements is also provided elsewhere, but it is appropriate to state here that the writing of *Fighting Fire: A Century of Service* would not have been possible without assistance from a number of individuals and organisations. Members of the Board, especially Kristine Klugman and past President Bill Weston, the Chief Officer and Secretary have given their assistance and encouragement throughout. All staff (both past and present) have extended their cooperation but none more so than the Publicity Section, with Bill Rowlings and his staff meeting my endless requests for aid.

At the Urban Research Unit of the Australian National University, encouragement and advice was forthcoming from Pat Troy, whilst typing and research assistance support was provided by Wanda Dziubinski, Sue Craig, Pamela Denoon and Jan Wells. The publishers George Allen and Unwin, especially publisher John Iremonger, designer Martin Hendry and copy editor Judy Vago, have provided encouragement and an undoubted professionalism throughout the project.

Special thanks is due to firefighters Ray Manser, Steve Woods and Warwick Richardson for information supplied for Chapter 1 and firebuff Brian Blunt for sharing his knowledge of fire appliances. Whilst all errors remain the responsibility of the author, Bill Rowlings, Kristine Klugman and Jan Wells all made invaluable comments during text revisions.

Finally, I am indebted to my wife Ashlyn and young son Tristan for patiently bearing my extended absences from Canberra, and to Nin and Nan for providing an abode during my Sydney sojourns.

COOLING THE FLAME.

ABBREVIATIONS

AAV	assessed annual value
AGL	Australian Gas Light Company
ARP	air raid precautions
BFC	Board of Fire Commissioners of NSW
BFCAR	Board of Fire Commissioners of NSW, *Annual Report*
bhp	brake horsepower
CABA	compressed air breathing apparatus
DCO	Deputy Chief Officer
DO	District Officer
FCO	Fire Control Officer
FD	Fire District
FS	Fire Station
gpm	gallons per minute
IFE	Institution of Fire Engineers
kL/m	kilolitres per minute
km/h	kilometres per hour
kW	kilowatt(s)
L/s	litres per second
LGA	local government area
MFB	Metropolitan Fire Brigade
MFBAR	Metropolitan Fire Brigade, *Annual Report*
mph	miles per hour
MWSDB	Metropolitan Water, Sewerage and Drainage Board
NES	National Emergency Service
NSWFB	New South Wales Fire Brigades
NSWPD	New South Wales Parliamentary Debates
NSWPP	New South Wales Parliamentary Papers
NSWVP	New South Wales Votes and Proceedings
ohv	overhead value
PF	Permanent Fireman(men)
psi	pounds per square inch
R/T	radio/telephone
SO	Station Officer
SUPT	Superintendent
TL	turntable ladders
UAP	United Australia Party
UCV	unimproved capital value
VF	Volunteer Fireman(men)
WT	water tanker
WANS	Women's Auxiliary National Service
WFA	Women's Fire Auxiliary

1

WE STRIVE TO SAVE

Founding Sydney Fire Services

SINCE SETTLED BY GOVERNOR ARTHUR Phillip's First Fleet in 1788, Sydney has faced the terrors of fire. As early as 1792, on a scorching December's day, a grass fire raced through the country around Parramatta and Toongabbie, destroying a house and fencing in the process. During the Colony's first drought in 1797 fire destroyed most of its precious wheat crop. Responding to a despatch from Governor Hunter, the Duke of Portland wrote:

> In order to remedy so alarming an evil in future, it occurs to me that it will be proper to oblige all persons holding farms adjoining to the waste and uncultivated lands to keep plowed up so much thereof, between the cultivated parts and the wastes as shall be

A symbol of steam power—Big Ben—purchased in 1892 and capable of pumping 1000 gpm

Skyscrapers surround the monument on the site of Australia's first church—'The Wattle and Daub'—destroyed by fire in 1798. Seating 500 worshippers the church cost the princely sum of £67.12.11½d

judged to be sufficient to stop the progress of the fire from the latter. It will also be highly proper to take the same precaution with regard to all lands belonging to the Crown, and in addition thereto, to make a wide trench or ditch where the situation will allow of it. (Jervis, 1952:151)

This practical step of firebreaks was not enforced, but Governor Hunter did instigate the first fire regulation in the General Orders of 15 October 1801:

> No person whatever is to set fire to any stubble, without giving his neighbours sufficient notice: and not then, until every person is prepared by having their wheat stacked and secured. Should any person neglect this necessary Regulation, and any property be destroyed thereby, he will on conviction be obliged to make good all losses sustained by such neglect. No persons whatever are to smoke pipes or light fires near any wheat stacks, either public or private. (Reprinted in the *Sydney Gazette*, 1 December 1805)

It appears little heed was taken of the order when first issued, for it was reissued in 1805 after the Wiltshire (Parramatta) Wheatfields were totally destroyed by fire the previous summer.

The earliest building fire of note in the new Colony was the suspected arson of St Phillips Church on 1 October 1798. Built by the Reverend Richard Johnson, Chaplain to the Colony, the church was the first in Australia, its location marked today by a monument in Richard Johnson Place (cnr Hunter, Castlereagh and Bligh Streets). Like all early buildings in the Colony, the slab timber and thatched roof construction was easy prey for fire.

With the proliferation of small, ill-built dwellings in streets which were narrow, crooked and dirty, the setting was ripe for a major conflagration. On 4 December 1803, on a hot and windy afternoon, sparks from a chimney lodged in the thatched roofs of three houses in three separate streets. The houses were rapidly enveloped by flames. With violent shifts in the wind a calamity was avoided only by the prompt action of John Harris and several others who kicked in the walls to smother the flames. Harris and one of the other men were severely burnt on the arms and legs. With three houses and their

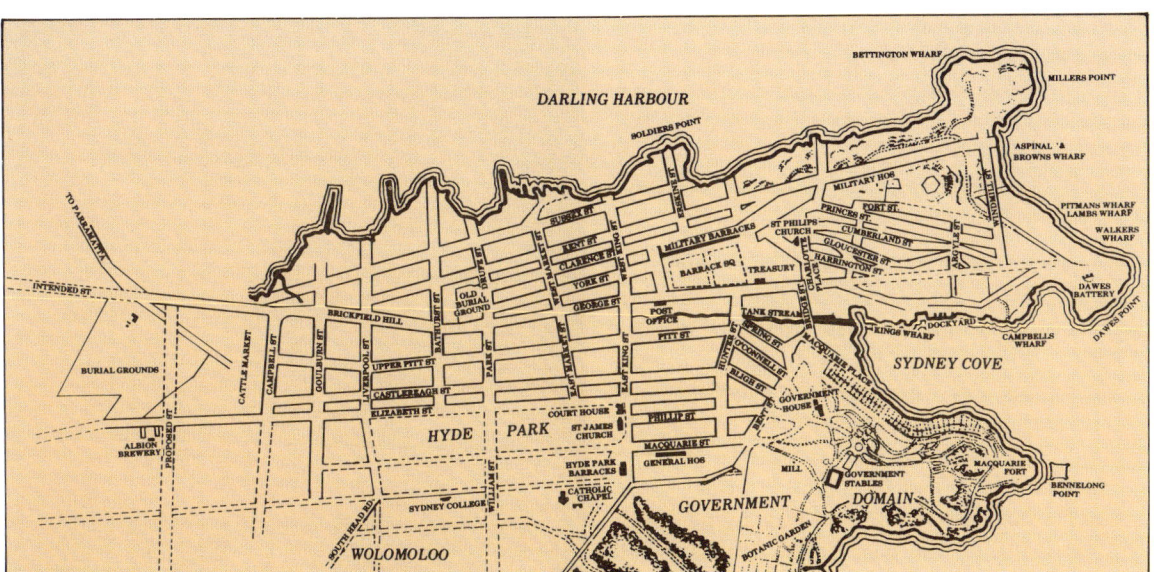

Sydney in 1836—a town of 18 000 people protected by two fire engines housed at the George St Military Barracks

contents destroyed and the lucky escape of a woman and her four-day-old infant, Sydney had been given dramatic warning of the dangers of fire.

On 10 March 1810 the *Sydney Gazette* recorded the Colony's first ship fire when HMS *Dromedary*, a 33-gun frigate, caught fire in Sydney Cove. The cause was never discovered and the ship was only saved by the use of scuttles, pumps and buckets to flood her hold and subdue the flames.

Under the direction of Governor Macquarie, Sydney grew to a population of over 12 000 by 1821. Renamed streets were now laid out in an orderly fashion and a number of fine buildings erected, but fire protection of the bustling township appears to have been limited. In 1805 a Mr Hartley of Chapel Row had lodged the following advertisement on his imminent departure from the Colony: 'A strong Fire Engine, very easy to work and capable of throwing water to a considerable height: it would not only be found extremely useful in any case of accident but be very advantageously employed as an expeditions [sic] conductor' (*Sydney Gazette*, 27 January 1805). Unfortunately there is no record of the engine's purchase or use.[1] The first record of 'fire engines' in the Colony is in January 1822 when two engines 'recently acquired by the Government' were used to extinguish a fire in the Military Barracks. Whilst the evidence of 1822 is unclear it appears from later records that the engines were in fact operated by soldiers from the Barracks in George Street, and housed there in the Ordinance section.[2]

The engines appear to have done little to protect life and property. In a description of the loss of the brig, *Ann Jamison*, and eight lives following a gunpowder explosion, a reporter wrote of 'the fire engines (if we must call them so) arriving on the scene' (*Sydney Herald*, 2 December 1833).

It is probably no coincidence that eight days after the fire aboard the *Ann Jamison*, Governor Bourke requested the Agent for the Colony in London despatch urgently, 'two good fire engines according to the most approved construction' (Colonial Secretary, 1833). In February 1834 tenders were called for the supply of hose and suction pipes for the new fire engines by the Acting Barracks Master at the Military Barracks. However, it was not until 22 October 1835 that the *Sydney Herald* was able to record the arrival of two new fire engines in the town.

By then Sydney, nearly 50 years' old, had grown to a population of some 18 000. Water was supplied both from the Tank Stream and from Busby's Bore, which ran from Lachlan Swamps (Centennial Park) to Hyde Park. Even when completed in 1837 Busby's Bore was totally inadequate for the needs of the growing Colony. Wharf development in Darling Harbour was extensive: the town was laid out to Campbell

Street in the south, in much the same fashion as we know it today. At Pyrmont the first industrial waterfront suburb was being opened up to allow the unloading of timber and coal (Kelly and Crocker, 1978:17).

On 23 November 1837 the *Sydney Gazette* observed:

> A great number of the houses in Sydney ... have lately been insured. The Australian Insurance Company has followed up the plan pursued by the London Insurance Company of placing a small device [firemark] on some conspicuous part of the building. The device adopted by the company is a guild kangaroo, about eight inches high [20.32 cm], with the name of the company and the date of its establishment raised round the border.

To protect the buildings marked, the Australian Insurance Company (established on 1 May 1836) stationed fire buckets, ladders and axes on the premises of Messrs Barker and Hallen in Sussex Street and at Lambs Wharf, Darling Harbour. A brigade of sorts was formed at the Wharf with seven or eight watermen (wharfies) under the charge of 'the boss', Parish, who wore a green coat with a 'kangaroo' on the sleeve.

OUR FIRST BUILDING CODE

A series of building fires in the colony forced Governor Bourke to outlaw the use of bark as a roofing material and to order a supply of slate from England in an endeavour to replace timber roofs. The same year, Sydney's first building code was introduced. In September 1837 an Act 'For Regulating Buildings and Party-Walls and for Preventing Mischiefs by Fire in the town of Sydney' was passed by the Legislative Council (City of Sydney Building Act, 1837). The Act permitted the Police Magistrate to erect 'stopblocks or firecocks' on water mains within any street or pavement. Such firecocks were to be masked and used in the event of a fire. Access was provided by a turn-key and pipe which were to be kept in the house nearest to each firecock.

As an incentive to fire companies the Act provided for 30s ($3) to be paid to the engine-

Firemarks of Australia's earliest fire insurance companies designated which risks were accepted by the fiercely competitive insurance brigades

keeper of the first engine to put 'water on fire', 20s ($2) to the second and 10s ($1) to the third. Such payments were at the discretion of the Police Magistrate.

A concession was also made to the watermen employed by the 'insuring houses'. They were 'free from being impressed or compelled to go to sea to serve as mariners'! (City of Sydney Building Act, 1837:745).

To discourage arson for insurance collection the Act authorised the Governor or Director of an Insurance House to make payouts in suspicious cases only when the money was spent in rebuilding. The Act also allowed for a fine of £100 ($200) or eighteen months' imprisonment for any servant found guilty of negligence or carelessness, 'causing a house to be fired'.

The building section of the Act identified six building classes based on height and number of squares. In each class the Act specified the thickness of external walls and of party-walls. For example, the first class of buildings were those in excess of 31 feet (9.45 m) in height or more than nine squares. In such buildings the party-wall had to be of brick, in excess of 30½ inches (77.47 cm) thickness at the base graduating to at least 13 inches (33 cm) thickness in the top floor (17½ inches (44.45 cm) if abutted by an equally tall building).

The common practice of having timber supports lying through party-walls was also outlawed, and regulations specified the thickness separating chimneys and flues in party-walls to prevent the rapid spread of fire between attached buildings. Precise specifications on the construction of chimneys outlawed the use of timber supports. In 1838, 1839 and 1845 the Act was slightly amended to widen its application.

It appears that soon after the formation of the Australian Insurance Company fire brigade in 1836-37 the Alliance Insurance Company followed suit, for they and the Barracks brigade attended the 'Theatre Royal and Hotel' blaze of 1840. The fire on 18 April 1840 was the largest up to that time in the Colony, killing one person (whose identity was never discovered) and destroying the hotel, theatre, four tenements and stables. Running from George to Pitt streets (between King and Market streets) the 'old Royal', as the theatre was known, and the Royal Hotel, with over 100 rooms, were city landmarks owned by Mr Joseph Wyatt (later lessee of the Victoria Theatre).

The inadequacy of the engines at the fire (with streams able to reach less than one storey in height) and the behaviour of the soldiers, many of whom were caught looting, saw moves by Captain James, the Assistant-Superintendent of Police, to form an 'effectual body of firemen'. Soon after this fire, the engines, hoses and ladders were taken from the Military Barracks to the Police Office yards in George Street, where an engine house was erected.[3] A brigade was formed with an inspector in charge, two sergeants and eight constables. For their 'extra' duties the police/firemen received £2 ($4), £10 ($20) and £8 ($16) per annum, respectively. Their operation appears to have been short-lived, however, because in 1842 the newly founded Sydney Corporation objected to the sum involved, arguing that 'the number of men now under the several insurance companies in the city renders the presence of constables at fires unnecessary otherwise than as protection to property on such occasions' (City of Sydney Archives, 1842-43:576).

These insurance brigades had also been formed as a result of the 'Royal Hotel and Theatre' blaze. In 1841, sixteen businessmen grouped together to form the Mutual Fire Insurance Association (located initially in A Sillitoes, Actuarial Firm, in King Street East). The Association immediately sought the formation of its own brigade and with this in view sent to England for two fire engines and two experienced firemen. In August 1842 the engines arrived, and were housed at the premises of a Mr Beavers, in Pitt Street. Two firemen, Thomas J Bown and Edward Harris, whose passage had been paid by the Association, arrived with the engines. The men were engaged for three years on weekly salaries of £2 5s 0d ($4.50) and £1 15s 0d ($3.50).[4]

Despite the success of the new fire engines, which were recognised as the best in the Colony, the Mutual Fire Insurance Association was wound up in August 1843, having over-extended its risk. Trustees of the Association then approached the City Corporation with an offer of both the engines and the services of Bown and Harris. On 31 January 1844, the appliances were turned over to the Corporation [for £200 ($400)] and Harris and Bown employed under the direction of the City Surveyor.

In April 1844 T J Bown resigned as Principal Fireman and Superintendent of Water Works to

'The Squirt' manual pumper provided the main fire power for the Insurance Companies' Fire Brigade in 1851

pursue his plumbing business at 284–286 George Street, Brickfield Hill.[5] Harris was promoted to Principal Fireman at a salary of 42s ($4.20) per week. It appears that at the same time the Corporation brigade was re-formed at the Police Court yards, with Harris in charge of twelve men, each of whom was trained in firefighting and dressed in Colonial cloth with a distinguishing badge.

The brigade appears to have operated with some efficiency until October 1848, when Harris was suspended for dereliction of duties. His principal duty as Superintendent of the Water Works was to act as a turncock, to draw the fire plugs at various locations for access to the water supply.[6] It was also his responsibility to replace the plugs, a task which he neglected after workmen had done some repairs to the mains, hence allowing water to escape into the street throughout the night. His replacement, Bartholomew McMahon, committed a similar offence in June 1850, and after being found drunk on duty, was 'removed' by the City Corporation.

For some six months after McMahon's dismissal the brigade appears to have ceased to function. Although it was reformed in 1851 the cost of its operation [£107 12s 1d ($215.21) in 1852] was considered to be excessive, and on 10 January 1853, the Corporation decided to wind up the brigade and sell all equipment.

By 1852 Sydney City housed a population of 42 200 and in the surrounding suburbs a further 9700. The Incorporated City was now a major centre of trade, commerce and industry. According to a public inquiry into Sydney's water supply, the only limiting factor to the City's industrial growth was the lack of a pure and regular water flow (Report, 1852). The inquiry recommended that a new water supply be obtained from Botany swamps. However, it was not until 1853, when the City Corporation was dismissed and replaced by three commissioners, that the Botany project was commenced (Clark, 1978:59). The temporary cessation of the Sydney Corporation brigade in 1850, and its inefficiency, appear to have caused the insurance companies to reconsider the closure of their brigade in 1843. The fire risk had increased appreciably and to counteract this risk the Sydney Insurance Company, along with the London and Liverpool, the Alliance and the Imperial Companies, formed an Insurance Companies Fire Brigade (later called the Sydney Fire Establishment). Under the charge of T J Bown, the Brigade operated from Bown's engineering works at Brickfield Hill, firstly with a small engine called 'The Squirt', and, from 1852, with a more powerful engine.

It was the practice of the newly formed Insurance Brigade to attend fires only at those premises with a firemark, signifying they were insured by one of the affiliated companies. The absence of a truly public fire service aroused considerable dissatisfaction. The fire at Tooth and Company's Brewery (Kent Street) in 1853, which burnt for five days, brought home the extent of the City's fire risk. In response, 'A Bill for the formation and regulation of a Fire Brigade and to authorise the destruction of buildings with a view to preventing the extension of fires within the City of Sydney was introduced to the Legislative Council on 10 October 1854. On 3 November the Legislative Council resolved that a Select Committee be formed of eight members, chaired by the Member for Sydney, Henry Parkes, to investigate the Fire Brigades Bill.

The Committee interviewed ten individuals —eight insurance company representatives, the Superintendent of the Insurance Brigade, T J Bown, and the Metropolitan Superintendent of Police, John McLerie. On 24 November 1854 the Committee presented its report. The report concluded that 'the evidence clearly proves that the formation of a Fire Brigade, such as is provided for in this Bill, is a matter of urgent necessity for the safety of the City' (Select Committee, 1854). The Committee also found in favour of the brigade being administered by the Police Authorities, with an inspecting engineer, four engineers and sixteen firemen constables. All favoured a special rate to fund the brigade. The levy of one penny in the pound was to be made on all property in the City according to its assessed annual value (AAV), and was to be collected by the City Commissioners. In addition the insurance companies (as a whole) agreed to contribute £1,000 ($2000) annually towards the expenses of the brigade [which were estimated at £5,480 ($10 960)].

The most contentious issue in the new Bill concerned the proposed powers to demolish buildings in the face of the fire and hence prevent its spread. While the insurance companies did not object to buildings being pulled down, they did object to such damage being treated in the same manner as if the buildings were destroyed. In the case of insured property, the Bill, as written, required Fire Insurance Offices to provide compensation for both fire damage and authorised demolition in the face of fire.

In delivering its report, the Committee agreed with the insurance companies' objection and recommended that: 'provision should be made, by a rate to be levied in the same manner as for the support of the Fire Brigade, to raise a fund for the compensation to all persons whose properties may be destroyed ... by authorised personnel ... to arrest the progress of fire and in cases of great danger' (Select Committee, 1854).

Given the composition of witnesses interviewed by the Select Committee, with its clearly biased representation, the Committee's findings are not surprising. When the Committee's Report went to the Legislative Council, the Fire Brigades Bill, despite its 'urgent necessity for the safety of the City' was not debated further. When reintroduced on 21 June 1855, members could not resolve the question of non-fire property damage. The Bill did not pass the Second Reading but, following the path of its predecessors, was withdrawn.

Sydney's first volunteers—the Victorian Volunteer Fire Company—with a motto of 'We Strive to Save'

Andrew Torning poses proudly with his No. 1 manual 'Pioneer', imported in 1855 for £500

VOLUNTEER BRIGADES

The failure to proceed with the Bill, and the failure of the Insurance Brigade to respond to all fires, prompted the formation of the first organised volunteer brigades. In October 1854 whilst the Bill was before Parliament the following notice appeared: 'Volunteer Fire Company—a meeting of members will take place this evening at 4 pm at the Company's Office Pitt Street' (*Sydney Morning Herald*, 19 October 1854). The notice refers to the Victoria Theatre Fire Company which appears to have been formed soon after the Royal Theatre fire of 1840.

Following the fire the proprietor, Joseph Wyatt, moved to the adjacent Victoria Theatre and purchased an engine. Details of the brigade in the 1840s are sketchy, although the Victoria Theatre engine appeared at a number of fires in these years. One of the actors at the Theatre and also a member of the brigade was Andrew Torning, who on taking over the lease of the theatre in October 1854 called the meeting for the formal constitution of the brigade as the Victoria Volunteer Fire Company No 1.[7]

On 3 March 1855 the brigade, at Torning's expense, imported a new fire engine for £500 ($1000). With the expiration of his lease with the

'The Camb' manual (left), members of No. 2 Volunteer Fire Company and rival brigades

Victoria Theatre, Torning's brigade, under the new name of the Australian Volunteer Fire Company No 1, moved into a new engine house in June 1857.

Only one year prior to the construction of No 1 Volunteer Company's new station, a second brigade (No 2 Volunteer Fire Company) was formed under William Camb, and located in a Government-built station in Phillip Street adjoining the Water Police Court.

Both volunteer brigades operated under a proper constitution and by-laws. Officers consisting of a foreman, a first and second assistant, a secretary, engine keeper; two trustees were elected at Annual General Meetings on 1 January each year. To join, members paid an initiation fee of 10s ($1) and 1s (10c) monthly [or an annual payment to become an honorary member of one guinea ($2.10)]. Other funds were raised from business houses, gratuities, benefit nights (held at the Victoria and Prince of Wales Theatres) and subscriptions from insurance companies. In the case of No 1 Volunteers, over half the cost of the new station of £486 2s 0d ($972.20) was met by insurance companies [the Sydney, £145 ($290); London and Liverpool, £50 ($100); Imperial, £20 ($40); Northern, £15 ($30); Royal, £12.10.1 ($25.01); and the Alliance, £12.10.0 ($25)]. At the same time the insurance companies' Fire Board agreed to subscribe to the brigade £100 ($200) per year commencing on 12 January 1859. Soon after, the first suburban volunteer brigade was established at Parramatta in October 1859.

The 1860s heralded the great suburbanisation of Sydney. Between 1861 and 1871 Sydney's population increased by some 5 per

AUSTRALIA'S OLDEST FIRE STATION

No 1 Volunteer Fire Company—Pitt St, Haymarket

IN 1856 Andrew Torning approached Governor William Denison for a grant of land on which to build a new engine house for the Victoria Volunteer Fire Company. When granted a small block in Pitt Street South (No 477) the Company immediately set about fund raising, holding a number of benefits at the Victoria Theatre.

With further contributions from a number of insurance companies and donations from business houses the cost of £500 ($1000) for a new engine house was raised.

In June 1857 the station built by J Sutherland, and designed by architects Clarke and Downey, was opened. A contemporary newspaper gives the following account:

> The completion of the main portion of the Fire Engine House of the Australian Volunteer Fire Company (No 1) is satisfactory to those residents in the city and suburbs who have carefully [sic] observed the energy and perseverance of the members of both this and the No 2 Company since the initiation of the valuable movement by Mr Andrew Torning six years ago, by importing at his own expense a powerful engine from London at the cost of about £500.00 [$1000]. The new engine house stands on the site of the ground granted by the Governor-General, in Pitt Street South, new [sic] the Haymarket. It is a solid building of brick (30 × 30 [9.14 × 9.14 m]; height, 24 feet [7.32 m]. It is erected on strong arches of ironstone, and is in the Italian style, executed by Alderman Sutherland, from a design by Messrs. Clarke and Downey. The portion now finished includes the engine-room, the watchman's apartment and the belfry, in which is placed an alarm bell weighing 3 cwt [152.4 kg]; and the Governor General, in addition to the original grant has lately granted another piece of ground, 30 × 20 [9.14 × 6.09 m] in the rear of the new building, for the erection of committee room, engineers office, stables etc. . . . Over the doors of the building is placed a large

Australia's oldest purpose—built fire station (1857) still stands today in Pitt St Haymarket

lamp, with stained glass and appropriate ornaments. It is the work of Mr Robinson of George Street. This and the inside banners will be gratuitously supplied with gas by the Australian Gas Light Company when their works near the Haymarket are opened ... The No 1 Company celebrated the opening of their new building by [sic] a dinner on Monday last, to which they invited the members of the No 2 Company ... (*Sydney Morning Herald*, 18 June 1857:6).

Between 1857 and 1885–86 the engine house and the No 1 Volunteers continued to serve the City of Sydney. When the company disbanded the engine remained chained to the floor until the building was sold at public auction to the Australian Gas Light Company on 25 September 1900. Since then the former fire engine house has been modified and used for a variety of purposes, today serving as a gauge and test room for AGL.

An architect's description today, reflects the changes wrought in 126 years:

> The building, which is approximately 6 m × 9 m, is of 340 mm brick in Flemish bond. The Pitt Street elevation, which is rendered, contains a central arched doorway dominated by a large projecting key stone. The facade with its rectangular parapet is decorated in an elementary way with recessed rectangular panels and several projecting string courses. The corners are emphasised by attached piers. The hipped roof is galvanised iron with a central ventilator. Alterations by the Australian Gas Light Company have bricked-in the arched opening, altered the joinery and interior. Nothing appears to remain of the belfry or of additions to the rear to house a caretaker, committee room, engineers office or stables.
>
> There are two interiors. The eastern interior features painted brickwork, and its utilitarian character reflects its functional role—of housing the fire engine.
>
> The ceiling is probably modern and conceals the original raked boarded ceiling.
>
> Separated by a boarded glazed partition is the western interior which may have formed an office for the fire company, or watchman's apartment.
>
> Plastered wall, good quality Victorian joinery, a raked boarded ceiling, a gasolier ceiling rose, and other details convey a comfortable domestic scale. (Howard Tanner and Associates, 1983).

Listed by the National Trust as an historic building the engine house presents a physical reminder of small-scale Sydney in the mid-nineteenth century. It is also a fitting monument to the foundation of volunteer fire brigades in Australia.

cent each year, reaching a population of 138 000 (Kelly and Crocker, 1978). Whilst much of the increase occurred in the City area an increasing proportion took place in Redfern, Glebe, Surry Hills, Woolloomooloo, Darlinghurst, Paddington, Balmain and on the North Shore, at St Leonards (now North Sydney). With growth came an increase in the frequency of fires. On 3 October 1860 the Prince of Wales Theatre was destroyed with three lives lost and on 29 June 1865, St Mary's Cathedral was burnt to the ground.

St Mary's was forty years old at the time of the fire. The destruction of the historic church was so great and swift that a journalist of the day was moved to say: 'No spectacle ever beheld by the city exhibited such fearful grandeur—such magnificent desolation' (quoted in *Sunday Times*, 22 August 1897). Watched by a crowd of over 30 000 the fire completely destroyed the church and its contents [including vestments worth over £1,000 ($2000)]. The Catholic Church seemed fated to be menaced by fire for later, on 5 January 1869, the temporary St Mary's Cathedral was also razed. Whilst a variety of allegations were made concerning incendiarism, no evidence was ever produced as to what caused either fire. Descriptions of both blazes criticised the location of fire plugs and the water pressure. In the latter case only 'one feeble jet was brought to bear on the flames', and it took almost half an hour to find the water plugs and attach a hose of sufficient length. The inadequacy of the City water supply had been fully detailed by a Royal Commission in 1867, which recommended a new scheme based on the Nepean River. Split by dispute and dissension, however, Parliament took no action.

In 1865 Shand, Mason and Company, English manufacturers of fire engines and equipment, exhibited a new steam fire engine at the Dunedin (New Zealand) Inter-Colonial Exhibition. After the Exhibition, the steamer was brought to Sydney and offered to the Insurance Companies Fire Brigade for £900 ($1800). The Brigade agreed to its purchase and at the christening, Miss Emily Bown, daughter of Charles Bown (nephew of T J) delivered these words:

Good Engine—Do thy work.
Be thy motto 'Never fail'

Illustrated Sydney News artist's impression of the destruction of St Mary's Cathedral on 29 June 1865. A temporary replacement suffered a similar fate only four years later

and for thy name I do proclaim
that good word 'Nonpareil'.
(Quoted in *The First century*)

The engine was first put to work, four days before Christmas, at John Hill and Company, furniture dealer in King Street. Despite its satisfactory performance the four-storey furniture factory was totally destroyed.

In the following year No 2 Volunteer Fire Company also acquired a steamer, the *Camb*, paid for by public subscriptions, insurance company contributions and benefit nights. The steamer was housed in the Phillip Street station while the manual appliance was shifted to a branch of the Company established on 4 August 1866, in James Wyatt's premises adjacent to the School of Arts in Pitt Street.

A significant day for both city volunteer companies, was 12 March 1868. On that day, No 1 Volunteer Company received the following dispatch from Government House: Sir—In reply to the address sent by you to H.R.H. the Duke of Edinburgh on behalf of the No 1 Volunteer Fire Company, I am directed to acquaint you, for the information of the members, that his Royal Highness has gladly acceded to their request, and has much pleasure in becoming patron of so useful an institution' (*Empire*, 19 March 1868). It was then moved and carried unanimously that the name of the company be changed to the Royal Alfred Australian Volunteer Fire Company No 1. His Royal Highness was then visiting Sydney and also on that day, whilst he was attending the Sailor's Home Picnic at Clontarf, an assassination attempt was made by a 'ruffian O'Farrell'. The Duke's life was saved by the swift action of a No 2 Volunteer Company fireman, William Vial, who grabbed the assailant and pinned him to the ground. At a benefit night at the Prince of Wales Opera Theatre, Vial's bravery was rewarded by a gold medal:

> On one side bears a well-executed engraving of the steam-engine of No 2 Company, and on the reverse the following inscription: "Presented by the Sydney Volunteer Fire Company to their brother fireman, Mr William Vial, in recognition of the bravery displayed by him at Clontarf on the 12th instant, when, at the risk of his own life, he was the means of preserving that of H.R.H. Prince Alfred, Duke of Edinburgh, (*Sydney Morning Herald*, 25 March 1868)

CONFLICT AND RIVALRY

By the late 1860s relations between the volunteer companies and the Insurance Brigades had deteriorated. The supporters of insurance brigades spoke of the volunteers as disorganised rabble whilst the volunteers accused the Insurance Companies of being motivated solely by profit. The *Sydney Punch* expressed its partisanship in verse:

> OUR VOLUNTEER FIRE BRIGADE
>
> Hurrah! hurrah! for our Fire Brigade
> Of gallant Volunteers,
> By peril or danger ne'er dismay'd,—
> Whose bold hearts spurn all fears!
> When the boding knell of the hoarse fire bell
> Full loudly calls for their aid,
> Then never will lag or was known to flag
> Our Volunteer Fire Brigade!
>
> Where the raging flames shoot toward the sky
> And fire fiends burst their bands;
> When the rafters fall and the windows fly
> And thick dart burning brands,
> Then the fire to quench—from its jaws to wrench
> Whatever may be stay'd,
> They are ever there, to save and to spare;—
> Our Volunteer Brigade!
>
> Full swiftly they hie at duty's call
> (A duty self-impos'd),
> And cheerily labour, one and all,
> Nor reck their lives expos'd.
> And they toil and strain, but 'tis not for gain.
> By hope of which they're sway'd;—
> They earn but renown, and honour's bright crown
> Our Volunteer Brigade!
>
> Oh! shame, foul shame on th' Insurance Brigade
> Who basely toil would shirk,
> And wherever their labours are not paid
> Refuse to aid or work;
> Who to save don't care any building where
> No policy is made;

An artist's impression of the Blackwell Wool Stores fire at Circular Quay in 1870

But 'tis reached then by readier men,
Our Volunteer Brigade! (*Sydney Punch*, 17 July 1869)

The 1870s was heralded by a further increase in the severity and number of fires. On 9 February 1870 Blackwell Wool Stores at Circular Quay, with over £50,000 ($100 000) of stored wool bales, was burnt to the ground. Worse was to follow. On 6 January 1872 the Prince of Wales Opera Theatre (rebuilt after the 1860 tragedy) was engulfed by flame. The report of the blaze indicated its extent and severity:

> Theatre with contents totally destroyed; four houses in King Street crushed by falling of Theatre wall, two considerably injured by the same, seven houses in Brougham place partially destroyed, three houses in Castlereagh Street considerably injured. Flour Mill attached to Theatre on western side totally destroyed, three citizens named, Vaughan, Tost, and Coates, lost their lives by the falling of Theatre wall. [Sydney Fire Establishment (Insurance Brigade), 1872]

The dramatic loss of the Prince of Wales Theatre led to some disquiet as to the adequacy of the water supply and the efficiency of the two volunteer companies and the Insurance Brigade:

> SIR—It has been a matter of general regret in this city that our firemen are periodically seized with a mania for fighting one another rather than combining to suppress our common foe.
>
> The late fire at the Prince of Wales Theatre has been the scene of another series of rows and threats, commingled with the foulest language, playing their stream of water at their rivals rather than at the fire, which was gaining on all sides. I would appeal to your powerful agency in assisting to put down such unseemly conduct in those who ought, by example and courage set a pattern to those around, and show that firemen are something more than mere bullies and cowards.
>
> Truly we are degenerating into the old Yankee volunteer style, when it was usual to knock off at the fire and have a good fight, cutting hose, smashing engines and various other sports . . .
>
> In conclusion, Sir, I assure you that no one more appreciates the spirit that actuates those who, as volunteer firemen, give their services to the citizens, without any pay or even hope of profit, than I do. Not noting the cost of clothes destroyed, time lost, business neglected, and often times pay from their own pockets to meet current expenses incurred. It is not that such services are unappreciated, but a feeling of apathy has arisen soley, caused by the loose manner the whole service is done in being totally disorganised, and ungovernable by any recognised authority.
>
> It is positively stated by gentlemen well qualified to judge, that the fire brigades were perfectly useless at the Prince of Wales Theatre, except at the cottages in Broughamplace, and did not exert any influence on any other part (because the fire had burned all it could get at, for it is a well-known fact that our colonial timber will not burn easily), all arising from a want of mutual understanding and a supreme head to direct their efforts.
>
> I am Sir, yours very respectfully,
> THE GHOST OF THE MAN ON THE ROOF. (*Evening News*, Letter to the Editor, 15 January 1872)

Responses such as these prompted the introduction of a new Fire Brigades Bill into Parliament on 27 November 1872. As with its predecessors, however, the Bill raised a stormy debate in Committee concerning the proposed sweeping powers of the Superintendent and the

---

Members of Sydney's early volunteer companies were justly proud of their community service

THE FOUNDING FATHER
Thomas John Bown (1810–1872)

BORN in Southwark in London, Thomas Bown trained as a plumber and later helped maintain and build fire engine equipment for James Braithwaite, Superintendent (and 'Father') of the London Fire Engine Establishment.

In 1842 Bown arrived in Sydney with his wife of ten years, Sarah, to take up appointment as Principal Fireman and Superintendent of Water Works with the Mutual Insurance Association. After having established a plumbing works in George Street, Brickfield Hill in 1843, Brown resigned his position as fireman in the following year. The firm of T J Bown and Company was listed in the Sands Sydney Commercial Directory as: 'Fire Engine and Pump Manufacturers, Manufacturers and Importers of sundry hardware and equipment/supplies for Plumbers, Gas Fitters, and Brass Finishers'.

In 1851 Bown accepted an approach from a consortium of insurance companies to act as Superintendent of a new Insurance Companies Fire Brigade. The Brigade operated firstly from the Bown premises in George Street and then, from 1864, from the new site of T J Bown and Company in Bathurst Street (opposite St Andrews Cathedral).

As Superintendent of the Insurance Brigade (known as the Sydney Fire Establishment) Bown tried without success to coordinate the activities of all the Sydney brigades. His clash with the volunteer brigades, particularly at the fire scene where each fought to be first to 'put water on the

question of who was liable for damage done by the fire brigade. Eventually passed by the Legislative Council, the Bill was not read to the Assembly before the close of session in 1873.

The Insurance Brigade was now located at 105 Bathurst Street in a two-engine bay fire station originally erected and leased by T J Bown in 1864. The Brigade housed an impressive array of equipment and had an operating budget of some £2,000 ($4000).

By the mid-1870s Sydney's suburban growth was extensive. The Saturday Land Sale was commonplace and subdivisions seemed to arise from nowhere.[8] The suburbs of St Peters, Marrickville, Ashfield, Five Dock, Leichhardt, Balmain, Randwick and Waverley were part of this land boom as large estates were carved up. The City's water supply still came from the totally inadequate Botany Water Supply and it was not until 1879 that work began on the Nepean scheme. It was to be another eight years before the first Nepean water reached Sydney, under the auspices of the newly created Board of Water Supply and Sewerage (Clark, 1978:64).

The rapid growth of the City and suburbs, combined with the procrastination of politicans, saw a rash of new volunteer companies formed. On 8 January 1875, No 3 Volunteer Fire Company was formed by William Hinchy at Barleymow Hotel (cnr Castlereagh and Park Streets) and the following year the Company established a branch station at 91 William Street. On 18 March 1875, a Newtown and Camperdown Volunteer Company was also formed setting an example for other 'suburbs' which were shortly to follow suit and form their own local brigades (Nos 4, 5, 6, Glebe and Woollahra brigades were all formed in the second half of 1875). The equipment and efficiency of these new brigades left much to be desired. The *Sunday Punch* commented on the performance of the newly formed Glebe Company:

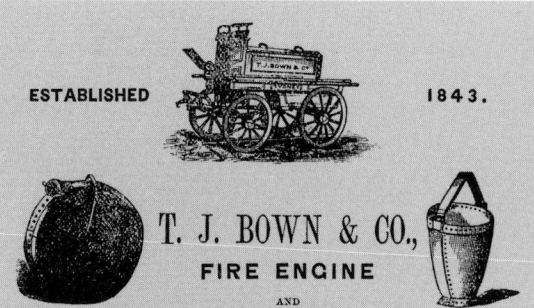

T J Bown & Co.—Sydney's foremost fire engine manufacturer

fire', was widely featured in the press of the day. It was in the 'professionalisation' of the Insurance Brigade that T J Bown was more successful. On his retirement at the end of 1867 the Brigade had twelve full-time firemen, a foreman (his nephew, Charles), assistant foreman (William South), watchman and three engineers. Its equipment consisted of a large steam fire engine (the *Nonpareil*), three manual engines, one hose reel and one hose and ladder carriage.

Bown's skills as an engine-maker within the Colony were unsurpassed: he was awarded first prize for fire engines at the International Colonial Exhibition in Sydney in 1870 and acted as agent for Shand, Mason and Company, London. The success of his company with Showroom, Fire Engine Station (leased to the Sydney Fire Establishment), Brass Foundry and Plumber's shop is further testimony of his organisational skills. In addition Thomas Bown acted as Secretary to the Sydney Fire Establishment and, in the late 1860s, was elected an Alderman on the City Council.

His death on 8 January 1872 did not end his family's influence on the development of Sydney fire brigades, for his nephew Charles Bown was then Superintendent of the Insurance Brigade. The 'Father of the Sydney firemen' was given a full fireman's funeral and was laid to rest at St Peters Cemetery.

DESTRUCTIVE FIRE AT THE GLEBE
BURNING OF A PAPER COLLAR.
Partial destruction of a Neck-tie.
(Not reported in the *Evening News*.)
It is with feelings of the greatest regret that we have to report that shortly after 9 o'clock on Friday night, a most destructive fire broke out in the house of one Michael O'Flannagan, at the Glebe. William Bartle, a jolly young waterman, first saw the flame and gave
The Alarm
to every engine station in the city. Millions of people ran to view the conflagration. M. Flannagan had been to the O'Connell Centenary, and was returning home, when informed of the fire by Dr. Barry. The fireman at one of the stations, on hearing of the fire, caught up a small syringe and immediately commenced playing thereon.
The Premises and Stock
The premises extended from George to Pitt Streets, and were stored with lollipops, paper collars, lucifer matches, lobsters, oysters, and Windsor soap.
The Origin of the Fire
Miss Angelina Flannagan lit a match; the cat mewed; she was frightened and dropped the match, which fell upon a paper collar, and in a moment
A fearful Blaze
illumed the hall of the Flannagans.
Two Thousand Engines
were soon upon the scene, and played their 'jets d'eau' in rapid succession on the burning mass, when
An accident happened to
the Steam Fire-engine,
a bolt in which becoming loose, turned the water in the direction of the gutter instead of on the roof. Three firemen, with unparalelled [*sic*] courage, went up

A Ladder
and then came down again.
The adjoining Premises
were saved, save that three small blister spots were apparent on the paint on the following morning. The whole property
Was Insured
in several fire offices, for far more than it was worth. Amongst the incidents at
The Fire
it may be noted that the captain of the Brigade sneezed, and had no 'pocket-handkerchief to wipe his little nose'; a dog barked; and one courageous individual actually took off his coat and pumped.
The Paper Collar
was consumed, besides one copy of PUNCH, for which the owner had refused
Ten Thousand Pounds
About one o'clock all was over, and as the rosy god arose, no trace of the fire could be seen, save the charred figure of MR PUNCH on the title page of his Journal. (*Sunday Punch*, 20 August 1875)

Their efficiency may have been in question, but there is little doubt that the volunteers enjoyed their pastime. Monthly picnics, cricket matches and torchlight processions kept up morale and gained the public eye. Because many of the volunteer superintendents were also publicans, the processions had frequent stop-overs to quench their thirst (the volunteer firemen's version of the 'pub-crawl'). The result was often an unusual outbreak of minor fires to which the volunteers responded with competitive zeal!

Inadequate water supply and the increased competitiveness amongst the volunteer companies led to more heated disputes over the use of fire plugs. At the Castlemaine Brewery fire in September 1875, the volunteer companies were first on the scene and refused to give way to the more powerful steamers of the Insurance Brigade, and even drew axes to enforce their stand. These actions and resultant publicity resurrected the Fire Brigades Bill, dormant since 1873. A 'Bill to make better provision for the Extinction of Fires' was introduced and on 25 November a Select Committee of the Legislative Council, under Chairman Saul Samuel, was formed to investigate the Bill. The Committee interviewed representatives from the volunteer companies, the insurance companies, the Inspector of Police and City Commissioners. In presenting its Report in April 1876, the Committee recommended that a Superintendent of Brigades be appointed and that 'Parliament should be invited to appropriate annually a sum of money equal to that contributed by the Insurance Companies for that purpose' (Select Committee, 1876). When put before the Legislative Council the President of the House argued on a point of order that the new Bill was a Taxing Bill and hence amendments should originate in the Assembly. Mr Samuel was thus forced to withdraw the Bill and return it again to the Assembly. When read in the Assembly in June 1876, the new Bill aroused heated debate both inside and outside the Chamber. Both Andrew Torning and William Camb (Superintendent of No 2 Volunteers) threatened to resign if the Bill was passed and Charles Bown (T J Bown's nephew) appointed as the new Superintendent. Other volunteers, however, petitioned the Parliament to pass the Bill. The squabbling over the Bill's provisions saw debate adjourned when Parliament recessed in August.

In 1880 a number of brigades, led by the Insurance Brigade, formed the Metropolitan Associated Fire Brigades, holding their first annual meeting in the Temperance Hall, Pitt Street, on 10 January 1881. The following brigades formed the Association: the Insurance Brigade, City Brigade, North City Brigade, St Leonards Brigade, Paddington Brigade, Newtown Brigade, Waterloo and Alexandria Brigade, Surry Hills Brigade and the Hook and Ladder Brigade. With Charles Bown as Superintendent, the Associated Brigades lobbied Parliament extensively and served to intensify popular support for a Fire Brigades Bill. At the same time a United Volunteer Fire Brigade Association was formed by the Nos 1, 2, 3, Wollahra, Glebe, Hudson's and Mount Lachlan brigades, with Mr E Oram appointed Superintendent General. This group sought to act as a strong anti-insurance lobby to counteract the Associated Brigades.

Both groups sought to maximise their influence and standing within the community. The United Volunteer Fire Brigades held a Grand Intercolonial Fire brigade Competition at Prince Alfred Park on the Prince of Wales' Birthday (9 November 1881). Some sixteen visiting brigades attended from Victoria and country areas, as did the city companies. The events included engine practice (four, seven, and eight men), ladder race, steam engine practice, disabled ladder practice and hose reel practice, in a format similar to the Volunteer Demonstrations of today. The Metropolitan Associated Fire Brigades responded with its First Annual Gathering, held at The Garden Palace on 22 March 1882.

In January 1881, the Parkes Government introduced a Fire Brigades Bill to Parliament. The nine-clause Bill proposed a Fire Brigades Board of five members (three from the insurance companies) with the costs of the brigades being met by insurance companies and the Government.

Sir Henry Parkes' lukewarm support for the Bill saw it lapse once again. In September, Parkes replied to an Opposition question regarding the state of the Bill by saying, 'it will probably be introduced within a fortnight'. The fortnight passed without the Bill being brought forward and in January 1882, against strong opposition from the volunteers who demanded representation, the Bill was withdrawn.

THE PALACE BURNS

On 22 September 1882 the most 'costly' fire in the history of the Colony took place. At about 5.40am on a Friday morning, smoke was seen rising from the Garden Palace Exhibition Building in the Botanic Gardens. Within an hour the largely timber building and its contents, valued at more than £500,000 ($1 000 000), was reduced to tons of debris. Opened on 17 September 1879, the Palace was one of Sydney's grandest sights. More than 800 feet (243.84 m) long and with a glass dome 200 feet (60.96 m) in height, the Palace was modelled by the Government Architect on the famous London 'Crystal Palace' building. After the Colonial Exhibition of 1879 the building was used for smaller displays and concerts and as well was occupied by a number of Government departments. Among the contents lost were over 320 paintings valued at £6,000 ($12 000); Railway Construction Branch plans worth £100,000 ($200 000); and the only complete record of the 1868 Population Census.

The cause of the disastrous outbreak was never discovered, but the publicity surrounding the fire led to yet another Fire Brigades Bill being introduced to Parliament. Its reception from the disillusioned insurance companies was hostile: 'Instead of the comprehensive measure which was anticipated as the result of the valuable experience obtained by Sir Henry Parkes in his travels through Europe and America, it proved to be nothing more than a replica of the bill introduced twelve months since' (*Australasian*

The Garden Palace Exhibition Building in the Botanic Gardens (1882). Within an hour Sydney's most dominant landmark, with contents valued at more than £500 000, was razed by fire

WERE OUR EARLY THEATRES JINXED?

THERE is little doubt that theatres—by ill-fortune or deliberate arson—were the most fire-prone establishments in Sydney's early days. Equally unlucky were the theatre owners, who were by law restricted in the size of their insurance coverage.

When the Royal Theatre and Hotel were destroyed in 1840, their owner was Joseph Wyatt. He had recently paid £9,000 ($18 000) for the property but was insured for only £3,000 ($6000—that being the maximum allowable in those fledgling insurance company days). With the loss of his new acquisition and some £6,000 ($12 000), Wyatt took up a lease on the adjacent Victoria Theatre in Pitt Street.

To protect the theatre, Wyatt purchased a small manual fire engine to keep on the premises. Presumably this engine was used to put out a fire in the theatre on 25 September 1844. The fire was the subject of an arson inquest into the role of a former theatre employee, James Bunce. The allegation was made that Bunce, who had recently been dismissed by Wyatt, had placed material, props and costumes under the eaves of the theatre loft and set fire to them. As the evidence against Bunce was circumstantial, the jury found him not guilty and the case was dismissed.

When his lease on the Victoria Theatre was not renewed in 1857, Wyatt bided his time for a further theatre opening. In 1860, after the Prince of Wales Theatre was destroyed, Wyatt decided to rebuild.

Opened on 23 May 1863, the Prince of Wales Theatre cost an estimated £30,000 ($60 000). The opening was a gala affair, with the Governor, Sir John Young, and Lady Young present to see Lyster's famed opera company performing *Martha*. Designed by Mr J F Hilly, the building was the pride of the Colony, with a 'comfortable' seating capacity of more than 900. Luckily for Wyatt, he sold the theatre to the Fitzgerald family—the owners on the fateful morning of 6 January 1872, when the uninsured theatre was consumed by flame with a loss of three lives. The site appears to have been jinxed, for when the theatre was rebuilt as the Royal, it, too, was destroyed by fire in 1892.

The longest-surviving Sydney theatre, after the loss of the Prince of Wales, was the Victoria Theatre, built in 1836. It was saved from flames twice: in 1844 when under Joseph Wyatt and again in 1866 when a large fire was ignited under the stage by an incendiary. However, on 11 July 1880 the old 'Vic', was also totally destroyed by fire. Discovered by four actors after the night's performance, the lavish curtains and drapes were readily consumed by the flames, which had taken hold well before the arrival of the Insurance and volunteer brigades. Whilst a number of the surrounding buildings damaged in the blaze were insured, both the Josephson family who owned the old 'Vic' and James Myer, the caretaker, were uninsured. Total uninsured loss was estimated at £12,000 ($24 000).

Following the inauguration of the Metropolitan Fire Brigades (MFB) in 1884, the number of theatre fires diminished, although the second Theatre Royal was burnt out in 1892, as was Her Majesty's Theatre in 1902. It was after this latter blaze that an Inquiry was held into theatre fire safety, culminating in the Theatre and Public Halls Act (1908), which still forms the basis of public entertainment fire safety codes today.

Saved from fire in 1844 and 1866, the 'Old Vic' Theatre finally succumbed in 1880

Sydney fire brigades 1883. Despite the existence of the Insurance Companies brigade and 22 volunteer fire companies, the metropolis of 225 000 residents had only minimal fire protection

Insurance and Banking Record, 10 November 1882).

With the defeat of the Parkes Government in the election of 1883 the stage was at last set for the passing of a Fire Brigades Bill by the new Stuart Government. Twenty-nine years had passed since the introduction of the first ill-fated Bill—years in which the conflict and jealousy between the volunteers and the insurance company brigades had magnified. These jealousies were to come to a head in the presentation of the 1883 Bill (see Chapter 2).

'If the 1870s can be seen as the decade of estate subdivision, then the 1880s must surely be the decade of the builder. In fact investment in residential building reached boom proportions as existing suburbs were consolidated and new ones created' (Kelly and Croker, 1978:39). The focus of the boom was an intensification of development within existing suburbs. As the Gibbs, Shallard Map of Sydney and Suburbs (1885) shows, the density of streets and buildings had increased appreciably. It was over this metropolis that the opposing volunteer and insurance brigades provided fire protection. Despite the proliferation of volunteer 'suburban' fire companies, Sydney was poorly protected from fire in 1883. The brigades were inadequately equipped, mostly part-time, ill-trained and undisciplined, housed mainly in temporary sheds, and lacking in overall control and direction. As with other basic services such as roads, water, sewerage and lighting, Sydney's fire services were inadequate for the needs of Sydney in the 1880s. A new dimension of size brought on by the 'Long Boom' required a new dimension in thinking.[9] No longer could public services be treated in a cavalier fashion and no longer could the necessity for city-wide co-ordination and funding be ignored.

OUR EARLIEST VOLUNTEER
Andrew Torning (1814–1900)

Artist, set designer, actor and Sydney's first volunteer firefighter! Andrew Torning received notoriety amongst his comrades for his habit of 'trumpeting' commands at the fire scene

ANDREW Torning was born in England on 26 September 1814, and married at eighteen years of age. His wife, Eliza (née Crew), was to become a popular actress, and the couple arrived in Sydney from England with a troupe of actors in 1842. Brought out by Joseph Wyatt, proprietor of the Victoria Theatre, Eliza appeared as the character 'Ernestine' in the play, *Somnambulist*, at the 'Vic' on 27 October 1842. Andrew Torning's starring role appears to have been in the *Barber of Pekin*, performed early in 1845.

Torning's most significant contribution to the theatre, however, was as a set designer, painter and decorator. In 1854 he took over the lease of the Victoria Theatre and set about reorganising the theatre fire brigade. Known as the Victoria Volunteer Fire Company No 1, the brigade operated from the theatre until 1857, and, during its three years there, held a number of benefit nights to raise funds for a new fire station. In June 1857 the station in Pitt Street South (Haymarket) was occupied under the new name of the Australian Volunteer Fire Company No 1, signifying its status as the first organised volunteer brigade in Australia.

In 1858 Torning and his wife visited the United States. In his nine years in the US, Andrew Torning took out American citizenship to enable him to join the San Francisco Fire Department. In 1861 he was joined by his son Thomas (a member of No 1 Volunteer Company), who also joined the San Francisco Fire Department.

Because of his son's ill-health, Torning and his family returned to Australia in 1867. His return was triumphant: a hero's welcome from Nos 1 and 2 Volunteers awaited him at Circular Quay. The welcome was followed by a procession through the city to Bondi, where Torning was re-elected as Superintendent of No 1.

As the founder of the volunteer movement, Torning championed its cause in the bitter clashes with the Insurance Brigade. In the press, in deputations to Parliamentarians and in his public addresses, Torning preached the need for self-financed voluntary and community service, independent of the 'profit motives' of the Insurance Brigade. His opposition to the Insurance Brigade was emphatic and he told a Select Committee Inquiry in 1876 that under no circumstances would he or his company serve

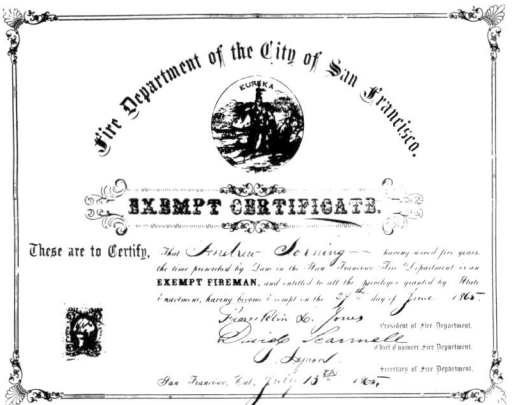

After five years service to the San Francisco Fire Department, Andrew Torning qualified as an 'Exempt Fireman'

under Charles Bown, Superintendent of Insurance Brigade.

Torning also achieved notoriety for his practice of 'bellowing orders' at the fire scene through his trumpet—a practice William Camb (Superintendent of No 2 Volunteer Company) played on amusingly. Following a dispute over who was first on the scene of a Pitt Street fire, Camb scored a point from Torning by stating, 'I shall never rush into print, as Mr Torning has done, in order to trumpet my own praise'. In 1876 Torning resigned as Superintendent. However, he was elected honorary 'Captain' by the No 1 Volunteers. In the following year Torning formed the City's first Hook and Ladder Company.

In the bitter Parliamentary debate over the 1883 Fire Brigades Act it was Torning, along with the newly elected head of the United Volunteers, Mr W S Kelly, who successfully lobbied for a Volunteer Representative on the new Board. Elected to the position, Torning made a last ditch stand to preserve the independence of the volunteers. In this he failed and in 1886 Torning resigned and No 1 Volunteers, along with some of the other volunteer companies, disbanded rather than serve under Charles Bown.

It was a sad end to the career of a man who founded the volunteer movement, and whose traditions and values of community service survive to the present day. In his obituary of 1900, the *Sydney Morning Herald* described Andrew Torning as 'an artist, fireman, pantomimist and humanitarian.

2

STATUTORY AUTHORITY

Constitution, Function and Personality

LIKE ITS PREDECESSORS, THE 1883 FIRE Brigades Bill had detractors. In February 1883 the Bill was presented to the Assembly by the Colonial Secretary, Mr Stuart, and at its second reading drew strong opposition on a number of grounds, foremost being the proposed powers of the new Superintendent described in Clause 9. The Superintendent was to have authority over all brigades present at any fire, including volunteer brigades. Opposition members believed that if the Superintendent was to have such powers, then volunteers should be given representation on the Board. The extent of the Superintendent's powers at the fire scene also raised the hackles of many members. Among other powers, the Bill proposed that the

The Board of 1898 pose in Headquarters' yard with staff, the Big Ben steamer and Sydney's 'oldest' fire engine, 'The Squirt'

Superintendent: 'may take any measures which appear to him necessary or expedient for the protection of life and property and may cause any buildings or tenements to be entered, taken possession of, pulled down or otherwise destroyed for the purpose of extinguishing or preventing the spread of fire' (NSWPD, 1883:663).

Such powers were seen to be unprecedented in the Colony and open to abuse. It was also alleged that such a clause rendered it necessary for all property-holders to insure and was thus explicitly designed in the interests of insurance companies. The issues were not new and in fact had prevented the passing of a Fire Brigades Bill since the first attempt in 1854.

Much debate also took place on the Colonial Secretary's proposal that the Superintendent be appointed from abroad. It was clearly the Government's intention to defuse the strong jealousy existing between the Insurance Brigade, which was lobbying for the appointment of Charles Bown, and the volunteer brigades, which were supporting Mr W S Kelly, Superintendent General of the volunteer brigades.

The dissent concerning the new Bill was such that in April 1883 Mr Stuart requested the Bill be withdrawn for further amendment. When reintroduced in October the only substantive change was the inclusion of a volunteer brigades' representative on the Board, thereby recognising the principle of community service which had characterised the volunteer brigades since 1854. This spirit of service given with minimal monetary reward, set the new statutory Board apart from other statutory authorities established in the late 1800s—a distinction which survives in much the same form to the present day.

Whilst there was little opposition to the new Bill at the second reading on 18 October (40 to 3 in favour), the Bill was sent to Committee where a number of amendments were made, among which was a clause allowing for additional insurance company representation: 'That after the word "companies" there be inserted the words "namely one [representative] by other fire insurance companies whose headquarters are in New South Wales and one [representative] by other fire insurance companies carrying on business within the colony",' (NSWPD, 1883:163).

THE FIRST BOARD
Metropolitan Fire Brigades (1884–1909)

On 24 January 1884 minor Legislative Council amendments were approved by the Assembly and on Thursday, 14 February 1884, the Fire Brigades Bill became law and the Metropolitan Fire Brigades (MFB) a reality (see Appendix 2.1).

Contributions to the Board's finances came from fire insurance companies, municipal councils and the Treasury in equal proportions. Contributions by the insurance companies were calculated on a percentage of the amount they held at risk on fire insurance policies within the metropolitan district, whilst the municipal contribution was based on a pro rata apportionment of the assessed ratable property situated in each municipality.

The six-member Board consisted of a Governor-appointed Chairman (with casting vote), one member elected by the City of Sydney Municipal Council, one by suburban municipalities, two by insurance companies and one by

Liverpool & London & Globe Insurance Company provided insurance representative Mordaunt Clarke on the first Metropolitan Fire Brigades Board

volunteer companies. With the exception of the volunteer representative, the Board reflected the philosophy of the day that those groups which provided the funds should have Board representation and hence control of Board policy.

Given the very similar constitution of the Board today it is perhaps not surprising how little the 1884 Act and its extension state-wide in 1910, has changed.

Following Royal assent, the most pressing concerns were the appointments of the Chairman and Superintendent by the Governor. In March 1884 deputations from both the volunteer brigades and the Associated Fire Brigades approached the Colonial Secretary with their recommendations. There is little doubt that the latter group proved the more influential, as Mr Charles Bown was appointed Chairman on 29 March 1884. There was apparently some confusion for a number of days however, for the popular press consistently referred to the appointment of Mr T J Bown (Charles Bown's uncle) as the new Chairman. With the appointment of Charles Bown the new Board was complete: the elected representatives were Mr William Kippax (representing the City of Sydney), Mr Walter Church (local insurance companies), Mr Mordaunt Clarke (the Liverpool, London and Globe, and other insurance companies), Alderman Richard McCoy (suburban municipalities) and Mr Andrew Torning (volunteer companies) (see Appendix 2.2). The latter election was the closest: Andrew Torning (No 1 Volunteer Company) defeated James Horan (No 2 Volunteer Company) by thirteen votes to eleven with the votes of North City and Surry Hills being declared invalid on the grounds that they were branches of the Hook and Ladder Company. The first meeting of the new Board took place on 16 April at the temporary office established in a house on the corner of the south side of Bridge Street's intersection with Elizabeth Street. The following day the Colonial Secretary announced the appointment of Mr William D Bear, former Engineer and Third officer of the London Metropolitan Fire Brigade, as the new Superintendent. The appointment was based on the strong recommendation of Captain Eyre Massey Shaw, Chief of the London Brigade.

On 4 July 1884 the MFB regulations were presented and approved by Parliament, the most contentious issue being the clause relating to the membership of volunteer brigades, which stated:

'Under no circumstances shall a Licensed Victualler be allowed to remain or be admitted as a member' (MFBAR, 1885:7).

At a meeting of the United Volunteer Fire Brigades the view was expressed that the new regulations were a gross insult to many volunteer companies (with active publican firemen) and had been framed by Superintendent Bear without consultation with the volunteer movement. Despite a threatened strike the regulation stood; but Bear was to prove an embarrassment to the new Board in the months ahead as he pushed to the limit his authority as Superintendent.

In the first *Annual Report* of the new Board, the limitations of the 1884 Act were given detailed consideration and some 33 amendments proposed. The Board also pointed out the inadequacies of the existing Kerosene Act, Gunpowder and Explosives Act and the regulations on 'lofty buildings'. But the Board's earnest requests regarding a reformulation of the Fire Brigades Act fell on deaf ears.

The inadequacies of the Act were not the only difficulties facing the Board in its formative years. In 1886 a vacancy was created on the Board by the failure of the volunteer companies to elect a representative. The failure was based on the requirement of the Act that only registered volunteer companies had a vote. At a meeting of volunteer companies indignation was expressed at this requirement (Torning's brigade being one of those unregistered) and by a vote of fourteen to nine the volunteers decided to ignore correspondence from the Board and formulate their own code of election rules. When the day gazetted for elections (19 March) passed, a five-member Board was formed and for over a year and a half the volunteers were without a representative. Rather than enact the clause allowing for a Governor's appointment, the Government held an extraordinary election on 14 December 1887 at which Edward J Love from Parramatta Volunteer Company was elected.

In 1886 defalcations were discovered in the accounts of the Secretary of the Board, Andrew Bone; subsequently indicted at Quarter Sessions he pleaded guilty and was sentenced to five years' penal servitude. Evidently Bone's demise was no lesson to this successor, William Ager, for in 1890 he absconded to the bush with some £780 ($1560) of the Board's money. Three years later he too was brought to trial and received a two-year sentence (Appendix 2.3).

In 1887 the Board framed further amendments to the Fire Brigades Act and submitted them to the Chief Secretary for ratification. However, as with its 1885 recommendations, no changes were enacted. It was in fact not until 5 September 1900 that 'A Bill to Consolidate and Amend the Law relating to the Prevention and Extinguishing of Fires, for the Protection of Life and Property from Fire; and for the purposes consequent on or incidental to those objects' was submitted to the Legislative Assembly by the Chief Secretary, the Honorable J See. The Bill was a far-sighted departure from the existing Act. It called for the replacement of the elected Fire Brigades Board by three permanent Commissioners, to be appointed by the Governor. The Bill also made provision for the extension of Board authority to Harbour waters and the control of fire floats.

The Bill drew an adverse reaction from funding bodies (particularly the insurance companies), who argued that if they were forced to contribute they should also be entitled to representation. The strong opposition in Parliament and inconsistency with sections of the Harbour Trust Bill saw the Bill withdrawn at the second reading.

In October 1900 a far less radical Bill was introduced. However, the slowness of its passage through Parliament brought the following reaction from the Board in 1901: 'The Board recommends that the Government assume entire control of the Fire Brigades service, appoint a Chief Commissioner and two or three Assistant Commissioners as an administrative body, and give it jurisdiction over the whole State, the cost of maintenance to be borne by the Consolidated Revenue Fund,' (MFBAR, 1901:2). In the light of current (1983–84) inquiries into funding and Board structure. this represents a perceptive stance. It would suggest that the Board of 1901 was happy for the removal of a 'vested interest' Board structure only if responsibility for funding was transferred to the State Government. The Board's wishes were not to be: on 15 September 1902, a totally innocuous Consolidation Bill (Fire Brigades Act 1902, Act No 80) was passed. The Board's reaction was curt and to the point: 'the long-desired thorough amendment of the Act has not been undertaken, nor has Fire Brigade legislation been further advanced' (MFBAR, 1901:2)

The years 1902–07 were relatively uneventful, although in 1905 the first Interstate Fire Brigade Conference was held in Melbourne on 15 March, to negotiate a joint submission to the Federal Postmaster-General for a reduction in Fire Brigade telephone charges. The success of the meeting (and of the submission) saw the Conference initiated as an annual event, with the second held in Sydney on 14 May 1906.

Throughout this period an increasing number of 'country' councils were making application to be covered by the Fire Brigades Act. By 1907 Campbelltown [101 square miles (261.59 km^2)], Richmond [20.5 square miles (53.09 km^2)] and Penrith [13.55 square miles (35.09 km^2)] were all contributing to the Board and operating brigades. Other applications from more distant local governments and a shortfall in the funds of fire brigade boards in country towns convinced the Board to make submissions to Parliament for a Fire Brigades Bill to cover the State as a whole.

The main difficulty faced by local country fire boards was their lack of adequate revenue. As the 1884 Act applied only to the County of Cumberland, insurance companies (and for that matter, local councils) were not bound by law to contribute to country fire boards. Following an earlier decision in 1888 when the Deniliquin Fire Board was found to be improperly constituted, many insurance companies refused to contribute, while in the Newcastle area the local councils were the principal defaulters.

During the period from 1884 to 1909, the lifetime of the Board, it expanded considerably. Expenditure increased from £18,357 ($36 714) to £57,300 ($114 600) (see Appendix 2.4). The insured value of risks rose from £8,977,000 ($17 954 000) in 1872 to £89,971,992 ($179 943 984) by 1909, a risk covered by some 63 insurance companies. This expansion was indicative both of the growth of Sydney and the increased prominence of the property insurance industry. Administratively, the Fire Brigades Board had expanded to include a Secretary/Accountant (Zachary C Barry), a Chief Clerk (Henry M Webb), a clerk and three junior clerks, a storekeeper and messenger (W South). All support services under the Principal Electrician (Edward Smith), the Principal Mechanic (Ephraim Stoneham) and the Storekeeper (J E Peters, JP) were provided by firemen at Headquarters (Castlereagh Street) as part of their duties (the permanent Headquarters staff

THE FIRST CHAIRMAN
Charles (Chas) Bown JP (1836–1918)

THE death of Charles Bown (who retired as Chairman of the Board in 1910) on 20 November 1918 brought to a close an era in Sydney fire services.

Born in London on 21 October 1836, Charles Bown arrived in Sydney in 1857 to work for his uncle, Thomas J Bown. Employed in Thomas's business, plumbers' and gasfitters' supplies and fire-extinguishing requisites, Charles also joined the Insurance Brigade of which his uncle was Superintendent. Promoted to Brigade foreman in his first year, Charles took over as Superintendent at the beginning of 1868 when his uncle departed for England. Following his uncle's death in 1872 Charles Bown became manager of the business, T J Bown and Co., which in 1864 had moved to 101–107 Bathurst Street.

Between 1868 and 1883 Charles Bown remained Superintendent of the Insurance Brigade and was a prime force behind the 1883 Fire Brigades Bill. As first Chairman of the MFB Board (in 1884), Charles Bown was instrumental in drafting the new Board's regulations (many of which remain in force 100 years later). During his period as Chairman (from 1884 to 1909), he never missed a Board meeting!

As foundation Chairman of the new Board of Fire Commissioners of NSW in 1910, Charles Bown was again instrumental in the formation of Board regulations and procedures. Whilst T J Bown is generally recognised as the 'Founder of Fire Services' in Sydney, it was Charles Bown who was the most influential in the formulation of fire service administration and legislation.

The last MFB Board, 1909. Seated (left to right) Alderman W Taylor, G S Arthur, Chas Bown (Chairman), Edward Love (Vice-Chairman), Alderman A Kelly and T M Tinley. Standing in front of 'Big Ben' are Superintendent Alfred Webb and his Deputy, Nicholas Sparks

in 1909 numbered 38). As a consequence, the demarcation between the Secretary, who was the head of all support services, and the Superintendent, as operational head, was far less clear than in today's service.

STATE-WIDE POWERS
The Board of Fire Commissioners of New South Wales

In September 1909 a new Fire Brigades Bill was introduced in Parliament after an abortive attempt the previous year. The Bill proposed the abolition of the Metropolitan Fire Brigades Board and other fire boards in NSW and the placement of fire brigades under one central authority. It was proposed that the new Board be called the Board of Fire Commissioners of New South Wales (BFC) and consist of five members: one each to be elected from country municipal councils, metropolitan councils, fire insurance companies, volunteer fire companies, plus a President, appointed by the Governor. The Bill also proposed that the basis of contributions remain unchanged from that which had existed during the period of the MFB, that is, proportional contributions from insurance companies, municipalities and the NSW Government.

Not surprisingly, it was the questions of representation and funding on which most of the second reading debate was focused. Country members took exception both to the increased charges to be borne by country municipalities and shires and the idea of control from a central Board, resident in Sydney. They further argued that election procedures would ensure four city representatives and only one from the country, with the strong likelihood that monies collected from country pockets would find their way to the city.

When the Bill was sent to Committee on the second reading, a series of amendments were proposed to improve the position of country municipalities and shires. Most were defeated by close votes; for example, an amendment to alter the constitution of the Board to a president and five members, with two from country councils, was defeated by 25 votes to 23.

Two important amendments, however, were passed. First, the stipulation that the maximum contribution by any municipality be one farthing in the pound on the unimproved capital value (UCV) of its land, and that this amount could not be increased without the consent of the Minister and the relevant council. Second, that the Board expend within each fire district an amount approximately equal to 90 per cent of contributions from each district. Both these amendments (with slight alterations) exist to the present day.

Delays through both the Committee and the Legislative Council, where a number of further amendments were made, saw the new Bill delayed until 1 December 1909. Subsequent administrative delays in the election of Board members meant that the new Board was unable to take office until 16 February 1910 (from 1 January until 15 February the new Act was administered by the Chief Secretary, W Wood). The series of delays created an unusual anomaly for the new Board—it had no funds and was not entitled to raise monies from contributors until the year after its constitution! This embarrassing situation arose from the assumption that the Board would be elected in 1909. To fund the new Board the Government advanced £42,000 ($84 000) and passed a short amending Act on 27 August 1910.

A vital aspect of the new legislation was the provision of limited borrowing powers, with Government approval, for the Board. The purpose was to relieve the Government of the responsibility for funding site acquisition and the construction of new stations. This direct control over its own finances, both from loan raising and statutory contributions, put the Board (after the 1910 amendments) into a strong and autonomous role as a statutory body.

The first years of administering the new Act saw a number of difficulties arise. Country brigades were generally inadequately housed and equipped and in many cases the cost of replenishment was far in excess of their contribution. Compounded by the financial stringencies associated with the First World War, the Board was often blamed for the obsolesence of equipment from MFB days. At the same time other councils protested at the increased charges they were forced to bear. In many cases requests from councils for extension of the Fire Brigades Act to their vicinity were rejected by the Board on the grounds that contributions could not sustain a brigade. Stormy protests from the affected councils ensued, and Crookwell, Hillgrove, Wentworth and Wilcannia withdrew

VOLUNTEER RIGHTS
Edward James Love JP (d. 1912)

A VOLUNTEER fireman since the late 1840s, Edward Love made a significant contribution to the respectability of the volunteer movement, being the volunteer representative on the MFB from 1887 to 1909 and on the Board of Fire Commissioners from 1910 until his death on 17 February 1912.

A one-time employee of the Sydney Municipal Council, Love accepted a position as engineer with Parramatta Council, which he held until retirement. An early captain of the Parramatta Volunteer Company, Love devoted a lifetime to the volunteer movement.

With the non-appointment of a volunteer representative to the MFB in 1886 the Government (under strong pressure from insurance lobbyists) contemplated a Board reconstitution. It was largely Love's standing and persuasive arguments which saw the Government maintain the status quo. When the same arguments opposing volunteer firemen representation on the Board resurfaced in 1909, it was again Love who fought for 'volunteer rights'. The Honorable E H Farrar, speaking in the Legislative Council in 1926, stated: 'Had there been no Edward Love at the time [1909] . . . there would have never been any representatives of the partially-paid men on the Board of Fire Commissioners' (NSWPD/LC, 1926:977).

Thus he established a tradition of volunteer representation which remains in 1984. His other legacy was to leave behind a nephew, Victor Trumper, who was to entertain Australian cricket fans for many years.

---

from coverage by the Act. There was only one council which was prepared to take advantage of section 34 of the Act to authorise an increase in the limit of contribution. Whilst unpopular at the time the precedent created by the Shire of Gilgandra was to be used to good effect by many other councils in the years to come.

Bown's retirement at the end of 1911 was accompanied by the appointment of a caretaker President, George Henry Pitt, Secretary of the Department of Audit, whilst a Royal Commission of Inquiry was conducted 'into certain matters in connection with the administration of the Fire Brigades Act'. Conducted by Mr Walter Edmunds, barrister-at-law and acting district court judge, the Inquiry resulted from allegations in Parliament that Board vehicles and men were used in connection with a political election campaign; that rail fares were reimbursed to a Board member who had a free rail pass; and that a member of the Board had a suit paid out of the Board's uniform account.

The Royal Commission, which ran from 21 January until 7 April 1911, received widespread publicity from the press (although it failed to rate a mention in the Board's *Annual Report*). Unfortunately for the long-serving members of the Board (Bown, Love, Taylor and Secretary, Barry) the publicity and evidence from the Inquiry revealed significant (if financially minor) improprieties. Royal Commissioner Edmunds found the Board was deserving of widespread censure for its method of operation: whilst the Board should be commended for implementing the new Act with diligence, the use of Board funds for the purchase of cigars and liquid refreshments, for dinner and theatre parties and for the purchase of private footwear and clothing could not be condoned. He also found that pleasure trips in Board vehicles, use of motor

Foundation members of the Fire Brigades Employees Union, 1911. Standing immediately right of the standard is the first President, Charles Butcher

cars for electioneering and dinner and sherry parties for the Board were immoral. Finally:

> The public exposure which has resulted from Mr Alcock's [Inspector of Public Accounts] inquiry, and the resulting humiliation of gentlemen, who in other respects have done efficient and honorable service for the public, ought to be sufficient to prevent the repetition of such abuses, provided that the safeguard of an effective annual audit of the board's accounts is established. (Royal Commission of Inquiry, 1911)

All Board members survived the Inquiry, but there is no doubt their personal standings were somewhat tarnished, and for Charles Bown it was a sad end to three decades of community service. Following the Inquiry, Frederick Coghlan, former Under Secretary, Chief Secretary's Department, was appointed the new President. His appointment was made under the direction of the Acting Chief Secretary, Frederick Flowers, who was quoted in the *Evening News* as stating: 'I have no hesitation in saying—and I am accepting the full responsibility of it—that as far as the administration is concerned this [the Fire Brigades] is the worst managed service in this Department' (*Evening News*, 1 June 1911).

Flowers was to have some input into the Board's rejuvenation, for in 1914 he was appointed President after the resignation of Frederick Coghlan. It should perhaps be noted that, not coincidentally, other critics of the Board in 1911 were also to gain office in later years. John F Beswick (a former motor officer at Headquarters, Union treasurer and a leading Royal Commission witness in allegations against misuse of Board vehicles) was appointed Volunteer Representative in 1916, whilst Hugh Shedden, Mayor of Newcastle and a strong lobbyist for country interests, was appointed the Country Council Representative in 1913.

On Friday 8 January 1911 a Fire Brigades Employees Union was formed at Trades Hall, with Mr C Butcher elected President and Captain Dakin, Secretary. From its earliest days, when members gave evidence at the Royal Commission, the Union has acted as a major watchdog on Board policy, particularly concerning worker conditions.

With the possibility of war in Europe, the Government failed to authorise Board borrowing, despite repeated requests, until 1914 when it agreed to act as guarantor to a loan of £100,000 ($200 000) with the Australian Mutual Provident Society. In the same year, following the death of Zachary Collis Barry, Henry Mayo Webb (the son of the former Chief Officer, Alfred Webb) took over the position of Board Secretary. In 1919, after strong representation from the Board, borrowing power was raised from £100,000 ($200 000) to £150,000 ($300 000) by the Fire Brigades Amendment Act 1919, which gained assent on 23 December 1919.

The early 1920s were uneventful. In 1925 Edward Harkness was replaced as Board President by the Honorable Thomas Januarius Smith. Smith, who had been appointed by the Lang Government, was a Labor member of the Upper House, and this led to accusations that his appointment was purely political. T J Smith was to hold the position (through governments of a variety of political persuasions) until 1956, creating a record period of Board presidency which stands to the present day.

One of T J Smith's earliest and most publicised endeavours was his promotion of the Fire Brigades Art Union. On 30 June 1926 a spectacular gathering was held at Headquarters in the presence of His Excellency the Governor of New South Wales, Admiral Sir Dudley De Chair, to present cheques totalling £86,711 ($173 422) to various charities. The display was highlighted by a number of historic fire appliances (including replicas of 'engines' from 120 BC made in the Board's workshops and held today by the Fire Museum) and the issue of a special commemorative photo album.

THE ERA OF 'T J'

Board Reconstitution

On 29 January 1927 the Fire Brigades (Amendment) Act (No 4) was given Royal Assent. Initiated by the Colonial Secretary, Mr Lazzarini, in the Lang Labor Ministry, the Act followed similar action of the earlier Railways Bill by bringing about employee Board representation. As such the move exemplified the Lang view that worker representation was a first step to improving worker conditions. Debate within both Houses on the issue of Board representation and funding was heated.

Initially it was the Government's proposal that the reconstituted Board should consist of seven members instead of five, the new representatives being an additional insurance representative and a permanent firemen's representative. Mr Bavin (Leader of the Opposition in the Assembly) summed up the Opposition view to this proposal: 'The effect will be that three members of the board, two of them employees and probably members of the Fire Brigades Association, and one of them Mr Smith, an ex-Labour [sic] member of this House, and an appointee of this Government, will be able to out vote the representatives of the insurance companies which provide half of the cost' (NSWPD, 1926:395). Other Opposition members argued that the idea of employee representation was 'communistic' and that if the insurance companies were 'being called to pay the piper' (refering to the increase from 33⅓ to

The 1926 Headquarters display of Ancient and Modern Fire Appliances (top). In attendance were (above left to right): H M Webb (Secretary), T J Smith (President), Elaine De Chair, Dudley De Chair (Governor of NSW) and F Jackson (Chief Officer)

50 per cent in the insurance contribution), they should 'be able to call the tune'. This view was endorsed by a petition from the insurance companies read to the Legislative Council on 4 November 1926.

When passed to the Legislative Council, the Honourable E H Farrar, former Under Secretary and President of the Board (1915–21), and a member of the Opposition, spoke at length on the Bill. He was particularly averse to the idea of a permanent firemen's representative, whom he argued 'would undermine the authority of the Chief Officer' (NSWPD, 1926:977). In his speech it is clear that it was common knowledge that the likely permanent firemen's representative would be James McNamara, a sacked fireman and then Secretary of the Fire Brigade Employees' Association.[1] The Act was so worded that the firemen's representative did not have to be a permanent fireman, but rather a member of the Association.

Despite strong Legislative Council opposition the new Bill was returned to the Assembly with only two amendments: firstly an eight-member Board, to facilitate two additional insurance representatives (rather than the Government's proposal of one); and secondly, to increase the limit of the Board's borrowing powers to £250,000 ($500 000).

In summary the changes to the constitution of the Board were:

(a) that the Board consist of eight, instead of five, members, with the additional representatives being from the insurance companies (two) and permanent firemen;
(b) that all volunteers (and not simply each brigade) have a vote in the election of the Volunteer Representative on the Board;
(c) that the President be appointed to a full-time position, for a period of five years, with a salary to be determined by the Governor-in-Council;
(d) that the basis of contributions be insurance companies, 50 per cent; local government councils, 25 per cent; and NSW Government, 25 per cent;
(e) that the Board's borrowing power be increased from £150,000 ($300 000) to £250,000 ($500 000); and
(f) that the Board be entitled to make by-laws dealing with fire escapes, fire protection and storage of inflammable material.

In accordance with these provisions the

Driver J S Willis with Board President E H Farrar as passenger delivering the first motorised appliance to Broken Hill in 1917

Honorable Thomas Januarius Smith MLC (who remained silent in the Legislative Council debates), was re-appointed as President at a salary of £750 ($1500), [the Secretary then receiving a salary of £800 ($1600)!]. William Clarke and Edward Haythorpe were elected as the additional insurance company representatives, while as foreshadowed, James McNamara became the first Permanent Firemen's Representative.

The new Act was clearly a victory for the Labor Government and its policy of employee representation. At the same time it represented a blow to the insurance companies which, despite an increase in representation, faced a large increase in their contributions. Indeed, from a contribution of £100,723 ($201 446) in 1926 [6.58 per cent per £100 ($200) of premium income in the Sydney Fire District], their contribution rose to £162,552 ($325 104) [10.43 per cent per £100 ($200) of Sydney FD premiums], whereas the municipal and State Government contributions actually declined.

The reappointment of 'T J' as President was also not without its controversy. Five days after the defeat of Lang by Bavin, the *Sunday Times* ran a feature article which mounted a vitriolic attack on the President—arguing that he had 'the tenacity to carpet the experienced Chief Officer, Mr Jackson', that 'he knew as much about fire-fighting as a child knows about aviation' and 'that his appointment was purely political'. The article called on the new Bavin Ministry to 'dispense with the services of the President, reappoint an Under Secretary from the Chief Secretary's Department, and let the Chief Officer get on with running the brigades' (*Sunday Times*, 23 October 1927). To the credit of T J Smith, the allegations against him were not pursued in the House; Jackson retired in December and Smith survived as both an Opposition member in the Legislative Assembly (until its reconstitution in 1934) and President of the Board.

Whilst 'T J' consolidated his position throughout the 1930s, his rapport with the union movement and the 'Labor' cause lessened. It was the 1938 unrest over working hours (see Chapter 5) that brought the growing resentment between Smith and the Fire Brigade Employees Association to a head. From that time until his retirement in 1956, disputation with the left-wing Association was to reverberate throughout the service.

DISSENT AND DISCONTENT
The Demise of 'T J'

The most pressing Board concern in the years immediately after the Second World War was the increasing cost of the Brigades' operations. In 1945 the Board's aggregate expenditure was £563,724 ($1 127 448)—[£439,880 ($879 760) in the Sydney FD], and by 1949 the figure had risen to £904,820 ($1 809 640)—[£726,820 ($1 453 640) in Sydney FD]. The increased costs were in most part due to the introduction of the 56-hour week and three platoon system in 1945 (see Chapter 6). Despite the closure of 23 fire stations in the Sydney FD (and others at Newcastle), the number of permanent officers and firemen increased from 766 in 1944 to 1012 in 1949. The Board's salary bill had doubled from £338,596 ($677 192) to £668,830 ($1 337 660).

With the Board's borrowing fully extended to its limit of £250,000 ($500 000) and councils unwilling to increase their rate of one farthing (0.25c) in the pound ($2) of UCV, the Board was facing a mounting cost squeeze. In fact, by 1949 the Board found that despite stringent cost

James McNamara (seated behind left) the first Permanent Firemen's Representative on the Board watches as President T J Smith (standing left) presents a cheque for £4270 to St Margaret's Hospital for Women 'Where 1/– a day keeps baby a day'

savings the estimate of revenue would be insufficient to cover expenditure. The President of the Board had for a number of years made representation to his former government colleagues for amendments to the Act and in 1949 the Colonial Secretary, J M Braddeley (Labor), introduced a Fire Brigades (Amendment) Bill to the Legislative Assembly. The Bill proposed three amendments to place the finances of the Board on a sound and viable basis:

(a) an increase immediately in the limit of the Board's borrowing power from £250,000 [$500 000] to £500,000 [$1 000 000];
(b) provision for the Governor to proclaim the maximum rate that may be levied by councils; and
(c) the alteration of the basis of contributions from the ratio of 2:4:2 to 1:6:1; i.e., councils to pay 12.5 per cent, the insurance companies 75 per cent, and the Government 12.5 per cent. (NSWPD, 1949:2363)

Opposition in the House to the proposed Bill was heated with Liberal and Country Party members arguing that the changes represented a severe impost on insurance companies and left the 'door open' for an actual increase in the costs borne by local government. Mr D Clyne (Labor member for King), Chairman of the 1938 Committee of Inquiry into the 'Working Conditions of Firemen', responded: 'We must either have firemen who are over-worked and underpaid, or provide for increased contributions for the management of firefighting services. We cannot have it both ways' (NSWPD, 1949:2372). Despite representation from the insurance companies and further Parliamentary opposition, the (Amendment) Bill was quickly passed to take effect from 1 January 1950.

The effect of the new legislation was to almost treble the insurance company contribution between 1949 and 1956. To partially cover the increased burden the share of premium income for fire service contributions increased from 17.9 to 32.8 per cent. Over the same period the local government contribution increased only marginally with the rate per £100 ($200) of AAV actually declining from 8s 9d ($0.88) to 5s 6¾d ($0.56). It is little wonder that the insurance industry representatives on the Board were the most vocal in demanding that stringent control be maintained over expenditure. It is worth noting that despite these attempts expenditure within the Sydney FD in the 1950s kept pace with the rate of increase in the value of property (as measured by AAV, Appendix 2.4).

Keeping pace, however, was not sufficient. The whole nature of Sydney's urban area and, consequently, the areal distribution of fire risk was in the midst of dramatic change. Low density building development in suburbs such as Bankstown, Parramatta, Sutherland and Ryde was proceeding at an unprecedented rate. As the enforced contributions of councils within these growth areas rose (being based on a percentage of their AAV), so did their demand for better fire protection. Sutherland, with the fastest rate of population growth of any Sydney local government area (LGA), had a threefold increase in its contribution to the Board between 1950 and 1956.

By the mid-1950s strong representations were being made by these fringe councils (particularly Sutherland and Blacktown) for an upgrading of fire protection. At the same time the firemen's association (which now included station officers and had changed its name in 1948 to the Fire Brigade Employees Union) was agitating for a further reduction in working hours and higher wages. The fight against these agitations was led by Board President, T J Smith.

At the Board level T J Smith's principal protagonist was Maurice Stolmack, elected to the Board by the permanent firemen in 1949. Stolmack was the first elected Board member who was also a Board employee: conflicts immediately arose concerning his 'personal interest' in many of the matters being debated at Board meetings. The issue came to a head at a Board meeting on 15 December 1952 when matters concerning employee working conditions were to be discussed. The Chairman of the meeting, T J Smith, immediately requested Mr Stolmack to withdraw, which he did under protest. The section of the By-laws (No 8) which the President utilised, states: 'A member of the Board shall not vote in any matter in which he may be personally interested by way of profit. During the discussion of the matter, the member so interested shall withdraw from the board room unless by the unanimous consent of the members present he be permitted to remain.'

Mr Stolmack immediately sought an injunction against the Board, but the Equity

Court upheld its actions. Stolmack's militancy continued the actions initiated by his predecessor, Sid Jordan, a member of the Communist Party. Jordan, along with Union President Harry Evans and Secretary Jim Lambert (both Labor men), had led the attack on the Board during the 1940s. During this period a bitter antagonism had developed between the left-wing union leaders and the Board President, T J Smith. His last term, begun in 1952, saw the bitterness intensify and permeate every facet of the brigades' operations.

During the 1950s the Union campaigned vigorously for T J's removal from office and the introduction of a 40-hour week. In April 1955 the Fire Brigades Act was amended to provide for an ordinary working week of 40 hours; however, the Industrial Commission ruled that a 48-hour week should be worked with eight hours' compulsory overtime at a time when the Cahill Government was due to go to the polls in December. At the same time the Colonial Secretary, Mr C A Kelly, following strong lobbying from the Union, twice sought the resignation of T J who, in the opinion of many Labor members, had become a political embarrassment. A lengthy interview with T J in the *Daily Telegraph* of 16 November 1955 did little to dampen the friction. T J argued that communist elements within the union were 'out to get him'.

In the final analysis it was the NSW Parliament which resolved the issue of T J's future. The Colonial Secretary of the returned Cahill Government introduced a Fire Brigades (Amendment) Bill to Parliament in August 1956, the principal specifications of which were:

(a) the reconsititution of the Board to consist of five members: the President, one member each from insurance companies, local government, volunteer and permanent firemen;

(b) a retiring age of 65 years for all Board members;

(c) five-year terms of office for all Board members.

T J Smith had been reappointed as President on 1 April 1952 for a five-year term and had turned 65 on 13 January 1955. As the Opposition parties vehemently argued, the legislation was aimed at removing 'T J' from office. Despite denials from the Government benches there is little doubt that this was indeed the aim. In his closing remarks at the Second Reading, Colonial Secretary Kelly stated: 'Let me say quite frankly that if I were asked my opinion I would say that it will be a very good thing when he [T J Smith] does go out' (NSWPD, 1956:1722).

In addition to effectively removing T J, the legislation also removed Mr Hector MacKenzie (the representative of country municipalities and shires) and Mr A H Campbell (the volunteer's representative) both of whom were older than 65. Both were seen as 'anti-Labor' men.

It is worth viewing the years of dissent and discontent in retrospect. Until the 1940s the working conditions of firemen fell well behind those of the community-at-large. Any improvements (for example, a decrease in working hours) always postdated those in the rest of the workforce and were only 'won' under strong opposition from the Board. The intractable stance of the Board on almost all issues served to consolidate a groundswell of popular support for the more radical members of the Union. Once set-in-motion the *esprit de corps* within firemen ranks (similar to that among nurses today) served to spread the view that strike action was necessary to bring about improvements.

Thus at a time when the communist 'red scare' dominated the Australian political scene the firemen's Union was undergoing popular radicalisation. Firemen were no longer prepared

Chief Secretary C A Kelly with Chief Officer Horrie Pye inspect volunteers at the 1962 Wagga Wagga Volunteer Demonstration

THE DOYEN OF PRESIDENTS
Thomas Januarius (T J) Smith (1890–1975)

BORN in Ireland, T J Smith worked his way to Australia aboard the steam tub, the SS *Irishman*, earning £3 15s 0d ($7.50) per month. He was only 22 when he arrived in Sydney in May 1912. After a short time as a shop assistant he headed northwest to Moree and Walgett, where he became a jack-of-all-trades around the shearing sheds. Following a successful stint as an Australian Workers' Union (Western Branch) organiser, he returned to Sydney.

In Sydney T J joined the 'No Conscription' organising committee, fighting tooth-and-nail Prime Minister Billy Hughes' referendum on Conscription. His organising ability and the contacts made during the campaign proved invaluable a year later when he won the seat of King in the Legislative Assembly. Entering Parliament on 24 March 1917 at the age of 27, T J was then one of the youngest-ever State Parliamentarians.

Defeated in the 1920 elections following the move to proportional representation, T J cultivated his real estate interests and at the same time accepted a seat on the executive of the 'radical' Irish Self-Determination League.

In 1922 T J returned to politics, appointed by the Lang Labor Government to the Legislative Council—a position he was to hold until the reconstitution of the Legislative Council in 1934. His long period of service entitled him to retain the title of 'Honourable' for life.

In 1925 T J was offered the then part-time position as President of the Board of Fire Commissioners by his parliamentary colleague and friend, the NSW Chief Secretary, Carlo Lazzarini. He held this position for a record 30 years—through political administrations of both persuasions.

T J was instrumental in the far-reaching changes brought in by the Fire Brigades (Amendment) Act of 1927. His appointment to a full-time position as President (on a salary less than the Board Secretary) coincided with the introduction of the two-platoon system, the introduction of senior fireman rank and the first promotion by examination. T J was popular and a champion of improvements in the working conditions of his growing band of recruits.

Despite the stringencies of the Depression years, morale within the Brigades was high. It was T J's foresight which took the Spanish Civil War as a sign of things to come and the Board embarked on an extensive re-equipment program to combat fires from incendiary bombs.

The bitterness surrounding the 1938 Committee of Inquiry into the working conditions of firemen, caused the harmony within the Brigades to deteriorate. The second half of T J's reign was to prove a bitter battle between a seasoned and stubborn President fighting for Board autonomy and an increasingly militant Union seeking reform.

By the 1950s the feud between T J and the Union had become a personal obsession (on both sides). T J's age and loss of political power were to prove his undoing. After the Cahill Labor Government introduced legislation in August 1955 compelling Board members to retire at 65, T J (who had reached 65 the previous year) was forced to retire on 2 December 1956.

From T J's standpoint it was a sad but honourable defeat. 'A man' said T J Smith 'must not run away... And running away I would be if I resigned...' (*Daily Telegraph*, 16 November 1955).

Perhaps T J's career on the Board is best encapsulated by one of his Union adversaries, Maurice Stolmack: 'Although one of the toughest, T J was without question one of the shrewdest and most talented of all [Presidents]'.

to accept the view that strike action was unacceptable in an essential government service. Indeed the evidence suggests that the intransigence of the Board was in part based on the misconception that the Union would not resort to the industrial leverage of strike action. Ironically, this radicalisation had been partly brought about by the gulf separating the financiers of the Brigades and the firemen themselves. It is only in very recent years that this gulf has been narrowed and much of the bitterness dissipated.

The reconstitution of the Board from eight to five members also drew strong opposition in Parliament, particularly from Country Party members. The removal of a separate country council representative and alteration of voting procedures effectively ended country representation on the Board. Under the proposed legislation the number of votes each council had in the election of the council representatives was proportional to the contributions: less than £100 ($200): one vote; £100–500 ($200–1000): two votes; more than £500: two votes plus an additional vote for each £100 ($200) in excess of £500 ($1000). This dramatically altered the voting ratios (for example, the City of Sydney now had 83 votes compared with its previous 4), and gave city councils 387 votes to 249 for country councils.

Despite the opposition, the amending legislation was passed and only two members of the old Board survived to take office on the five-man Board on 3 December 1956. One was Maurice Stolmack, who continued to represent the permanent firemen, and the other was Leslie Edye Duff, formerly the city council representative, but now the new Government-appointed President.

THE FIVE-MAN BOARD
Harmony Returns—Briefly

Duff immediately set about improving morale within the fire service and improving relations between the Board and its employees. His first task was the renovation of 'Rat's Castle', as the firemen's quarters at Headquarters was less-than-affectionately called. His other plans included the restoration of the Band, the pooling of all the workshops and improvements in recreational amenities at fire stations. In Duff the Government had chosen a

The five-man Board of 1957 (left to right): A H Mallam, M Stolmack, D A Webb (Assistant Secretary), L E Duff (President) W O Wiggins (Secretary), C J Edwards, A E Shaw

man who set out to please everybody—an impossible task, but at least one which soothed many of the Brigades' troubles. His reign was brief, however, for on the morning of Monday, 16 February 1959, Leslie Duff died in Sydney Hospital. The *Wentworth Courier* drew the following profile:

> On Monday, Les Duff, probably the most popular Mayor Woollahra has ever had, died, at the age of 62. President of the NSW Board of Fire Commissioners, Les Duff was that admirable personality, a brilliant administrator and a born sportsman. What he did to get Australia the Olympic Games will always be remembered in athletic circles. Les had managed the Australian team to the Olympics in 1928 to Amsterdam and his interest in boxing and in the sport he shone in at Fort St School, swimming, made him a much demanded man at the Melbourne 1956 Olympic Games.
>
> Les was alderman at Woollahra Council from 1941 to 1956, and he was Mayor in 1954, the year of the Royal visit of Her Majesty the Queen and also in 1948.
>
> His funeral from St Mary's Cathedral on Wednesday, given full Fire Brigade honours and led by a detachment of both the NSW Police and his men at the Fire Brigades, was one of the biggest held in Sydney. For Les Duff was a man who will be well remembered and when he went to take over the Fire Brigades, the loss was Woollahra Council's, for he was universally respected and admired in our district. (*Wentworth Courier*, 17 February 1959)

During Duff's brief period as President, the Fire Brigades Act was amended once, in March 1958. The Amendment aimed to lessen the burden on those 174 insurance companies and 65 firms, contributing an average 31.11 per cent of their premium income to the Board. Under the Amendment, insurance companies with motor vehicle and household insurance policies covering fire risk were for the first time required to contribute. The net effect of the legislation was an increase of 40 contributing insurance companies and a reduction in the average contribution to 17.22 per cent of assessable premium income. It was the first legislative concession to 'fire insurance interests' since before the war.

On 4 April 1958 after protracted negotiations the Board of Fire Commissioners became responsible for fire protection in the Australian Capital Territory. The former staff of the Canberra Brigade was augmented by four officers and 26 firemen from the NSWFB, led by Inspector C Holdom. Although the NSWFB provided men and expertise, all costs were borne by the Commonwealth Government. The arrangement was to last until the creation of the autonomous Australian Capital Territory Fire Brigade in 1974.

Benjamin Andrews, the new President, took office on 9 March 1959. From the Chief Secretary's office, Andrews had a working knowledge of fire services, having been executive officer of the New South Wales Bush Fire Committee. He took over a fire service of 4500 employees (including volunteers) with an administrative staff of 70. The upper echelons of the administrative staff included:

Secretary: Mr W O Wiggins
Assistant Secretary: Mr D A Webb
Accountant: Mr N G Hinchcliffe
Industrial Officer: Mr R T Gosling
Stores Officer: Mr R Blanchard
Property Officer: Mr G M Butler
Paymaster: Mr C James
Architect: Mr F A Ross (retired 1959 and replaced by Mr A Cunningham)

It is perhaps significant that during the reign of Benjamin Andrews (1959–65) industrial disputation was minimal. On 29 January 1965 he retired as President to be replaced on 28 June by Leonard George Verrills.

In 1967 a most unusual Board appointment took place. John Francis Ford, an alderman of Randwick Municipal Council, was elected to the Board in the stead of Alderman Edward Shaw (who had served in the position for eleven years). In addition to being an alderman, John Ford was also a Superintendent in the Board's employ. This meant the five-man Board consisted (potentially at least) of a three to two voting block in favour of 'employee interests'.

At a Board meeting on 23 August 1967 this potential coalition of interests was put to the test. At an earlier Board Finance meeting of three of the Board members (President, insurance representative and volunteer representative), a recommendation was passed for an appeal against the decision of a Conciliation Commissioner concerning a new award. When brought to the full Board meeting of 23 August, Jack Bennetts (Permanent Firemen's representative) sought details of the legal advice on which the Finance Committee's recommendations was made. The President, Verrills, refused to give such information unless an assurance was given that it would not be passed on to the Fire Brigade Employees' Union. Mr Bennetts' reply was that he could not make such an undertaking. When put to the vote the Finance Committee's recommendations were adopted three to two (with Mr Bennetts and Mr Ford dissenting). The President's power held, with the volunteer representative, V A Riley, voting to adopt the Finance Committee's recommendations.

At the recommendation of the Union, Jack Bennetts contested the issue in the Equity Court, arguing that the Board was not entitled to refuse to produce details of the legal opinion. In his judgment Mr Justice Street rejected the appeal, arguing that the over-riding duty of a Board member was not to the group who elected him, but rather to the Board and the interests of the public as a whole. While the judgment was widely praised by similarly constituted statutory Boards it was also widely condemned by the union movement.

Despite the judgment of Justice Street, there is little doubt that in many cases the interests of the electing group have been a primary concern of Board members. Equally, the constitution of the Board itself has been a primary concern of the political parties. The potential voting situation which had arisen in the five-man Board prompted the Chief Secretary of the Liberal–Country Party coalition to introduce a Fire

FAMILY TRADITIONS
Henry Mayo Webb (1880–1964) and Derek Alan Webb (1914–)

THE eldest son of Chief Officer Alfred Webb (see Chapter 5), Henry Mayo Webb spent his childhood in and around Headquarters fire station. On 1 July 1900 at the age of twenty, he joined the MFB in the first intake of auxiliary firemen. His stay was short, however, and in 1901 he went wool-classing, spending a number of years in the outback.

Returning to Sydney he was appointed clerk in the administration section of the MFB. Having served as Second Clerk, he was appointed Chief Clerk (Paymaster) in 1909 and in 1914, on the death of Zachary Barry, Henry Mayo Webb was appointed Board Secretary. In the same year his son, Derek, was born. Henry's reign as Board Secretary was to last 31 years—a record that is unsurpassed.

In 1932 Derek joined his father's staff as a junior clerk with a yearly salary of £92 12s 10d ($185.29). Amongst his early duties was report writing for the later Deputy Chief Officer, W Beare (who had joined as an auxiliary with Henry Webb in 1900). When Henry Mayo Webb retired on 31 January 1945, Derek Webb was still a clerk; eleven years later he had reached the position of Assistant Secretary to Bill Wiggins.

Henry Webb (left) and Derek Webb (right)

On 8 November 1963 Derek Alan Webb was appointed Secretary, a position he held until retirement in 1975.

The Webb family connection with Sydney fire services is unique. From 1888 until 1975, Alfred, his son Henry, and Henry's son, Derek, all rose to the highest echelon in either the firefighting or administrative sides of the service.

Brigades (Amendment) Bill to Parliament in 1970. The Bill received assent on 26 March 1970, and introduced the following amendments to the Fire Brigades Act:

(a) The Board was enlarged from five to seven members to comprise—
  (i) A full-time President appointed by the Governor.
  (ii) A Deputy President appointed by the Governor (new position).
  (iii) One member elected by the municipalities and shires to which the Act applies.
  (iv) Two members elected by Insurance Companies (formerly one member).
  (v) Two members elected by employees—one by volunteer firemen and one by permanent officers and firemen.
(b) The Board may deal with personal property (not being leasehold property) without the consent of the Minister.
(c) Limitation on the Board's borrowing powers is removed.
(d) The President of the Board is the Executive Officer of the Board. (BFCAR, 1970:8)

As with previous Fire Brigade (Amendment) Bills reconstituting the Board, the Parliamentary debate was bitter. For the first time in the post-war era the Liberal–Country coalition had 'the numbers'. The Chief Secretary, Eric Willis, argued that two government appointees were necessary to further the public interest and that two insurance industry representatives were in accord with the substantial financial contribution they made to the Brigades. The Labor Opposition, lead by the member for Maroubra, Bill Haigh, suggested that insurance companies had 'wielded the whip' and that the legislation was designed to further weaken the minority position of firefighters on the Board.

A $100 MILLION SERVICE
The Modern Era

The early 1970s saw a growing conflict between the seven-member Board and employees. Resentment between the Board President and the Fire Brigade Employees Union over manning and pay peaked in 1976. The growing climate of discontent, particularly over staffing of the new Alexandria complex, saw direct approaches from the Fire Brigade Employees Union to the Minister for Services, Mr Ron Mulock (Labor). With a Labor Government now in office, the Union was of the opinion that direct lobbying could further its case. In December 1976 the Board was informed by the Minister that he proposed to establish a Committee of Inquiry and that it was the Government's intention to bring the Board under Ministerial control.

The Board's response was as follows:

(a) The Board could not agree to the establishment of the Committee of Inquiry, as proposed. The Board would not be acting properly or legally in passing to such a Committee its statutory responsibility as laid down under the Fire Brigades Act;

(b) whilst the Board would at all times be prepared to discuss with the Minister, and seriously consider opinions he may care to express on any matter affecting the fire service, it could not undertake, in the absence of legal powers vested in him, to accept directions from him contrary to the Board's views on what it should properly do;

(c) when Parliament amends the Fire Brigades Act providing for ministerial control, the Board would accept any directions from the Minister consistent with the powers given to him by Parliament. (BFCAR, 1876:35)

Despite the strong stance taken by the Board it was effectively powerless to prevent the proposed Government actions. In March 1977 the new Minister for Services, Haigh, introduced a Fire Brigades (Amendment) Bill to Parliament, with the following provisions:

(a) to bring the Board of Fire Commissioners of New South Wales under the control and direction of the Minister;

(b) to require an insurance company that is required to pay a contribution to the fund established under the Fire Brigades Act, 1909, in respect of a year commencing on 1st January to make payments based on premiums received by or due to it during the year ending on the preceding 30th June, instead of the year ending on the preceding 31st December;

(c) to require an insurance company referred to in paragraph (b) to furnish a return as to premiums paid in respect of the period

Chief Officer William Henry Beare received the awards (top, left to right) of: Kings Fire Service Medal; King George V and Queen Mary Silver Jubilee Medal; King George VI and Queen Elizabeth Coronation Medal; Thirty years long service medal and bar. Alderman John Clement Beare (left), his son William Henry (right) and his son in turn, William Robert (centre) gave 90 years of service to the States fire brigades

1st January, 1977, to 30th June, 1977, and thereafter in respect of each year ending 30th June; and

(d) to enable the Minister to fix the remuneration, including travelling and subsistence allowances, payable to members of the Appeal Committee constituted under section 40A of the Fire Brigades Act, 1909, instead of the expenses and fees payable being prescribed by regulation. (BFCAR, 1977:13)

The principal amendment recommended in the new Bill was that in exercising its functions, the Board would be subject in all respects to the control and direction of the Minister. Despite strong opposition in the House by Liberal Party leader Peter Coleman, the Act was passed and given assent on 13 April 1977. The following month the Minister for Services announced formally that a Committee of Inquiry was to be conducted into the operations of the NSW Fire Brigades. The three-man committee consisted of Mr K Parkinson, then manager of the Govern-

90 YEARS OF SERVICE
John Clement BEARE (1832–1902)—Board representative
William Henry BEARE (1884–1965)—Chief Officer
William Robert BEARE (1922–   )—Secretary

BILL Beare's retirement as Secretary on 16 July 1982 brought to an end 90 years of service by the Beare family to Sydney fire brigades. It was the younger Bill Beare's grandfather, John Clement Beare, who began the family tradition in 1890, when he was elected as the City of Sydney representative on the MFB. A tram driver, Alderman John Beare served a term of ten years on the Board. For his nineteen years of continuous service as Alderman in Fitzroy Ward (1881–99), reclaimed land at Elizabeth Bay was dedicated as Beare Park on 25 September 1909.

The youngest son of John Clement Beare, William Henry aspired to be a fireman from the days when he followed his father to view the city's major fires. In opposition to his mother's wishes for him to enter the clergy, William Henry Beare joined the MFB in 1900 with the first intake of auxiliary firemen. On a salary of 15s ($1.50) per week, William Henry learnt the rudiments of firefighting whilst assisting in the workshops. In 1904 he became a probationary fireman with a salary of £106 ($212) per year and later the same year married. By 1918 William Beare had reached the rank of sub-station officer with one of his tasks being to represent firemen on the Police, Ambulance and Fire Brigades Art Union Committee. On 19 February 1922 William and Ethel Beare (née Jones) had their sixth child and first son, William Robert, who was born in their married quarters above Annandale Fire Station.

By 1926 William Henry had reached the rank of station officer and two years later was appointed District Officer in charge of education at Headquarters. His early task was the educating of many an 'old hand' for the new senior fireman's exam. William Henry worked progressively through the senior officer ranks, and was appointed Deputy Chief in 1936 and Chief Officer on 27 September 1944, a position he held until retirement in December 1947.

By the time of his father's retirement William Robert Beare was established as the Board's fire records clerk, having joined in 1940 (although serving in the RAAF during the war). The younger Bill Beare was to establish a history of service on the administrative side to match that of his father on the firefighting side. In 1958 he became Assistant Paymaster, four years later, Assistant Industrial Officer and in 1968, Industrial Officer.

As Volunteer Demonstrations Secretary (1960–68), Bill's cheerfulness and friendliness endeared him to thousands throughout the State's volunteer brigades. In August 1974 he reached the pinnacle of the administrative side of the service when he was appointed Secretary, a position he held for eight years.

The record of the Beare family speaks for itself, although it would not be complete without mentioning their favourite pastime, lawn bowls. Like father, like son—both Bill Beares have promoted the Brigades' sporting teams, particularly lawn bowls. It should go without saying that Bill jnr's contribution to the first Bowls Club Committee in the 1950s was as Secretary, and today he is patron of the NSW Fire Brigades Bowling Club, reformed in 1982.

A UNIQUE RECORD
John F Ford (1914–   )

WHEN born on 7 November 1914 the third John Francis Ford had a formidable fire brigade record to live up to. His grandfather (John F Ford, 1857–1943) had joined the MFB in the first intake of 1 July 1884 and had risen to the rank of Third Officer.

Leaving school during the Great Depression, John Ford enrolled in the intake of six cadets to the NSW Fire Brigades in February 1932 (working a 40–hour week). At 21 he was appointed a Fourth Class fireman, working an 84–hour week.

In 1936 and 1937 John Ford toured as a breakaway with the victorious Fire Brigades Rugby teams. His skills were not only on the football field however: in his senior fireman's exam in 1945 he topped later Chief Officer Charles Milledge by seven marks. He was one of the first NSWFB firemen to qualify as Graduate and in 1953 Member, of the Institute of Fire Engineers.

In 1958 whilst serving as District Officer (DO) at No 13 Waterloo, John Ford rescued a woman in a house fire at Redfern and was later awarded the Royal Shipwreck Relief and Humane Society's Bronze medal and Certificate of Merit. In 1962, whilst still a DO, John Ford was elected Alderman to Randwick Council (under Mayor W Haigh, later Minister for Services). In his capacity as alderman, Ford was elected as the local councils' representative on the Board in 1967 (whilst still in the Board's employ as a Superintendent).

In 1968 John Ford lost his seat in local government and was automatically ineligible for Board membership. However, on regaining his seat in 1971 he served three years on the Sydney County Council. In 1973, one year prior to his retirement from the NSWFB, John Ford was awarded the Queen's Fire Service Medal.

John Francis Ford's contribution to the fire service was not yet complete. In 1977 he was elected as Deputy President of the Board, holding the position until his retirement in 1979. Leaving the Board, John Ford returned to local politics and was elected Mayor of Randwick in 1980.

John Francis Ford (the third) has achieved a unique record of community service in local government and fire brigade affairs.

---

ment Stores Department; Mr J Meeve, a former Deputy-Chief Officer of the NSW Fire Brigades; and Mr F Bryce, Secretary of the NSW Fire Brigade Employees Union.

The Liberal Opposition reacted angrily to the proposed Inquiry and, in particular, its membership. In the House of Assembly in June 1977 the Liberal leader attacked the 'extraordinary state of affairs': 'Mr Bryce is the main accuser and this Government has turned the accuser into judge. The accuser will be required to adjudicate on his own accusations against the board. That is the sort of inquiry that this Government has committed itself to in a cowardly acquiescence in the demands of a union executive' (NSWPD, 1977:6446). The Board President also strongly opposed the Inquiry, publicly attacking the Government over the Inquiry's constitution. With the Board now under Ministerial control such open opposition had only one possible outcome. Under strong pressure from the Government, Leonard Verrills retired as Board President on 3 July 1977, after 12 years' service in the position.

The new President was William Weston, former Deputy Commissioner of the Department of Corrective Services. His appointment closely followed that of Deputy Board President, John Ford, in February 1977. The new Board, on 13 July 1977, agreed to assist the Inquiry, providing a comprehensive statement of the Brigades' organisational history, status and role, functions, policy, constitution and structure, staffing, plant and equipment, staff training and development, special services and, importantly, the major problems facing the Board. Indeed, when the Committee of Inquiry report was presented to the Minister in November 1978, many of its 113 recommendations were already in the process of being implemented. The changed nature of the relationship between the Board and the Minister is reflected in the fact that the Board was empowered to consider the Inquiry's recommendations and to make decisions concerning the appropriateness of implementation.

In his reign as Board President from 1977–83, Bill Weston made a number of major changes to the operation of the NSWFB. Whilst many are discussed elsewhere in this book, particularly in Chapter 9, they closely match the list of initiatives documented during the Brigades' first-ever management seminar in December 1982. Significant were the:

- establishment of the Staff Training and Development Division
- establishment of the Breathing Apparatus Section
- provision of the Computerised Control Centre (Alexandria)
- conception of new services complex and completion of Stage 1
- establishment of Bush Fire Hazard Reduction Section
- creation of additional Deputy Chief Officer position
- creation of position of Manager (Technical Services)
- acceptance of rescue responsibility
- appointment of Media Liaison Officer
- introduction of rescue monitors and hydraulic platforms
- personal issue of breathing apparatus for firefighting staff
- provision of protective clothing for firefighting personnel
- reintroduction of Fire Brigade Band
- attendance of Chief Officer at all Board meetings

The initiatives reflect an attempt by Weston to forge a new era; one of innovation, modern management and fresh ideas. In the words of Chief Officer Rex Threlfo, 'During his presidency, he endeavoured to take the fire service out of the 19th century and into the 20th century'. Critical to the organisational change which has taken place is the input of new management techniques, including both outside appointments to senior positions and advice from consultancy bodies. The consultancy bodies cover public relations, equal employment opportunities, management training and records control.

A fundamental change introduced during Weston's term in office was an amendment to the Fire Brigades Act in 1979. Amongst other alterations, the new Bill gave the Board explicit powers to engage in both preventive burning in areas prone to bush fires and the rescue of persons and property even where there is no fire or no immediate threat of fire. It is in the area of an expanded rescue role that the Brigade has undergone its most recent transformation (see Chapters 3 and 9).

The modernisation of fire service equipment, escalating pay rates and the general rate of inflation have seen the cost of Brigades operations rise appreciably since the early 1970s. From a total expenditure of $12.2m in 1970 the Board's estimate for 1984 is a staggering $107.7m, the first year the estimates have exceeded $100m. The proportional contribution of the three contributing bodies has remained unchanged since the Act was amended in 1949, but as discussed earlier, the burden has varied enormously over this period. During the 1960s insurance companies and local councils contributed at a relatively low rate on their respective incomes. Insurance companies consistently paid less than 20 per cent of their premium income whilst local councils contributed under 20c per $100 of AAV (Appendix 2.4) until the early 1970s. More recently insurance companies have contributed an increasing proportion of their premium income, reaching 32.6 per cent in 1982. It is for this reason that insurance companies have become more vocal (as they did in the 1950s) in their calls for a reformulation of fire service funding (see Chapter 9).

The most recent change to the Board, following the retirement of Bill Weston, has been the appointment of the Board of Fire Commissioner's twelfth President, Phil Gallagher, on 17 October 1983. It is under his presidency that the Sydney fire services move into their second century.

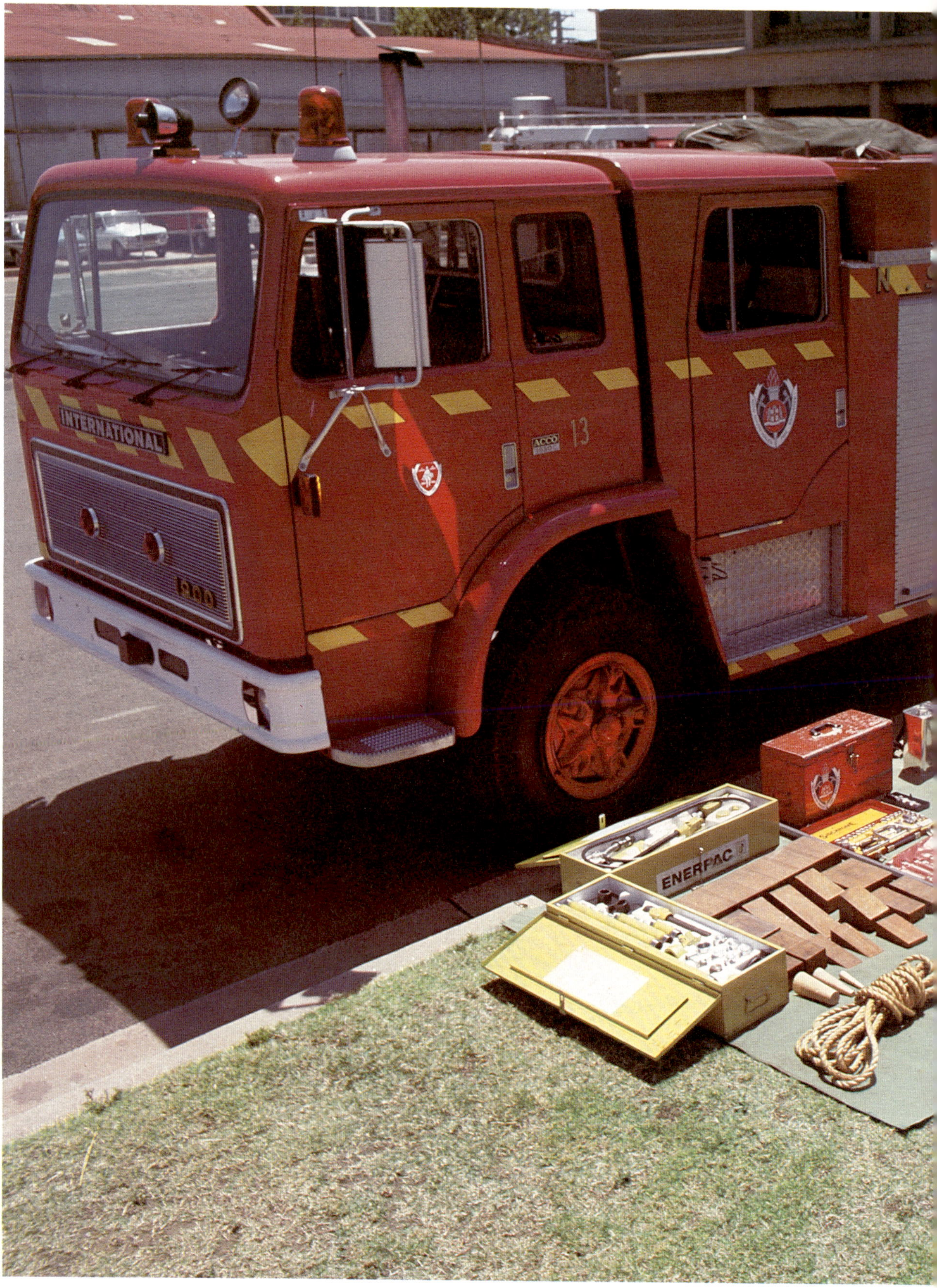
INTERNATIONAL
13
ENERPAC

3

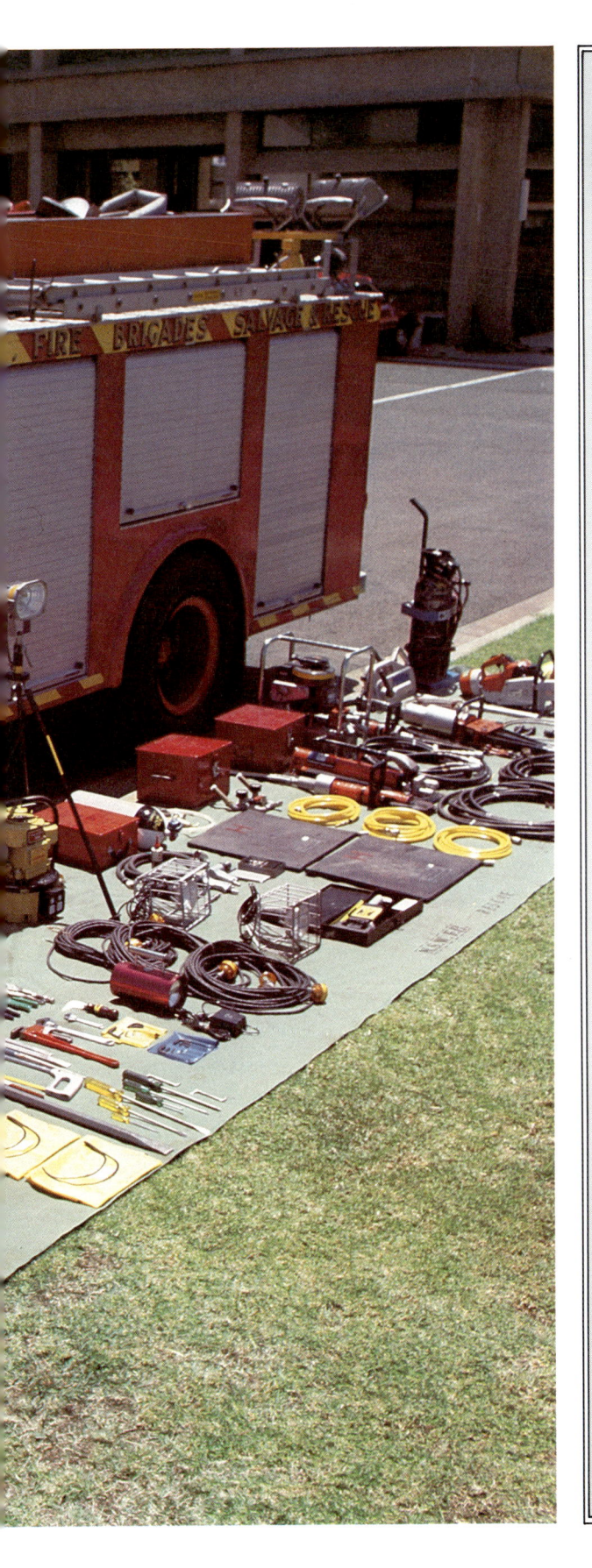

WHAT BURNS NEVER RETURNS

Prevention and Protection

ON 24 JANUARY 1884 THE METROPOlitan Fire Brigades Act, 'An Act to make better provision for the protection of Life and Property from Fire and for other purposes', was passed by the NSW Parliament. As remarkable as it seems today, the Act, despite its title, gave no legislative power to the MFB for fire protection. Nor had the MFB been given any powers of administration or inspection under such earlier Acts as the Kerosene Act (1871), the Gunpowder and Explosives Act (1876), the City of Sydney Improvement Act (1879) and the City of Sydney Building Act (1837).

From the reports issued by the Board in the 1880s it is clear that its members were deeply concerned about the inadequacy of the existing

Modern rescue equipment displayed beside the International Salvage motor

An early telephone fire alarm and the first Headquarters' switchboard—rudimentary—but essential elements of fire protection in Sydney prior to 1910

legislation. Nonetheless its recommendations for substantial amendments to the Act had fallen on deaf ears (Chapter 2).

RUDIMENTARY LEGISLATION

One incident in the late 1880s typifies the Board's lack of power. A consignment of 50 000 cases of American oil with a flashing point below 100°F (37.8°C) was condemned in Brisbane and forwarded to Sydney at a reduced price. The dangerous oil was then stored at Towns' Wharf, within 50 feet (15.24 m) of shipping and other warehouses containing combustible material. A Kerosene Act restriction that kerosene oil be stored more than 50 feet from any building occupied by other persons was easily circumvented by the same lessees securing buildings in the vicinity. On attempting to inspect the consignment Superintendent Bear found that the only authorised inspector was the Kerosene Inspector from the Government Analytical Department, who was 'away in the country'.

The Board at the same time pointed out the inadequacies of legislation on fire protection in tall buildings, stating: 'The Modern Sydney Warehouse, looming up 100 feet [30.48 m] in the air, with its enormous cubic capacity, in some instances ten times that allowed in other cities, its shafts for lifts, gas-engines, and other modern developments to aid the fire fiend, is beyond the capacity of any fire department to protect', (MFBAR, 1884:3). As revealed by the death of First Class Fireman Fisher in 1886 (see Chapter 4) many buildings violated existing building codes, which in any event were poorly constituted and unenforceable. Most insurance companies simply refused to have anything to do with such properties.

The Board's only success in its protestations to the Government was the appointment of Superintendent Bear as Kerosene Inspector in 1886, following the disastrous Jones' Kerosene Bond fire in Melbourne during the previous December. Bear's appointment, however, did not prevent two destructive kerosene fires, one at Miller's Point in 1890 and another, two years later, at Waterloo.

On a more positive front, two revolutionary changes were taking place in fire prevention technology. In 1882 a telephone system introduced to Sydney provided a significant improvement in fire reporting. It replaced the existing

A turncock outside Chatswood pumping station c. 1895. The services of Water Board staff to ensure maximum water pressure during fire emergencies is as essential to the Brigades today as it was then

system of fire reporting by large fire bells and messengers on foot. Later that same year the Insurance Brigade at Bathurst Street became the 105th telephone connection with the GPO Exchange; by 1884 there were nineteen connections from Headquarters to volunteer stations, wharves and public buildings.

In January 1890, thirty telephone fire alarms, imported from America, were installed on telegraph poles at city corners (the first at the corner of George and Park Streets). When these alarms replaced the bell-type alarm introduced in 1885, Sydney became the first city in the world to install telephone fire alarms. The alarms, connected to the 200-shutter exchange at Headquarters, were operable by keys given to the police, public bodies and nearby residents, or by breaking a small glass panel.

In the previous year, the newly created Water and Sewerage Board agreed to begin replacing the old-fashioned fire plugs in the City with some 1500 screw-down hydrants and in the suburbs with ball-hydrants. Following the disastrous Great Fire of 1890 (see Chapter 8), the program of fire plug replacement was also accompanied by the gradual replacement of three-inch (7.62 cm) and four-inch (10.16 cm) water mains in the City by six-inch (15.24 cm) mains installed at a greater depth to avoid fracture in the case of falling walls. By 1892 the last of the fire plugs was removed from the City. Their replacement also saw the end of the practice of paying turncocks to be present at

Headquarters, ready to travel to the fire scene with the Brigade.

The Kerosene Act was amended in 1895 increasing the minimum flashing point to 110°F (43.3°C). However, attempts by the Board to bring a Bill before Parliament to 'Amend and Consolidate the Law relating to the Keeping, Selling and Conveyance of Inflammable Liquids' were unsuccessful. In almost all its attempts to improve fire prevention regulations the Board was thwarted by the powerful political lobby of property and business interests.

In 1898 the MFB adopted its first smoke helmet, the Vajen Bader from the United States of America. Weighing about 7lbs (3.18 kg) and made of leather coated in a fire-resisting solution, the helmet had a small air cylinder attached which contained ten minutes of compressed air. Later the MFB added a Denarouze model with a 60-foot (18.29 m) line of flexible tubing through which the wearer inhaled clean air. In 1909 the MFB also had 'MFB Pattern' and 'German Pattern' helmets, based on the Denarouze model but with voice communication.

By the turn of the century the Brigades' inspectional duties had increased dramatically, covering 4000 hydrant inspections, 900 telephone inspections and 198 building inspections. Under the Shop and Factories Act (1896), the Superintendent (now Alfred Webb) also visited numerous factories giving advice on fire safety. Because of his inspectional duties the Board successfully sought the release in 1901 of Superintendent Webb from his time-consuming task as Kerosene Inspector.[1] They also approached the metropolitan transit authorities to amend traffic regulations and give 'priority to the Fire Brigade when proceeding to a fire'. By now there were 190 telephone alarm connections, covering 165 miles (265.65 km), to 19 fire stations (36 to Headquarters, which had just installed a new telephone switchboard).

The introduction of the electric tramway system to Sydney on 8 December 1899 concerned the Board, especially when it was extended along Castlereagh Street in 1901. The Board believed that the trolley wires were an impediment to the operation of rescue ladders when fighting fires. The wires caused a continual dropping of shutters which activated the alarms, necessitating significant alterations to the telephone fire alarm system.

The years 1901 and 1903 saw two disastrous fires which were to have a significant influence on fire safety legislation. The tragic Anthony Horderns fire of 1901 resulted in lengthy public and political debate over building regulations. In 1904 the Board approached the Government 'for legislation to limit the height of buildings to 90 feet [27.43 m], exclusive of architectural features; and to have outside fire-escapes and balconies provided upon every building higher than 60 feet [18.29 m] from the pavement, (MFBAR, 1904:3).

The legislative response was slow and it was not until 1908 that a Select Committee was

Resembling the grotesque masks of Greek tragedies, early smoke helmets (below) and the Vajen Bader and Denarouze smoke helmets (right) used by the Metropolitan Fire Brigades

The Headquarters' switchboard from 1909 to 1970. Constructed by principal electrician Edward Smith, the switchboard occupies a special 'communications' room at the Fire Service Museum

appointed, under Chairman J M Creed, MLC, 'to inquire as to the dangers to which Sydney and its suburbs are liable from fire, and as to what means of control or prevention would be practicable for the future'. The Committee's report, submitted in December 1908, reiterated much of the Board's argument during its 24-year history! One novel recommendation sought an independent system of mains in the heart of the City through which sea water could be pumped for fire-extinguishing purposes.

Following the Her Majesty's Theatre fire of 1902 and the horrific Chicago Iroquois Theatre fire of 1903 (in which 600 lives were lost), the Government set up a Sub-Committee in January 1904 to investigate theatre fire safety. The Sub-Committee, which consisted of Acting Superintendent Sparks, the Assistant Government Architect, the City Building Surveyor and the Inspector of Theatres, delivered its report on 8 November 1905.

As a result 'The Theatres and Public Halls Act' was passed on 8 December 1908. When it came into operation the following year, 247 theatres and public halls were registered, requiring inspection by the incoming Chief Officer of the new Board of Fire Commissioners. In the same year, four 'special service staff' were appointed to inspect fire protection equipment in Commonwealth and State government buildings.

In 1909 the telephone exchange at Headquarters was moved from the front watchroom (because of tram noise and vibration) to

Headquarters' Control Room c. 1930. From this room Brigade staff serviced all emergency calls and automatic fire alarms

the former billiard room. At the same time a new switchboard, built and designed by the Board's first Principal Electrician, Edward Smith, was installed. Constructed of colonial rosewood, cedar and Tasmanian blackwood, the switchboard was described as the finest in Australasia. One section serviced the three types of automatic fire alarms: the Grinnell, the Kirkby thermostatic alarms and the May-Oatway system. The Grinnell system was first installed in Sydney in 1889 by the partnership of Russell and Wormald which gained the Australian agency. It provided both an automatic alarm and sprinkler system, activated when a temperature of 100°F (37.8°C) was reached. The Grinnell system had been patented by Frederick Grinnell of Providence, Rhode Island (USA) in 1882 and its first Australian installation was in Melbourne in 1886 (Marryatt, 1971). The May-Oatway thermal alarm was introduced into Sydney in 1909 when it was installed at Angus and Robertson's, the offices of the *Daily Telegraph, Evening News, Sydney Morning Herald* and G Johnston and Sons. It was described at the time as the 'magic fire alarm'.

ENLIGHTENMENT
A New Era

In contrast to its predecessor, the Fire Brigades Act (1909) provided an explicit recognition of the need for fire prevention. Section 19 (1) of the Act states: 'It shall be the duty of the board to take all practicable measures for preventing and extinguishing fires and protecting and saving life and property in case of fire . . .' (Fire Brigades Act 1909:15). The Act also provided the Board with powers to make by-

A CARPENTRY WIZARD
Edward Smith (1863–1930)

BORN in the Shetland Islands, Edward Smith arrived in Sydney in 1875 at the age of twelve. During the voyage he learnt the rudiments of ship carpentry. On 7 May 1891 he joined the MFB as a fireman, rising to the rank of Station Officer in 1902. At the beginning of 1905 he was appointed the Brigades' first principal electrician. Awarded a long-service medal in 1906 and bar in 1921, he also received the King's Police Medal in 1925. A Justice of the Peace, Edward Smith rose to the highest echelons of NSW Masonry: in 1929 he received a commission as Knight Grand Cross, the first time the honour was bestowed outside the British Isles.

On 13 November 1928 Smith retired and went on long-service leave to his homeland, where he died two years later. He is best remembered within the Brigades for his design and supervision of the Headquarters switchboard, now exhibited at the Fire Museum. Installed in 1909 this masterpiece of electrical and carpentry wizardry served as the Brigades' communication heart until 1969. Whilst many would argue it was an error, perhaps some of Smith's character is contained in the switchboard's carved facade, where a five-leaf clover sits among others of the four-leaf variety. Until its replacement the extra leaf was used to test the observational powers of new recruits.

---

laws prohibiting or regulating the lighting of fires and reinforced the powers of the Chief Officer. The general powers of the Chief Officer in relation to fire prevention were threefold:

> [he] may at any time enter any theatre, hall, building, or place, used for the purpose of public entertainment or public concourse, to ascertain whether the provisions of any Act, ordinances, regulations, or by-laws for the prevention of fire or for the safety of the public have been contravened or have not been complied with; . . . [he] may at any time enter any land, building, or vessel for the purpose of ascertaining whether the provisions of any Act, ordinance, regulation, or by-law relating to the storage or keeping of explosives, or of kerosene or any inflammable matter, or relating to the lighting of fires, have been contravened or have not been complied with; . . . [he] may cause to be served personally or by post on the occupier of any land or building, or the master, owner, or agent of any vessel on or in which any inflammable matter or explosive is stored or kept contrary to any Act, ordinance, regulation, or by-law, a notice requiring him to remove such matter or explosive within a time therein named. (Fire Brigades Act 1909:27)

The reinforced powers of the Chief Officer closely followed the guidelines of the Select Committee Report of 1905. Other aspects of the Committee's Report, however, remained unresolved and the subject of bitter community debate. In 1911, for example, the Board noted that the proposed Building Act, limiting the

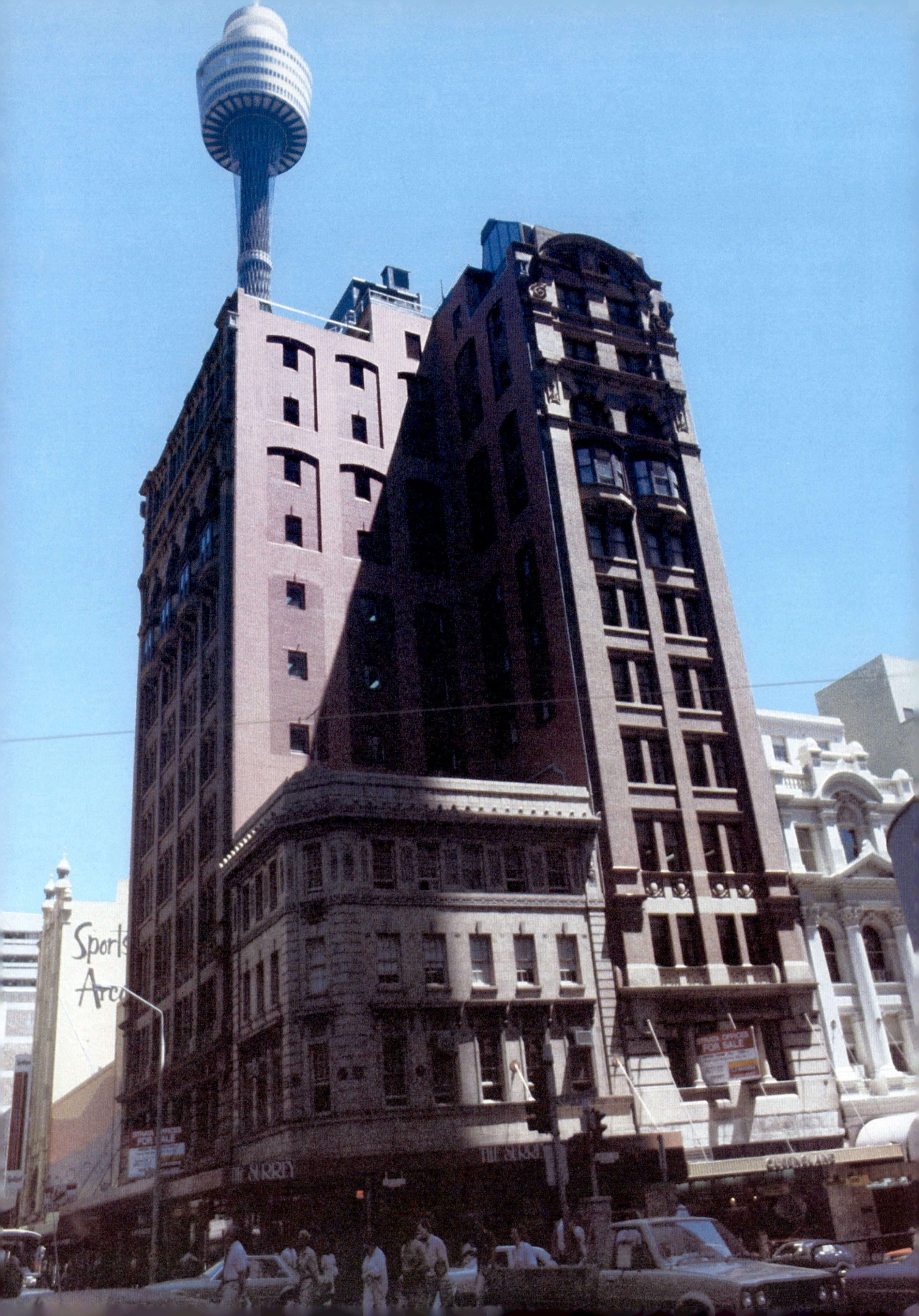
FOR SALE
THE SURREY

height of buildings and ensuring means of fire escape, had not been enacted. As a consequence the City authorities were powerless to regulate the height or construction of city buildings.

At this time Culwulla Chambers in Castlereagh Street, a building of thirteen storeys and 165 feet (50.29 m) in height [35 feet (10.67 m) higher than any other Sydney building], was under construction.[2] Other plans were being proposed for a building of 22 storeys, in excess of 200 feet (61 m). In a series of public statements, Chief Officer Webb came out strongly against such buildings. Bitter debate took place in the City Council between the 'pro-skyscraper' lobby which argued for progress, less congestion and a means of counteracting rising property values (and rents), and the 'anti-skyscraper' lobby which favoured regulation, conservatism and fire safety. Even the press took opposing stands: the *Daily Telegraph* described the skyscraper as an 'innocuous thing' while the *Sun* supported Alderman Lindsay Thompson who referred to skyscrapers generally as 'tragic monstrosities'.[3]

The debate was not resolved until December 1912 when an Act 'to regulate the height of buildings within the Metropolitan Police District' was passed. The Act limited buildings to 150 feet (45.72 m) within the District and to 100 feet (30.48 m) outside: 'Provided that in the case of any buildings exceeding one hundred feet in height, the Fire Commissioners of New South Wales shall first certify to the Chief Secretary that adequate provision has been made in respect of such building for protection against fire' (Height of Buildings Act 1912:784). The Board's only disappointment was that it lacked similar powers for buildings under 100 feet.

In the ensuing years the Board was successful in pressing for a number of new fire prevention bills. In 1915 the Kerosene Act of 1871 was repealed and replaced by an Inflammable Liquids Act; the Height of Buildings Act of 1912 was amended in 1916, as was the Theatres and Public Halls Act in 1922. The Local Government Act of 1919 also included a new ordinance (Ordinance 71), although the provisions were essentially the same as those previously contained in the City of Sydney by-laws.

A minor modification was the introduction of fire alarm pillars in 1916, when the City's telephone lines were placed underground. Of more significance was the growth in the number of fire alarms. By 1920 there were 487 street fire alarms in Sydney and suburbs and in the same year there were over 360 automatic fire alarms connected to Sydney FD stations. Of the 1350 alarms reported in the Sydney FD in 1920, 104 came from automatic alarms and 191 from street fire alarms. In both cases the major drawback was their high frequency of spontaneous false alarms—accounting for some 60 per cent of the 273 false alarms in 1920. Thefts of fire alarm instruments and parts were also common (though convictions were few).

A major innovation in personalised fire protection was the introduction of the first two 'Proto' respirators at Headquarters in 1922. The Protos consisted of an oxygen cylinder, sufficient for two hours, a breathing bag with a supply of caustic soda to absorb carbon monoxide, a mouthpiece, nose-clip, goggles and skull cap. Before these units, the Brigades were dependent on the Burrell gas mask, smoke jackets and eight Bellows Smoke Helmets.

Culwulla Chambers (left) at 22 storeys was Sydney's tallest building in 1912. Designed by Spain and Cosh, who also designed 29 NSW fire stations, the building was at the centre of both heated and whimsical debate over fire safety in skyscrapers

GETTING INTO THE ACT

Amendments to the Fire Brigades Act 1927

Following strong representations by the Board throughout the 1920s, the Fire Brigades (Amendment) Act 1927 contained seven provisions for the making of new by-laws:

(a) prescribing for various classes of buildings the means to be provided to enable occupants thereof to escape from the building in case of fire, and for the inspection and maintenance of such means of escape;

(b) prescribing for any building used for a purpose which in the opinion of the Board is of a hazardous nature or for any building the construction or use of which is, in the opinion of the Board, likely to allow the rapid spread of fire, the installation of fire alarms, sprinklers, and other devices or appliances approved by the Board designed to prevent or retard the spread of fire, and for the inspection and maintenance of such alarms, sprinklers, appliances, and devices;

(c) prohibiting or regulating the storage of inflammable matter on the roof, in the basement, or in any other part of a building;

(d) prohibiting or regulating the storage of inflammable matter in light areas or in close proximity to any building in any municipality or shire;

(e) regulating the deposit of inflammable matter in yards or on vacant blocks of land in any municipality or shire;

(f) regulating the burning off of waste inflammable matter in any municipality or shire;

(g) regulating the disposal of hot ashes and providing for proper receptacles for holding the same. (Fire Brigades Act (Amendment) 1927: Section 21)

Amendments to other Acts in relation to fire prevention took place in subsequent years. In 1931 the Inflammable Liquids Act of 1915 and the Shop and Factories Act of 1896 were amended. The latter amendment required that the efficiency of fire escapes be certified in writing by the BFC. In December 1932 a Local Government (Bush Fires) Amendment Act was passed revising the Local Government Act (1919) and the Bush Fires Act (1930). The amendment gave more comprehensive inspectional powers to shires and municipalities for the prevention of bush fires (although in practice these were rarely enforced). At the same time the amendment allowed regulations under the Careless Use of Fires Act (1912) to be altered. The alterations provided for the installation of spark arrestors and trays on engines used for traction, agricultural or railway and tramway purposes.

On 22 December 1933 new by-laws dealing with the storage and deposit of inflammable matter were gazetted. Whilst the by-laws, made under the 1927 alterations to Section 21 of the Act, were extensive, the penalties for noncompliance were set at a maximum of £20 ($40). As with so much of the fire prevention legislation in other Acts, the by-laws lacked teeth and any real monetary penalty for non-compliance.

In the 1930s a major concern of Chief Officer Richardson was the inefficiency of the existing system of hydrants. For a number of years he and the Board had unsuccessfully requested that the MWSDB introduce pillar hydrants, but these were never introduced into Sydney because in 1936, tests of a new valve-type double elbow hydrant proved satisfactory. These hydrants facilitated multiple connections and portability.

Recognising the imminent danger of war in Europe, the Board in 1935–36, on the recommendation of President T J Smith, embarked on a major campaign to up-grade NSWFB supplies of breathing apparatus. In 1934 the Brigades held fifteen smoke helmets and five Proto respirators within the Sydney FD; by the end of 1939, in addition to the original smoke helmets, Sydney fire stations held 169 gas masks and 34 Protos. Each station was supplied with at least one gas mask; the Protos were all held by the Smoke and Resuscitation Officer (SO H Brown) at Headquarters.

An extensive training program in the use of the new equipment was implemented and by 1939, 55 officers and 214 firemen within Sydney had qualified in the use of Protos. Many a retired fireman today remembers the tortuous training sessions in special smoke 'huts' at Headquarters during the 1930s. A number of the qualified officers and senior firemen provided the nucleus of the special instructional group set up during the war for Air Raid Precaution and gas training (Chapter 6).

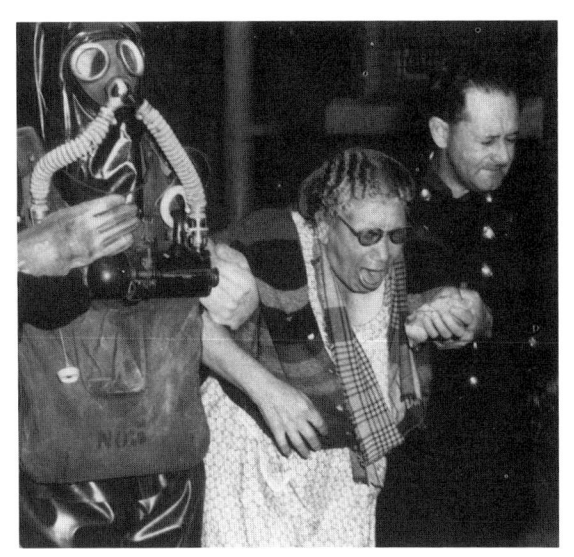

The value of Proto breathing apparatus is brought home in this dramatic rescue

Of the 6343 alarms recorded in the Sydney FD in 1939, 158 came from automatic fire alarms, 305 from automatic sprinkler alarms and 628 from the 505 street fire alarms. Whilst there had been an overall increase in the number of false alarms the proportion from the above sources had decreased substantially from the figures recorded in the 1920s.

POST-WAR ADVANCES

Following disastrous bush fires throughout NSW in the late 1930s a Bush Fires Advisory Committee was established on which the Chief Officer represented the Board. Further fires during the war years saw the implementation of Bush and Rural Fire Prevention Orders (see Chapter 6) and amendments to the Careless Use of Fires Act 1912. It was during the years 1947–49, however, that the most dramatic changes in combating bush fires took place.

Bush fire brigades were organised in a few council areas on the fringes of the Sydney FD, most notably the Blue Mountains. In these and other council areas hose box posts were established. Under the supervision of a force of 1686 reservists, the hose boxes were equipped with standpipe, branch and several lengths of hose. By 1949 some 60 of these posts ringed Sydney. At the same time the Board embarked on the purchase of bush firefighting equipment. Water tankers were based on the suburban perimeter and at Katoomba, and a range of knapsack pumps and rakes were supplied to brigades throughout Sydney.

On 9 December 1949 a new Bush Fires Act came into force replacing the 1930 Act and the Careless Use of Fire Act (1912–1946). The Act represented the first serious attempt to coordinate volunteer bush fire brigades throughout the State, in areas outside the Fire Brigades Act. Centralised authority was empowered to the Bush Fire Committee on which Fourth Officer G M Gilmour was the Board's representative. Funding was centralised in an Eastern and Central Bush Fire Fighting Fund, with contributions from State (25 per cent), local councils (25 per cent) and insurance companies (50 per cent). Disbursement to the now 'official' bush fire brigades was made through the shires and municipalities, reorganised under the Local Government (Amendment) Act 1947. For the first time field days and exercises were held by bush fire brigades in the Blue Mountains, Sutherland and Hornsby under the instruction of Board staff.

Despite these precautions, 1951–52 was marked by severe bush fires, resembling those of 'Black Sunday' in 1938 (Chapter 8). An abnormally dry spring and summer accompanied by record temperatures created conditions for disaster. From early November 1951 until February 1952 a dense smoke haze hung over Sydney, forcing the frequent closure of Sydney airport. Each day brought new threats: Frenchs Forest, Menai, St Marys and countless other suburbs suffered heavy property losses in November. In December the Blue Mountains were devastated—over 50 homes and businesses were destroyed. Despite the efforts of permanent and reserve firemen along with volunteers, the antiquated equipment, both war and pre-war, and the poor water supply proved no match for the flames. During the crisis Deputy Chief Officer G M Gilmour was appointed Controller of Operations within the Blue Mountains area. By the end of February NSW had lost 20 lives, over 200 homes, and millions of dollars worth of property.

Following the fires, consultations between local government authorities, the Bush Fire Committee and the Board resulted in major alterations to the system of hose boxes and deployment of reserve firemen. The corps of reserve firemen was disbanded and the reserves given the options of applying for paid volunteer

Opening of a two-way radio system at Headquarters in November 1948 significantly improved Brigade communications

positions with Board brigades, becoming unpaid auxiliary firemen at Hose Box posts or becoming unpaid volunteers in bush fire brigades under the control of local councils.

In the light of the current inquiry into a rationalisation of all fire services within NSW (Chapter 9) the views expressed in a newspaper editorial following the 1951–52 fires, are of interest:

> Responsibility for firefighting can no longer be left to local authorities whose resources are limited and whose action is rarely properly coordinated. Bush fires do not respect shire boundaries nor do they wait upon haphazard organisation. A state-wide control on the lines of Victoria's Country Fire Authority with broad powers of direction is the only effective answer.
> (Sydney Morning Herald, 1 February 1952)

Many, including Board President T J Smith, held similar views; T J argued that the appropriate body of control was the BFC. The new Colonial Secretary, Mr C A Kelly, did not agree, however, and plans for a more broadly based BFC were dropped.

The most significant innovation in the immediate post-war years was the introduction of two-way radio communication. In 1948 the firm of Thorn and Smith Ltd began equipping all patrol cars (Chapter 5) and first-response motors with two-way radios. Inaugurated on 17 November 1948 by the Governor-General of NSW, the system operated with a call sign of VL2BF, first from a temporary base at Headquarters and then from a main base at Crows Nest. Following the Blue Mountains fires, a permanent two-way radio base was also established at Katoomba.

One of the earliest uses of the new two-way radios was in patrol cars which were also used for the transfer of staff on concourse duty. The radios, however, had to be removed from vehicles used in the transfer of staff to Randwick race meetings (or an alternative vehicle found), following the discovery that they were being used 'illegally'. An enterprising racegoer had found that he could catch the result of an interstate race by 'listening-in', then signal a mate in the betting ring.[4] The role of Brigades' staff in these activities was never disclosed!

The growing sophistication and scope of the Brigades' communication systems resulted in a complete reappraisal of the system in the mid-1950s by the Board's principal electrician, Harry Watson. New 80-line switchboards were provided at the District Stations of Stanmore and Waterloo, and 100-line relay boards at Newtown and Crows Nest. By 1955, 795 street telephone alarms were connected to Sydney FD stations as were 82 special fire alarms, 142 private alarms, 870 automatic sprinkler alarms and 279 automatic thermostatic alarms.

The immediate post-war years witnessed major changes in the other Board workshop areas. With the closure of 25 fire stations in 1945 (Chapter 4) and the temporary transfer of carpenters, plumbers and painters from Headquarters during the war (Chapter 6), the Board sought a further redistribution of support services. In 1946 the carpenters' shop was transferred to Bexley FS, and the painters and plumbers to Rozelle FS. In 1949 the transport section was moved from Headquarters to Pyrmont and the clothing and boot factories and hose department to Stanmore FS.

In 1956 following extensive renovations at Headquarters, a site was purchased in Spencer Street, Five Dock, to establish new workshops. Completed in 1958 the new complex provided for an assembly shop, machine shop, spray painters area, blacksmiths shop and lubritorium.

As telephones became more widely accessible to the public, a much higher percentage of fire calls were received by phone: some 6744 of the 10 012 Sydney fire calls in 1955. Automatic alarms accounted for a further 2054 calls, of which 1951 were false alarms. In contrast, the number of calls from citizens reporting to fire stations (586) and street fire alarms (266) decreased.[5] Consequently the Board began a policy of phasing out street fire alarms in the Sydney FD. The last year in which a new street telephone alarm was installed was 1958, the same year in which a record of 807 street fire alarms was received, their number declining to 276 by 1963. By this time all mobile appliances in the Sydney FD were equipped with radio/telephone (R/T) communications.

In 1957, after lengthy consideration by a Height of Buildings Committee (on which Chief Officer Pye represented the Board), the Height of Buildings Act was amended to allow for buildings higher than 150 feet (45.72 m). The Amendment created an 11-person Height of Buildings Advisory Committee to advise the Chief Secretary on any development applications for buildings in excess of 150 feet.[6] An Interim Fire Protection Code was developed and approved by the Committee in 1964. The Code detailed specifications (amongst others) for fire-isolated stairways, fire-resisting doorways, fire detectors and sprinkler systems, and hydrants with a minimum pressure of 30 psi (206.7 kPa), on all floors. Much of the work in formulating the Board's criteria for buildings in excess of 150 feet was undertaken by Building Inspecting Officer DO Jack Meeve (later Deputy Chief). Subsequently a new Fire Protection Code for buildings between 80 and 150 feet (24.38–45.72 m) in height was also approved by the Chief Secretary's Department. Acceptance of both Codes within the Height of Buildings Advisory Committee had not been achieved easily. Developers and architects were critical of the stringent nature of provisions for sprinkler systems and smoke-proof stairways. Architects were principally concerned about the constraints on building aesthetics whilst developers were concerned about the increased costs of construction.

The major impetus for change to the building height regulations came in 1957 when the Australian Mutual Provident Society approached the City Council and the Chief Secretary, Mr C A Kelly, with plans for a 13-storey, 250-foot (76.2 m) high building, the tallest in Australia. Opened in February 1962, the building was the forerunner of a new era in Sydney buildings and a new hazard for the NSWFB.

On 20 July 1963 the Brigades suffered their first fatality in sixteen years and the eighteenth since 1884. Senior Fireman Ronald (Hookey) Jenkins died from carbon monoxide poisoning in an electricity substation fire in Napoleon Street (off Kent Street) in the City. An ex-army artillery sergeant, Jenkins had joined the fire service in 1948 after a short stint in the police force.

The exact circumstances of Jenkins' death remains both a mystery and a quiet source of discontent amongst some older members of the Brigades. Thorough checks by the Mines Department of the Proto set Jenkins was wearing when he entered the substation ruled out equipment failure. Allegations of a breakdown in correct procedures, poor supervision by senior officers, out-of-date equipment and a 'cover-up' at the Inquest have never been substantiated.

What is known however is that the death of Jenkins had a major impact on the use and supplies of breathing apparatus within the service. Most of the existing equipment had been purchased just before the war and many of the younger members of the service had little training or practical experience in its use. In 1964 the first of twelve sets of Compressed Air Breathing Apparatus (CABA) were introduced and Vista-Vision masks were attached to a number of existing Proto sets. The older all-service canister type gas masks were progressively withdrawn. By the end of 1968 all permanently-manned stations in Sydney, Canberra, Newcastle, Wollongong and Broken Hill had been supplied with CABA.

NEW DIRECTIONS
The Past Fifteen Years

The major communications innovation in the late 1960s and early 1970s was the installation of direct telephone lines from Headquarters to all stations in the Sydney Fire District. The existing system required many of the incoming calls on the emergency '000' number to be relayed from Headquarter's Control through a District Station to the responding brigade/s. The new system allowed multiple, simultaneous connections from Headquarters to Sydney stations following a '000' call. Introduced at the same time was a PABX switchboard, giving five direct lines to Headquarters, allowing the segregation of fire calls from business lines and from the sprinkler/thermal alarm relay section. With the separation of calls, the '000' Control Centre was relocated at the rear of Headquarters in the former electrical workshop building. The Headquarters' watchroom, which had previously handled the whole communications function, was redesigned as a 'relay room' for the domestic telephone switchboard and as a monitoring centre for the 916 automatic fire alarms in the City area. Equipment was also installed enabling the activation of station sirens and volunteer house bells at Mortdale, Rhodes and Merrylands. In 1970 this system was also extended to Engadine, Avalon and Berowra.

With the establishment of a new Control Centre, the electrical workshops staff of 27 (under Chief Engineer-Electrical, Ken Griffiths) moved to the Five Dock workshop complex, ending a continuous era of workshop operations at Headquarters since 1888. The electrical workshops joined the Building and Maintenance Section (Chapter 4), motor workshops (Chapter 7) and stores and purchasing section. The stores and purchasing officer, Nigel Button, supervised the Five Dock stores staff of twelve, the clothing factory (24 staff), boot factory (seven staff) and hose department (staff of five at Stanmore FS).

By the end of 1970 stations in A, B, C and E districts were directly turned out from Headquarters Control and the old fire call number of '2233' had been withdrawn. The availability of public and private telephone lines to the '000' number saw the last of the street pillar box alarms removed from the Sydney FD in 1972 and at the same time, Sydney fire stations dispensed with the ubiquitous bicycle. An 82-year span had come to an end.

The introduction of direct turn-outs from Headquarters dramatically improved both the speed of turn-out and the amount of information which could be orally exchanged between Control and senior officers at the fire scene. A 'Red' alert signal was introduced giving airway priority and allowing for extra brigades, ambulances, police or electrical services to be 'ordered on'.

In 1970 a major change took place in bush fire organisation with the formation of the Bush Fire Council. The 27-person Council, which replaced the Bush Fire Committee set up in 1949, included two BFC representatives, Leonard Verrills (Board President) and Superintendent John Ford. The principal objectives of the new organisation were to allow for a more centralised and standardised distribution of funds and equipment, and for a greater coordination of all interested parties in bush fire suppression. At the same time the Board's Bush Fire Section was upgraded. A Bush Fire Control Centre with an emergency bush fire radio base was established at the new Headquarters Control. Four senior officers were nominated as Emergency Fire Controllers for the County of Cumberland, under section 41F of the Bush Fires (Amendment) Act 1970. Other officers attended the five-day Bush Fire Council School at Kurrajong for the first time. Extensive bush fires around Sydney in October 1971 fully tested both the Board's Bush Fire personnel and the new Control Centre, with 352 call outs being processed in one 24-hour period (the greatest number since 'Black Sunday' 1938).

The other major change in the early 1970s was the formation of the Fire Prevention

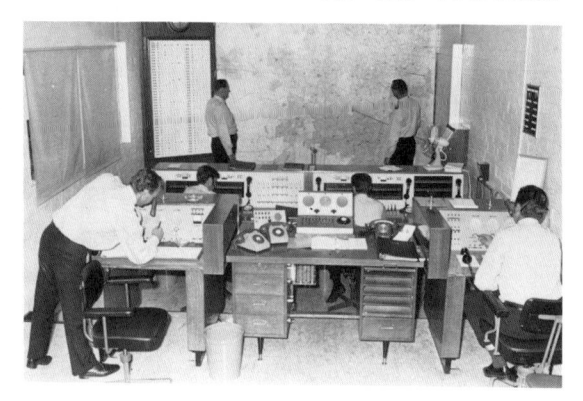

In 1970 the Headquarters Control Centre was modernised and reestablished in the former electrical workshops (top). The old Control Centre was redesigned as a relay room (above)

Department in 1970. With the sustained construction activity throughout the city, the Brigades' inspectional duties had escalated to a record 4865 on-site inspections and building development applications. Between 1957 and 1970, 79 buildings over 150 feet (45.72 m) in height had been built in Sydney. With the increased workload, the fire prevention officers lost their reputation as the 'silvertails' of the fire service. Inspections were now carried out on the means of escape and fire protection based on regulations and codes in eleven separate Acts:

1. Factories, Shops and Industries Act;
2. Theatres and Public Halls Act;
3. Private and Public Hospitals Act;
4. Child Welfare Act;
5. Local Government Act;
6. Height of Buildings Act;
7. Inflammable Liquids Act;
8. Explosives Act;
9. Liquified Petroleum Gas Act;
10. Bush Fires Act;
11. Fire Brigades Act.

The formation of the Fire Prevention Department followed the 1967 transfer of responsibility for the Height of Buildings Act to the State Planning Authority under the Minister for Local Government. By then the range of specifications within the Interim Fire Protection Code had been expanded and architects and planners had developed architecturally pleasing and economically practical new designs.

In 1974 Local Government Ordinance 71 was replaced by a more detailed building code, Ordinance 70. Ordinance 70 is administered by the Building Regulation Advisory Council (BRAC), originally constituted in 1945 with eleven members and answerable to the Minister for Local Government. Essentially, Ordinance 70 deals with buildings up to 25 metres (82 feet) in height whilst buildings in excess of this height are covered by the Interim Fire Protection Code. The Board's powers under the latter Code, administered through the Height of Buildings Committee, are far more comprehensive, it being obligatory for all plans for buildings in excess of 25 metres to be approved by the Fire Prevention Department. On the other hand, plans under Ordinance 70 are only submitted to the Brigades if local councils think it necessary to seek the Board's advice (which may in any case be rejected).

Today the Fire Prevention Department operates with a staff of 24 officers. One of the two Deputy Chief Officers sits, in lieu of the Chief Officer, as the Brigades' representative on the Height of Buildings Committee, which is administered by the Minister for Planning and Environment, whilst the Superintendent of Fire Prevention remains on the Building Regulation Advisory Council, answerable to the Minister for Local Government. To remove problems of demarcation between the two groups (and between the Interim Fire Protection Code and Ordinance 70) a three-year transition period has been proclaimed from 1 January 1983, in which the Interim Fire Protection Code and Ordinance 70 will be reconciled.

Despite the initiatives in the area of fire prevention, particularly since 1970, the fact remains that the NSW Fire Brigades have, with a few exceptions, no direct statutory power to initiate, supervise or enforce the laws on fire protection and prevention.

The communication innovations initiated in the late 1960s accelerated during the 1970s. In 1975 a selective-calling radio system and a multi-channel 24-hour tape recording system were installed in the Headquarters Control Centre. The following year it was decided to centralise all automatic fire alarms within the Sydney FD. The existing system had 3804 automatic fire alarms each connected to one of ten terminal stations (the District Stations plus Drummoyne, Hornsby, Liverpool and Manly).

The centralised automatic alarm system was to become only one component of a $2m Control Centre for all fire calls in Sydney. Operative in October 1980 and based at Alexandria, the new Control Centre contains the centralised automatic alarm system, the '000' emergency lines and the bush fire control centre (previously located in the old Headquarters' workshops). The new computerised central control system has totally revolutionised the Brigades' communications system (Chapter 9). Despite the advances, a high proportion of the Brigades' 18 938 false alarms in the Sydney FD emanate from faults in the centralised automatic alarm system.

Communications are not the only area in which the Brigades have taken giant strides in equipment modernisation. Based on strong arguments advanced by President Bill Weston, the Fire Brigades Employees Union and the 1977 Committee of Inquiry, the Minister and the

Board agreed to an expanded role for the Brigades in the area of rescue. The Fire Brigades (Amendment) Act 1979 gave the Brigades power to undertake rescues which were not associated with fire. By 1983, 5.9 per cent of the calls (1239) to 'fires and other emergencies' within the Sydney FD were to non-fire rescues. Three categories of rescue capability have been developed: support, light and medium. The six District Stations in the Sydney metropolitan area have medium rescue capability, possessing advanced hydraulic rescue sets, air bags, air drills, air saws, winch sets and lighting. All other Sydney FD stations have a light rescue capability. Whilst well-equipped, the Brigades' greatest difficulty has been coordination with other rescue groups (Chapter 9).

In 1978 a special Breathing Apparatus Section with a staffing of one DO and four SOs was created and in 1980 moved to premises in Allen Street, Alexandria (No 9 Station). The section is in charge of some 1000 CABA sets, 65 oxygen sets and 150 resuscitation sets in Sydney and selected country centres. Following extensive testing throughout 1979, it was decided to adopt a new oxygen-breathing unit, the Drager Model BG 174, with the old Proto IV sets being gradually phased out.

In 1980 the Breathing Apparatus Section acquired a second special-purpose Breathing

Fire brigade rescue units are often called to Sydney road accidents (top), whilst chemical spillages such as the overturned petrol tanker, Beverly Hills (above) constitute an increasing threat to Sydney residents

Apparatus Van equipped with CABA sets, gas detection equipment, Oxy-Viva resuscitator and chemical suits. In addition to its maintenance, inspection and re-charging duties, the Breathing Apparatus Section handles over 350 calls yearly to major fires, chemical spillages and gas leaks. An increasingly significant portion of calls are to spillages: in 1983 the Brigades attended 2612 spillage calls within the Sydney FD. The transport of hazardous substances such as liquified petroleum gas, petroleum, propane, mixed-chemical loads and toxic insecticides poses a major threat to safety, particularly in densely populated areas. Two of the more serious incidents have been the petrol tanker fire which destroyed Hornsby fire station in 1971 (Chapter 8) and the accident on QANTAS Drive, Mascot in October 1977, when a tanker driver was killed and 12 000 litres of burning fuel were discharged over a large area.

The necessary coordination of rescue resources in 'spillage' situations was vividly displayed on 16 November 1982 when an Esso

Chemical suits worn by today's firefighters

Whilst not removing the danger, compulsory Hazchem codes on chemical tankers enable brigades to identify and contain spillage situations

petrol tanker overturned in Stoney Creek Road, Beverly Hills. Whilst police cordoned off the area and with Salvation Army assistance evacuated 83 homes, Breathing Apparatus personnel monitored the area and motors from Hurstville, Kogarah, Mortdale and Bankstown blanketed the tanker and surrounds with 1700 litres of foam. After electricity workers deactivated power lines brought down in the accident, Esso engineers began the hazardous task of pumping to a recovery tanker. Brigades' staff remained at the scene until the final righting and removal of the overturned tanker—in all, nine hours elapsed between the initial call and the 'stop' message.

In July 1980 the Hazchem Emergency Action Code was introduced whereby Brigades staff had access to information cards with the precise details on what to do at an emergency involving chemicals. At the same time Clause 188 of the Dangerous Goods Regulation was introduced requiring a Hazchem placard, indicating the substance being transported, to be displayed on bulk road transports.

Despite the advancements made in fire prevention since the early 1970s it remains the poor second cousin within the overall context of the Brigades' activities. Two factors are most prominent in this regard. First, the Board lacks the ultimate legislative power in the area of fire prevention. Local government, builder, developer and architect interests have been the most potent forces in influencing Sydney's building codes. In many cases their interests are far removed from questions of fire safety. Second, fire prevention has been viewed by many Brigades' staff (and members of the public) as an 'academic' exercise of bureaucratic 'red tape' removed from the 'real' world of extinguishing fires. Overcoming this nineteenth-century conceptualisation of the fireman's role (both inside and outside the fire service) is a matter for an extensive re-education program. It may well require the active involvement of outside expertise in the form of engineers, designers, and private fire prevention consultants.

74

4

A HOME AWAY FROM HOME

Fire Stations

ONE OF THE EARLIEST CONCERNS OF the fledgling MFB in 1884 was the question of fire station sites, particularly in the city area. Whilst the 1884 Fire Brigades Act empowered the Board to hold property, it did not include the right to purchase land and erect fire stations. As a consequence the Board remained dependent on the Government to initiate land purchase, approve plans and fund construction.

The Board's most pressing demand was for a new Central Fire Station; the Headquarters brigade (the only MFB brigade in 1884) was operating from the old Insurance Brigade Headquarters in Bathurst Street. In July 1884 the Government announced the purchase of a site on the west side of Castlereagh Street (217), between

Fireman Alfred Gibbs, wearing bicycle-clips, ready to mount Liverpool Fire Station's only transport in 1916. Nozzles and hoses surround the station's fire appliance, the hose-cart

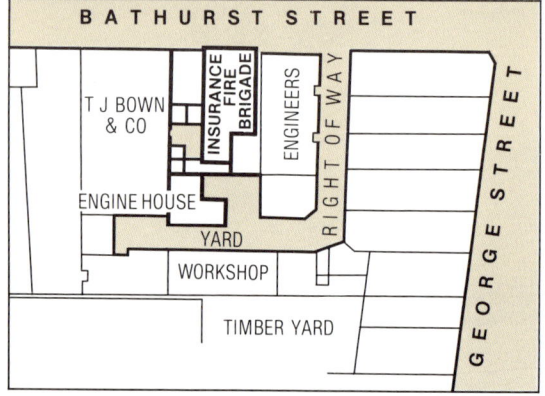

The southwest corner of George and Bathurst Sts c. 1880s. The headquarters of the Insurance Fire Brigade and later the Metropolitan Fire Brigades 1884–1888 stands on the far right with lookout tower (top)

Bathurst and Liverpool Streets, for £10,000 ($20 000).[1] By March 1885 plans had been drawn by the Colonial Architect's Department under James Barnet and approved by the Board and by September tenders called. Unfortunately for the MFB the successful tenderer, Millett Bros., became insolvent in 1886. This, combined with a dissolution of Parliament, meant little progress was made. However, when new tenders were called in 1886 John Baldwin obtained the contract and on 17 February 1888 gave notice of completion. On 1 March 1888 the MFB occupied their new Headquarters station.[2]

In the meantime the MFB had been more successful with its plans for one of two other city stations. On Superintendent Bear's advice, the Board in 1884 envisaged two stations at either end of the city to complement the new Central Station. In opposition to the Government's policy, the MFB purchased a site at 57 George Street in 1884 for a southern branch station and

CENTRAL STATION
Headquarters—1888[a]

THE following abridged description comes from the *Sydney Morning Herald* the day after the new building was opened for public inspection:

> The building may be looked upon as a decided acquisition to the city in as much as it has been built on the most modern style, combined with American ideas for quickness in turning out fire engines and the necessary apparatus for fire extinction. The station which is of four floors, with two winged

Tiles adorning the engine room walls at Headquarters' Fire Station, Castlereagh Street

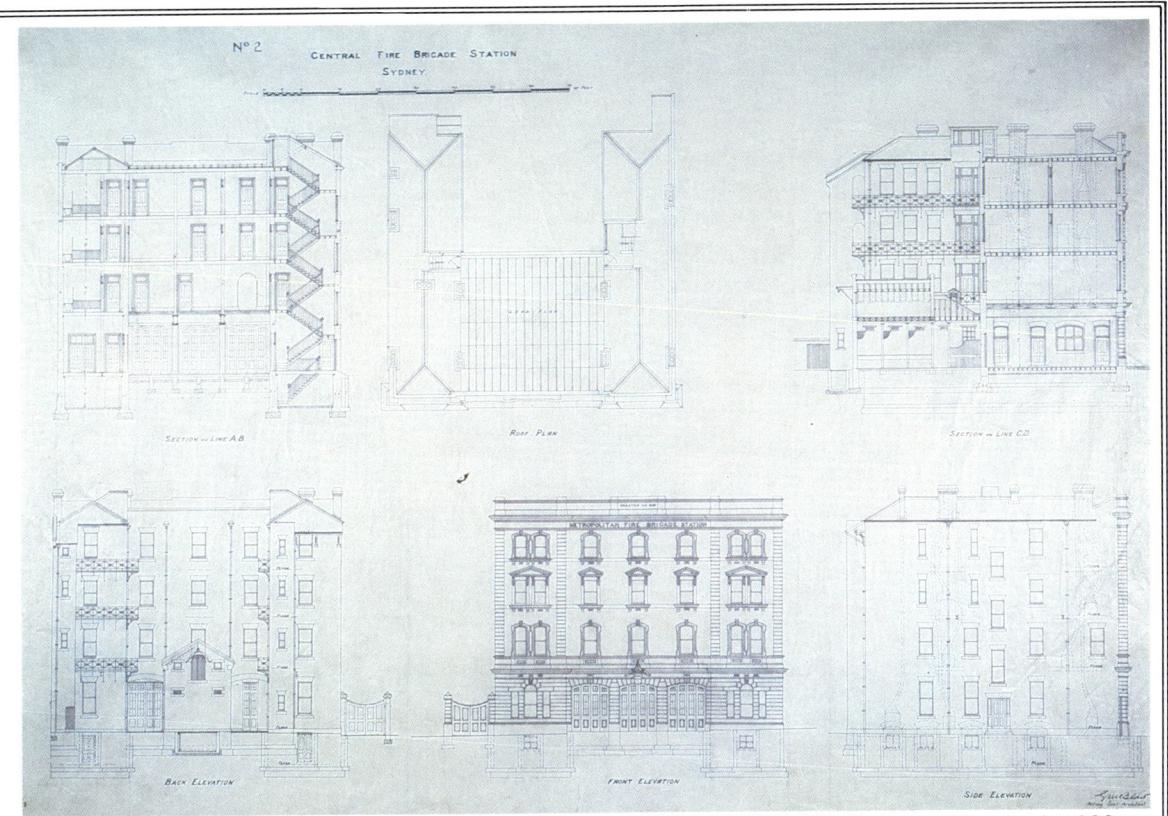

Metropolitan Fire Brigade Headquarters, designed by the colonial architect and occupied in March 1888

basements, stands on a piece of ground 88ft × 120ft [26.82 × 36.57 m]. The structure itself, has a frontage of 75ft [22.86 m] with a right-of-way on the southern side of 13ft [3.96 m] width. The front which is about 60ft [18.29 m] in height, is built in red brick, with cement piers, but the middle part, containing the piers and arches of the three doors of the engine-room up to the first floor, is built with Pyrmont stone in rusticated style, having a carving of the head of Her Majesty the Queen on the centre keystone, and an emblematical carving of a fireman's helmet, branches, nozzles and an axe on each of the other two keystones. The depth of the main building, with the two side wings, with stables for the accommodation of five horses attached to the middle of the structure, is about 68ft [20.73 m]. The ground floor on the northern side consists of a watchroom in which the whole of the telephones, telephone exchange board, fire alarms and electrical apparatus are worked. The electrical contact in this room, when pulled, rings the whole of the house-bells throughout the entire building, turns up the gas full in the engine-room, stables, drill ground, staircases, and passages, releases the stable doors which immediately fly open by means of springs and also releases a weight situated in the single men's bedrooms on the first floor, which opens two flaps to enable the firemen to slide down a pole. This pole is hung from the joists in a corner of their bedrooms, and the men descend on it into the engine-room. Speaking tubes extend from this room to the whole of the superintendent's apartments, which are situated on the first floor northern and to the whole of the principal foreman's quarters, which are situated on the second floor, to the tower[b], and to the superintendent's office. At the rear of the watchroom and staircase is a recreation room for the men, about 16 × 21½ft [4.88 × 6.55 m], which will contain a billiard table. At the southern end of the building the offices of the superintendent and secretary to the Board are situated, likewise the single men's messroom and kitchen. In the centre of the station, between the watchroom and offices, the engine bay is situated. This is a clear spot of 37½ft [11.43 m] and a depth of 34ft [10.36 m], for the accommodation of two steam fire engines and one manual. Directly in the rear of this apartment, with the doors facing into the engine-room, are the stables, which enable the horses to be hitched up at once to either [sic] of the three engines. Between the stables and the single men's messroom is another small engine-room which can be entered from either the main engine-room or the drill-ground, and which is occupied by the large steam fire engine.[c] This engine is only used for very large fires. On the southern side of the building on the first floor is the Fire Brigades Board board-room, three single men's quarters, with the necessary lavatories and bathrooms. The rest of the building is divided off for the accommodation of five married men, each having a suite of rooms. On the roof is situated the lookout tower which stands between 70ft [21.34 m] and 80ft [24.38 m] from the pavement level. From this tower a magnificent view of the whole of Sydney can be obtained. At the rear of the whole is situated a workshop, built on iron columns about 18ft [5.49 m] in height.[d] In this department is a lathe, a kiln for making copper-heaters hot for repairing canvas hose, and the necessary carpenters' benches and engineers' plant for doing the whole of the repairs for the brigade. Under the workshop will be placed a large extension fire-ladder, 30ft [9.14 m] in length, which when hoisted extends to over 70ft [21.34 m], and will be drawn by two horses to large fires. In connection with this ladder, in the back part of the main building, about 60ft [18.29 m] in height from the drill ground, is a platform for drilling the brigade members in ladder practice. There is also stationed under the workshops a reserve steam fire-engine, a light life-saving ladder and a manual engine for drill purposes and fires in the immediate vicinity. In this ground is a large covered tank[e] built for the purpose of working the steam and manual engines from, for washing hoses after a fire, and also for the purpose of topping the boilers of the steam fire-engines, and a room for keeping the heater. This heater will keep the steam fire-engines supplied with 5lb to 10lb [34.45–68.9 kPa] of steam both day and night. The roof of the main building is a large lead flat, covered with wooden grating. This will be utilised for the purpose of a ground for drying clothes. The total number of rooms, exclusive of basement, bathrooms, laundry and workshop, is 46, for the accommodation and general working of the whole station, viz: one superintendent, one principal foreman,

Flower pots identify Superintendent Webb's sitting room (top) on the first floor of Headquarters' Fire Station c. 1900

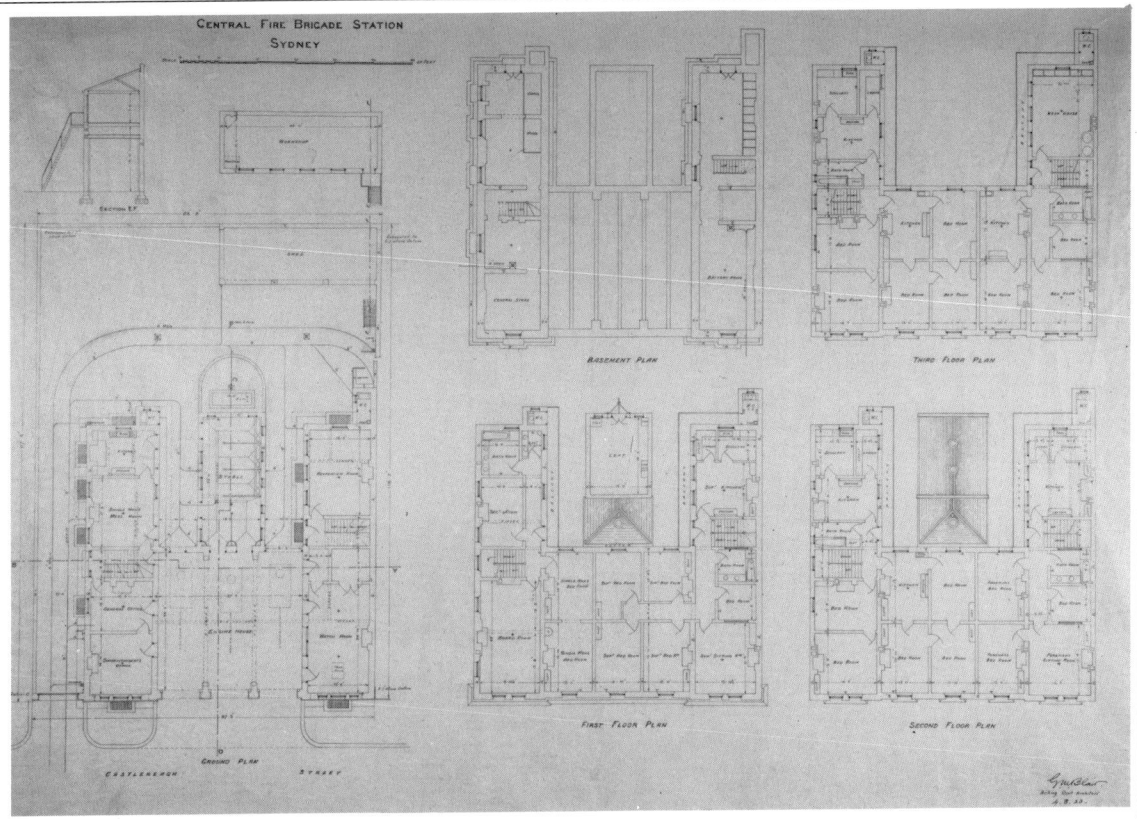

The floor plan of Headquarters' Fire Station

five married men and about eight single men. Four other married men belonging to the station live out in their own dwellings, within a few yards of the station. In the drill ground is a salvage waggon built at the expense of the different insurance companies, and a waggon with the necessary salvaging plant will be stationed there after a time. The harness for the horses is similar to that used in America. The harness together with the sway bars, is kept suspended over each horse in the stables by means of weights running into tubes, which trip themselves when the collar is snapped to, and the horses go into the engine. (*Sydney Morning Herald*, 2 March 1888)

Notes
a All brigades were given a number as they were established, starting with the original Headquarters (No 1) in 1884.
b The tower was commonly called the 'pigeon box'. Junior firemen took three-hour duties 'fire spotting' from dusk to dawn.
c 'Fire King'.
d The workshops were enlarged in 1893 under plans prepared by Charles Hellmrich and were the first of many 'alterations and additions' to take place at Headquarters (see Hughes, 1981).
e The hose tank appears to have been used for other purposes as well, as the following humorous account from the diary of Probationary Fireman Francis Arthur Tuck (1895) suggests:

> After breakfast we held a court martial on one of the men. The charge was he did knowingly and wilfully ignite certain explosives to wit: fireworks, and place the same above and below the beds of several of the men. The charge being clearly proved, the verdict of the Court was that he should be taken and dipped in the Hose Tank which had been filled for the occasion. The Prisoner was then taken hold of by five of the Jurymen and despite all his struggles was launched into the (cold, cold) tank and on regaining Mother Earth once more he flew into a terrible rage and things were humming for an hour or so (Tuck, 1895).

80 / *Fighting Fire!*

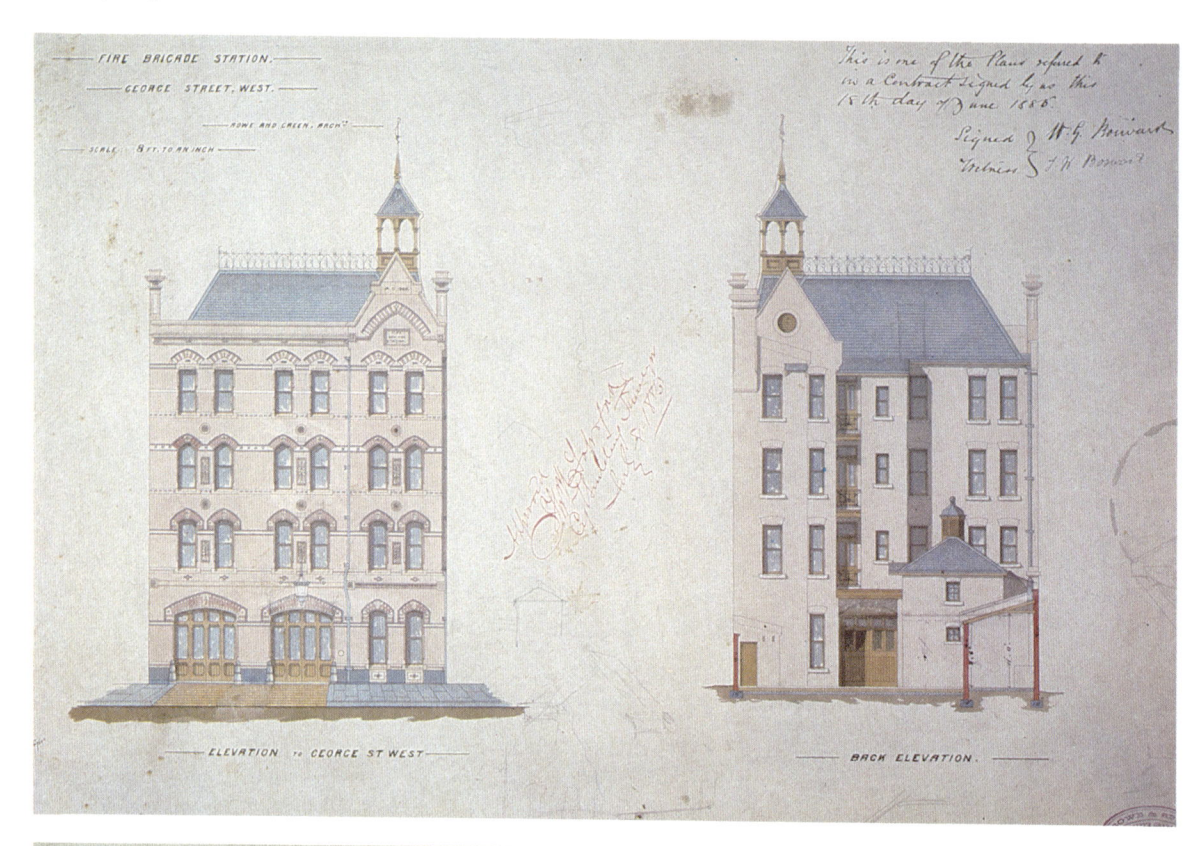

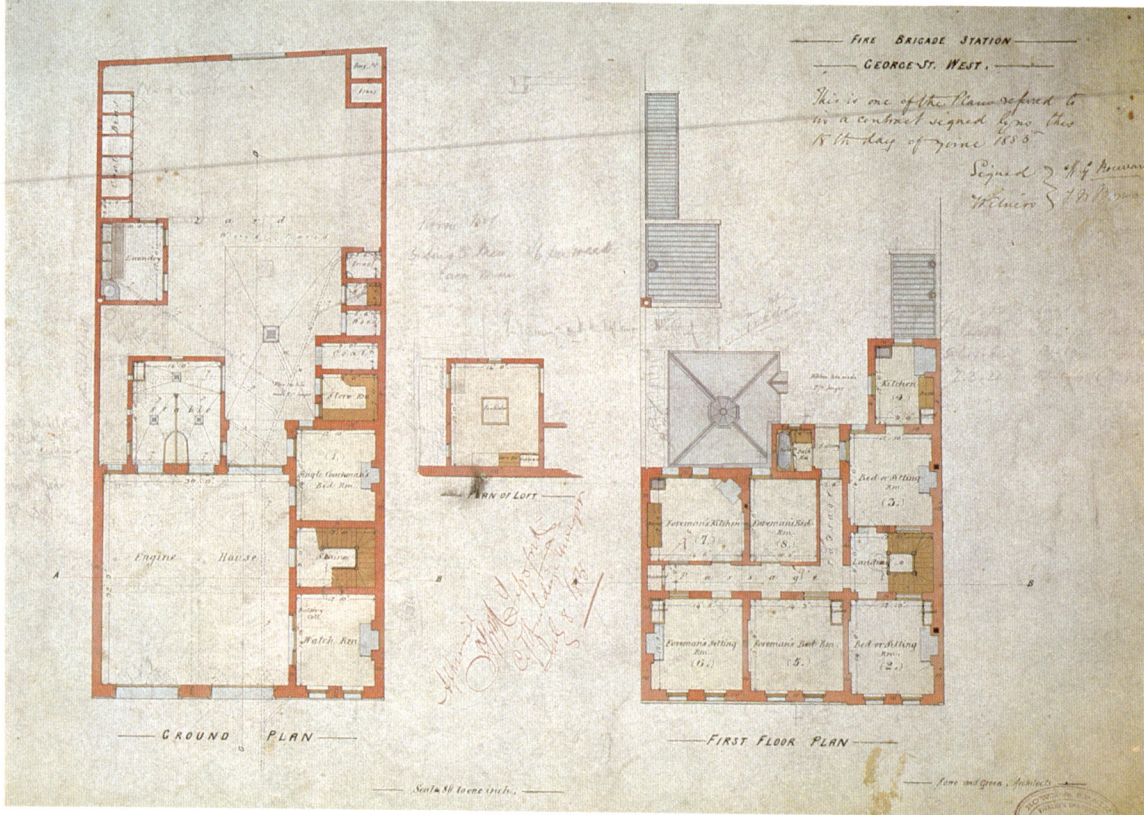

George Street West fire station, designed by Rowe and Green, opened in 1886 and was demolished in the mid-1950s to make way for Sydney Technical College

under plans by Messrs Rowe and Green, architects, George Street West (No 2) was completed and formally opened on 9 August 1886. The station provided accommodation for six married and two single firemen (one being the Officer-in-Charge, Foreman Edward Ashdown), stalls for two horses, and engine bays for two steamers and one manual. Nick-named the 'Workhouse', George Street West was to serve the railway-end of town until closed in 1955 and demolished to make way for the Institute of Technology.

At the other end of town, the Board recommended to the Government that a piece of land in George Street North, adjoining the Sailor's Home, be resumed as a site for a Northern Branch station, noting in 1884: '[the site] is close to the water, and where the Steam Floating Engine, which the Government is about purchasing, is proposed to be stationed' (MFBAR, 1884:2).

The lack of authority in the Fire Brigades Act over the waterways and delays in the purchase of a floating engine proved a festering sore in relations between the Board and Government.[3]

As a consequence a decision on a southern branch station was delayed.

The station which has the honour of being the first station built for the MFB was in fact not a city station. In May 1886 (three months before George Street West) a station designated as Marrickville No 3 was opened in Stanmore Road, Marrickville, to 'protect the districts of Petersham, Stanmore, Newtown, Leichhardt, Marrickville, St Peters, Cooks River, and other western suburbs' (MFBAR, 1886:1). This station survives today as a District station (re-named Stanmore No 7) and stands as the oldest operational fire station in Sydney.

Between 1884 and 1890 the MFB permanent Brigades operated from these three stations: No 1 Headquarters, No 2 George Street West and No 3 Marrickville. The stations were supported by the volunteer companies, most established prior to the MFB and operating from stations owned by the volunteer company or local council. In 1884 there were 22 (six unregistered) volunteer companies in the city and suburbs. By 1890 only three of the city companies survived as Superintendent Bear pursued a policy of closing

Marrickville No. 3 (now Stanmore). Having being opened by the Metropolitan Fire Brigade in 1886, it is the oldest operational fire station in Sydney

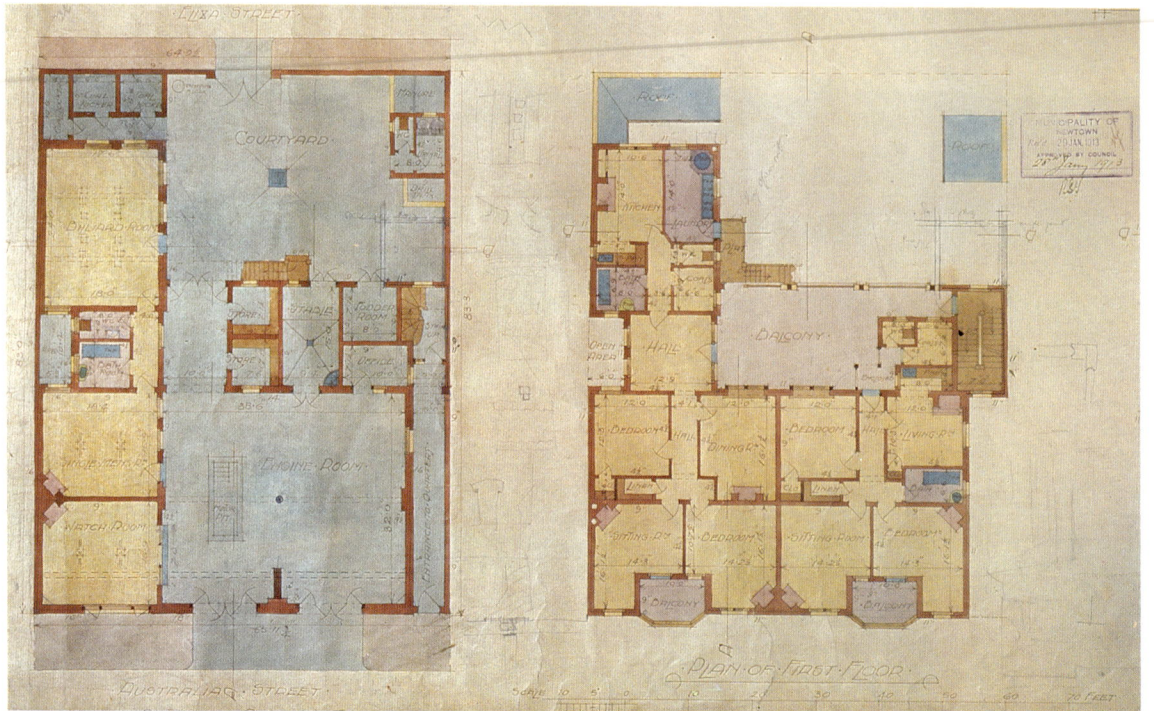

The two-engine bay Newtown Fire Station designed by Spain, Cosh and Minnett and completed in 1913. The station still operates today in Australia Street with a staff of 25 firefighters

volunteer companies in the city area. However, it was Board policy to encourage the formation of suburban volunteer stations and to this end the Board solicited sites from the Government and local councils in districts which were 'becoming urban in character, containing a large population ... and outgrowing protection' (MFBAR, 1891:3). In 1892 the Board obtained a sum of £1,200 ($2400) from the Government for the erection of a station in Balmain. Plans were drawn up by architect, Mr Charles Hellmrich, JP (an alderman and local council representative on the MFB) and the building erected by Messrs Folster and Heels:

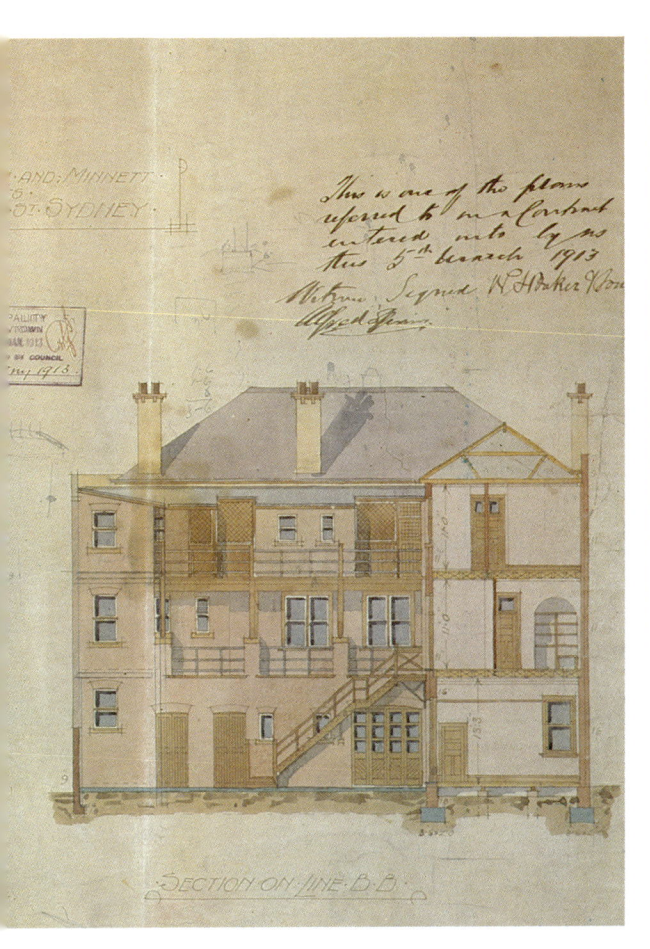

> The selected site is at about the highest elevation in Balmain, having the great advantage of down-hill runs for the fire appliances when called into service, and of commanding a distant view. It has a frontage of 50 feet [15.24 m] to Darling Street by a depth of 150 feet [45.72 m], and is close to the town-hall, post and telegraph offices, and the main business portion of the suburb. (MFBAR, 1893:2)

The local Balmain volunteers, with a Head Station in Booth Street and a Branch Station in Wise Street, closed these quarters and moved into a new station in August 1894, becoming the first fully volunteer brigade to occupy an MFB-owned station.[4] Some two years earlier the Newtown Volunteer Company had disbanded, being replaced by two permanent firemen plus a number of auxiliaries, in a station in Australia Street, Newtown. This was the first MFB station to be manned by a 'mixed' staff system.

In the same year, the Board had at last convinced the Government that a station at Circular Quay was required to protect the northern end of the city. On 4 July 1891 building commenced, based on plans prepared by the Government Architect, W L Vernon. Sited at the junction of George and Queen Streets, it was occupied by the MFB on 25 January 1893:

> It stands in a magnificent position to control outbreaks of fire on ships lying at wharves, and in the bonds and other buildings, with their immensely valuable and often very inflammable contents, in that quarter of the metropolis. It is a substantial structure, and reflects great credit upon all connected with its erection. The plans of the building were drawn by the Government Architect, and the utmost has been made of the limited space of ground available. It is fitted with the most modern appliances for ensuring speed in turning out to fires, and a detachment of eight of the Metropolitan Fire Brigade has been stationed there, with two steam fire-engines, horses, etc; and a fire ladder capable of extension to eighty feet [24.38 m] will be added on its arrival from London, whence it has been ordered. To this station the fire-float must eventually be attached. (MFBAR, 1892:2)

The Circular Quay Fire Station heralded Vernon's appointment as Government Architect. It signified the revival of the former Colonial Architect's Office which had been under attack and threatened with abolition following Barnet's retirement in 1889.

By the 1890s the population of suburban Sydney was more than double that of the City of Sydney. Despite the depression of the early 1890s, the suburbs continued to expand as both the steam tramways and railways penetrated south, west and north. In the south the suburbs

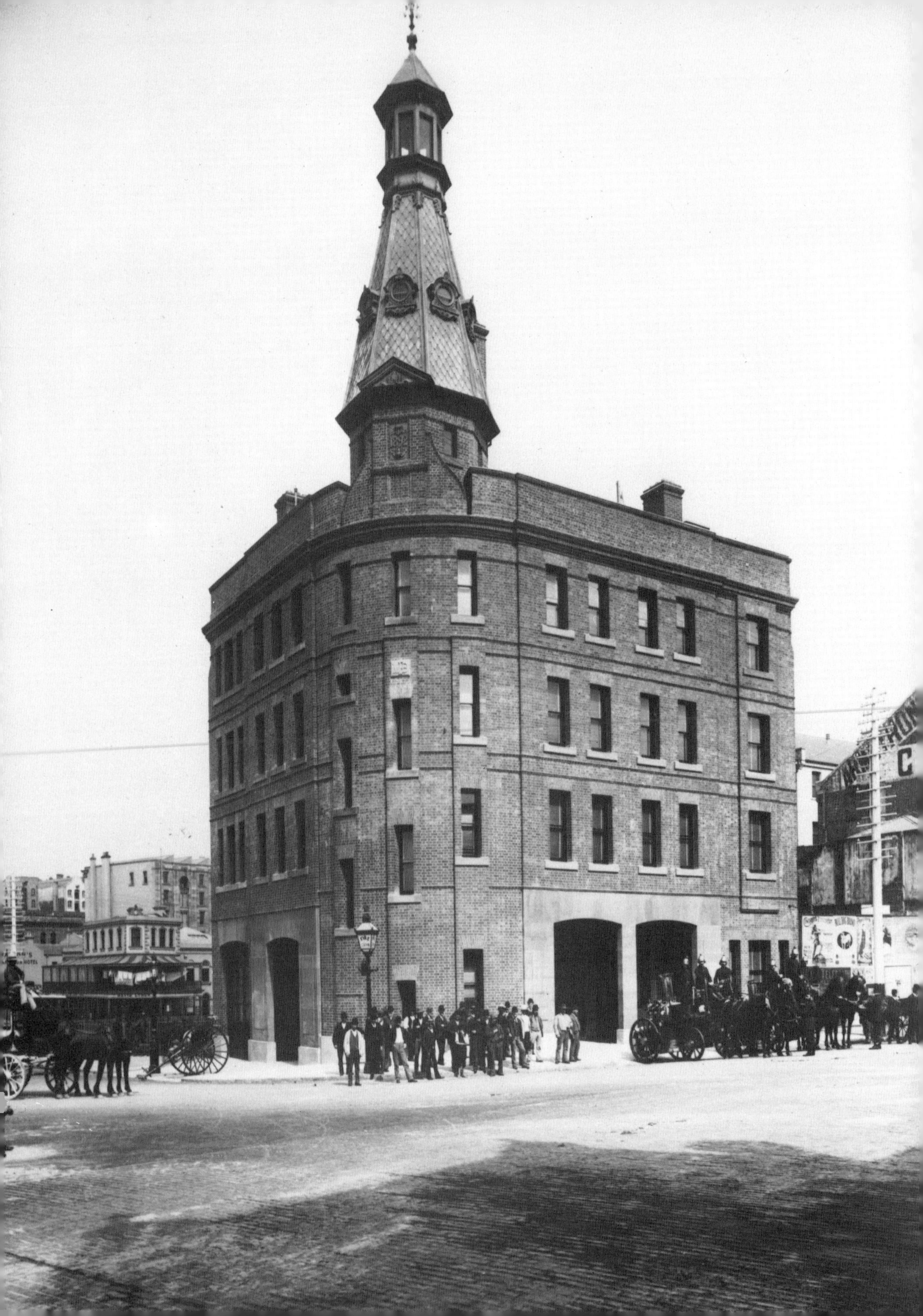

The original Drummoyne fire station (No. 17). Opened in 1896, the station was owned and operated by volunteers until replaced by a new station with permanent staff in 1910

of Kogarah and Rockdale were being developed along the rail line which crossed the Georges River to Sutherland. To the west suburbs opened up on the Sydenham to Belmore line and the Strathfield line. Areas in between the rail lines were served by an ever-expanding tram system. In the 1890s growth on the North Shore boomed with North Sydney, Mosman and Manly being opened up.

During this period many local councils petitioned the MFB for the establishment of a local fire brigade and for a new fire station. In some cases councils or a volunteer brigade approached the Government directly for a building grant, offering a suitable site, often on council-owned property.

Granville is an interesting example. Under strong lobbying from Edward Love, the volunteers' representative on the Board, the area of Granville was brought under coverage of the Act in 1891. A brigade of twenty members, with a hose-reel, was established under the captaincy of Love in a small 'shed' in Good Street. Six years later a temporary fire station was established in Sydney Road on weekly rental to the MFB, whilst a new station was built on the Good Street site. The purchase of the site and cost of the station were funded by a government grant and operation of the station placed in the hands of the volunteers. In 1901 the volunteers handed ownership over to the MFB. With some additions in 1909 and the appointment of the first permanent staff on Captain Love's death in 1912, Granville FS remained operational until closed in 1945. The Good Street building still stands today, remodelled as a shop.

The strong lobbying from local councils during the 1890s caused major dissension between the Board and Superintendent Bear. It was Bear's view that the Board should approach the Government for a loan of £25,000 ($50 000)

Circular Quay fire station (left) opened in 1892

for the express purpose of purchasing land and building stations. The majority of the Board was against this proposal, however, because the loan foreshadowed a considerable increase in contributions. Their suggestion was that the Government should be approached for a special annual advance. Whilst the Government would not agree to the advance it did agree to provide irregular amounts in the Government Estimates for the purchase of sites and the building of branch and suburban fire stations. On this basis new stations were built on freehold or long-term lease land at North Sydney (1895), Darlinghurst (1896), Rockdale (1897), Hurstville (1897) and Manly (1898). Most were designed by the Government Architect, Walter Vernon (although North Sydney was built as the 'mirror image' to the design produced by Charles Hellmrich for Balmain).

A powerful force on the Board in the negotiations with local councils over fire protection was Alderman William Taylor (Councils' representative, 1894–1922). Elected Mayor of Rockdale in 1893 at 32 years of age, William Taylor was a wily administrator and an adept lobbyist. At a time when the 'southern' suburbs of Hurstville, Canterbury, Kogarah and Rockdale were the fastest growing areas of Sydney, Taylor strongly promoted the formation of local volunteer fire brigades. Brigades at North Botany (1892), Rockdale (1892), Kogarah (1895) and Hurstville (1897) were all formed under his patronage with the councils providing land and in many cases holding the fire station in trust. In subsequent years Taylor (appointed MLA for St George in 1908) continued his role as spokesman for local government interests, particularly in his own constituency; as a result, 'during the next 20 years fire stations were erected at Rockdale, Arncliffe and Bexley and those at Kogarah and Hurstville were rebuilt, making the St George District the most fireproof part of the metropolitan area' (St George Historical Society, 1971:18–19).

Another feature of the 1890s was the application for registration by a number of volunteer companies outside the immediate Sydney area. They did so with the encouragement of their councils who realised that the subsidy they would enjoy would be in excess of the compulsory council contribution. This immediately pointed to the inadequacies of the

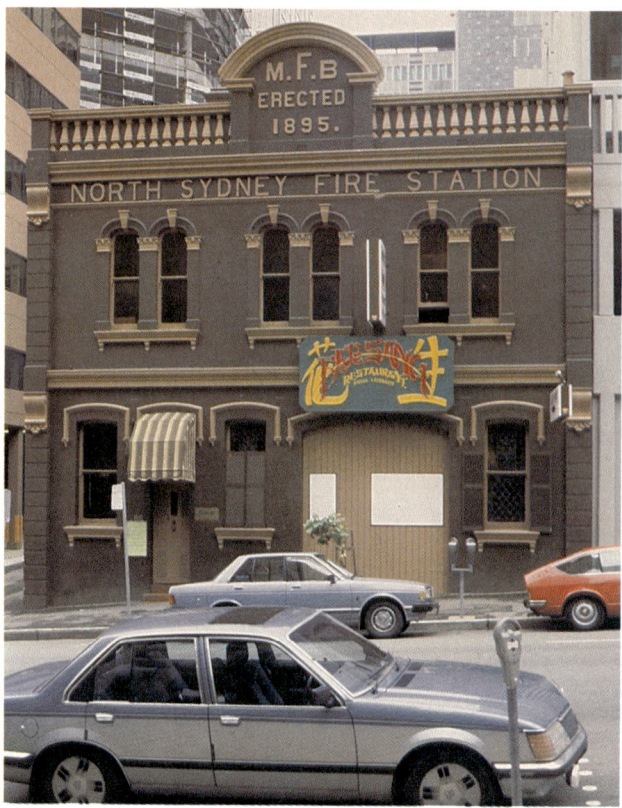

Granville Fire Station (top) and North Sydney Fire Station (above) both closed in 1945 but exist today as a shop and restaurant respectively

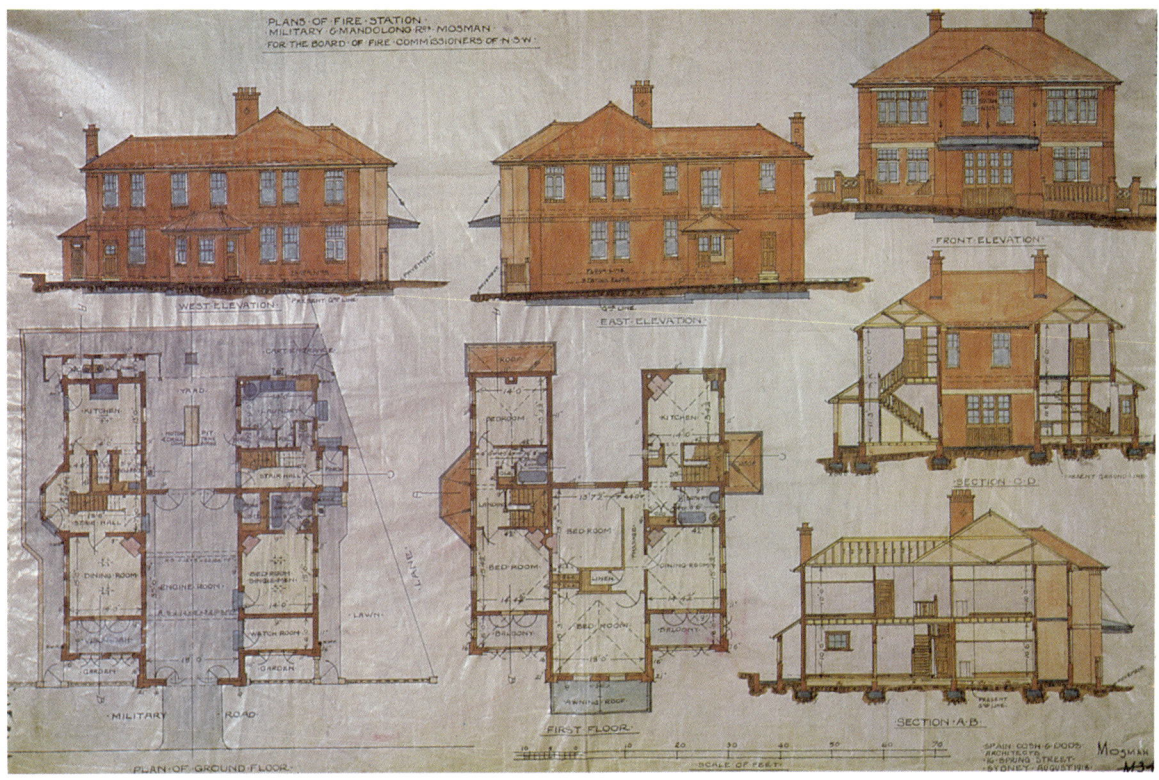

Mosman Fire Station opened in 1919. Designed by Spain, Cosh and Dods the station cost £3319 and replaced the original station in Myagah Road

Silver trowel presented to Board President Charles Bown at the opening of Paddington Fire Station, 257 Oxford Street in 1899

Act (and foreshadowed the later demise of the MFB and formation of the State-wide Board of Fire Commissioners in 1909). Despite reservations in 1898 the Board gave a subsidy of £25 ($50) to Liverpool and of £30 ($60) to Richmond, with the Liverpool Volunteers occupying a small station built with a Government grant. Other brigades were to follow suit; Penrith in 1905 and Campbelltown in 1907.

The years 1898–1905 represented a period of fluctuating fortune for the Board and new Superintendent, Alfred Webb, in their plans to extend the network of suburban stations. In 1898–99 an unprecedented number of stations were built, with over £6,300 ($12 600) spent on 'buildings'. Stations built were Redfern (No 10—conversion of old courthouse and lock up), Parramatta (No 27), Granville (No 19), Willoughby (Chatswood No 32), Rookwood (Lidcombe No 30), Burwood (No 15) and Paddington (No 11). Plans were also proposed for new stations at Ashfield, Chatswood, Mosman, Randwick and Woollahra. In a number of cases (for example, Alexandria and

Leichhardt Fire Station is typical of the design employed by Assistant Government Architect, E L Drew in 1905–06

Woollahra) the volunteer brigades disbanded at the request of the Board and were replaced by a staff of permanent and auxiliary firemen.

In 1900 submissions from the Board to the State Government for the funding of station construction and land purchase were successful and £55,000 ($110 000) was set aside in the loan estimates for 'land and stations'. However, the delayed effects of the 1890s depression had diminished the public purse and the loan votes lapsed. The Government's response to an irate Board delegation was short and terse: 'the matter must stand over, no funds being available' (MFBAR, 1904:3).

To alleviate the lack of space at Head-quarters the Board obtained a 21-year lease on 211 Castlereagh Street in 1904 (having held a yearly renewal lease since 1902) and a five-year lease on 213–215 Castlereagh Street. With other station plans the Board was less fortunate and it was not until early 1905 that money was released from the 1902–03 Loan Vote, and tenders called by the Government Architect.

With a further influx of funds in the 1905–06 vote the Board was able to embark on a period of feverish construction and land purchase. In almost all cases, designs were by Vernon's assistant, E L Drew from the Government Architect's Branch of the Public Works Department. In all, between 1905 and 1909, some £87,600 ($175 200) was allocated by the Government for station construction and land purchase. Two styles predominated in this period. Those built in 1905–1906 (Botany, Glebe, Leichhardt and Woollahra) were in the English architectural style popularised by Charles F Voysey. Those built later (Arncliffe, Bexley, Five Dock, Rozelle and Neutral Bay) were variations on the Edwardian Free Style. Almost all these buildings stand today as symbols of both the imagination of their architect, E L Drew, and the busiest construction phase in the history of Sydney Fire Brigades.

The location and distribution of stations within Sydney were based on principles developed in London by Eyre Massey Shaw and brought to Sydney by Alfred Webb. Writing in 1905 Webb stated:

> Fire stations and alarms should be so arranged as to protect, in a methodical way, the areas, so that no part is more that [sic] five minutes from the nearest fire station; that is, from the time the fire is observed until the arrival of a fire engine at a fire. This is to include the time occupied in giving the alarm, and time of the brigade turning out and travelling to a fire. In the suburbs the time may be extended. In order to cover the area systematically a standard of time is necessary; and although it may at the present moment not be practicable, owing to money considerations, to establish fire brigades throughout the whole of the Board's area, it would be well to distribute the various sections so that ultimately they may be at regular intervals. This matter is urged owing to the rapid developments which have taken place in the suburban areas. (Superintendent's Report to Board, 1905)

Most of the stations were located on the highest points of main thoroughfares to ensure the most rapid response by the horsedrawn steamers.

Many of the negotiations between the Board and local councils over stations sites and new brigades were protracted affairs. Randwick, whose volunteer brigade had been disbanded by the Board in 1897, 'found the lack of fire protection in the face of an ever increasing levy irksome' (Lynch and Larcombe, 1959:230). In 1900 a special committee of Council selected a fire station site adjoining the police station, but Superintendent Webb preferred land in Belmore Road. A series of alternative sites was considered between 1901 and 1904, but it was not until 1905, after a council deputation approached the Chief Secretary, that a brigade was formed in rented premises in Avoca Street. It was to be another three years before Randwick gained a permanent station in The Avenue.

Towards the end of the five-year lease on 213–215 Castlereagh Street the Board sought allowance in the Public Works Fund Estimates for its purchase. In 1908–09 £5,000 ($10 000) was set aside and in May 1909 the property was purchased from Sir William Manning for £4,675 ($9350).

By the end of the MFB reign in 1909, a network of 52 stations covered the 352 square miles (911.68 km^2) of the Sydney FD. Twenty-one were permanently-manned and 31 operated by volunteers. It was a far cry from 1884 when the MFB had only one permanently-manned Central Fire Station and volunteer brigades defending the centre of Sydney.

THE SPAIN AND COSH ERA

A major change heralded by the Fire Brigade (Amendment) Act 1909 was the provision of powers for the Board to raise a loan, to the value of £100,000 ($200 000), to purchase sites and erect fire stations. Whilst the loan was not immediately authorised, Superintendent Webb initiated planning for new stations and sites in Sydney and throughout the State. For the Government Architect's Department it was the end of an era of being principal architect to the Board. However, in the initial two years of the new Board, the Government Architect did design the Darlinghurst, Crows Nest and Enfield stations (funds having been allocated in the 1908–09 Estimates).

The Hunters Hill (Gladesville) Station in Pittwater Road has the honour of being the first station acquired by the Board of Fire Commissioners (BFC), being taken over on 1 January 1910, when Hunters Hill was included in the Sydney FD for the first time. However, the first fire station actually built by the BFC was Drummoyne, in Lyons Road, on 30 June 1910. When members of the Drummoyne Volunteers did not apply for positions in the new station, the Board appointed an officer and three permanent firemen to man the station.

Darlinghurst Fire Station designed by Government Architect Vernon

VERNON'S SWANSONG
Darlinghurst—1911

DARLINGHURST Fire Station was completed by the Public Works Department at the end of 1911 for a cost of nearly £10,000 ($20 000) and occupied by a brigade of eight permanent firemen on 22 January 1912. It replaced the old station at 250 Victoria Street which had been operated by the MFB on a 21-year lease since 1 May 1896.

The building represented a dramatic departure from tradition, both in terms of fire station design and in Government architecture:

> Such buildings as the Police and Fire Stations at Darlinghurst, built in ginger brick with stone dressings, display unconventional massing and whimsical detailing bordering on Art Nouveau. This was a local manifestation of the international succession, a revolt against academic rules, awkward maybe, but quite successful in the context of suburban Sydney (Weirick, 1976:8).

The year 1911 was Walter Liberty Vernon's last year as Government Architect, and Darlinghurst Fire Station his swansong. Vernon had served for over two decades as Government Architect, with his first major work being the imposing Circular Quay Fire Station in 1891.

Darlinghurst, in its original layout, consisted of three storeys. On the ground floor (from the junction of Victoria and Darlinghurst Streets) was the Watch Room adjacent to a motor bay and ladder bay. Both bays had double-door access to Victoria Street and Darlinghurst Road. Adjacent to the Ladder Room were the horse stalls and fodder room and hose-drying yard. Single men's quarters were provided plus a recreational room (dominated by the obligatory billiard table). The rear of the ground floor was occupied by two sets of married quarters (No 1 House and No 2 House). Each consisted of a paved yard area, bathroom and toilet, storeroom, kitchen, two bedrooms and living room. The first floor provided accommodation for four families (Nos 3, 4, 5, and 6 Houses) with the largest, No 6, having four bedrooms, kitchen with pantry, living room, bathroom and toilet plus the half-moon balcony facing Queens (Kings) Cross. Identical quarters to No 6 were provided on the second floor (No 7 House), plus clothes-lines, two laundries and drying shelter. On the flat roof additional space was provided for drying, plus a third laundry.

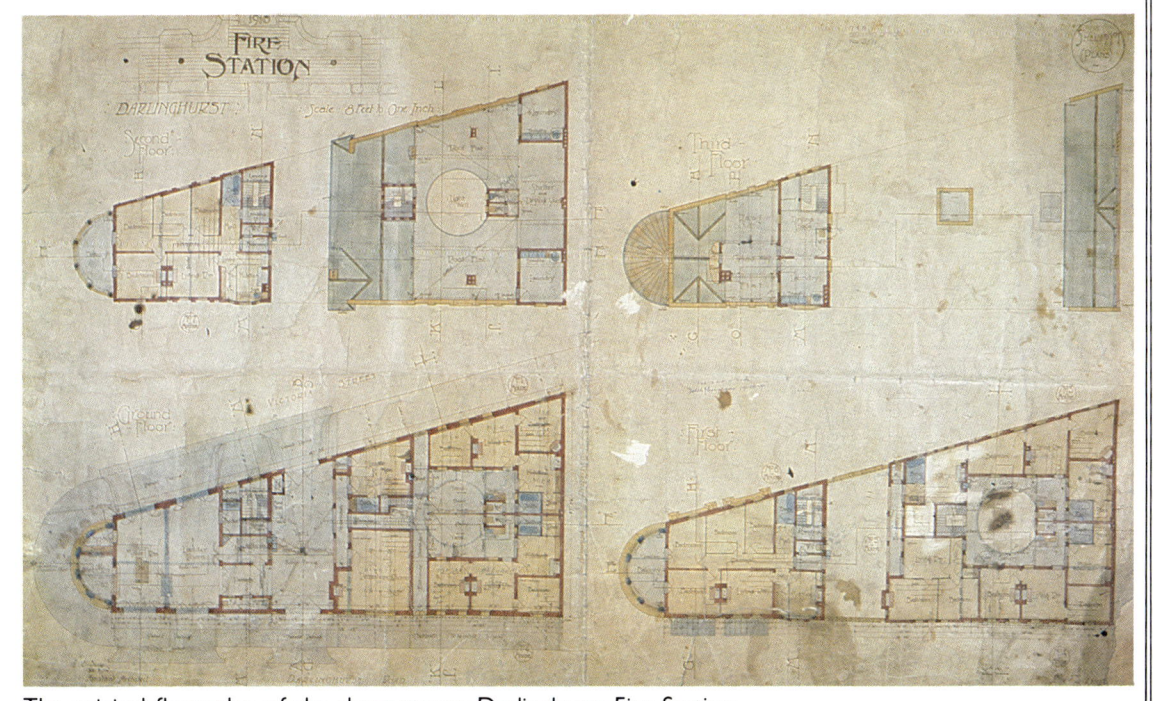

The original floor plan of the three-storey Darlinghurst Fire Station

Between 1910 and 1927 (and the end of the continuous shift system) the Board embarked on a major program of site acquisition and station construction throughout the State. The principal architects to the Board were now the private architect firm of Spain, Cosh and Minnett—an association which was to last until 1922.

Founded by Colonel Rowe in 1855 the firm had been associated with the MFB in designing George Street West (1886), Paddington (1899) and Ashfield (1901). In 1898 Alfred Spain became senior partner and continued the firm with Thomas F Cosh, who had joined the partnership in 1893. In 1910 Rupert V Minnett became the third partner, having done his articles with the firm.

In addition to their fire station designs, the firm was responsible for a number of other important works including St Clement's Anglican Church, Marrickville; the Trades Hall, Goulburn Street; the Blashki Building, Hunter Street; and Federal Paper Mills, Botany.

The firm's earliest works for the Board were the extensions to Headquarters and in 1912 Hurstville, Mascot and Campsie stations. The successful tender of £9,668 ($19 336) for the Headquarters' extensions (213–215 Castlereagh Street) was by Messrs Wall and Sons. Wall and Sons were prominent building contractors of the period and operated as Robert Wall and Sons until 1970 when they were wound-up (Hughes, 1981). The building was of four storeys, with the ground floor housing the Board's office and Boardroom (hence its common name of the 'Administration Building'). The second floor contained offices and the third and fourth floors rooms for single firemen plus messroom and kitchen. Two laundries were constructed on the roof, with the existing laundry of the old MFB building being converted to residential quarters. Other sections of the MFB building were renovated to provide more quarters for married senior officers. By August 1913 the extensions were complete. In 1915, with the end of the horse-drawn era at Headquarters, the building at 211 Castlereagh Street which was still under lease and had been used as a workshop and horse stables, was renovated. The workshop section was expanded at a cost of £1,099 ($2198) and a stores section added. It was not until 1923 that the Board was able to achieve its goal of purchasing the site [at a cost of £20,400 ($40 800)].

The new Board of Fire Commissioners replaced the 213–215 Castlereagh Street quarters (top) with an 'Administration block' adjoining the original MFB fire station (above). It was not until 1929 that the ground floor offices were replaced by two additional engine bays (right)

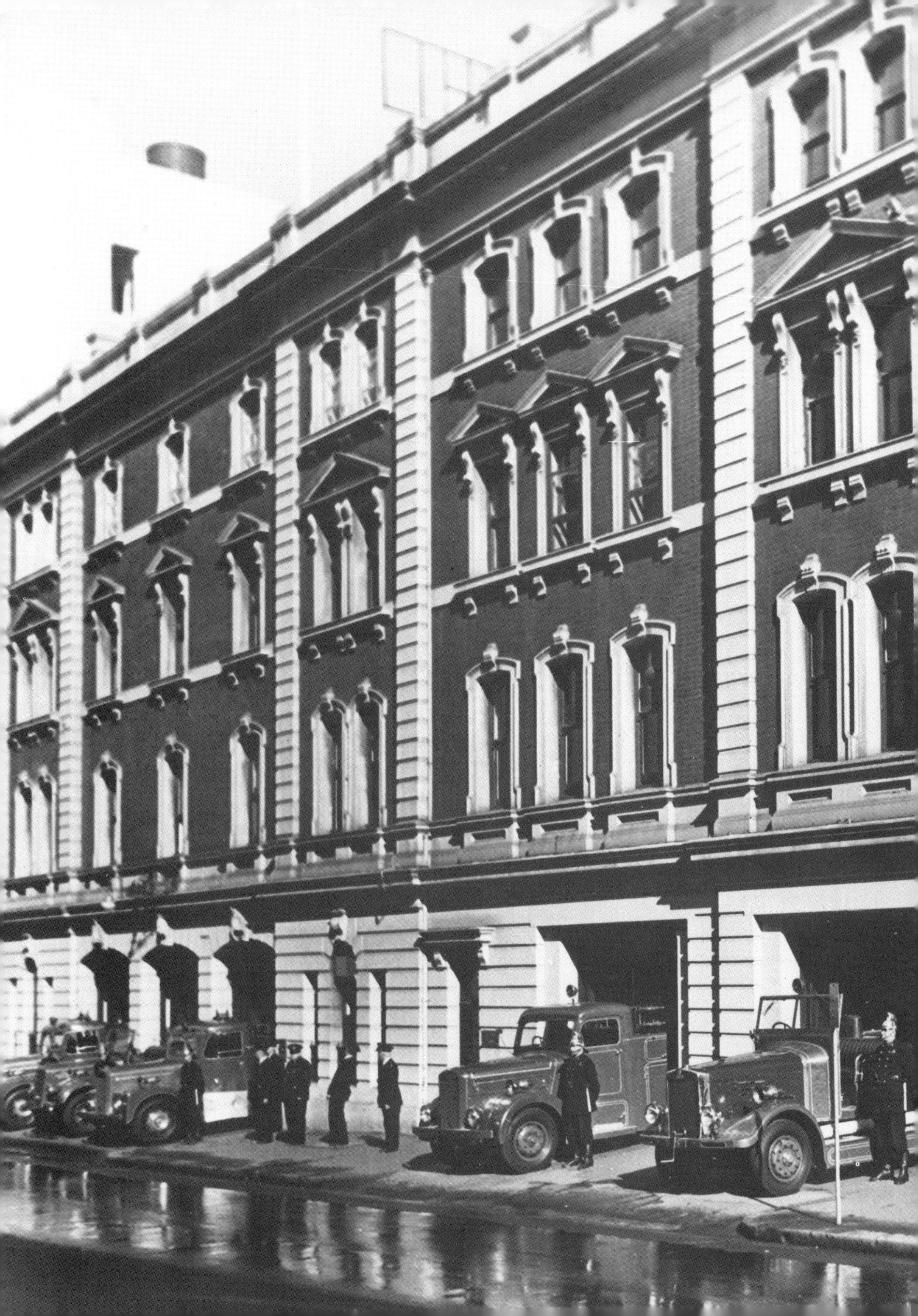

ERAS PAST
Freshwater (Harbord)—1914

Harbord staff in 1931 with Captain Jack Oliver and Station Officer Devenport at the helm. Closed in 1945 Harbord Fire Station serves today as a baby health clinic (right)

FRESHWATER'S weatherboard houses and surrounding bush created a considerable fire risk. Moreover, communication difficulties and the slowness of transport often allowed a bushfire to get out of control before the Manly Brigade could reach the scene. In 1914 the community decided to organise Freshwater Fire Brigade. The first headquarters was in Charles Street in a building previously occupied by Mr Hennessey, a butcher. The station was manned by Captain S Sterland, Senior Fireman J Oliver, and Firemen J C Olsen, F W Dains, G Phillip and J Allen, all of whom were partly-paid volunteers. Jack Oliver succeeded Captain Sterland in command.

Following an alarm, the firemen rang the bell then manhandled a large two-wheeled cart to the fire. The 'cotton-reel', as the cart was called, was equipped with a thousand feet [304.80 m] of hose and was a great attraction to children. After use, the fire hose was attached to a tall post to dry. The bell which had a good tone and could be heard all over the district was later donated to Harbord Public School.

With the aim of building a new fire station, a trust fund was organised by William Nixon, Chairman, Thomas Toor, secretary, and T A Sterland, treasurer. The new station, in Lawrence Street, was opened on 26 January, 1925 by the president of the Fire Commission Board, Mr Harkness, in the presence of about three hundred people. Jack Oliver, the brigade Captain at that time, remembers how the station operated: 'We had a Garford Fire Engine with solid rubber tyres. When a fire broke out, bells working from a switchboard inside the station rang in the firemen's homes. Available men immediately responded to the call, most of them arriving on push bikes.'

When modern, faster moving vehicles were introduced into the Manly district, Harbord station was closed down. Jack Oliver, who takes an active interest in local affairs, still complains about 'them' closing the station. The tree which stands beside the station building today, was planted by H Devenport, the Brigade's first full time Station Officer.

Thanks to the efforts of a group of local people led by Frank Booth, the building was put to good use when it was made into a Baby Health Centre in 1949. It was the first clinic established by Warringah Shire Council, an achievement that owed much to the efforts of two local councillors, S Raffo and C Walsham. (Gordon, 1978)

In 1914 the Government eventually approved the £100,000 ($200 000) loan for the purchase of sites and the creation of fire stations. An exhaustive survey of the Sydney FD was undertaken by the new Chief Officer, N Sparks, under the time criterion for station coverage proposed by his predecessor Alfred Webb. A critical element of the survey was the recognition that motorised appliances were now rapidly replacing the slower (and more expensive to maintain) horse-drawn appliances. Sparks' view was that motorised central stations could be established (some on new sites), eliminating those now poorly positioned stations built to facilitate horse-drawn responses.

The Board's program of site acquisition was extensive: between 1914 and 1917 sites were purchased at Marrickville, Vaucluse, Waterloo, Beecroft, Ryde, Lane Cove, Annandale, Hunters Hill, Bankstown, Canterbury, Homebush, St Peters, Daceyville, York Street and Mosman.

During the same period an extensive program of station construction, under the architects Spain, Cosh and Dods[5], began with stations being built at Waverley, Vaucluse, Beecroft, Ryde, Mortdale, East Willoughby (Willoughby), Guildford, Lane Cove, Annandale, Hunters Hill and Bankstown. With loan limitations and financial restrictions during the war, designs were kept simple, with single bays and spartan facilities. In other cases (Eastwood, Gordon, Freshwater) stations were leased. Improvements were also carried out at the many stations where permanent staff replaced volunteers, to upgrade accommodation and provide officer quarters.

Many of the new brigades were established on the fringe areas of the expanding suburbs. They were generally poorly equipped and ill-housed but lacked nothing in spirit and keenness. The account of the Freshwater Fire Brigade, (from Gordon, 1978), which was formed in 1914, typifies the smaller suburban brigade of this period.

On 22 November 1917 the President of the Board, Ernest Farrar, presented a lengthy proposal to the Board entitled 'Consolidation of Fire Stations, Sydney Fire District and Reorganisation of District Officers'. The proposal was a culmination of planning underway since 1914 and was 'not for today or tomorrow, but covers a period of from fifteen to twenty years hence' (BFC Minutes, 1917:929).

The plan evaluated each existing station in terms of age, manning, appliances and location. It further considered the suitability of vacant sites held by the Board, and possible site purchase. It proposed that vacant sites at Surry Hills, Kensington, Strathfield and Rose Bay be sold and that the following stations be closed: George Street West, North Sydney, Alexandria, Matraville, Canterbury or Campsie, Rozelle and Turramurra plus one station in St George District. At the same time the proposal was to upgrade adjoining stations. For example, the elimination of North Sydney was to be accompanied by a motorisation of Neutral Bay and the construction of a new, permanently staffed station with a motor appliance at Mosman. The Maroubra station was, in part, a response to a deputation from Randwick Council which argued that the Matraville hose post was totally inadequate for the fire protection needs of the area. Many of the changes were strongly influenced by individual councils.

The second part of the President's proposal was a reduction in the number of District Officers from seven to four, with four of the older DOs retaining pay and entitlements but operating essentially as Station Officers. It was proposed that the three younger DOs, Grimmond, Nance and Lister, be stationed at Burwood, Kogarah and Crows Nest and Divisional Officer Lamborne be brought from Broken Hill to Headquarters as the DO of 'A' District.

In 1917 the Board sought amending legislation from the Government to allow for an increase in its borrowing powers and to allow properties previously acquired by the Government to be 'vested in the Board'. The Board's rationale in both cases was to enable implementation of its program of station consolidation and, at the same time, sell unwanted properties (many of which were under Government ownership).

The Government's immediate response was to initiate an inquiry in 1918 by the Auditor-General, Mr F A Coghlan (Board President, 1911–13) into 'The Board of Fire Commissioners Scheme for the Consolidation of Fire Stations in Sydney'. The inquiry was sparked both by the Board's request for Property Bill legislation and a newspaper series critical of the Board's plans for the reorganisation of District Officers (Chapter 5).

Whilst most of the Coghlan Report addressed the question of District Officer appointments it also concluded that:

> The scheme [of reorganisation], so far as it relates to the motorisation of stations, is undoubtedly in the public interest. The Scheme as approved by the Board may need to be adjusted from time to time, but the motorisation of stations and the eliminations of unnecessary stations are in accordance with approved practice elsewhere, and ... while economical, appears to be consistent with public safety. (Auditor-General's Report, 1918:635)

With this approval and the transfer of a number of Government-owned properties, the Board embarked on the program of 'consolidation' in 1919. The vacant sites were sold and plans for the construction of the new stations plus alterations to others were drawn up by Spain, Cosh and Dods.[6] The years 1919 to 1928 saw a total of fourteen new stations built in the Sydney FD (an additional 40 were built in other Fire Districts). The only section of the Board's consolidation program which was not pursued (with the exception of Turramurra which closed in 1920) were the plans to close stations, because of strong union and local government opposition and delays in passing the Real Property Act.

In 1923 the Board decided, as an economy measure, to cease the practice of employing architects on a contract basis, thus severing their connection with Spain and Cosh. The last of the Spain and Cosh designs were Manly (1921), Lakemba (1921), Maroubra (1924) and Hornsby (1925). In all the firm had designed 29 fire stations throughout the State.

THE ROARING TWENTIES
The First Architect to the Board

Between 1923 and 1928 most new stations and quarters were designed by the Board's first in-house architect, W McNiven. Bill McNiven first joined the MFB as a probationary fireman on 1 May 1900, rising to the rank of SO at Balmain. His training as a carpenter saw him appointed Clerk of Works in 1916, on the death of the Board's first Clerk of Works, George T Broadhurst.[7] In 1918 the position was upgraded to Officer-in-Charge of Construction and in 1923

McNiven became registered as an architect under the Architects Act (1923).

McNiven's first designs in the Sydney FD were Dee Why (1924) and Burwood (1925), very much in the traditional lay-out adopted by Spain and Cosh. Burwood station, with a fully permanent staff of six men, provided double engine bays, two storeys of single men's quarters plus married dwellings (later sold) on either side of the station. Dee Why provided officer accommodation on the second floor with a standard ground floor layout for single men. Whilst other stations and quarters were constructed in the Sydney FD under McNiven's plans, his major contribution in the period 1923 to 1927 was in country towns, where many of his designs still stand today.

By 1922 Sydney's population had passed the one million mark and the city was in the midst of an unprecedented building boom: 'Almost 40 per cent of Sydney's population growth between 1921 and 1929 took place in the western and southwestern suburbs, slightly less than a quarter in the eastern suburbs, around seventeen per cent in the southern suburbs and the remaining nineteen per cent north of the harbour and the Parramatta River' (Spearritt, 1978:34). Growth, as in earlier decades, was closely tied to the rail lines: to the west the Strathfield–Parramatta line, the Belmore–Bankstown line and the extensions to Villawood and Regents Park. In the south further development took place in Hurstville and Mortdale; in the north Willoughby, Lane Cove and along the coast from Manly to Dee Why. The terrace style which predominated in early 'housing booms' was replaced by semi-detached houses and bungalows (Boyd, 1960). Most developments, particularly those along the rail lines, were served by a nearby fire station built in the preceding two decades. For example, the expansion along Strathfield–Parramatta rail line was serviced by Concord (1901), Homebush (1919), Rookwood (Lidcombe 1899), Auburn (1908) and Parramatta

Manly Fire Station at Fairlight, one of the last Spain and Cosh fire stations, completed in 1921

(1899). In fact the 1920s saw the formation of many brigades, such as Wentworthville and Fairfield (1920) and Baulkham Hills (1924), on the urban fringe where population numbers were few and housing widely scattered. There is little doubt that by the late 1920s Sydney and its suburbs were as well covered by fire brigades relative to the fire risk as they would ever be.

With the adoption of the two-platoon system in 1927 (see Chapter 5) a gradual change took place in the design and layout of fire stations. Most Board-owned cottages adjacent to stations were sold, whilst station quarters were rented to firemen. Where stations became permanently manned under the new shift system it was necessary to provide officer rooms, along with recreational area, lockers and change rooms, in sections previously utilised for single or married quarters. In many cases (for example, Hurstville) areas previously used as stables were also converted into mess or recreation rooms.

It was at Headquarters where changes of the greatest magnitude were required. In 1927 a new watchroom was opened (Chapter 3), and in 1928 work commenced on alterations to the Administration Building. During these alterations the Board's offices were temporarily relocated across the street at 242 Castlereagh Street (later Boyded Showrooms). Completed in September 1929, the alterations were carried out under the supervision of McNiven and his assistant Fred Ross.[8] The ground floor (previously used as a Boardroom) was converted into two engine bays, bringing the total at Headquarters to five, plus offices for the District Officer and Station Officer. At the rear of the building additional toilet and shower facilities were provided along with engine access to the drill yard. On the first floor, provision was made for the Board's office and Boardroom, whilst the second and third floors, previously used as firemen's bedrooms and messrooms, were converted into offices for the administrative staff. On the roof provision was made for a games room, which had previously occupied a section of the area taken over by the new watchroom.

With the retirement of Bill McNiven in 1931, Fred Ross was appointed the new architect to the Board. Ross had joined the Board in 1919 as a draughtsman and while in the Board's employ gained his architecture degree part-time. A slowdown in Sydney's growth, the onset of the Great Depression along with war preparations

OLD NUMBER 10
Redfern

THE transformation from horse and steam to motorisation ended a nostalgic era of Sydney firefighting. Along with the passing of horse and steam went many of the 'old' characters, men from the MFB days, who had joined in the 1880s when professional firefighting in Sydney was in its infancy. Each of the old metropolitan stations had at least one of these characters but none is as well remembered as the Officer-in-Charge of Redfern (No 10) from 1904 to 1926, Henry T Dawes.

Known as 'Rufus', 'Dickie', 'Daddy' and 'Izes', SO Dawes was a seafaring Englishman, round and thickly set, with a swaggering walk and a shrewd, jovial temperament. Redfern station opened five years prior to his arrival when the old Redern police court was converted by the Government Architect. With a staff of six men in its early years Redfern was a busy station turning out to all the big inner-city fires along with those in Redfern's bustling commercial area.

Redfern possessed three horses, all Irish greys—'Belfast', 'Shannon' and 'Limerick'. Two pulled the steamer whilst the third pulled the set of curricle ladders. The following account gives some insight into the character of the horses, 'Rufus', and the life at Redfern fire station:

> One day when 'Limerick' was about to be taken out with the curricle ladders for exercise, Station Officer Dawes, a bit of a card who liked to imagine himself as a good judge of horseflesh, remarked: 'That horse looks fit enough to pull a blinking house down'. The boys at the station thought that old 'Rufus' had suddenly become psychic for soon after word was received that 'Limerick' and the curricle ladders had in fact broken a cast iron shop awning support! The horse had backed on to the support when frightened by the noise of a steam tram chugging up a nearby hill. (*Fire News*, 1 July 1958:10)

In 1913 Redfern's first motor fire engine was installed—a Dennis 'Aster' two-cylinder motor turbine. The faithful 'Shannon' and 'Limerick' were sold, but 'Belfast' was retained, to pull the curricle ladders. By 1913 Redfern's population had grown to over 25 000 and it was now at the heart of a major commercial area. On 9 February

1915 gas lighting was replaced by electric lighting and only a few months later, 'Belfast' was sold. DO George Caller recalls:

> 'Belfast' was a magnificently-built grey; I shall never forget him. After his fire-fighting career had finished, 'Belfast' was sold to a Bedding Company situated about a hundred yards [91.44 m] from the Redfern fire station. I often used to see him pulling a load of feathers around the district. And he was really fire-brigade minded; whenever he passed his old station he knew it. If the bells happened to go on when he was near he would become hard to handle and likely to upset his load of feathers and 'turn out' with the Brigade. A fire-fighter through and through was old 'Belfast'. (*Fire News*, 1 October 1959:13)

By the end of 1915 Redfern brigade had slipped into another era. It was to be a number of years before the last links were severed. In 1926 'Rufus' Dawes left Redfern and a year later the end of the continuous shift system saw many firemen leave the neighbourhood to establish residences elsewhere. No longer were they required to live either on the station or in one of the nearby terraces or boarding houses.

The final serverance came in 1972 when the old Redfern fire station was demolished and replaced by a smaller but more modern station (see Appendix 4.1).

The opening of Redfern Fire Station (No. 10) in 1900 (above). From 1904–1926 the officer-in-charge was 'Dickie' Dawes (top, seated centre)

from the mid-1930s saw only six stations constructed in the Sydney FD during the 1930s. In country areas, however, the program of station construction and alteration intensified. By the end of 1938 the Board's building assets had increased to £388,222 ($776 444). This reflected not only the magnitude of the Board's construction program with its own architects but also the transfer of Certificates of Title to the Board under the Real Property Act (1925).

The most controversial issue during the 1930s was the scheme of station closures put to the Board by a deputation from fire insurance companies in October 1930. With the increase in levies on insurance companies in the 1927 amendment to the Fire Brigades Act, companies were looking to reduce the costs of fire brigade operations. To this end their scheme proposed staff reductions and the closure of twelve stations—Woollahra, Bondi, Marrickville, Ashfield, Wentworthville, Toongabbie, Northmead, Campsie, Arncliffe, Bexley, Neutral Bay and Chatswood. The response of Chief Officer Thomas Nance was total rejection of the scheme:

> The risks which confront the fire brigade today are infinitely greater and more dangerous than those of a few years ago, and it is more than ever necessary to get to a fire in the shortest space of time ... The imperative demands of the public are for efficiency, and if one life should be lost as a result of the closing of any station, the responsibility is wholly and solely on the Fire Department, which must answer to the outcry of public opinion. (*Sunday Guardian*, 26 October 1930)

There is little doubt that public opinion was firmly on the Chief Officer's side, with an outraged newspaper editorial stating, 'There can be no tampering with the only too inadequate fire protection now existing. Not even for insurance company profits' (*Sunday Guardian*, 26 October 1930). With that the issue ended, at least for the time being.

POST-WAR BLUES
Station Closures

With the introduction of the 56-hour week at the end of the Second World War, the closure of 23 fire stations was the most significant single Board action in relation to fire stations throughout its 100-year history (see Chapter 6). It was in direct contrast to the views expressed by Chief Officer Nance in 1930 (although not to those held by the insurance representatives on the Board at that time). The number of fire stations covering the 352 square mile (911.68 km^2) Sydney FD dropped from 76 to 53.

The Board's rationale for the closures was that it represented an attempt to 'increase efficiency by a re-allocation of personnel, having regard to changes which have occurred over many years in the character and situation of fire risks, the more modern and efficient fire fighting appliances and equipment available, vastly improved road conditions and other similar factors' (BFCAR, 1945:2). In the case of changes in the older, inner areas of Sydney there is little doubt that this rationale was in most part justified, but there is also little doubt that the timing and extent of closures was closely related to the bitter clash between the union and the Board at this time (see Chapter 2).

'C' District indicates the changes which took place throughout the Sydney FD. Four stations were closed—Arncliffe, Bexley, Canterbury and Mortdale—with adjacent stations remaining at Rockdale, Kogarah and Hurstville. Most of the permanent firemen from the closed stations were redeployed at the District Station, Kogarah, which had an increase of one fireman per shift (and a net increase with the change to three platoons of 25 firemen). Hurstville also received additional staff. Rockdale, however, was demoted to a shift staff of an SO and one fireman. In hindsight the closure of both Arncliffe and Bexley has left a significant gap in the area served by stations within a five-minute radius. A section from Kingsgrove to Bardwell Park (areas which were developed in the immediate post-war years) remains outside this 'immediate' coverage even to the present day.

At the same time as the 23 fire stations were closed, Sydney was about to embark on an unprecedented era of suburban growth. Between 1947 and 1954 Sydney's population increased by almost 400 000 to 1 863 161. The influx of migrants, the trend to home ownership (from 39.7 per cent in 1947 to 59.6 per cent in 1954), the large-scale Housing Commission developments along with speculative building and the efforts of 'owner-builders' resulted in an outward spread of the Sydney urban area. In particular, sections of Bankstown, Blacktown, Fairfield, Holroyd,

Hurstville, Parramatta, Rockdale, Ryde and Sutherland had dramatic expansions in residential area. Sutherland's population, for example, increased from about 29 000 in 1947 to 65 757 in 1954.

In contrast many of the inner areas of the city were losing population as manufacturing replaced the older residential neighbourhoods. Manufacturing was strongly clustered in the inner suburbs of Alexandria, Waterloo, Pyrmont, Redfern and Balmain, and was tending, increasingly, to shift to the immediate west, Concord and Ashfield, or to the south, Marrickville, St Peters and Mascot.

With the rapid post-war growth came a corresponding increase in the number of fire calls; from 5950 in 1945 to 9592 in 1954. The magnitude of growth in the suburbs meant that an increasing proportion of calls were being received from suburban areas.

The scale and rapidity of Sydney's urban growth, the wage demands of a three-platoon manning system, financial stringencies after the war and the Board's policy of station closures all served to weaken station coverage in the immediate post-war years.[9] In many cases even the remaining stations were now ill-positioned, having been located during Sydney's rail and tramway era when most suburban development was clustered at nodal points along the public transport network. Sydney's post-war growth was based on the mobility given by the motor car, with the result that areas between the rail routes were 'infilled' at the same time as whole suburbs were being built on the urban fringe with very little, if any, public transport.

Despite an increase of over 200 per cent in expenditure within the Sydney FD between 1945 and 1955, little went toward new stations and/or new brigades.[10] There were exceptions. In 1948 a temporary building was built on a new site at Castle Hill; in 1952 Mortdale was reopened as a volunteer brigade and in 1953 a new brigade was established at Caringbah. These exceptions do not hide the stark contrast between the immediate post-war inactivity and the 'boom' construction years between 1900 and 1927.

Many of the stations placed on the 'inactive' list in 1945 were sold. Although some such as Alexandria, Homebush, Canterbury, and the 'Workhouse', George Street West, have been demolished, most survive today in a variety of guises:

'For Sale' and barely recognisable, the former Vaucluse Fire Station as it is today

> *Arncliffe*: council library
> *Annandale*: residence and storage
> *Bexley*: vacant (owned by Board)
> *Chatswood*: shop
> *Enfield*: part residence
> *Five Dock*: police station (vacant)
> *Granville*: shop
> *Hunters Hill*: baby health centre
> *Harbord*: baby health centre
> *Mascot*: reopened 1960
> *Mortdale*: reopened 1952
> *Maroubra*: reopened 1957
> *North Sydney*: restaurant
> *Pyrmont*: reopened 1960
> *Ryde*: reopened 1960
> *Rozelle*: bush fire station (No 99)
> *St Peters*: baby health centre/kindergarten
> *Vaucluse*: residence
> *Woollahra*: reopened 1951
> *Waverley*: convention centre

Pyrmont, Five Dock, Bexley, Rozelle and Arncliffe stations served as Board workshops for many years. However, the most novel conversions were to baby health centres. Sold to local councils, three of the former fire stations were converted to cater for the needs of the post-war baby boom.

Lacking finance to build new stations, Fred Ross and his staff were principally occupied with station alterations. The increases in staff associated with the three-platoon system placed further pressures on space within stations. Billiard rooms and recreational areas were altered to provide more locker space and mess facilities. The major project of the Board's building staff in the post-war years was the alteration of the former Paddington FS to a training college.

A REASSESSMENT
Stations for the Fringe

In 1956 a newly constituted Board took office under the Presidency of Leslie Duff. Although Duff was to die in office three years later, his presidency saw a major redirection in Board policy toward the planning and construction of fire stations. In December 1956 Paddington Training College was opened and exactly one year later major alterations at Headquarters were also completed. The extensive alterations provided improvements in the administrative workspace and, more importantly, in the accommodation of firemen. 'Rats Castle', as the firemen's quarters on the top floor of the Headquarters building was known, was now a thing of the past. The Chief Officer's quarters on the first floor (last occupied by W Beare) and Deputy Chief's on the second floor (last occupied by E Griffiths whilst Chief) were converted to offices. At the same time the Board began taking steps for the purchase of adjoining properties in Bathurst Street to facilitate the further extension of the Headquarters property.

In 1957 the Board initiated a major review of fire protection within the Sydney FD. Largely under the supervision of DCO (and later Chief Officer) Horrie Pye, the review looked at the location and staffing of stations and the boundaries of the Sydney FD vis-à-vis the post-war growth of Sydney and the changing distribution of Sydney's fire risk. The review was long overdue and in part had been brought about by the growing agitation by many suburban councils that they were receiving very little fire protection in return for a rapidly escalating contribution to the Board.

The trend to a suburbanisation of Sydney begun in the immediate post-war years continued. Areas such as Bankstown, Ryde and Sutherland consolidated their development, with Bankstown's population increasing from 102 000 in 1954 to 152 000 in 1961. Indeed Bankstown, Parramatta, Ryde and Hurstville were almost fully consolidated by the early 1960s (Neutze, 1977). By the mid-1950s the dispersal of manufacturing from many of the older port/central city-tied locations was also well underway. Under the impetus of a labour supply established in the previous decade, greater land availability and cheaper land prices, suburbs such as Parramatta, Bankstown and Auburn had dramatic increases in the area of land utilised for manufacturing. The dispersal of manufacturing served to reinforce the increasing fire risk of suburban areas of Sydney.

The review of the Sydney FD, in the light of the above changes to the area of Sydney's urban development, was comprehensive and far-reaching, particularly in relation to the 'urban fringe'. The review proposed that five Fire Districts on the fringe of Sydney be included in the Sydney FD and that 'replacement' stations be built in many of these areas. In 1959 the first of the proposed changes was implemented with the opening of Revesby FS, serving an area which had been opened up with the completion of the Kingsgrove–East Hills rail line in 1931. In the Sutherland area major changes were also made to the network of fire services, although in this case extreme doubt must be cast on their appropriateness. In 1959 both Cronulla FD and Sutherland FD were disbanded and added to the Sydney FD. In conjunction with this change the Board decided to close Cronulla FS and transfer the permanent staff to a new station in Mansfield Avenue, Caringbah. At the same time it was decided to close the the Caringbah FS operating from President Avenue and to transfer some volunteers to the new Caringbah FS. These changes were effected in March 1959. The net effect of the changes was that Sutherland was served by two stations with four SOs and 27 volunteers in the place of three stations with a total complement of four SOs and 33 volunteers.

As early as 1956 Sutherland Council made written submissions that the whole of the Shire be included within the Sydney FD. The representations were based on the rapid post-war population and housing growth and were made despite the Council's own estimate of an increased cost to Council of up to £8,528 ($17 056) per year. In February 1958, following the Review of the Sydney FD, the Board responded to Council submissions with a four-point proposal that:

1 Sutherland Council establish a Bush Fire Brigade at Kurnell;
2 a new Caringbah FS be established to replace both Cronulla FS and the existing Caringbah volunteer brigade in President Avenue;
3 a replacement station be built at Sutherland once a suitable site was found; and
4 Sutherland FD and Cronulla FD be added to the Sydney FD.

The Sutherland Council's response to the Board's plans was two-pronged. In April 1959 Council applied to the Bush Fire Committee that areas of Sutherland Shire outside Fire Districts be designated a Bush Fire District and the formation of 'official volunteer' brigades under Council supervision be initiated. Council's second strategy was to express its dissatisfaction with the Board's decisions by way of deputation, firstly in July 1958 to protest the closure of Cronulla FS and secondly in February 1959 to discuss changes in general to Sutherland fire services. At both meetings Council members expressed concern that despite a rapid increase in Council's funding requirements, Sutherland was receiving a lower level of service than previously. They argued this was especially the case in Cronulla which was now 'distant' from the nearest FS, and even further from a 'back-up' brigade. It is significant that the Board's major defence in the July meeting was that Caringbah would be a two-appliance station. However, in the February 1959 meeting, six months after Cronulla FS closed, the Board stated, 'it *hoped* Caringbah would be a two-appliance station' (Sutherland Council Minutes, February 1959). But this was not put into effect.

By mid-1959, with Council pleas ignored, opposition to the Board's changes intensified. Local community groups, notably the Engadine Progress Association, protested against the high fire insurance premiums and inadequate fire protection in growth areas outside the Sydney FD. To co-ordinate opposition the NSW Fire Brigade Employees' Union organised a public meeting at Sutherland School of Arts in July 1959. At the meeting council and union representatives voiced concern at the inadequate level of service, particularly in relation to the lack of permanent manpower and to the large areas covered by an individual brigade, especially when the size of Council's contribution was considered relative to other municipalities.

Further meetings with BFC members followed in late 1959 and opposition culminated in the presentation by Council delegation of a petition signed by 8000 residents, requesting permanent fire protection in Sutherland Shire. The result was the opening in 1961–62 of a replacement Sutherland FS in Moore Street, with four permanent officers and volunteers. At the same time, however, the Board voted against extending the FD boundaries.

In 1960 a replacement fire station was opened at Avalon (the Warringah FD being included in the Sydney FD in 1959) and in the same year Mascot, Ryde and Pyrmont stations, closed in 1945, were reopened. Based on recommendations of the 1957 Review of the Sydney FD, the Board announced an extensive rebuilding program on the western fringe of Sydney where Liverpool and Cabramatta FDs had been disbanded and placed into the Sydney FD in 1959. In 1961 replacement stations were opened

Avalon—typical of the smaller fire stations built on Sydney's fringe in the early 1960s

at Blacktown, Cabramatta, Campbelltown, Liverpool and Rydalmere. All were designed by Board architect, Fred Ross, and his successor, Arthur Cunningham.[11] They were to be the last of the stations designed by a Board architect. Arthur Cunningham's retirement in 1961 heralded the end of a 38-year era, as the Board decided to abolish the position of Architect to the Board in favour of independent architects. The stations, as with those throughout the rest of the 1960s, were simple in design and based on a minimisation of cost.

Under the administration of President Ben Andrews (1959–64) there was a continuation of station rebuilding and in some cases the establishment of new brigades on Sydney's urban fringe. Brigades were established as far afield as Berowra, Engadine and Busby (Green Valley) as the post-war spread of the urban area continued through the 1960s. New suburbs sprang up in Blacktown, Ku-ring-gai, Sutherland, Warringah and Liverpool, Liverpool's population increasing by 176 per cent between 1961 and 1966.

As with other public service authorities providing localised community services such as sewerage, roads, schools, hospitals and clinics, the BFC was faced with the difficult task of providing service to an increasingly far-flung and low-density urban area. Despite the rebuilding program pursued during the 1960s and the establishment of new brigades, not everyone could be satisfied. Most opposition came from councils and community groups on the fringes of the Sydney FD, where urban growth was most spectacular and where contributions to the Board had increased rapidly. For example Blacktown's contribution increased almost sevenfold between 1955 and 1969.

Blacktown represents a typical example of the problems faced during the 1960s. The replacement Blacktown station built in 1961 was manned by a station officer and twelve volunteers, the nearest brigade being the fully volunteer Toongabbie, five kilometres to the east. Even by the mid-1960s extensive housing and some industrial development had taken place in areas such as Doonside, Rooty Hill and Lalor Park. A proposed station at Lalor Park was rejected by the Board due to limited funds and at the same time the Board deferred Council requests that the new 'urban' areas of Blacktown be brought into the Sydney FD.

In 1967 and 1968 two special meetings of Blacktown Council were convened to discuss fire provision within the LGA. Present at the first meeting was the local government representative on the Board. He was also present at the second meeting, attended by the President of the Board, Chief Officer, Employees' representative on the Board, Secretary of the Fire Brigades Employees' Union and two Councillors from Baulkham Hills. Blacktown aldermen expressed their own and the community's disquiet with the level of fire protection within the Blacktown LGA. Specific details of the area's expansion and demand for protection were documented. The main areas of concern were:

1 the Board's failure to extend the Sydney FD to areas Council felt required Board coverage;
2 the failure of volunteers to respond to alarms, particularly at Toongabbie FS;
3 the increasing number of cases where bush fire brigades were responding to 'house' fires;
4 the inappropriateness of often having an SO only respond to a fire call;
5 failure to build a new station in the Lalor Park–Seven Hills area (a recommendation for which was made by the Board's own technical committee in 1958);
6 the increasing funding to the Board with only minor fire service improvements;
7 with a number of multi-storey buildings appearing, the lack of turntable ladders in the Western District;
8 the lack of a direct phone link to the Blacktown FS.

As a result of these meetings and correspondence with the Board, a delegation from Blacktown Council was received by the Board in May 1968. The Board at this meeting announced that Doonside was to be included in the Sydney FD, that the permanent staff at Blacktown would be increased by one man per shift, that station offciers would be stationed at Toongabbie and that a new brigade was proposed for Mt Druitt.

It was to be another three years before the Mt Druitt Brigade was established and during those years the Blacktown Brigade (and Blacktown Council bush fire brigades) had to service a widening urban area. In 1971 (prior to the establishment of Mt Druitt) Blacktown Brigade attended 724 first-call alarms, with more than 60 per cent in excess of a five-minute response.[12]

Macquarie Fields (Campbelltown Fire District) presents the most futuristic design of the newer Sydney area fire stations

Despite the station building program on the urban fringe during the 1960s the weight of evidence would suggest that the supply of men and stations did not match the 'demand' brought about by Sydney's suburbanisation. In some cases, for example, Bankstown, where a 'temporary' station, with an SO and two firemen per shift plus ten volunteers, covered an extensive area it appeared that the suburb had been 'by-passed' in fire services provision. The reasons for the difficulties in servicing many of the suburban areas lies in the scale and extent of urban growth combined with a cost-conscious Board. Between 1958 and 1969 the AAV of Sydney FD property increased by 177 per cent whereas over the same period expenditure within the Sydney FD increased by only 113 per cent. The percentage of premium income contributed by insurance companies over the same period declined from 31.11 per cent to 18.26 per cent. Similarly, the contributions of local councils declined from 4s 6¼d per £100 (23 cents per $100) of AAV to 16 cents per $100 of AAV.

DESIGN FOR THE FUTURE

The 1970s saw little respite for the Board, as Sydney's fringes extended even further to accommodate an apparently insatiable appetite for home ownership. Areas outside the Sydney FD—such as Camden, Campbelltown, St Mary's, Penrith, Terrey Hills and Menai—were showing all the signs of an urban 'take-off'. Between 1976 and 1981 Campbelltown had the largest growth in new dwellings (11 025) of any council area in Sydney.[13]

At the end of 1983 the Sydney FD embraced an area of 1260 km^2 and contained 73 brigades, from Engadine in the south to Mt Druitt in the west and Berowra and Avalon to the north. The surrounding fire districts of Bundeena, Campbelltown, Camden, Penrith, Riverstone and Windsor contained a further eleven brigades, including the one most recently established, on 28 May 1981, at Macquarie Fields. The futuristic design of Macquarie Fields, by the architectural branch of the NSW Public Works

Department, signifies a return to a direct Government involvement in station design and construction—an involvement which had its origins in the 1880s.

The distribution of stations throughout Sydney today is a far cry from the formative years of the MFB when only one central station and 22 volunteer companies provided Sydney's fire protection. In other towns and cities throughout NSW the Board administers a further 239 brigades, the most recently formed brigade being Mulwala, established in 1984.

Most Sydney stations built during the 1970s have been in the outer areas of the Sydney FD, for example, Avalon (1970), Northmead (1973), Miranda (1974), Smithfield (1975) and the most recent within the Sydney FD, Cronulla (1977). Replacement stations have also been built at Redfern (1972) and Alexandria (1975). Of brick construction, most of the stations on Sydney's outskirts have been built with two bays to house both a fire engine and water tanker. By far the most prominent amongst the independent architects employed by the Board has been J W Roberts.[14] From its first design, Liverpool (1958), the firm has designed more than 60 stations, the most recent in Sydney being the replacement Wentworthville station completed in 1983. In addition to fire station design the firm has also been prominent in the design of theatres, including Skyline Drive-ins and Her Majesty's Theatre. Supervision of station construction and maintenance sections (plumbers, painters and carpenters) was the task of the Works Supervisor, two Clerk-of-Works and the Building Maintenance Officer and, more recently, a consultant.[15]

Despite a continuation of the Board's building program through the 1970s a number of difficulties remain with both the current distribution of stations and the procedures for implementing new construction. The example of a recent Sydney FD station, Cronulla, indicates the inordinate delays which may occur from the time when the need for a station is recognised and its actual opening (in this case, six years). In July 1971 the Board sent Sutherland Council a letter detailing plans for upgrading the level of fire protection in the Shire. Included were details of negotiations with the MWSDB for vacant land on Captain Cook Drive (cnr Elouera Road), North Cronulla.

Following the Board's July 1971 letter Council responded favourably, noting that it expected to vacate the North Cronulla sullage dump by the end of 1972. At the end of 1973, following a number of letters concerning zoning on the North Cronulla site, the Board notified Council that it felt the Cronulla–Woolooware area would be better served by a new station at Woolooware. This was a result of a lowering of the priorities attached to the inclusion of Kurnell peninsula in the Sydney FD.[16] The Board asked Council to approve a site at Lots 11 and 12 at the

Wentworthville Fire Station, designed by J W Roberts and completed in 1983

corner of the Kingsway and Wills Road. Council replied in February 1974 rejecting the Board's proposal on the grounds that it did not want to cut the Kingsway median strip and that a fire station in Wills Road would decrease the residential amenity of the area.

In April 1974 the Board rejected Council's recommendation, stating that it was proceeding with acquisition. Council then took the case to the Minister for Local Government and the Minister for Planning and Environment in November 1974. The latter's response was to agree with Council and to suggest that Council put up some alternate sites to the Board. In early 1975 three sites were considered by an Assistant Town Planner from Sutherland Council. His conclusion was that a site at 35 Croydon Street, Cronulla, was the most favourable, being geographically central, zoned commercial (and hence not a 'noise' problem) and having two old weatherboard cottages on-site. The analysis and conclusions were sent to the Board which appears to have 'backed-down' from its earlier stand on the Wills Road site. No sooner had the Board received Council's report than it was discovered that 35 Croydon Street was in fact a block of eight units! Council immediately sought to rectify its mistake by suggesting a number of further sites in Croydon Street and in Wilbur Avenue.

In August 1975 the Board rejected all sites arguing that as a back up station to Miranda, Cronulla needed to be further west. The BFC announced in the same letter that it was negotiating a site at the intersection of The Kingsway and Franklin Road, Woolooware. Council immediately responded that the Franklin Road site possessed the same difficulties as that at Wills Road. The Council then requested a joint 'field inspection' with Council town planners, Alderman C Tregear (the Local Government Representative on the Board) and Senior Fire Officers to consider 'all' sites. Prior to this (February 1976) inspection, details of the Board's proposals for a Franklin Street site leaked to the press. Following a press release in local newspapers a number of letters and a petition with over 100 signatures was received by Council in opposition to the Franklin Street site. The petitioners' arguments were that the fire station would be noisy and lower real estate values, that it represented an accident hazard and was not a central location in the Cronulla–Woolooware locality. Council submitted these objections to Alderman Tregear.

Cronulla's International pumper, facing the rear of the station yard

Following the February 'field day' Alderman Tregear responded in detail to Council stating that after weighing all considerations both he and the Deputy Chief Officer felt the Franklin Street site was the best alternative. His argument was that the site was of sufficient size (that is, no operational difficulties), possessing excellent access, centrally located, cheap and sufficiently close as a Miranda 'back-up'. Further, he noted that a modern fire station was aesthetically pleasing and of little noise nuisance. Finally, in March 1976, Council acceded to the Board's request, plans were submitted in July 1976 and Cronulla FS opened in 1977.

A similar situation has arisen with a proposed new brigade at Chester Hill. Identified as the most poorly fire protected area in the Sydney FD (Adrian, 1982) plans for a new station at Regent's Park/Chester Hill have been 'in the air' for some four years. Staff ceilings imposed during the economic recession and an inability for the Board and Bankstown Council to agree over final site development mean that the urgently needed station and brigade are still no further than the drawing board.

On a more positive front the Board initiated a continuing review of the deployment of manpower and the location of stations within the Sydney region in the early 1980s. Whilst not yet ratified plans exist for a reorganisation of the current district system with two new districts centred at Liverpool and Blacktown. New stations and the relocation of existing stations will also be recommended to better match the distribution of stations with the 1984 pattern of fire risk.

108

5

A CENTURY OF SERVICE

Firemen From Past to Present

DURING THE DEBATE ON THE FIRE Brigades Bill in 1884 Opposition members had been enraged at the extensive powers to be granted the Superintendent of the Fire Brigades. As described in sections 8–12 of the Fire Brigades Act (gazetted 24 January 1884), at fires the Superintendant could:

> take and direct any measures which appear to him necessary or expedient for the protection of life and property or for the control and extinguishment of fire and may cause any buildings or tenements to be entered, taken possession or pulled down or otherwise destroyed for such purposes or for preventing the spread of fire. (Fire Brigades Act 47 Vic, No 3, 1884:5)

Burwood Volunteers, 1912, with horse and mascot

THE MFB
Firemen and Brigades (1884–1909)

The Act contained no explicit regulations concerning day-to-day running of the Brigades but provision was made for the Board, at the direction of the Governor, to formulate such regulations. The initial regulations presented to Parliament on 4 July 1884 specified 43 rules 'under which the Fire Brigades Board will Register or Subsidise Volunteer Fire Companies'. The rules were explicitly designed to regulate, discipline and standardise these companies. Many of the rules were foreign to the history and traditions of the volunteer movement, which had relished its picnics, torchlight processions and independence at fires. Some of the rules—for example, 'At no time will any of the apparatus be permitted to attend a demonstration without the written consent of the Superintendent. Members of Companies (volunteers) shall abide by the instructions given by the senior Member of the Metropolitan Fire Brigades present' (Regulations under the Fire Brigades Act, 4 July 1884: 3)—brought a storm of protest from volunteers. The brigades were given the choice of registering with the MFB and being subsidised, disbanding, or operating as an unregistered company. Subsidation was based on four classes:

First class (Steamer and twenty effective registered members): up to £175 ($350) per annum
Second class (two manuals and twenty men): up to £125 ($250) per annum
Third class (one manual and fifteen men): up to £100 ($200) per annum
Fourth class (hose reel and fifteen men): up to £50 ($100) per annum

In 1884 the list of companies was as follows:

Registered:
No. 2 Volunteer Company, Head Station, Phillip-street, Circular Quay*

* Brigades linked to Headquarters by telephone.

Theatre Royal Volunteers—the first volunteers to register with the Metropolitan Fire Brigades in 1884

No. 2 Volunteer Company, Branch Station, York-street, Markets*
No. 4 Volunteer Company, George-street, opposite Railway*
No. 5 Volunteer Company, Campbell-street, Surry Hills
Alexandria Volunteer Fire Brigade, Raglan-street*
Balmain Volunteer Fire Company, Head Station, Booth-street*
Balmain Volunteer Fire Company, Branch Station, Wise-street*
Burwood Volunteer Fire Company, Station-street
Glebe Volunteer Fire Company, Mitchell-street*
Paddington Volunteer Fire Company, South Head Road
Petersham Volunteer Fire Company, Crystal-street
Redfern Volunteer Fire Brigade, Regent-street*
St Leonards Volunteer Fire Brigade, Mount-street

Standard Brewery Volunteer Fire Company, Foveaux-street*
Surry Hills Volunteer Fire Company, Palmer-street*
Theatre Royal Volunteer Fire Company, adjoining the Theatre, Castlereagh-street*

Unregistered:
No. 1 Volunteer Company, Pitt-street, Haymarket*
Albion Volunteer Fire Brigade, Buckland-street, Waterloo
Manly Volunteer Fire Company, Manly Beach
Pyrmont and Ultimo Volunteer Fire Company, Union-street*
Waverley Volunteer Fire Company, near Charing Cross*
Woollahra Volunteer Fire Company, off Ocean-street*

The following unregistered Volunteer Companies disbanded during the year:
No. 3 Volunteer Company, Bathurst-street

St Leonards (North Sydney) Volunteers c. 1890

Paddington No. 2 Volunteers outside their station on the corner of Dowling and Oxford Streets, 1898

City Volunteer Fire Brigade, Druitt-street
Hook and Ladder Company, off Bathurst-street
North City Volunteer Company, Queen's-place
Mount Lachlan Volunteer Fire Company, Raglan-street, Waterloo

The loss of their Board representative (Andrew Torning) in 1887 marked the beginning of the end for many companies, particularly those within the Sydney City area. By the mid-1890s the last of the City volunteer companies, North City (then in Cumberland Street) and Standard Brewery (in Foveaux Street) were disbanded, in accordance with Superintendent Bear's policy of removing volunteers from the City district. It represented the end of a 40-year era from the formation of Torning's No 1 Volunteer Brigade in 1854. Despite the loss of the City brigades, others were being established in the suburbs as the 'Long Boom' continued.

Whilst rules and regulations for volunteers were defined in 1884, it was not until December 1885 that similar rules for permanent staff were presented to the Colonial Secretary. The hours, duties and restrictions were harsh. The MFB fireman of the 1880s was almost certainly single, aged between 21 and 32 (unless previously an active fireman), taller than 5 feet 6 inches (168 cm) and with a 37 inch-plus (94 cm) chest. He had to be 'generally intelligent, capable of acquiring instruction, and able to read and write ... physically strong, free from any defect in limb, hearing or sight, from colour-blindness, from any organic, infectious, or contagious disease, and not subject to chronic ailments, or fits, or to nervousness' (MFBAR, 1885:7). He was 'on duty' for the entire 168-hour week, although he could apply for six hours' leave once every ten days and was encouraged 'to attend his place of worship and pay proper attention to the observance of the Sabbath-day'. He either lived at the station in dormitory quarters (if single) or in rented accommodation within a few hundred yards of the station.

His 'working day' was full: rising at 5.45 am (or 6.45 am outside summer), starting yard cleaning duties after roll call at 6.00 am, breakfasting at 8.00 am (cooked by a fireman cook) and back at work by 9.00 am. Another roll call at 10.00 am was followed by station duties until lunch between 1.00–2.00 pm. Station duties involved polishing, cleaning and checking appliances, harnesses and other equipment and a full turn-out drill on one of the steamers. Depending on rank (ranging from 3rd class fireman through to 1st class fireman) his afternoon duties, after 2.00 pm roll call, included general station, workshop or stable duties and instruction by the engineer in driving the steamer and its operation. Once duties were completed he was allowed to turn-in. The turn-in period allowed the fireman a chance to play billiards, read, study for his exams and relax (unless the bells sounded) within the station bounds until dinner and roll call at 7.00 pm. At 10.00 pm the station doors were 'closed-down' by the new watchroom shift (10.00 pm to 6.00 am) and it was 'lights out' (unless the bells sounded) until 5.45 am.

KILLED IN ACTION
Second Class Fireman, Frederick Patrick Fisher (1863–1886)

A NATIVE of Gibraltar, stonemason by trade and former member of No 1 Volunteer Company, Fisher joined the MFB as a single man in the initial 1884 intake. Promoted to Second Class Fireman in 1885 and placed in charge of the 'Express' manual, Fisher's future seemed assured until the fatal night of Tuesday, 25 May 1886.

Because Marrickville's manual was out of order, No 1 Brigade from Bathurst Street, and Newtown and Standard Brewery Volunteers responded to a call from four shops alight in Parramatta Road, Leichhardt. The blaze was easily subdued within an hour but during the final moments of mopping-up operations, the front wall of Howe's stationery shop (in which the blaze had apparently been started by fireworks) suddenly collapsed, crushing Fisher and four Brewery volunteers.

Superintendent Bear, bystanders and other firemen rushed to their aid and hauled the men from the mass of brick, mortar and charred timber. Whilst the volunteers were fortunate to escape with lacerations and broken bones, Fisher's skull was fractured and crushed, despite his brass helmet. Death was instantaneous; Fisher was the first of only eighteen Sydney firemen to die in the course of duty between 1884 and 1984 (Appendix 5.2).

Fisher's funeral procession from Bathurst Street fire station to Waverley Cemetery on 27 May was the largest in the City for years; a crowd in excess of 5000 massed in Bathurst and George Streets. Carried on a manual engine fitted with bunting and draped by the Union Jack, Fisher's coffin was conveyed up Oxford Street in the direction of Paddington while a band played the 'Dead March in Saul'.

At midday the cortege reached the Waverley gates, where the coffin was borne through lines of Fisher's comrades to its final resting place. To the last rites of the Catholic Church, Fisher, the first permanent fireman to make the ultimate sacrifice, was laid to rest.

Postscript: Whilst evidence given to the Coroner's Inquiry indicated faulty construction of the Howe building (and, in fact, the whole terrace of which it was part), Fisher's death was described as accidental and no further action was recommended by the jury or the coroner.

THE FIRST CHIEF
Superintendent William Douglas Bear (n d)

DOUGIE Bear served for fifteen years in the London Fire Brigade, rising to the rank of Third Officer and Engineer. At the recommendation of the London Chief, Eyre Massey Shaw, Bear was appointed by the Governor of New South Wales as the first Superintendent of the Metropolitan Fire Brigades.

From his arrival in Sydney aboard the Orient steamer, *Garonne*, on 19 June 1884, to his resignation on 26 September 1898, Bear's period in office was tempestuous. Within a few months of his arrival he was in conflict with the volunteer companies, the Board and the Deputy-Superintendent, James Dawson. Bear was an outspoken critic of existing fire protection in Sydney, the lack of brigade discipline and lack of funds, and the inadequacy of the Acts covering building structures, theatres and storage of inflammable material. As a result of his petitions to the Board and approaches to Parliament, Bear was appointed Kerosene Inspector in 1886 with powers to inspect properties storing kerosene and the kerosene itself, and to recommend prosecutions under the Kerosene Act.

Superintendent Bear's annual reports to the MFB provide insight into his efforts to organise the brigades into a coordinated, disciplined and efficient service. Unfortunately his outspokeness and self-assertion brought him many enemies, inside and outside the service. This was compounded by his liking for alcohol which, by 1894, had caused him to become so ill that the Board recommended he visit San Francisco to recuperate.

In February 1895 Bear was found guilty by a Civil Service Board of breaching Section 37 of the Civil Service Act—'dereliction of duty due to drunkenness'. His fine of £25 ($50) appears to have had little impact, for on 2 April 1895 Bear was suspended by the Colonial Secretary subject to an Executive Council investigation into Board allegations of further intoxication. Bear's apology and subsequent reinstatement brought an angry response from the MFB Board, which sent a delegation to the Chief Secretary, complaining of its lack of control over the matter (MFB, 1895:235).

On 7 May 1898 Bear was again suspended

for intoxication. Under strong pressure from the Colonial Secretary, Bear resigned on the 26 September 1898. It was a sad end to a career which had set the Metropolitan Brigades on their feet. Bear had instigated many improvements in equipment and organisation. Perhaps his career is best summed up by the following newspaper story of popular mythology:

> In conversation with some Americans who did not know him as Superintendent of the MFB, he voiced the opinion one night in a public place that ... the MFB of Sydney was the equal of anything of the kind on earth—including New York's splendid system ... and was called on to make good his boast that, for a turn-out to a fire the Sydney men could show all-comers something in the matter of speed. He was laughed at. Very well, he would show them! Taking an opportunity, he stole down to a street alarm just outside the door of the place in which they were, called the brigade to a fire there, and returned ... 'Come with me,' he said to one of the strangers. He took him to the fire alarm. 'Poke your stick through that,' he said. 'Want me to get in gaol?' enquired the American. 'I'm the Superintendent of the Fire Brigade, and you'll not get in gaol,' said Bear. 'You tell me to smash that glass?' asked the visitor, 'Yes.' The stick was driven through at once. Almost instantly the first fire engine showed at the top of Market-street, others came into sight directly, and in a few minutes steamers from outlying stations were along—the street was filled with fire engines, salvage waggons, hook and ladder carriages, all the equipment of a big brigade. Hoses were out, steam was up, men were standing-by, and the usual fire crowd of spectators was there. It was a big demonstration. The stranger tendered his hand to the local Chief. 'Say,' he said, 'I haven't seen anything just as smart as that in my life. I reckon your fire station is round the corner' he said. 'Jump into this cab with me and I'll take you to it,' replied Bear. And he gave the cabman the address of the MFB, with instructions to get there by going round the Haymarket half-way to Surry Hills and back!! (*Sunday Times*, 5 September 1920)

Given the hours 'on-duty', annual rates of pay were low by today's standards:

Deputy Superintendent: £400 ($800)
Foreman: £182 ($364)
Senior Fireman: £162 ($324)
1st class Fireman: £150 ($300)
2nd class Fireman: £130–140 ($260–280)
3rd class Fireman: £112–120 ($224–240)
Probationer: £106 ($212)

In the early years recruits were taken on three months' probation, from a variety of backgrounds, although Regulation 5 stated, 'all other things being equal, preference will be given to seamen' (MFBAR, 1885:7). Of the initial intake of 30 permanent men, half were from the Insurance Brigade, most others from volunteer companies, two from the London Fire Brigade[1], and two 'late Royal Navy'.

As the number of stations/brigades grew so did the intake of permanent men. When Superintendent Bear resigned in 1898 and was replaced by Alfred Webb, the nine permanently manned brigades had a complement of 71 permanent (including eight probationers) and thirteen auxiliary firemen (Appendix 5.3). The auxiliaries were drawn from the ranks of the volunteers (generally at the stations where the volunteers were replaced by permanent staff) and were paid a small retaining fee of 10s ($1.00) per month and 1s 6d (15 cents) turn-out fee [for the first hour and 1s (10 cents) for each hour thereafter]. In addition, the 21 suburban volunteer stations had a total complement of 316 men.

It was under Webb and his deputy, Nicholas G Sparks (appointed in 1897, after service in the Royal Navy and London Fire Brigade) that a number of significant MFB changes were instigated. On 31 December 1899 the partially paid auxiliary corps was disbanded and reformed by enlisting youths aged 17–20 to train for future service in the Brigades. Amongst the twelve recruits were Charles D A Richardson (later Chief Officer), Sydney A Tuck (later Third Officer), William H Beare (later Chief Officer) and Henry M Webb (later Secretary). Until disbanded in 1911 the Auxiliary Corps continued to recruit youths who were later to serve the Brigades in a distinguished capacity—the most notable being Edward James Griffiths ('Griffo') (later Chief Officer), recruited on 2 August 1907.

The most significant and long lasting of Webb's changes to the operation of the Sydney

Brigades was the division of Sydney into a number of districts and the creation of a new position of District Officer (DO) in 1899. Five districts were created:

Central (Headquarters No 1): DO Frank Jackson
Southern (George-Street West No 2): DO John F Ford
Northern (Circular Quay No 3): DO Sydney Watson
Mid-West [Marrickville (now Stanmore) No 7]: DO George Lang
Eastern (Paddington No 11): DO Thomas Gorman

In their formative years District Stations operated with manning strengths similar to other stations. However by 1906 their staffs were boosted, all having a complement of twelve permanent men (Headquarters 32) and one or two auxiliaries. Sydney Watson was raised to the new position of Senior District Officer (equivalent to Third Officer) in 1903 and in 1906 Strathfield was made a District Station under DO George Dadd, to cover the new Western District (the council areas of Auburn, Burwood, Concord, Enfield, Granville, Parramatta, Rookwood and Strathfield).

With the introduction of District Officers, the positions of Foreman and Assistant Officer were abolished; Station Officer (SO) position was introduced in 1899 and Sub-Station Officers (SSO) in 1906. The new arrangements recognised the growth of Sydney and signified a decentralisation of authority away from Headquarters to District and suburban stations. Each station came under the authority of a District Officer and, if permanent, under the day-to-day control of a Station or Sub-Station Officer. As a consequence the Superintendent and his Deputy focused their time on administrative matters (except in the case of major fires).

As well as changing the permanent system, major changes were made to the volunteer system. In 1901 the system of subsidising volunteer brigades was abolished, and a system of partial payment of volunteers introduced. Payment took the form of a retaining fee, plus fees for attending fires and drills. Brigades were restricted to a maximum of eight to ten partially paid men who were registered with the MFB. Captains of volunteers were no longer subjected to annual election but rather would 'hold office,

The carpenter's shop at Headquarters' fire station after the installation of electric power in 1905

permanently during the pleasure of the Board' (MFBAR, 1901:3). Most volunteer brigades welcomed the changes, although others opposed the idea of payment and more Board control (including Waterloo Volunteer Brigade, which disbanded after 22 years' service).

As an incentive to permanent staff, a five years' 'good conduct and energetic service' medal (with an honorarium of a penny a day) was introduced in 1902. In addition, a fifteen-years' bronze service medal was instituted and first presented at Headquarters on 30 June 1903 by Sir John See, KCMG, Premier and Chief Secretary. The ceremony—including presentation, guard-of-honour, drill and athletic display—set the foundation for a regular series of similar displays over many years to dignitaries from State and local government and fire insurance companies.

Principally through the youth corps, Brigades training and displays emphasised physical fitness and athleticism in the early 1900s. This was most dramatically shown in the popular sport of whaler boat racing. The first MFB crew was formed in 1904 with Charlie Grimmond (later Chief Officer) as coxswain. It was the second Brigades crew between 1905 and 1912 which captured the imagination of the public. Unbeaten in match races for seven years, this crew ruled as 'Cock o' the Harbour' against visiting opposition from USS *Baltimore*, HMS *Powerful* and HMS *Challenger*.

The Fire Brigades whaler crew —'Cock-o' the Harbour' in 1906

The race against the HMS *Powerful* crew on 7 August 1907 was over a four-and-a-half mile (7.24 km) course from HMS *Powerful* in Farm Cove around Shark Island and back. Widely publicised, the race drew crowds of spectator craft. Substantial sums changed hands as each side had willing backers. It was the Fire Brigades' crew in their larger and heavier whaler which coped better with the 'moderate gale and nasty sea', to cover the course in 45 min 33 sec, a winning margin of 2 min 15 sec (some 30 lengths).

After the champion crew disbanded in 1912, whaler racing continued spasmodically from a boatshed in Woolloomooloo Bay. Through the late 1920s and early 1930s, Brigades crews under Bill Richardson and Sid Giles raced in many an Anniversary Regatta as well as against visiting navy crews. Whilst never achieving the fame of the earlier Brigades crews, they 'made good times over the measured mile'. In 1939 the boatshed and whalers were sold to the Navy for the use of Sea Cadets and a 35-year era had ended.[2]

By 1909 the nature and organisation of Sydney fire services had changed significantly from the formative days of the 1880s. The permanent strength of the Brigades had risen to 220 (comprising the Superintendent, Deputy-Superintendent, Senior District Officer, six District Officers[3], nine Station Officers, eleven Sub-station Officers, 134 firemen, 33 Coachmen,

Drills and physical exercise were formalised soon after the turn of the century

four Special Service[4], and twenty auxiliaries) at nineteen stations. The 28 volunteer brigades were manned by 248 partially-paid volunteers.

Training was now formalised into a series of rigorous drills involving dumbbell, chemical hose carriage, curricle ladder, hose, hose reel, hydrant, manual engine, pompier ladder, scaling ladder, steamer, squad drill and turntable ladder. It was the dumbbell drill, done to music, that so delighted the regular crowds at Wednesday public demonstrations at Headquarters (perhaps only rivalled by the practice turn-outs). Promotion was now by examination in writing, spelling, composition and drill based on a Fireman's Manual prepared by Deputy Chief Nicholas Sparks. Discipline was harsh by today's standards, generally run military-style by one of the many senior officers having a Royal Navy background. Operationally, both in equipment and men, Sydney fire services had matured into a fire service of world standing.

AUSTRALIA'S 'OLDEST' FIREMAN

Fireman William South (1823–1912)

WILLIAM South came to Australia from England as a lad with Sir William a'Beckett (afterwards Chief Justice of Victoria) and for a while remained in his employ. At seventeen whilst training to be a saddlier, he attended his first fire, the Royal Theatre fire of 1840. When four insurance companies formed a brigade under T J Bown in 1850, Billy South joined and remained a member until 1884, reaching the rank of assistant foreman.

When the MFB was formed, 'Old Billy South' was due for retirement. However, firefighting was in his blood and his popularity amongst staff saw him employed as head messenger to the Fire Brigades Board. Recognised as the 'oldest fireman in Australasia', Billy South was honoured by the Government when the Premier, Sir John See, presented him with a gold medal in 1903. His mates at Headquarters fooled the press of the day when they came to interview Billy by calling him Superintendent. The lengthy interview which appeared in the morning and evening papers referred to Superintendent William South—much to the amusement of MFB staff, including Billy.

In his interview Billy reminisced about the first engine used by Bown—the *Squirt* which was housed at T J Bown's engineering firm on Brickfield Hill, near Union Lane. He could also remember the Royal Hotel and Theatre between George and Pitt Streets, with over 100 rooms. Soldiers from Wynyard Square barracks, with their small manual, made no impression against the flames which destroyed both buildings in 1840. Among Billy's fondest memories was the introduction of the first steam engine to Sydney in 1859.

South's death in 1912 severed the last link with the foundation of firefighting in Sydney and his dedication to firefighting for more than 70 years established a record of service unsurpassed in Sydney fire brigades.

STATE-WIDE COVERAGE AND UNIONISATION

The creation of the Board of Fire Commissioners of NSW (BFC) in 1910 heralded a new era. Under Section 13 of the Fire Brigades Act (1909) the properties of a number of fire brigades boards, along with some 100 volunteer fire brigades, were taken over to be reformed into 77 Fire Districts, portioned into eight divisions—each under the supervision of a senior officer, with the new designation of Divisional Officer. The initial task of Divisional Officers was to compile an inventory of all equipment and its condition, and to assess brigades and their training. Many of the country brigades were poorly equipped and in the new Board's formative years most expenditure over and above wages and salaries went on replacement hose and appliances.

The Sydney FD was reduced by excluding the Municipalities of Campbelltown, Liverpool, Penrith and Richmond (which were included among the Country Fire Districts), while Hunters Hill was added. Thus the area of the Sydney FD (A Division) at the end of 1910 was 152.6 square miles (395.22 km^2), covered by 49 brigades. A number of these brigades were now manned by complements of both permanent and volunteer staff (for example, Rozelle with four permanent and four volunteers), a policy which has survived in the Sydney FD to the present day.

In 1911 Chief Officer Alfred Webb undertook a major review of the Brigades' strength, organisation and working conditions. On his recommendation the Auxiliary Youth Corps formed in 1900 was disbanded, due to the high attrition rate. The staff of permanent firemen was subsequently increased by 23 to cover both the loss of auxiliaries, and an extension of firemen's annual leave from ten to fourteen days.

The most significant changes recommended and adopted by the Board concerned the volunteer brigades. A number of Captains and Engine-keepers who were both physically fit and 'qualified', were taken into the permanent staff as second Class Firemen, with pay of 8s 6d (85 cents) a day and promotion entitlements. It was also decided to supply members of both Sydney and country volunteer brigades with uniforms: a tunic or galatea, boots, vest, cap and two pairs of trousers every two years (three years for country volunteers) plus a dungaree suit (overalls) for engine-keepers.

The net effect of the changes introduced by Webb was an increase in the number of permanent firemen in the Sydney FD from 214 to 291 between 1910 and 1914. More significantly the number of stations manned solely by volunteers decreased over the same period from twenty-six to seven.[5] Neither before nor since has such an important step been made in upgrading the permanent composition of Sydney FD staff.[6]

It is no coincidence that these improvements in working conditions and a general pay increase, averaging 1s (10 cents) per day, were initiated in the same year that the Fire Brigade Employees' Union was formed. The union was to prove a powerful force in the years ahead, winning a further increase of 1s per day in 1916.

In 1913 Chief Officer Alfred Webb died in office and was succeeded by his long-serving Deputy, Nicholas Sparks. One of Sparks' first initiatives was to introduce the rank of Inspector (above Divisional Officer). Two Inspectors were appointed in 1914, J Graham and G H Dadd (F Jackson having been promoted to Deputy Chief Officer), and were responsible for inspecting and instructing brigades in country fire districts. It was also Sparks who was given the task of placing the Brigades on a 'war footing' following the outbreak of the First World War.

In 1919 Sparks, along with Jackson and District Officer T G Cutts, was awarded the King's Police Medal. They followed Third Officer Sydney Watson and Fourth Officer J F Ford who were the first recipients of the

Station Officers from E District and their District Officer, Chris Digby (seated, second from left), 1913

A BORN INNOVATOR
Chief Officer Alfred Webb (1850–1913)

EDUCATED at Christchurch School, Hampstead Heath (London), Alfred Webb joined the Royal Navy at fifteen and three years later joined the London Fire Brigade. Rising through the ranks, he became an officer, eventually serving as Eyre Massey Shaw's deputy.

In 1888 Alfred Webb was appointed as Deputy Superintendent of the MFB under Superintendent Bear, and arrived in Sydney in March with his wife and four children (the second eldest of whom, Henry Mayo, was destined to become the longest-serving Board Secretary). Following Bear's resignation on 26 September 1898, Webb became Superintendent. In his eleven years as Superintendent of the MFB and three years as Chief Officer of the Board of Fire Commissioners, Webb transformed the Sydney and NSW fire service. Gone were the days of undisciplined, ill-equipped and untrained part-timers. By 1913, particularly in Sydney, the Brigades were equipped with modern, motorised appliances. The men were fit, well-trained and professional in their outlook on firefighting.

It was Webb who instigated many changes in the Brigades between 1898 and 1913 concerning rank structure, training, the district system, motorised appliances, smoke helmets, uniforms, and partially paid volunteers. In essence Webb brought a degree of standardisation of equipment and training to New South Wales unsurpassed in Australia, and provided the basis for firefighting as we know it today.

One of Webb's earliest innovations were 'In-Orders', a system of written communication within the Brigades which persists today. In April 1899 Webb directed through In-Orders that: 'Officers in charge of Stations are instructed that females are not to be allowed in single men's bedrooms'. (There is no record of the reason for this directive!)

Many of Webb's innovations were gleaned from his eight-month overseas tour in 1903–04 during which he attended the International Fire Prevention Congress and Exhibition in London and visited brigades in Europe and America.

Following the example of his predecessor, Webb was a strong proponent of fire prevention, particularly in public buildings. It was partly his evidence to the Commission of Inquiry into Fire Safety in Theatres in 1904 and 1908 which resulted in the introduction of the Theatres and Public Halls Act 1908. This Act gave extensive

Chief Officer Alfred Webb (left), who in the years 1898–1913 transformed Sydney fire brigades to a disciplined firefighting force. He was laid to rest at Waverley Cemetery in 1913 (right)

powers to the Chief Officer and enabled Webb to establish a Special Services section of Building Inspection (the forerunner of Fire Prevention as it is known today). An amusing sidelight to Webb's presentation of evidence to the 1908 Inquiry was his advice that women attending theatres should shorten their dresses. The popular press of the day (who no doubt found the proceedings rather dry!) latched on to this advice with much glee, and the *Melbourne Punch* produced the following tongue-in-cheek commentary:

> Superintendent Webb, head of the Sydney Fire Brigades, has undertaken a terrific task. He wants the ladies who attend theatres in evening dress to cut off their trains. The fox who lost his tail and tried to induce all other foxes to cut off theirs, undertook quite a trifling mission compared with this. Mr Webb points out that the long train is a terrible danger in the event of an alarm of fire at a theatre. In the rush for the door it gets about the wearer's legs and trips her, or other people trample upon it, or get entangled in it and the wearer is pulled down. This is all perfectly true, and reasonable, and wise, but it is not sufficient for a scheme to be wise, and healthy, and clean, and a commonsense provision against accident, maiming, or death, to induce a lady to change the cut of her dress, if the cut is fashionable. Mr Webb should know that facing death and disaster is nothing to a woman beside the horror of facing a fashionable audience in an unfashionable gown. (*Melbourne Punch*, 2 April 1908)

Until his death on 19 January 1913 the Brigades had for the first time a Chief Officer who held the respect and confidence of his Board. Webb was buried at Waverley Cemetery with a full Brigades funeral, leaving a son (Henry Mayo Webb, Secretary 1914–44) and grandson (Derek Alan Webb, Secretary 1963–74) to carry on an unsurpassed tradition of service to the NSW Fire Brigades.

Alfred Webb's name itself lives on in the NSWFB in the Alfred Webb Trophy, an award presented at the biennial Volunteer Demonstrations for the brigade with the highest aggregate number of points. The trophy was first won in 1932 by Lithgow Brigade at the Wagga Wagga Demonstration.

Station Officer Augustus Gerard who suffered fatal burns at a fire in 1920

decoration from the New South Wales Fire Brigades in 1917. The silver medallion was instituted in that year by King Edward VII and awarded to 'members of all recognised Police Forces and regularly organised Fire Brigades throughout the British Dominions in recognition of special and exceptional service, heroism, or devotion to duty' (BFCAR, 1919:4). It was also in 1919 that the Board approved a long service medal for volunteer brigades (that for permanent staff having being initiated in 1903), awarded to members completing fifteen years' continuous service with good conduct.

The hazards faced by firemen (both then and now) are exemplified by the bizarre death of SO Augustus Gerard from burns received following a fire at Elliott Bros, wholesale druggists, Terry Street, Balmain on 3 June 1920. The fire itself was relatively minor, confined to a quantity of phosphorus within the factory area. This was quickly subdued by firemen from Balmain, Pyrmont and Rozelle (including Gerard) who smothered the flames with sand. However, returning to Rozelle, Gerard's clothing suddenly burst into flame due to the friction of the air on red phosphorus adhering to his uniform and due to his proximity to the steam boiler. Within seconds Gerard was a living torch and despite the efforts of his comrades who immediately enveloped him in a blanket, he was

The NSW Fire Brigades and visiting Victorian cricket teams at Sydney Cricket Ground, 1920. Chief Officer N Sparks (seated centre) retired the following year

badly burnt about the arms, body and face. Gerard's burns proved fatal, and he died three months later on 10 September 1920.[7]

Whilst deaths such as that of Gerard emphasised the occupational hazards of firefighting there were other, more fortunate sides to Brigades life in the years after the First World War. Cricket was the most popular of the numerous sports in which Brigades teams participated. In 1921 after a successful visit the previous year by a Victorian team, the NSW Fire Brigades team visited Melbourne. Managed by Divisional Officer (former Chief at Broken Hill and later Chief Officer, Western Australia) J M Lambourne, the NSW XI wrested the firemen's 'Ashes' from a Victorian side which included the interstate cricketer, Arthur Liddicut. The successful NSW team comprised G Harper (top-scorer in the first innings with 35), F A Tuck, C D Franks, G Challis, A Baber, W Cooper, A Winter, W Jones, H Coghlan, H Cheal, L Watt (with a match-winning 77 in the second innings) and F Wilson. Scoring only 78 in the first innings, the NSW side was 44 behind, but their 154 in the second was far too good for the Victorians who were still 19 runs in arrears when Strownix was caught and bowled by Franks. A member of the NSW team, Nick Winter, was to achieve even greater sporting recognition when he won the Gold Medal for the hop-step-and-jump at the 1924 Paris Olympics.

By the 1920s the character of Sydney Brigades was again changing with many of the old-timers from MFB days retiring or dying. In 1921 Sparks retired to be replaced by Frank Jackson. Sparks [with a pension of £500 ($1000) per annum], along with Third Officer J Ford [£250 ($500) pa] and DO T Cutts [£200 ($400) pa] were the last officers to receive a pension from the Board: subsequent retirements were covered by the Superannuation Act (1919). The Superannuation Act represented a major change in

Chief Officer N Sparks (top) was replaced by Frank Jackson (bottom) who served from 1922–1929

tradition with pensions on retirement no longer subject to Board discretion.

Jackson had joined the Brigades on 7 February 1889 and by 1909 had been promoted to District Officer and assigned the highest fire-risk area of Central District. Prior to his retirement in 1928 Jackson initiated a number of major changes in the NSWFB. In 1921 'A' Division was expanded to include not only the Sydney FD but also Fairfield and Narrabeen Fire Districts, whilst in 1923 a major restructuring of officer ranks took place. The title 'Officer-in-Charge' was abolished, and men holding the position were promoted to the rank of Sub-Station Officer. In turn, all existing SSOs were elevated to Station Officer. Jackson also created the rank of Motor Inspector, to which the first appointee was H Coghlan in May 1923.

Under Jackson the Headquarters workshops were expanded with the addition of the clothing factory (1920) and boot factory (1921). A few of the older-hands, particularly ex-seamen, assisted in the workshops, sewing canvas, repairing rope lines and so forth. By the 1930s, however, almost all the workshop duties were carried out by full-time workshop staff—machinists, bootmakers, hose makers, etc.

Largely through the actions of the Fire Brigade Association of NSW in the Industrial Arbitration Court, a number of changes took place in leave and pay entitlements in the mid-1920s.[8] In 1923 permanent firemen in the Sydney FD (and two years later, country staff) were granted 48 hours' leave each week instead of 30 hours. The increased leave entitlements forced the Board to increase Sydney FD manning by 42 to 357. In the light of subsequent events, it is significant that the 1923 log of union claims included application for a 48-hour week (subsequently altered to a two-platoon, 84-hour week). However, this claim and a later appeal to the Full Bench of the Industrial Court were dismissed in November 1923.

In 1925 the Forty-Four Hours Week Act was passed by the Lang (Labor) Government. However, the Board utilised Section 6 (2) of the Act, 'ordinary working hours in any industry may be increased beyond those prescribed in this section if the Court or Board is of the opinion that in the public interest such increase shall be allowed', to maintain working hours at the existing 112 hours per week. In the new award negotiated in 1925 (operative until 11 August

1927), however, firemen received increases in pay from 2d (1c) to 8d (7c) per day, in annual leave from two to three weeks, and in rental allowance from 8s (80c) to 12s 6d ($1.25) per week. In addition, a new rank of Senior Fireman was created, for which a First Class Fireman could apply after ten years' service and satisfactory performance at a Senior Firemen's exam. Given the large number of firemen with more than ten years' service at the time, competition for the new position was keen, as the following humorous account portrays:

Brain Fag at Fire Station

The principle that one is never too old to learn is being given a severe test at Fire Brigade Headquarters this week.

Quarters are turned into studies, old service men are digging out their logarithm tables and Euclid, and not one of them has taken a day off since the announcement of the consent award between the Union and the Fire Brigades' Board.

It creates a new position, with a rise in pay: that of Senior Firemen.

The watchroom is quite a bright spot these days in consequence of the furbishing of educational accomplishments.

Instead of discussing the introduction of Oxford bags into the Brigade uniform, firemen exchange witty badinage about concentric circles, high pressure systems, the density of water and similarly interesting topics.

One old fireman was so interested in drawing diagrams on a blackboard in his room that he missed three meals. Another has gone cross-eyed from trying to take in two pages of an arithmetical work at the one reading.

They have all shown that they can put out fires, but it's explaining how it's done that makes the difficulty.

Senior firemen are appointed from the men of at least 10 years' service who possess two good-service badges.

The trouble is that they are all becoming so proficient through study that the Board is worried they may resign and become University professors. (*Guardian*, 4 September 1925)

Anticipating the likely introduction of a two-platoon system the Board ran a major public relations campaign in the *Sydney Mail* calling for new recruits. Part of the promotion read:

The firemen in Sydney have a career with possibilities, but they must put aside thoughts of a quiet life with nights at home by the fireside. Their fires are bigger and more exciting. The lowest paid man gets £4 13s 9d [$9.38] a week, and his home is the station. Others get £5 [$10], £5 10s [$11] and so on. A station officer's position is one for the ambitious to attain early, with pay at over £7 [$14] a week. They are well looked after, for men who live always at tension must be taken care of. Leave is generous, and there are no deductions of pay for time off. He has 21 days' annual leave, as well as time off each week. The day's work commences in the station at 7am (or 9 o'clock if he has been out on a fire during the night). The afternoons on duty are available for recreation and rest unless calls break in. (*Sydney Mail*, 23 June 1926)

By 1926 the Sydney FD was covered by 73 brigades (the same number as today) with 419 permanent men and officers and 152 partially paid volunteers. This represented an increase of 24 brigades and 215 permanent men in the sixteen-year period of the Board of Fire Commissioners. Over the same period the Sydney FD had increased in size by almost 90 square miles (233.10 km^2) to 242 square miles (626.76 km^2). Brigades stretched from Kogarah, Hurstville and Mortdale in the south, Bankstown and Fairfield in the south-west, Wentworthville in the west to Hornsby and Narrabeen in the north.

FREEDOM!
The Two-platoon System

In 1926 the Fire Brigade Employees' Conciliation Committee, consisting of Mr T M Jackson, Chairman, and Messrs T S Douglas, Fire Commissioner (an insurance industry representative), and H M Webb, Secretary, and Messrs C A Milledge and J McNamara (President and Secretary, Fire Brigades Association), was formed to renegotiate the 1925 Award. Their majority recommendation of a 112-hour week (averaging 56 hours' leave weekly) was adopted by the Industrial Court, to operate from 1 September 1926 until 11 August 1927.

The Fire Brigades' Association of New

The original Headquarters' 'Flyer' crew under Station Officer Shelley (centre), Wally Plumbe who was killed whilst turning out to a fire call in 1940, is standing second left

South Wales immediately lodged an appeal which was heard by Industrial Commissioner, A B Piddington in April and May 1927. His judgment, to become operative on 1 March 1928, introduced a two-platoon system in the Sydney and Newcastle Fire Districts, and lessened the on-duty hours for firemen from 112 to 84 hours per week, to be worked in two platoons of fourteen hours and ten hours respectively, with a shift change every third day. The judgment also allowed firemen to reside anywhere within their respective fire districts, although removal expenses for transfers within a district were abolished.

The introduction of the two-platoon system followed the precedent set in London in 1919 and first adopted in Australia by Brisbane Fire Brigades in the mid-1920s.

The end of the continuous system heralded a new era for Sydney brigades. Gone was the obligatory 24-hour attachment to an individual station; firemen of all ranks now had an independence between work and home in keeping with the community-at-large.⁹ This independence drastically altered the daily life-style of firemen, giving them freedom of choice of residence, home ownership, free-time and family-life, previously unknown. On the negative side this freedom necessitated more frequent and lengthier journeys to work, an end to the fortnightly dances at Headquarters for single firemen and their friends, and a loss of some degree of camaraderie in station life. Whilst promoted by the Fire Brigades Association, the changes were part of a broader movement within NSW society. Under the Lang Ministry the Labor-values of unionisation, reforms in work conditions, and higher rates of pay were felt throughout the working-class.

With the retirement of Chief Officer Jackson in 1928, much of the organisational restructuring of brigades within the Sydney FD was handled by the incoming Chief, Thomas Pierce Hains Nance. At Headquarters the 'Single Men's' Mess was abolished and replaced by a messroom for all firemen, containing a gas ring and heating-oven and small food lockers. Another change was the introduction of the *Flyer*—a motorised fire engine manned by a crew of SSO and six men (later reduced to five) who were not allowed to leave the Engine House during their shift. *Flyer* shifts lasted five hours, with the SSO working a full shift from 8.00 am to 6.00 pm or 6.00 pm to 8.00 am.

The two-platoon system necessitated an increase of 15 officers and 165 firemen within the Sydney FD to maintain existing duty levels. The increase saw the Board's salary bill for permanent staff jump from £159,154 ($318 308) in 1927 to £205,489 ($410 978) in 1928. Over the same period the Board's total expenditure increased by almost £72,000 ($144 000) (with the bulk of the increase being borne by the insurance companies).

To improve the quality of recruits the rank of probationary fireman was introduced. After six months' trial and training at Headquarters the new recruits sat for a 'Confirmation of Appointment Examination' and, if successful, graduated to become Fourth Class Firemen. Once confirmed in their appointments the firemen were also covered by the State Superannuation Act (officers being covered in 1919 but firemen not until 1926).

With the onset of the Depression in the 1930s the Board, on the advice of Nance, instigated a Cadet Corps (similar to that which had been operated by the MFB). In 1932 six youths were appointed.[10] In the same year a Volunteer Fire Brigades' Demonstration (the first since that at Corowa in 1909) was held at Wagga Wagga. Officially opened by the Governor of NSW, Sir Philip Woolcott Game, the Demonstration attracted some 63 brigades from NSW and Victoria. The Lithgow Brigade was triumphant, winning the Alfred Webb Trophy for aggregate points. Since 1932 Volunteer Demonstrations have been a major event in the Brigades' calendar, matching competitive skills in an atmosphere of camaraderie.

The year 1932 also brought tragedy. On 18 May 1932 the Armidale Brigade, led by SSO Fred Maizey, responded to a fire in the storeroom of Braund's produce store (see Chapter 8). Within minutes of arrival 9000 detonators in the storeroom exploded, destroying two motor lorries and a large part of the building. Volunteer Fireman Berry Jones was killed instantly and Volunteer Fireman Bill Robinson lay mortally wounded beside the critically injured Maizey. The remaining members of the Brigade pressed on with their attack, even though a nearby shed contained gelignite and dynamite, and managed to subdue the blaze. In recognition of their bravery and gallantry the Board instituted the 'NSW Fire Brigades Medal for Conspicuous Bravery' which was conferred on eight members of the Armidale Brigade, two posthumously, on 6 June 1933 (Appendix 5.4).

The two-platoon system and Depression years witnessed a change in the type of person being recruited into the Brigades. Many recruits were married, older, and out-of-work skilled tradesmen whilst others were well educated, often from private schools. Gone were the days when the bulk of recruits were British, ex-Navy, and with little schooling.

Despite the changing backgrounds of recruits, physical training and athleticism was still seen as an essential ingredient of fire brigade life.[12] Many a recruit of the early 1930s remembers the physical training (PT) at Headquarters, two or three times each week under the instruction of 'Professor' Stuart. The Wednesday public displays at Headquarters resumed after the Great War, though only on a monthly basis. At the end of the band's performance (under Bandmaster J Pheloung),[13] gymnastics and drill displays, spectators lined the footpaths in Castlereagh Street to observe a 'practice' turn-out. When the viewers were settled, the bells were sounded, the doors flung open and the motor engine, motor salvage engine and turntable ladders emerged with bells ringing. After circling the Elizabeth Street block they backed into the Engine House. Often young children were given a ride, and allowed to wear a fireman's brass helmet. Headquarters was then opened for public inspection.

As part of the Board's promotion of sport, teams were entered in the Rugby League 'City Houses' competition and from the early 1930s in the Rugby Union 'Presidents' Cup. The years 1935 to 1937 were the golden years of fire brigade Rugby. In 1935 the team coached by Les Ford visited Queensland, defeating Brisbane (which included nine members of the Queensland XV) 31 to 14. In 1936 the Brigades team toured South Australia and Victoria, and again was victorious against the two State XVs. A victorious return visit was made to Queensland in 1937 by a side which contained five NSW State representatives and an Australian representative (Bill White). It was in 1937 also that the NSWFB team played

NSW Fire Brigades Rugby Union team—Victoria/South Australia Tour, 1936

and defeated Western Suburbs and University, then the leading teams in the Sydney First Grade Competition. Is it any wonder that the Brigades Rugby teams of this period were touted throughout the service to tunes such as the following:

The Fire Brigades Footballers' Nonsense Song

Tune: (with apologies)—The Drunkard Song (Fare-thee-well for I must leave thee) RBL

Verse 1
There is a team in Sydney-town—in Sydney Town;
A Football Team of great renown—great renown.
The Fire Brigades play football fast and clean,
The best that ever has been seen.

Chorus
Fire Brigades are ever ready,
They have players cool and heady;
When they start to pass that ball, then you can say 'Good-bye'
Come on! Come on! Brigades; Come on!, you'll hear them shout;
They can no longer keep us out—keep us out.
We'll hang their scalps on a weeping willow tree.
FIRE BRIGADES; FIRE BRIGADES; FIRE BRIGADES.

Verse 2
Bill White is now our Captain true—Captain true;
He's like 'a bolt from out of the blue'—out of the blue.
Quinlivan and Col Hodgson, you'll agree
Are centres of ability.

Chorus

Verse 3
Ellsmore, McDonald, Billy White,—Billy White
Are first class wingers, and can fight—'Oh yeah'? Too right.
Winter and Hamilton, are our two half-backs.
And make their rivals look like 'hacks'.

THE FIRE BRIGADES' SANTA
Chief Officer Thomas Pierce Hains Nance (1869–1941)

BORN at Kempsey, NSW, the son of a carpenter, Tom Nance learnt the trade as a young man. On 6 December 1895 he joined the MFB as a probationary fireman. Most of his early career was spent at Headquarters where his skills were utilised in the carpentry shop.

Nance was an able leader and organiser and quickly rose through the ranks, being appointed a District Officer in 1913. His next eight years were spent at Kogarah in charge of St George District. During this period his every spare moment was devoted to charity work, particularly in aid of returned soldiers and the Smith Family. In 1920 his efforts were recognised when he was awarded an OBE.

In 1921 Nance was appointed Inspector of country brigades and, in the following year, became Third Officer. Whilst Deputy Chief in 1927 he received the highest Brigades award, the King's Police Medal. After serving as Frank Jackson's Assistant Chief Officer in 1928, Tom Nance became in January 1929 the first Australian-born Chief Officer of an Australian fire service. Until retirement in 1935, Nance devoted his entire time to his two loves: the NSWFB and charity. It was at Headquarters where he managed to combine the two.

The southern basement proved an ideal workshop and each year Nance (with the aid of 'seconded' firemen) produced over 1000 toys for donation to the 'Sun' toy fund. His favourite was, naturally, a toy fire engine. Over the Depression years 'Santa' Thomas Nance brightened the hearts of many youngsters through his Headquarters 'toy factory'.

A deeply religious man, Nance believed one should put into practice Christian values, although this sometimes worked to his personal detriment, as the following story (related by ex-Chief Officer Charles Milledge) shows:

> Nance bought a house at Ashfield some six months before his retirement. He knew the Archdeacon at the local Anglican Church at Ashfield who told him about the poor straits a family was in with nowhere to go. Thomas said they can move into his place until his retirement. So they moved in.
>
> He gave the man, they were out of work and the woman had a young kiddy, a pound or so now and then, for keeping the lawns mowed and looking after the place, where they lived rent free.
>
> When Tom Nance retired and he went to move in, the fellow objected to going, and made claim for wages as caretaker for the period he had been in it. Nance approached the dear old Archdeacon who was most upset at hearing the news that the man was an absolute rogue. When taken to court the magistrate (who Tommy knew) said, 'You have been a fool, Tommy a fool', and Tommy admittedly had, for he was forced to pay the rogue's claim!

Nance rose to the pinnacle of a fireman's career and his contribution to the community during hard times was immeasurable. Thomas Nance's death in 1941 did not end the family's link with the NSWFB. His nephew, Jack 'Chiefy' Nance, joined the Brigades, and became a top Brigades footballer in the late 1930s, and later rose to the rank of District Officer.

Chorus

Verse 4

And Charlie Eustace, our full-back—our full-back;
Just watch 'The Firemen's Jumping Jack'
—Jumping Jack;
He finds the line, and tackles with a will
'Oh Boy'! he gives the crowd a thrill.

Chorus

Verse 5

'The Pigs' are forwards hard to beat—hard to beat;
They ruck and heel, and use their feet—use their feet.
The front-row men—Paul, Collins and 'Champion'
Can rake like roosters full of corn.

Chorus

Verse 6

And don't forget the break-aways—break-aways.
Ford and Palmer 'Spare-me-days'—'spare-me-days'.
'I'll say that they could stop a kangaroo'
'Tin hares have nothing on those two'.

Chorus

Verse 7

'Shamrock' O'Brien is not 'green'—is not 'green',
Nor Tiger Harvey a 'has-been'—a 'has-been'.
They lock the scrum; But watch them in the loose
Go hard, when they step on the juice.

Chorus

Verse 8

Two more we never can forget—can forget
Is Chalky Ulvihill, the best yet—the best yet.
And three loud cheers for the Manager; He pays.
Come on—'Hoop-ray'; 'Hoop-ray'; 'Hoop-ray'.

Chorus

Following a brief reign by George Grimmond as Chief Officer in 1934–35, Charles David Alexander Richardson, who had joined the Brigades in 1900 as a cadet, was appointed Chief Officer in 1936. It was the hard-working Richardson who was to lead the Brigades through the difficult years of the Second World War, serving a total of eight years. His early years were also difficult ones, in another respect, as conflicts between the Board and the union over working hours intensified.

In 1934 the Fire Brigade Employees' State Award of 1927 expired, and discussions between

Members of the Fire Brigades Association besiege Parliament House in 1938 calling for a 54 hour week

GRIFFO, SYDNEY'S GREATEST FIREFIGHTER
Chief Officer Edward James Griffiths (1891–1980)

VARIOUSLY known as 'Ted', 'Griff', 'Griffo' and 'Nuts', Chief Officer E J Griffiths established an unmatched reputation as a firefighter within the NSWFB. His attributes as an athlete, 'smoke chewer' and above all, leader-by-example became legendary. Very few men become a legend in their own lifetime—Ted Griffiths was one man who did.

Born at Pyrmont on 18 July 1891 Ted Griffiths joined the Brigades' cadet corp at the tender age of sixteen. His pay was 42s ($4.20) per week. A natural athlete, he performed in the Headquarters' gymnastics displays during his cadet and probationary days. It was also in this period that he played Rugby League alongside Dally Messenger. Both were members of the victorious Eastern Suburbs 'Roosters' team in the first ever Sydney Rugby League premiership of 1908.

In 1913 he enlisted in an artillery unit and left Australia with the first overseas contingent. Serving in the Gallipoli and Egypt campaigns, Ted Griffiths was on his way home for leave when the Armistice was signed. Rejoining the fire service in 1919, he made the switch from coachman to motor driver and served at a number of metropolitan stations, becoming SSO in 1926. Transferred to Headquarters as a District Officer in 1928 it was to become his home until retirement in December 1954.

It was during his 22 years as an officer at Headquarters that Ted Griffiths earned his reputation as a 'nuts and bolts' firefighter. He knew every fire risk in the city and how to handle it. In 1932 DO Ted Griffiths was the first officer in charge of a fire appliance to attend a fire across the Harbour Bridge. In 1936 it was DO Ted Griffiths who was the first fireman to don an asbestos suit at a Sydney fire, when he was lowered into the engine room of the fire-engulfed Manly ferry *Bellubera* (Chapter 8).

Griffo's popularity and daily habit of strutting around Headquarters in un-dress uniform made him a regular butt of Headquarters pranksters. During the scrubbing of floors on a Saturday morning Griffo was 'accidentally' soaked by a bucket of water. He immediately ordered the bells rung for assembly. Still dripping wet Griffo's gruff voice boomed throughout the station as he bawled-out all and sundry—threatening the culprits with a fate worse than death.

At Headquarters Ted Griffiths rose through the officer ranks, and was appointed DCO in 1946 and Chief Officer on 1 January 1948. At the age of 61 Chief Griffiths still hadn't given up leading by example. In 1950 he was overcome by smoke and fumes while directing firefighting and rescue operations in the hold of HMAS *Tarakan*. Again in 1951 it was Griffo who was in the thick

---

the Conciliation Committee and the Board broke down. The Fire Brigades Association immediately made application to the Industrial Commission for a public inquiry into the working hours of all firemen throughout the State. In response to growing agitation among firemen the Industrial Commission in March 1938 reduced the ordinary working hours of firemen in Sydney and Newcastle from 84 to 78 hours per week on the two-platoon system (although officers remained on 112 hours per week on the continuous system). The small reduction incensed firemen, who had been anticipating a 54-hour week on a three-platoon system. As a result protest marches and deputations were made to Parliament House.

of an eight-hour battle to contain a fierce blaze in the copra cargo of the Motor Vessel *Bulolo*. It was during this blaze that he amazed younger firemen by stripping off his tunic and diving into the flooded hold to reach the flames on the other side of the vessel.

In 1951 Chief Officer Griffiths was presented with the King's Police and Fire Services Medal by the NSW Governor, Lieutenant General Sir John Northcott. It was a fitting tribute to a career which spanned 47 years and made the name Griffo not only a boxing legend but a firefighting one as well.

Ted Griffiths' only son Ken was also to make his mark in the NSWFB. Born at Newtown fire station in 1919 Ken Griffiths spent his adolescence at Headquarters, regularly playing pranks on the station firemen. The following tale is related by one of the sufferers, Ken Magor:

> At the entrance to the Griffiths' flat there was a small alcove for milk bottles, and as young firemen we had to polish the stairs from top to bottom. Young Ken Griffiths would wait until you started at the roof top and then would set an alarm bell ringing in the alcove. Of course, being young in the Service, all your thoughts were that you were turning out and did not want to miss your appliance. Thinking of the time delay to get to the station bay, you wouldn't think to look at the lighting system on each landing to learn what appliances were responding. On arrival at the station bay to see no movement, you would realise you had been duped. (*Fire News*, 5(2) 1983:44)

In July 1935 Ken joined the NSWFB staff as an electrical apprentice. After serving with the Navy during the war he returned to the Brigades and to a career which would span 44 years. He completed his service in the highest Brigade position in his profession—Chief Engineer (Electrical).

When Premier Stevens refused to meet the deputation of Union President, J Cranney, Secretary, J McNamara, and Permanent Firemen's Board Representative, M J Piper, on 13 April 1938, the firemen threatened strike action. Their cause was immediately taken up in the Legislative Assembly by the Leader of the Opposition, Jack Lang, and became a major subject of Labor attacks on the governing United Australia Party (UAP).

The union and Opposition argued that a 56-hour week would allow firemen to lead normal family lives in keeping with members of other emergency services who worked a 44- or 48-hour week, whereas the Board and Government retorted that much of the firemen's hours were 'free time' and, furthermore, a three-platoon system would require an increase in staff costing £80,000 ($160 000). It was the latter which was clearly at the hub of the Board's case, particularly from the viewpoint of the insurance and council groups which would bear the brunt of the increase.

In September the Government won a snap division by one vote on an Opposition proposal for a Committee of Inquiry into the working conditions of firemen. Then on 19 October 1938, six members of the UAP sided with the Lang Opposition and appointed a nine-man Select Committee 'to Inquire into and Report upon the working conditions of the employees of the Board of Fire Commissioners of New South Wales with particular reference to the weekly number of working hours'. It was over a year before the Select Committee recommended the adoption of the New York system (outlined but opposed by Chief Officer Richardson) of three platoons on a 50⅖-hour week. With the outbreak of war, the Mair-Bruxner Government decided to reject the Committee's findings and place the whole matter before Arbitration (see Chapter 6).

THE TED GRIFFITHS' ERA
A 56-hour Week and Three Platoons

Towards the end of the Second World War the recommendations of the 1939 Select Committee of Inquiry were adopted and a Fire Brigades (Amendment) Bill was passed in 1944, reducing the working hours of firemen to 56 hours per week. Officers, however, were not to gain a 56-hour week until 1949 (when Station Officers joined the Fire Brigades Association to form the New South Wales Fire Brigade Employees Union).[14] In response to the reduction in working hours the Board immediately closed 23 fire stations, thereby provoking the Fire Brigades Association to retaliate by seeking a pay increase. The increase of 10s ($1) per week for each rank of fireman was granted from January

1946, based on the increased duties and responsibilities for firemen due to station closures.

The end of the war and the introduction of a 56-hour week heralded a new era for the New South Wales Fire Brigades. Whilst disputation and discontent dominated the service, other more subtle changes were at work. Many of the Brigades' senior stalwarts from the continuous and two-platoon systems were now retiring. Amongst others, these included such personalities as Chief Officer W Beare (1947); DCOs B L Barber (1946), R J Currer (1948); Fourth Officers G H Parks (1947), J Walsh (1948) and B Rodney (1948); Inspectional Officer J W Barnaby (1946); and Officer-in-Charge of Auxiliaries, J J Neville (1946). Replacements such as J Edge, C Milledge and G H Gilmour were to form the backbone of a 'young' senior staff under the new Chief Officer, Edward James Griffiths. During his reign from 1948–55 Chief Officer Griffiths established a reputation amongst his peers as, 'Sydney's Greatest Fire Chief'. In many ways it was his character and ability as a firefighter which carried the Brigades through the Board and union conflict in the immediate post-war decade.

Following the introduction of a 56-hour week for officers on 30 April 1948 the Board introduced a patrol system within the Sydney FD. For patrol purposes the Sydney FD was divided into seven zones. In each zone a patrol car manned by an officer and three men and equipped with firefighting gear and two-way radio operated in two shifts—8.00 pm to 1.00 am and 1.00 am to 6.00 am. The objective was for patrols to respond to calls for fire received by radio, attend fire stations and to patrol premises and localities for instructional purposes. The more subtle aim of the patrol system was to have firemen active and awake during the night shifts.

There is little doubt that the introduction of the patrol system was an attempt by the Board to re-exert its influence as the body empowered by legislation to set the duties and working conditions of its employees. In July 1948 both firemen and officers (with the exception of the Chief and senior officers) held a two-day stoppage, demanding an abolition of the patrol system. As the Board prepared deregistration proceedings against the Fire Brigades Association, the Premier and Chief Secretary intervened promising to investigate the issues if the men returned on pre-stoppage conditions. This they did on Tuesday night, 13 July 1948.

The patrol system issue continued to surface as an area of disputation, with many Brigade staff treating their 'night patrols' in a cavalier fashion. In 1953 the patrols ceased and were replaced by day inspections of local business and industry premises. Such familiarisation tours survive today, allowing an on-the-spot training of firemen in the location of hydrants, fire risks and alarms within their station area.

The requirements of additional staff under the three-platoon system, numerous retirements and higher wages in other occupations placed pressures on the manning of brigades in the late 1940s. A number of measures were introduced in an attempt to upgrade recruitment and simultaneously to achieve the best deployment of existing manpower. Examination syllabuses were revised and, in 1950, First-Class firemen with only eight years' service were allowed to sit for the Senior Fireman's exam (previously they had had to wait ten yers). The ranks of the senior executive officers were reorganised to provide positions of Chief Officer, Assistant Chief Officer, two Deputy Chiefs and five Executive Officers (equivalent to Superintendents). Recruitment requirements were relaxed: the minimum height was reduced from 5ft 7in (170.18 cm) to 5ft 6½in (168.91 cm). It was also decided to establish for the first time a recruit training college: plans were developed to convert Paddington FS to a training college and transfer the Paddington Brigade to the closed Woollahra station. The actual opening of the new training college (all previous training being conducted at Headquarters) was not be to accomplished until 20 December 1956 when Paddington Training College was officially opened by the Chief Secretary, the Honourable C A Kelly. At this time all probationary instruction at Headquarters (in the yard and the old gymnasium) ceased.

In January 1951 the Board introduced a system of officer rotation (the 'rota' system) whereby officers were regularly redeployed around stations to give them the widest possible experience of fire risks. Although opposed by the union, the system was enforced by the Board. By 1951 the staffing position had worsened—the Brigades were under their authorised strength by 46 men at the beginning of the year, and suffered a further 86 retirements and resignations during

Paddington Fire Station converted to a training college in the 1950s under the control of District Officer Sid Giles

the year. To overcome this shortage, the strict entry requirements were temporarily relaxed allowing appointment of probationary firemen who 'exhibited a generally accepted standard of suitability for service'. In all, 92 recruits were appointed in 1951, easily the Brigades' largest single intake to that date. To supervise the new recruits a District Officer position was created, to which Sid Giles was appointed in 1951 (later assisted by DO 'Chiefy' Nance).

One of the most significant changes in the post-war years was the changing view on the education of Brigades personnel. Largely through the efforts of the then Executive Officer Charles Milledge, sixteen members of the Brigades (including Jack Meeve, Viv Lowther, Harry Clay, Rex Hopping, Jack Mundey, Jack Kinnear and John Ford) sat for the graduate exam at the Institute of Fire Engineers (IFE) in 1951, with ten passing (Jack Mundey with distinction). The earliest members of the NSWFB to have attempted the IFE exams were Tom Parks, Frank Hulbert and Charles Milledge in the mid-1930s—on their own initiative and through the Victorian Branch of the IFE. In many ways the introduction of IFE exams typified the changing nature of the NSWFB—a contrast between the old and the new. As with many progressive changes the 'old' did not give way easily. Many a senior officer opposed the increasing trend to 'book work', arguing that the only real firefighters were 'seat-of-the-pants' men who learnt by experience. To Chief Officer E J Griffiths' credit, whilst he himself was without doubt from the old school (having completed his formal education at the age of ten), he gave full encouragement to the introduction of IFE exams. His retirement in 1954 and the appointment of Charles Milledge on 1 January 1955 epitomised the transformation of the senior echelons. In stark contrast to Griffo, Charles Milledge was quietly-spoken, widely read and qualified as a member of IFE. Whilst not in the same mould as Griffo as a leader of men, Chief Officer Milledge did more than any other officer to improve and formalise the training of Brigades personnel. Most of the improvements in the exam syllabus for probationers, senior firemen, SOs and DOs, along with the new curriculum at the Paddington Training School, were instigated by Charles Milledge.

By 1954 the pressure on staff appointments had eased and the length of probationary training was extended from three to four months. Already another dramatic issue was arising, however, which was to further stretch the resources of the Board's training and manning. As early as April 1953 the Fire Brigade Employees Union had sought a new award before the Full Bench of the Industrial Commission. Among its claims was a new system of standard hours based on a 40-hour week. On 13 November 1953 the Industrial Commission rejected the 40-hour week claim, with the result that firemen and station officers refused to perform normal duties for a number of days. One change which was approved by the Commission was the abolition of the Sub-Station Officer rank and the introduction of five grades of Station Officers—A,B,C,D and E. All SSO's were appointed at grade E and advanced a grade each year.

Despite its first-round loss, the Fire Brigade Employees Union continued a vigorous lobbying campaign for the 40-hour week. In April 1955 it was successful and a Fire Brigade (Amendment) Act was passed introducing a 40-hour week. However, the Board approached the Industrial Court in June for a compromise: a 48-hour week, including eight hours' overtime. On hearing of the decision all station officers and firemen in the Sydney FD held a stop-work meeting and called a strike. The five-day stoppage was a bitter affair with neither the Board (led by President T J Smith) nor the union (led by President Harry Evans) prepared to give ground. In contrast to the 1949 dispute over a 56-hour week, both the press and the Government attacked the union action; Chief Secretary Kelly threatened to bring in the army and the *Daily Telegraph* referred to the stoppage as 'a near crime' and a 'strike against a city'. It was only the actions of Board member Alderman L Duff, who addressed a meeting of the firemen, which led to a return to work in return for a meeting with the Board.

At the meeting chaired by Mr Justice Beattie, union delegates and the Board agreed that a 42-hour week would become operative from 1 July. The 42-hour week was to be based on 40 standard hours and two hours of compulsory overtime over an eight weeks' roster cycle. Personnel were divided into four platoons and each day split into three shifts—morning shifts: 7.00 am to 3.00 pm, afternoon: 3.00 pm to 11.00 pm and night: 11.00 pm to 7.00 am. Each platoon then worked two weeks of six shifts and six weeks of five shifts over an eight-week cycle.

Despite the working week agreement the union continued action in the Industrial Court for new wage rates. On 12 October 1955 the Court ruled increases less than those demanded by the union. The result was another strike on 13 October 1955. It was to prove the longest and most bitter in the history of the NSWFB. For eleven days stations were manned solely by 'skeleton' senior officer crews. As the Board made application for the deregistration of the union, accusations were made that striking firemen were calling-in false alarms.

On this occasion the union was beaten and under a direction from the NSW Labour Council firemen resumed work on 24 October 1955. The union was deregistered and fined £500 ($1000) although on 30 November the order of deregistration was lifted and the fine 'deferred'.

THROW THE BEDS OUT
A 42-hour Week

The introduction of the four-platoon system immediately stretched the Board's manpower resources and late in 1955 a major recruitment drive was launched. Inducements were 28 days' annual leave, three months' long service leave after fifteen years and a further three months' every ten years. Rates of pay were as follows:

	Ordinary Weekly Wage £ s d ($)	Weekly Wage (incl. overtime) £ s d ($)	Year
Probationary Fireman	14 8 0 (28.80)		
4th Class Fireman	14 8 0 (29.80)	20 2 4 (40.23)	1
3rd Class Fireman	15 3 0 (3.00)	20 9 0 (40.90)	2
2nd Class Fireman	15 10 6 (31.05)	20 19 2 (41.91)	3
1st Class 'B'	15 18 0 (31.80)	21 9 4 (42.93)	4–5
1st Class 'A'	16 5 6 (32.55)	21 19 2 (43.91)	6–9
Senior Fireman	16 18 0 (33.80)	22 16 4 (45.63)	10

After two years' service a senior fireman was eligible to sit for a station officer's exam.

To accommodate new recruits (until the opening of Paddington Training College) temporary probationary schools were established at Waverley and Five Dock, and recruit training was shortened to only eight weeks. Concourse duties (see Chapter 6) were discontinued as were the activities of the Fire Brigades Band which had been in service since 1915. The Brigades were still heavily dependent on volunteer staff and many of the reservists (abolished in 1952) were taken on as partially paid volunteers. At the end of 1955 the manpower of 'A' Division had risen to 299 officers, 822 permanent firemen and 343 volunteers.[15] This represented an increase of 393 permanent staff and 54 volunteers from the two-platoon days of the immediate pre-war years.

On 29 July 1956 Chief Officer Charles Milledge announced his premature retirement upon reaching 60 years of age. In selecting a replacement the eight-member Board adopted a policy of not electing officers to senior positions if older than 58 years of age. Their recommendation to the Minister was that Mr H Pye be appointed, passing over Deputy Chief J S McGrath who was then 58 years of age. This departure from seniority was not accepted by the Chief Secretary, Mr Kelly, even when the new five-man Board (by a vote 3:2) confirmed the recommendation.

One of the dissenting votes was that of Board President Mr L Duff, who along with the Fire Brigade Employees Union lobbied the Chief

Secretary for McGrath's appointment. With Horrie Pye as Acting Chief the issue remained unresolved for fourteen months. At an extraordinary Board meeting on Monday 16 September 1957 the Board (under threat of dismissal by the Minister) reversed its decision.

Mr J S McGrath was appointed Chief Officer of the NSWFB the following day by the Governor-in-Council. It was clearly a victory for the Minister and the Board President and a loss for Horrie Pye who immediately took extended leave. Chief Officer J S McGrath was to serve for only four months, however, retiring due to ill-health in January 1958. His Deputy and former Acting Chief, H W Pye (member IFE) was appointed Chief Officer on 17 January 1958.

One of Board President Les Duff's actions in his short reign was the re-establishment of the Fire Brigades Band in 1957 (still under Bandmaster Jerry Pheloung). The Band's repeal was shortlived: on 30 April 1959 its activities were again suspended, 'due to a shortage of funds and staff' and it was not to reappear again until 1979.

During Chief Officer Pye's six-year period in office (1958–63) the Brigades continued to expand and working conditions to improve. In June 1960 Conciliation Commissioner Herron recommended 'just' increases in the wages of firemen and station officers. Increases ranging from 6s 3d (62c) per week for fourth-class firemen to 23s 9d ($2.38) for station officers 'A' Grade were granted by the Board. In all the increases between 1957 and 1960 represented a 25 per cent marginal increase on the award.

In 1961 agreement was reached with the union that a policy of the non-replacement of volunteers in Sydney FD be implemented. To initiate the scheme recruitment was again increased and 172 probationary firemen appointed. With 59 resignations and retirements, a net gain of 113 was achieved. By the end of 1961 'A' Division boasted a complement of 340 officers, 1110 permanent and 317 volunteer firemen. The officers consisted of the Chief Officer, Deputy Chief, six Superintendents (replacing the rank of Executive Officer), seven Inspectors, 12 District Officers and 313 Station Officers. Instruction of new probationary firemen utilised a complete 'Manual of Instruction'. Known as the 'Red Reader', the 339-page manual (written by instructor Harold Parker) became the

The Fire Brigades' Band re-established in 1957 but disbanded in 1959 due to a shortage of funds and staff

FIREMEN'S BRASS HELMETS TO BE REPLACED BY PLASTIC TYPE

Best Wishes
Lumsdon

Brigades' bible until replaced by the 'Green Reader' in 1975 (in turn replaced by the 'Blue Reader' in the early 1980s).

In 1963 Chief Officer Pye retired, his place being taken the following year by former Superintendent H Ray Barber. With the retirement of Deputy Chief C A Welsh, Inspectors V A Lowther and J E Meeve were both elevated to the position of Deputy Chief Officer on 10 March 1964. Lowther and Meeve were the 'bright young stars' as the Brigades advanced through the 1960s. Lowther's expertise was in bush fire control, having served under the first Bush Fire Officer G H Gilmour. By 1958 Viv Lowther had become the DO in charge of the bush fire section and a representative on the Bush Fire Committee. Jack Meeve's expertise was in fire prevention and it was essentially his guidance which had brought about the introduction of the Interim Fire

The change from brass helmets in 1964 was not achieved without opposition from some old-timers, however, Chief Officer H R Barber (above) was a staunch supporter of the change

Protection Code under the Height of Buildings Act.

In 1964 the age limit for appointment as a fireman was lowered from 21 to 18, allowing a further increase in the number of probationary firemen (208) in 1964. At the same time both firemen and officers gained a new award with four weeks' annual leave. But perhaps the most notable change was in the replacement of the traditional brass helmet in use since 1884. Resistance to the change, particularly amongst older firemen was strong; but the new helmets of polycarbonate had the advantages of strength, lightness and non-conductivity. White helmets were issued to station officers and firemen and red helmets to senior officers.

In 1967 Chief Officer Ray Barber retired, and on 19 May 1967 Vivian Alexander Lowther was appointed to the position. His appointment over the senior Deputy Chief, Jack Meeve, was a contentious issue, creating much debate within the Brigades. Both were highly respected, and most senior officers agreed that Jack Meeve, who was always his 'own man', was passed over because he represented a potential threat to the authority and dominance of the Board.

In 1968 a significant administrative change was made when Superintendents were taken off the standard roster. The Superintendents were engaged at Headquarters on day duty with specific areas of responsibility: Metropolitan, Special Services, Personnel, Equipment and Country. Whilst working day work, they also worked under a new rotation system whereby one Superintendent was 'on call' during weekends and nights.

THE MODERN FIREFIGHTER
Brigades Since 1970

The period 1970–76 was marked by further conflict between the Board and both the Fire Brigade Employees Union and the Senior Officers Association (Chapter 2). More than ten strikes and stoppages occurred during this period, principally concerning awards, manning and promotion. The disputation had a marked affect on morale; most Brigades personnel today look back on this period as one of bitterness and stagnation. But despite the disputation, day-to-day firefighting activities continued.

In 1970 the award of long service medals and bars for 15–30 years service ceased and was replaced by 'Her Majesty's Fire Brigade Long Service and Good Conduct Medal', to be awarded to both permanent and volunteer staff after 20 years' service. In 1970, 376 permanent staff and 425 volunteers were presented with the new award. In the same year Chief Officer Viv Lowther became the first Sydney Fire Chief to be invited as guest speaker to the Conference of International Fire Chiefs.

In 1972 Deputy Chief Jack Meeve retired and on 17 August, Superintendent Frederick Charles Davies was appointed to the position. The most pressing concern for both Davies and Lowther was the high attrition rate within the Brigades. Because of discontent within the Brigades and more attractive conditions elsewhere in the workforce, 223 permanent staff resigned in 1972 and by the end of the year the Brigades were 60 under their authorised strength. The result was a further delay in the implementation of permanent manning throughout the Sydney FD. Nonetheless, the position had changed dramatically from the early 1960s when 40 of the 66 stations in 'A' Division had volunteer staff. By 1975 this number had decreased to eighteen, with only five in the Sydney FD (Merrylands, Mortdale, Northmead, Rhodes and Engadine) being fully volunteer stations.

In February 1973 following disputation between the Board and the union, Justice Cahill of the Industrial Commission delivered judgment on a new award. Amongst other changes the new award altered the promotional structures of firemen and station officers. Promotion from First Class Fireman 'B' to 'A' was decreased to one year and from First Class Fireman 'A' to Senior Fireman, from three to two years. The 'E' grade of Station Officer was abolished, allowing the 'A' grade of Station Officer to be reached in seven rather than nine years.

The years 1974–76 were amongst the most troubled industrially in the history of the NSWFB. At both Gosford and Berowra major disputes occurred over manning. Agreement was reached that the stations be manned by a Station Officer and two firemen working two shifts during weekdays. At other times (nights and weekends) the stations reverted to fully volunteer complements. In 1974 the union demanded a standard roster of a Station Officer and three firemen at Gosford. The Board opposed the demand and a series of bans ensued. A compromise was finally reached with the weekday only duties of permanent firemen continuing, but manning during these hours was increased by one permanent fireman.

In 1975 the eight-hour roster system for firemen and officers was altered to a '10/14' roster. The introduction of the new system was authorised by Mr Justice Cahill, after he had ordered a secret ballot of officers and firemen to assess their preference (the first occasion in which an Industrial Commissioner utilised the secret ballot conditions of the Industrial Arbitration Act). The '10/14' roster, which took effect from 21 November 1975, was based on each platoon working two day-shifts from 8.00 am to 6.00 pm (ten hours) followed by two night-shifts from 6.00 pm to 8.00 am (fourteen hours) and then four days off-duty. The system applies today.

In August 1975 Chief Officer Lowther retired after 42 years' service (eight years as Chief Officer) and his Deputy Chief Officer, Fred Davies, was appointed to the position. In the same month the Industrial Registrar approved the amalgamation of the NSW Fire Brigade Employees Union and the Senior Officers Association.

AN INSTITUTION
Volunteer Fireman Wally Wright (1914–1982)

WHEN Wally Wright retired in 1981 he had completed 50 years and eight months' service with the NSWFB. His name had become an institution within the Brigades and his years of service a testimony to the dedication of volunteers.

As early as the age of eight Wally chased the horse-drawn fire engines as they passed his home in Mowbray Road, Chatswood. In Wally's own words:

> Firemen got to know me because I made a nuisance of myself, so they gave me the horses to look after. The officers would send me off on my pushbike with messages to Crows Nest station. They paid me a shilling [10c] a time and I decided this was the life for me. (*North Shore Times*, 29 April 1981)

During the Great Depression Wally, then 21, attempted to join the permanent staff but was under the regulation height of 5ft 7in (170.18 cm). Not to be rejected Wally joined the Chatswood Brigade as a volunteer in July 1930, at the same time buying a stretching rack in an attempt to increase his height.

Unsuccessful in his attempt to gain even half an inch, Wally remained at Chatswood until its closure in 1945 when he transferred to Lane Cove, remaining at No 61 until his retirement in 1981. Over these years Wally earned his living as a plumber, but his first love remained the fire brigades. Wally was always 'on call' and even in his last year attended 520 fires—a record that younger volunteers in 'quiet' stations would find hard to match in a lifetime.

On 25 January 1940, whilst responding to a bush fire call, Wally Wright was one of the six-man crew on a Dennis 'Ace' fire engine which overturned. Although badly injured he grabbed a pushbike and rode to the nearest fire alarm box to report the accident. Upon his return he helped extract the badly injured SSO W Plumbe (who later died in hospital) and only then would he allow ambulance officers to help him to the ambulance and hospital.

In 1971 Wally Wright was awarded the Queen's Fire Service Medal for his years of distinguished service, the first volunteer in NSW to receive this honour. His contribution to the NSWFB epitomises the service thousands of volunteers give yearly in protecting life and property throughout the State.

In 1976 the Brigades were again torn by industrial disputes—over the duties of Superintendents, the staffing of the new Alexandria training and control complex and minimum operational strengths. It was the union's view that all stations in NSW with permanent staff should have a minimum operational strength at all times of one SO and three men. They further argued that Merrylands, Northmead and Mortdale should be converted to permanently manned brigades. In the Board's opinion, such alterations would cost in excess of $15 million per year. As discussed elsewhere the apparent inability of parties to reconcile their differences resulted in ministerial control and the Committee of Inquiry in 1977 (Chapter 2).

The year 1977, under the new President Bill Weston, marked a dramatic transformation of the NSWFB. The period 1977–1983 has seen a resurgence in spirit and morale within the Brigades and some notable changes in direction and emphasis. Most importantly industrial relations have been put on a new footing of conciliatory negotiation.

After 1977 there was a further reduction in the number of volunteer stations in the Sydney FD with Engadine (1978) and Northmead (1979) gaining permanent staff and a number of other stations on 'the fringe' increasing in strength. In 1978 alone, 102 new positions were established with an intake of 175 trainee recruits. Forty-five new positions were specially designated for a relief section, with firemen in this section on stand-by to report for duty as directed wherever a vacancy due to illness, etc., occurred.

Perhaps the most significant change affecting the Brigades was the establishment of a Staff Training and Development Division at the Alexandria Training College, which became operational on 19 January 1979. Staffed by a Superintendent, five Senior Training Officers, twelve Training Officers and two firemen, the section was established to supervise and coordinate all training within the NSWFB including examinations, driving and aerial appliance instruction, instruction of volunteers, management courses for senior staff, a revamping of the 'Manual of Instruction' and special outside lectures.

In the same year an additional Deputy Chief Officer position was re-established to take charge of all specialised departments. Superintendent R C Threlfo was promoted to the position along-

Theory and practice go hand in hand at the new Alexandria Training College, opened in 1979

side the other Deputy Chief (Executive) C F Rose.

In addition to introducing staff training and development the Board adopted a policy of encouraging and sponsoring fitness within the Brigades. The Headquarters' gym was refurbished, sports teams sponsored and publicised and special events such as the 10 000 metres Annual Fun Run instituted. The Fire Brigades Band, inactive since 1959, was revived in 1979 under Bandmaster Arthur Satchell (and more recently, Mark Reay).

The year 1980 saw the retirement of Chief Officer Fred Davies, after a career of 39 years during which he was awarded the Queen's Fire Service Medal. His position was taken by Rex Threlfo (who was to retire in July 1984). By the end of 1981 the Board's authorised permanent staff ceiling of 2170 positions had virtually been reached, a ceiling imposed by the State Government during the depressed economic conditions of the early 1980s.

The announcement in 1983 by the Minister for Police and Emergency Services, Mr Peter Anderson, that 179 new positions could be established removed a major obstacle to further expansion of the Brigades. Advertising of the positions in September and October 1983

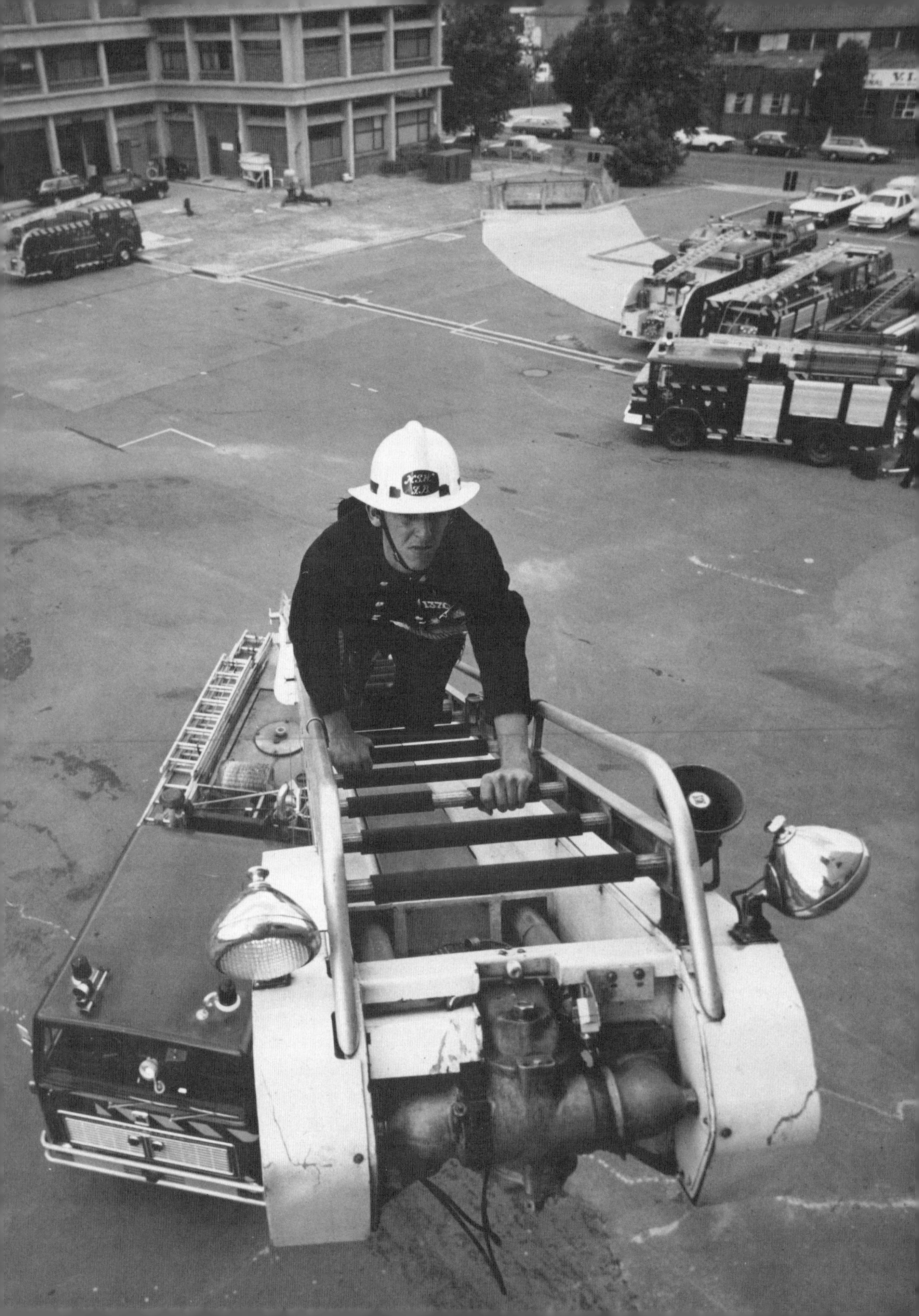

THE MODERN CHIEF
Chief Officer Rex Threlfo (1924–   )

BORN at Mullumbimby on the NSW North Coast, Rex Threlfo had aspirations to study law and joined a firm of solicitors upon completing school. His plans were interrupted by the Second World War and in 1941, at the age of seventeen, he joined the Army and served in the Middle East, New Guinea and Borneo.

On 6 May 1946 Rex Threlfo decided to join the NSWFB, to give it a trial for six months—he stayed a little longer, 38 years in fact! The following year he married and like many other war veterans built his own home, at Yagoona. Whilst moving through the fireman ranks he met two union representatives, Harry Evans and Maurice Stolmack. Both had an important influence on his political and union persuasions and following the successful 42-hour week campaign, Rex Threlfo joined the Union Committee. In 1957 on the retirement of Harry Evans because of illness he became President of the NSW Fire Brigade Employees Union—a position he was to hold for nine years.

In 1966 Rex Threlfo was promoted to District Officer and in 1968 he was appointed Building Inspector under Superintendent V Crum. During this five-year period Rex Threlfo established his reputation in the Brigades, acting as technical advisor to Deputy Chief Jack Meeve, the NSWFB representative on the Height of Buildings Advisory Committee. Promoted to Inspector in 1973 and Superintendent in 1977, he became the inaugural Superintendent of the new Staff Training and Development Division in 1979.

Early in 1980 Rex Threlfo was appointed to the Deputy Chief's position, and in October 1980 he became Chief of the NSWFB. His liaison with the President of the Board, Bill Weston, is now a matter of history. Being the first Chief Officer invited regularly to attend Board meetings, Rex Threlfo has been in the unique position of having a direct input to a sympathetic and progressive Board. Many of the recent major changes in fire prevention, staff training and staff management are attributable to his influence and foresight.

Looking to the future Chief Officer Threlfo sees a number of far-reaching changes:

> With the introduction of staff training and development courses the Brigades' efficiency on the fireground can only improve. Similarly our management courses will improve the capabilities of our senior officers, to be better administrators. The delegation of duties and the improvement in training and management will progressively lift the level of expertise within the NSWFB.

If these progressive changes come about they will in no small part be due to one of the Brigades most popular Chiefs, Rex Threlfo.

---

witnessed an unprecedented 3251 applications (including 68 by women—see Chapter 9). The first group of 76 successful applicants began training at the Alexandria Training College in 1983 with others to follow in 1984. Their training and working environment has changed immensely from that experienced by their 1884 counterparts. Spacious lecture halls, video equipment, detailed texts and 'hard study' are the probationers' lot for the first two months. Following an eight-week posting at a station the probationers return for a further six weeks' study. If successful they are then assigned to one of the 73 Sydney fire stations. There is little doubt that the working hours, salary and conditions of today's fireman are 'worlds apart' from those of 1884. However, the basic attributes of dedication and above all, courage, remain.

Aerial practice in the rear yard of the Alexandria Training College

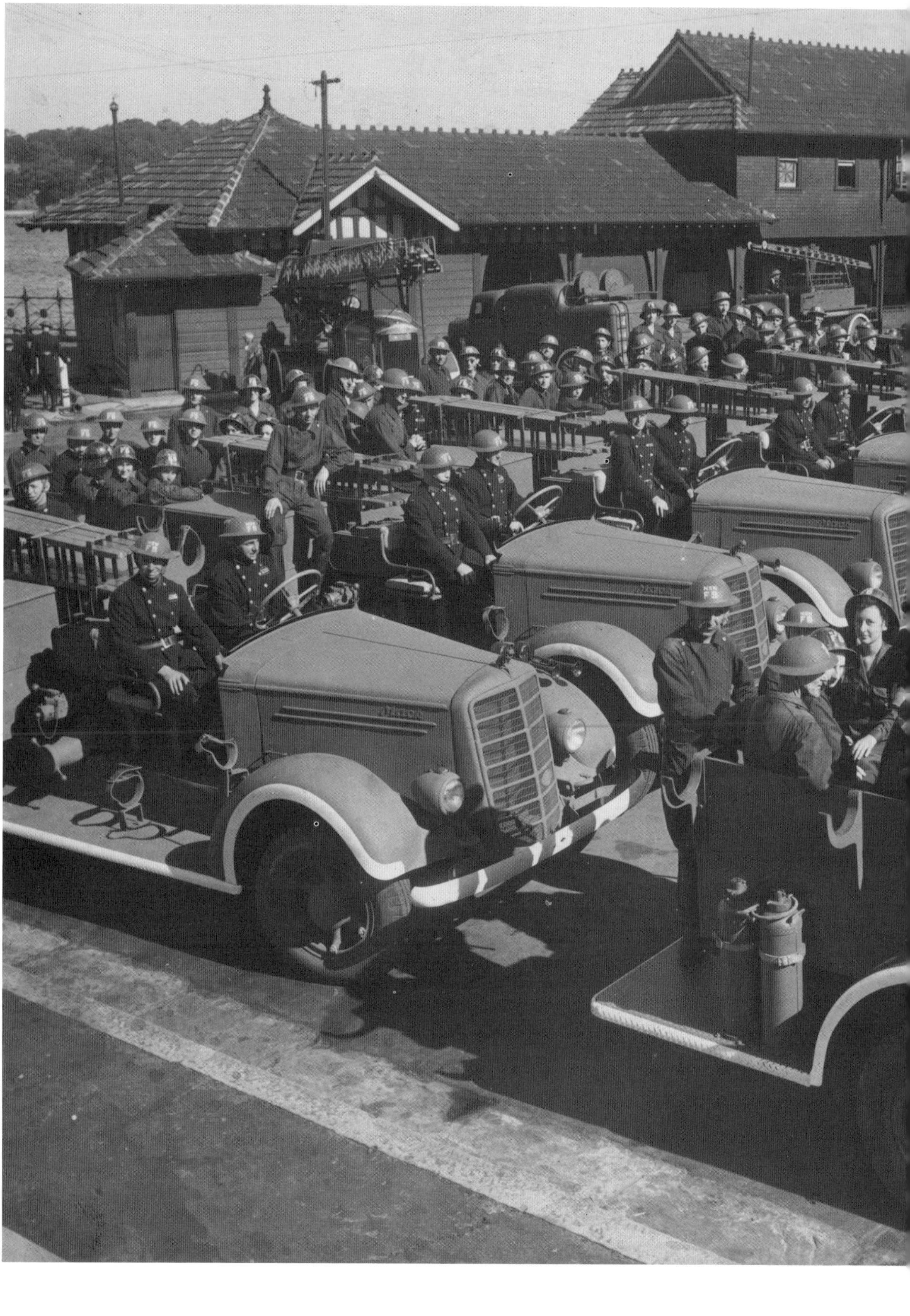

6

THE FOURTH ARM OF DEFENCE

Firemen at War

SYDNEY FIREMEN HAVE NEVER FACED the terrors of fighting fires during wartime aerial or naval attack. Our geographic position has (at least to date) provided almost total immunity from the devastation faced by Londoners during the German Blitz and Berliners during the Allied bombings at the end of the Second World War. Nonetheless, during both major world wars (1914–19 and 1939–45) NSW and, in particular, Sydney fire services underwent major changes as part of the war-footing. In essence they were placed on war alert as the 'fourth arm of defence'. Whilst many wartime changes were short-term, others were longer lasting. The Second World War in particular acted as a major catalyst to changes in Brigades' operations.

Members of the Women's Fire Auxiliary and their male counterparts wearing metal helmets at the handing-over of American 'lease-lend' Mack pumpers in 1943

THE GREAT WAR

With the outbreak of the first World War in August 1914, the Board adopted a number of precautionary measures to safeguard Sydney against fire resulting from enemy attack. All leave was immediately suspended and clerical, mechanical and electrical staff underwent training in fire drill. They were allotted to various fire stations where they would take up duty in the event of a conflagration.

Where permanent firemen reservists were called up for active service, the Board decided their positions would be filled temporarily by volunteers, with reservists able to resume their jobs upon return without losing seniority. Any deficiency in pay was also to be met by the Board.

It was decided the positions of permanent firemen who volunteered for active service would not be kept open. If they desired they could apply for reinstatement upon return, but would have to wait for a vacancy and be physically fit before reappointment. The Board's stance on permanent staff volunteering for active service was strongly opposed by the fledgling Fire Brigade Employees Union and in 1918 the Board agreed that 'it was desirable to make provision to enable them to rejoin at its [the war's] termination' (BFCAR, 1919:3).

The new policy of the Board was part of a package negotiated with the Returned Soldiers and Sailors Association and the Repatriation Department, whereby from the early part of 1918 the Board would make temporary appointments to returned soldiers. It was agreed that on war's end the Board would make such appointments permanent. By the end of 1919, 48 returned soldiers and sailors had been appointed. However, of the 51 members of the permanent staff who resigned, only eighteen sought and were granted reinstatement. In contrast to the decision taken by the Board in 1914, seniority was restored and the difference between military

Members of the New South Wales Fire Brigade who served during the Great War—including 26 killed-in-action

and firemen's pay was met. In all, seven of the permanent staff who volunteered made the supreme sacrifice. Of the twelve Imperial reservists conscripted, ten returned to the Brigades, and one (First-class Fireman, G W M King-Sergeant, Royal Horse Artillery) was killed in action. Of the ten members of the mechanical, electrical and clerical staff who had also enlisted, one was killed and the rest returned to support duties. Of the volunteer staff, over 212 had enlisted and those who returned were reappointed with all retaining fees paid during their absence.

On 2 May 1923 at Headquarters, the Honorable C W Oakes, Colonial Secretary, Minister for Public Health and Acting Premier, unveiled a Roll of Honour containing the names of the 316 members of the NSWFB Brigades who had enlisted for service in the Great War. In all, 26 men had died in serving their country.

An outcome at home of the Great War was the initiation of the Patriotic Carnival. The Carnival appears to have evolved from a 'Police and Firemen' Athletic Carnival first held at the Showground in 1912. The Carnival involved gymnastics, mounted police displays, fire drills and athletic events for adults and children. The highlight was the tug-of-war in which the Brigades' team defeated 'representatives of the law' two-to-one.

In 1914 an organising committee comprising Senior Sergeant Wallace, Fireman C D Franks and Constables Ferguson and Mackay was formed to plan a 'monster procession' from the Domain through the city to the Showground on 27 February 1915. The Patriotic Carnival, as it became known, captured public imagination and thousands of tickets were sold to raise funds for the troops abroad.

The procession, led by C D Franks on horseback, was more than two miles (3.22 km) long with over 46 distinct groups participating. About 100 motor cars were included, adorned with national flags, flowers and carrying representa-

Fireman C D Franks (on horseback) leads the Fire Brigade contingent in the 1915 patriotic procession

Members of the infamous Darktown (alias Pyrmont) Fire Brigade (top) formed by Jim Menzies (standing on the manual pumper). The first Fire Brigades' Band (above) with Bandmaster J Devlin seated third from left, was formed in 1916

tives of various nationalities in their national costume. Highlights included the 'Darktown Fire Brigade' and John Bull [alias Ephriam Stoneham, Principal Mechanic at Headquarters who weighed 22 stone (139.70 kg)].

The Darktown Brigade was formed specifically for the procession by Jim Menzies, a fireman and former showman. It followed the original Darktown Brigade constituted by members of the disbanded Theatre Royal Volunteers, which appeared at the Volunteer Demonstration at Corowa in 1909. With members from Pyrmont Brigade and Bill Rodney's fox terrier 'Dan' as mascot, the Darktowners proved so popular they gave regular performances around Sydney until the early 1920s. Whilst not perhaps the most 'efficient or disciplined' brigade to bless the service, it attained a notoriety which is nowadays attributed to those brigades lacking discipline and training. As ex-Station Officer 'Doc' Pearson recalled: 'Jim Menzies and us boys caused a mighty lot of laughter in our day, and what was more important, earned a lot of money to help the nation's war effort against Kaiser Bill' (*Fire*, Jan-Feb 1960:11). Another outcome of the Patriotic Carnival was the formation of the Fire Brigades Band in 1916 under Bandmaster John Devlin.

At the end of the Great War, although the Patriotic Carnivals ceased, community fund raising was perpetuated in the big annual 'Police and Firemen' carnivals and charity appeals of the 1920s. The highlight occurred in 1926 with displays of athletic events at the Showground and the raising of over £250,000 ($500 000). The money was raised by firemen selling tickets (first prize: a new motor car) in the Fire Brigades Art Union and Fire Brigades Queen Competition. With two free tickets for every book sold, was it any wonder that every station had firemen selling tickets at the door!

THE SECOND WORLD WAR

Following the declaration of war on Germany by England on Sunday 3 September 1939, the NSWFB, under the instruction of the Chief Secretary, was placed on war alert. Leave for all officers was deferred and all spare hose, boots, appliances, gas masks, hose reels and carts were despatched to stations within the metropolitan area. Stations were also issued with an order that 'all intruders seen about fire stations were to be questioned'. Following an appeal by the Fire Brigade Officers' Association to the Full Bench of the Industrial Commission, officers' leave was fully restored in December 1939.

For some time before the outbreak of war, a special staff of fourteen trained officers had been formed under Third Officer Sidney Tuck (no relation of his predecessor, Frances Arthur Tuck) to give lectures in Air Raid Protection (ARP) instruction. The lectures were given to permanent and volunteer staff, members of government departments, corporate bodies, private firms and National Emergency Service (NES) Wardens. A series of pamphlets was also produced by the Board instructing firemen in the detection of gases, air raid precautions, first aid, contamination and decontamination and neutralising bombs and projectiles.

To replace the fourteen officers on special duties, fourteen senior firemen were promoted to acting Sub-Station Officer rank and, in turn, an additional fourteen 'temporary' Fourth Class Firemen were appointed. To further supplement the ranks, a Reserve Corps was established under the Officer-in-Charge, J J (Gentleman Jim) Neville. The reserve firemen were drawn from local residents, with six or so being attached to each suburban station. A compulsory course of drill instruction was initiated for the training of reserves in basic firefighting as well as ARP work. The reserves received a badge (but no uniform) and were paid 2s 6d (25c) per hour if called to a building fire and 2s (20c) per hour for grass fires. By 1940 there were some 1453 reserves in training.

On 22 August 1939 the Select Committee on the 'Working Conditions of the Employees of the Board of Fire Commissioners' tabled its report in Parliament. The Committee was very much aware of the impact of the war emergency on firemen and their role as a 'fourth arm of defence' and concluded: 'for this reason, if for no other, the personnel of the fire service should be appropriately strengthened, and greater facilities provided for the training of firemen in air raids' (Select Committee *Report*, 1939:v). The philosophy of strengthening the Brigades had a major bearing on the principal finding of the Committee:

> Your Committee has carefully considered whether the inauguration of the three-platoon system would be in the public

interest—'public interest' having been given specific statutory recognition by the Industrial Arbitration (Eight Hours) Amendment Act, 1930. Your Committee's conclusion upon this point is that it would be definitely in the public interest that the three-platoon system (56 hour week) should be adopted and thus not only ensure a greater degree of general efficiency in the service, but also provide an increase of approximately 33 per cent in the number of trained firemen available to the community—especially in time of national emergency. (Select Committee *Report*, 1939:vi)

The Committee's findings clearly established 'in principle' the 56-hour week for firemen. However, the worsening war situation, lack of available manpower, cost [estimated at £82,741 ($165 482)] and the practicability (in a 'temporary' context) of the Reserve Corps system, led the Mair-Bruxner Government to 'shelve' the Select Committee Report. For the Fire Brigades Association it was to prove only a temporary setback in the campaign for a shorter working week. For the Board it provided some breathing space in which to ascertain the costs and logistics of a three-platoon system.

As part of 'war footing' the Board redeployed motorised fire appliances throughout the Sydney FD. A CO_2 and emergency tender were installed at Headquarters, with additional motors (previously spares) activated and stationed at nineteen suburban stations.

On 9 May 1940, the Industrial Commission brought down a new award for firemen, providing two grades of first-class firemen, abolishing rent allowances and increasing rates of pay, travelling and removal expenses. To further strengthen the Brigades the Board appointed thirteen additional SSOs and increased the strength of the Sydney FD to 616.

The Sydney, Blacktown, Cronulla and Sutherland Fire Districts were designated 'A' Division and the rest of the State divided into eight divisions (B to I). Within Sydney FD there were eight districts centred on:

'A' Headquarters	(No 1)	
'B' Crows Nest	(No 36)	
'C' Kogarah	(No 21)	
'D' Stanmore	(No 7)	
'E' George St West	(No 2)	
'F' Paddington	(No 11)	
'G' Parramatta	(No 27)	
'H' Drummoyne	(No 17)	

The greatest coordination problem within the Brigades was communication. Whilst Headquarters Control had direct phone lines to all district stations and to another nine stations, it was necessary to relay calls to all others. In many cases even the District Stations were not in direct connection to brigades within their area. Thus for Headquarters Control to contact Harbord it was necessary to go through the local exchange or to Crows Nest, relay to Manly and thence to Harbord. Similarly to contact Beecroft, it was necessary to go through Hornsby via Crows Nest or through Eastwood via Drummoyne.

The success of the Reserve Corps system prompted the Board to approve the recruitment of 2000 Auxiliary members to the Reserve Corps and the establishment of a 3000-strong Women's Auxiliary Fire Brigade Corps (WFA). The WFA Corps was recruited from Women's Australian National Service (WANS) Civil Defence units under the command of Lady Wakehurst. Following a ten-week course in ARP work, basic firefighting and first aid, women received a certificate and were assigned to a station within their local areas. Here they received weekly instruction in watchroom duties, location of major risks, fire alarms and station procedures. In an emergency they could be placed in charge of each station watchroom if the men were absent. The recruits were in the main housewives, over 30 years of age with a settled address and a good knowledge of their local suburbs.

By the end of 1941 the WFA program was fully operational. On 28 November the WFAs made their first public appearance, marching with the NSWFB unit on 'Prisoners of War Day'. The women were led by their commandant, Lola Douglas. There were now some 250 women firefighters in Sydney and Newcastle, each taking a two-hour night shift (7.30 pm–9.30 pm) at their assigned station watchroom.

On 9 April 1941 a Fire Brigades (Amendment) Act received Royal assent. The new Act enabled the extension of the Fire Brigade area to the Ports of Sydney and Newcastle and to Port Kembla and was to become effective on a day to be appointed by the Governor. Provision was also made within the Amendment for the funding by the Colonial Treasury of 'suitable fire floats'. The impossibility of securing suitable floats and resistance from the Maritime Services Board saw

Members of the Women's Fire Auxiliary show their skills during a presentation ceremony, 1942

the appointed day never arise! To the present day the Amendment has not been proclaimed, although investigations of just such an amendment are currently underway (see Chapter 9).

During 1941, with the deepening war emergency, the Board's program of ARP and firefighting instruction under National Emergency Legislation was intensified. By now 130 members of the permanent staff had qualified as Instructors in 'Fire Brigade Practice in National and War Emergency'. In 1941, 851 buildings were visited and instruction given to 60 253 persons, at 101 schools to 34 800 students, and at 199 public demonstrations to another 117 645 persons (BFCAR, 1941:3).

Because of the increased duties of firemen, the Industrial Commission authorised a 'War Allowance' clause, the wartime loading to commence on 3 October 1941. This provided an extra 6s (60c) per week for officers, senior and first class firemen, through to 3s (30c) per week for fourth class firemen.

With the entry of Japan into the war on 8 December 1941, the fire service was placed on a higher war footing. All the Board's mobile plant within Sydney was repainted for camouflage and headlamps masked. It was also necessary to repaint all street fire alarm pillars and mask all station windows to conform to 'brown-out' conditions. An air raid shelter was built in

NEWCASTLE'S FIRST FAMILY OF FIREFIGHTING[1]

'Wally' Walter M Plumbe (1898–1940) and Joyce Cummings (née Plumbe)

Wally Plumbe joined the fire service on 18 May 1923, rising to the rank of Sub-Station Officer. In 1939 he was posted to Chatswood as Officer-in-Charge.

Responding to a small scrub fire in Tambourine Bay Road, Longueville on 25 January 1940, with his crew of First Class Fireman John Darling, Volunteers Wally Wright, William Rudd and Thomas Neill and Reserve Fireman, George Suters, the Dennis Ace fire engine on which they were riding, overturned.

All except Wally Plumbe were thrown clear, suffering lacerations and fractures. Plumbe was pinned under the running board of the fire engine and was unconscious when local residents managed to drag him clear. Plumbe's skull had been fractured; three hours later he died in Royal North Shore Hospital.

The draped casket bearing Fireman Wally Plumbe is carried by a Dennis motor to Rookwood Cemetery, 1940

Wally Plumbe's funeral cortege was led by Deputy-Chief Officer W Beare. Four fellow officers acted as pallbearers, with the draped casket being borne by a 500/600 model Dennis fire engine to Rookwood Cemetery. One mourner at the funeral was his brother Dave, also a fireman and former dare devil pilot. Dave Plumbe was to remain in the fire service until retiring as Station Officer (Hamilton, Newcastle) in 1962.

Both Dave Plumbe's children, Joyce and Bill, took an early interest in their father's and uncle's occupation. At sixteen years of age Bill became an auxiliary and at seventeen a reserve fireman at Newcastle East. In 1948 he joined the permanent staff and in 1984 (at the time of writing) is in charge of Newcastle Headquarters' watchroom.

Not to be outdone by her brother, Joyce joined WANS and in 1941 trained to become a member of the Women's Fire Auxiliary. On receiving her certificate she was attached to the Cooks Hill station where she learnt the full routine of the watchroom and station duties.

As a WFA member, she wore WANS uniform with a WFA armband, FB badge on her epaulettes and a fire engine badge on the left collar. Her drill uniform consisted of a pair of overalls, rubber boots and Bakelite helmet marked NSWFB, a belt and pouches for axe and spanner. Despite reference to the WFA initials as 'weight for age', she and her colleagues were not deterred, proving themselves capable of mastering all the duties of 'firies'.

In 1946 Joyce married a Newcastle fireman, Ray Cummings. She and her husband showed a great interest in local politics and in 1968 (after rearing four children) she was elected to the Newcastle City Council as a Labor alderman for East Ward. In 1974 she was elected as Australia's first woman Lord Mayor and the following year was honoured with the Order of Australia.

To complete the story, Kathy Cummings (daughter of Joyce and Ray) applied to become a volunteer firefighter at Tighes Hill in 1978. Her rejection, along with others, was one incident prompting the Equal Opportunities Legislation facilitating the entry of women into the NSWFB (Chapter 9).

There is little doubt that the Plumbe/Cummings 'family' have made a unique (and in Wally's case the ultimate) contribution to the NSWFB.

Board President T J Smith and Lady Wakehurst present a successful WFA member with her certificate, 1942

the Headquarters basement and the watchroom structurally strengthened.

Auxiliary workshop premises were established at Pyrmont and Five Dock for the dispersal of plant and equipment repair from Headquarters. A Fire Brigade Control Centre was also built at Five Dock FS under the supervision of the Board's architect, Fred Ross. With a staff of eight, the 'decentralised' Control Centre was to maintain Brigades communication during the event of an emergency. A mobile 'shadow' control was also established and night roof duty was instigated at a number of stations close to the coast. The need for these precautions was reinforced when two Japanese submarines shelled Sydney and Newcastle on the morning of 8 June 1942. During the alert a complete blackout was enforced; WFA, Auxiliaries and reserves headed to their assigned duty points. Damage was fortunately relatively slight, with only one person injured, a resident of a block of flats at Rose Bay who suffered leg injuries when a bomb passed through his bedroom without exploding.

During 1942 a major press-based recruitment drive was initiated for more WFA personnel. To publicise its work and raise funds, a Fire Queen competition was arranged. The seven Sydney candidates raised £3,323 ($6646) in seven weeks; the winner, Mrs B L Baltzer of Dee Why, was crowned at Sydney Town Hall in October. The money went to a worthy cause—the first mobile canteen for firemen.[2]

During 1942 the Board approached the Commonwealth Government, through the Chief

Secretary, for funds to purchase more motorised appliances and other equipment for use by the 'enlarged' complement of permanent and reserve firemen and women. Early in 1943 the Board's requests were met. At a gathering at Bennelong Point on 30 January, the Federal Minister for Home Security, Mr H P Lazzarini, handed over the first eight 750-gallon (3409.57 L) Mack pumpers, to the Chief Secretary, the Honorable J M Baddeley.[3] The motors had been acquired under lease-lend arrangements with the American Government, together with almost 180,000 feet (54 864 m) of unlined canvas fire hose. At the handing-over ceremony the Brigades presented a public display, during which the newly acquired engines and other fire service appliances were manned for the first time by WFA members in service dress.

Additional engine bay space to house the new motors was provided at Alexandria, Bexley, Drummoyne, Matraville and Mortdale. During 1943 a further four Mack engine chassis with pumps, a stationary pump unit and 44 American La France fire engines, capable of pumping 1000 gpm (76 L/S) were received, modified and placed into service for reserve training.

The skills of the reserves and WFAs were displayed at a large 'demonstration' at Hordernian Park, Undercliffe, on 15 February 1943. Thirty-nine women's teams and 69 men's,

Members of the Reserve Corps and regular fireman at fire extinguisher drill, 1943

from throughout the State competed in the largest 'reserve' competition ever promoted by the Board of Fire Commissioners.

Further lease-lend fire engines were secured during 1944 and by year's end a total of 59 were stationed within the Sydney FD (the largest number, seven, at Bexley). In conformity with the National Security (General) Regulations, firemen were deployed 'ship watching' on vessels loading or unloading ammunition and explosives. It was also necessary to despatch engines and permanent and reserve staff to the Blue Mountains to combat record bush fires, which led to the introduction of a 'Bush and Rural Fire Prevention Order (No 2), 1944' under the National Security (General) Regulations. The four-part Order authorised the banning of the lighting of fires in certain areas in certain months, the establishment of bush fire brigades and reconstituted the Bush Fire Committee first formed in 1942. The new Chief Officer, William Beare, who replaced Charles Richardson as Chief Officer on Richardson's death on 16 September, was appointed to the Bush Fire Committee. Both Richardson and Beare had joined the Brigades as Cadet Firemen in 1900.

On 19 April 1944 a Fire Brigades (Amendment) Act was given Royal assent. The Act provided from the day following the end of the war that:

(a) the ordinary hours of duty and leave of full-time firemen should be arranged such that hours worked be on a system of three shifts per day;
(b) the average ordinary working hours for permanent firemen would be 56 per week;
(c) the average ordinary working hours for officers within the Brigades would be 84 per week.

The delay until war's end incensed the union, particularly its left-wing, which in 1943 elected Sid Jordan to replace Maurice Piper as the Permanent Firemens' Representative on the Board. From this point relationships between the Fire Brigades union and the Board deteriorated rapidly. The left-wing of the union, led by Association President Jim Lambert, began agitating for a number of improvements in working conditions whilst the Board, led by an equally determined T J Smith, argued that during the war contingency, funds were stretched to the limit. In July 1944 the conflict reached boiling point over the lack of overcoats for firemen on night fire-watch duties. The union delivered an ultimatum that a limited strike would ensue unless coats were provided to all firemen. At a Trades Hall meeting at 10.30 am on 3 July provoked by the suspension of nineteen men for refusing to perform duties, a motion was carried calling for the Board's dismissal and a refusal to return to work. The strike lasted eight hours, during which stations were manned solely by officers and volunteers.

At 4.30 pm Justice Taylor of the Industrial Commission called a compulsory conference of the Board and the Fire Brigades Association and at 6.30 pm he delivered details of settlement:

(a) all members of the Association to be issued with overcoats as soon as practicable;
(b) no man to be penalised for his participation in the strike (including the nineteen suspended); and
(c) all men to resume duty at once.

The first firemen's strike in Sydney had been short and bitter with a clear-cut victory for the Association. The question of where to obtain the overcoats was quickly resolved when the Board agreed to purchase blue Air Force overcoats. The Premier, Mr McKell, contacted the Prime Minister and Air Force overcoats were in Sydney the following day.

It was the same day that a stampede of 10 000 circus-goers tried to escape a fire in a Ringling Bros Circus tent in Hartford, Connecticut (USA). One hundred and fifty-nine persons, mainly children, were killed in the panic—worsened because of exits blocked by circus equipment. An investigating committee found that the tent had been sprayed with a waterproofing solution consisting of paraffin melted in petrol!

Resolution of the 'overcoat' dispute facilitated only a temporary cessation of hostilities between firemen and the Board. On 11 February 1945 following the suspension of Fireman W J Cruise (Stanmore) for refusing to do clerical duties, all firemen in NSW went on strike. The Association's stance was that firefighters would only return to work if men were not requested to do 'officers' work', defined as making out pay sheets, rosters and reports. The dispute flared after the first day, with the Association demanding an immediate reduction in hours from the 78 being worked, to 73½ hours per

"Hey! Don't you know there's a strike on."

The first NSW firemen's strike—the overcoat dispute in 1945—attracted its share of press publicity

week. After a bitter three days the strike ended when the Senior Officers' Association agreed to 'temporarily' carry out the clerical duties to which firemen objected. In contrast to the earlier strike, the press came out against the firemen's actions with vitriolic editorial attacks on the Fire Brigades Association.

Fortuitously no major fires occurred during the three strike days when stations were manned only by skeleton crews of officers. Following settlement of the dispute, negotiations continued over working hours. On 21 September 1945 (almost three weeks after the 'appointed day'), the long-awaited 56-hour week rosters were implemented. The rotation of hours over a six-day period was two day shifts of ten hours each, two night shifts of fourteen hours each, followed by forty-eight hours off duty; the cycle repeating every six weeks. The officers' roster, worked on the basis of 24 hours on and 24 hours off, averaged 84 hours over a week.

It was the Board's view that recruits and finance were simply not available to implement the three-platoon roster. On the day the new rosters were brought in the Board closed 23 fire stations in the Sydney Fire District. The stations closed were Alexandria, Arncliffe, Annandale, Bexley, Chatswood, Canterbury, Enfield, Five Dock, Granville, Homebush, Hunters Hill, Harbord, Mascot, Mortdale, Maroubra, North Sydney, Pyrmont, Ryde, Rozelle, St Peters, Vaucluse, Woollahra and Waverley. Men from these stations were reassigned to nearby stations to bring numbers up to the strength necessary for three shifts. Nonetheless the three-shift system still required an increase of seven officers and 130 firemen to man the Sydney FD.

Many of the station closures had been foreshadowed as far back as 1917 when the Board put forward a proposal for the 'Consolidation of the Sydney FD', based on the introduction of mechanised vehicles. Most of the closed stations were near other stations, having been constructed in elevated positions to facilitate horse-drawn response downhill. Despite opposition from both the Fire Brigade Employees Union and the NSW Fire Brigades Officers' Association and heated Parliamentary debate, the Chief Secretary, Mr Baddeley, supported the closures.

The war ended on 15 August 1945, and during the next year Brigade activities were normalised. The reserve, auxiliary reserve and WFA groups were disbanded, fire appliances repainted 'pillar-box' red, war loadings removed, warning sirens restored and on 7 September brass helmets restored (having been replaced in December 1941 by steel Army-type helmets). The Brigades also set about repairing more than 40 fire alarm boxes damaged in victory celebrations within the city. The jubilation heralded a new era of peace and substantial post-war recovery.

A TYPICAL FIREMAN?
Senior Fireman M L Griffen (1910–1942)

MICK Griffen joined the fire service on 14 May 1929 and from the start established a reputation as the Brigades' star athlete. The son of an Adelaide Fire Chief, Mick was a leading Australian Rules footballer and a better than average boxer, with lightning reflexes.

On moving to Sydney he changed football codes and in 1936 was scrum-half in the victorious Rugby tour of Victoria and South Australia. His fitness fanaticism had become legendary and he played the 'lead' role in the Fire Brigades' drill displays at Headquarters. Mick Griffen was the fastest man up the 100-foot (30.48 m) ladders and as a highlight to the display, would perform a somersault dive from the third floor into a 'catching net'.

In February 1942 Chief Officer Richardson was approached by the *Mirror* newspaper to pick out a 'typical fireman'; he chose Griffen! Griffen's acrobatic abilities and out-going personality had also established him as an excellent ARP demonstrator. For most of 1939–1942 Griffen acted as a demonstrator in Alec Coppel's Minerva ARP shows which toured schools and public gatherings, causing Coppel to comment: 'if he ever gives up firefighting he can become an actor'.

Neither was to be the case. On 11 June 1942, just four months after the *Mirror* feature, Griffen was crushed to death under red hot steel bars when fire destroyed the dye stamping section of R B Davies (Hardware) Pty Ltd, Marrickville. With four other Headquarters firemen, Griffen was extinguishing small fires when the roof collapsed and several hundred tons of steel rods slipped forward, burying him. Firemen and factory employees took more than two hours to release his crushed body from the tangled heap of hot steel and smouldering timber. In the process Fireman Reginald Cruse was electrocuted and was carried unconscious to hospital where he later recovered.

Mick Griffen's funeral was attended by his wife (whom he met in the Headquarters' tailoring section) and their two children, relatives, Board members, and about 200 firemen. The Fire Brigades Band led the funeral procession of firemen, in full wartime dress, from Kingsford to Botany Cemetery.

In everything he did, Mick Griffen excelled. Chief Officer Richardson had been more than a little cagey in presenting him as 'the typical fireman'. In death at the age of only 32, Mick Griffen had given the ultimate community sacrifice.

156

7

NEDDIES, COFFEE POTS & FLYING PIGS

Fire Fighting Equipment

WHEN THE MFB BECAME OPERATIONAL on 1 July 1884 all plant and equipment belonging to the Insurance Companies Brigade in Bathurst Street was transferred. At best the 'plant' of the new brigade can be described as rudimentary (Appendix 7.1). There were three steamers:[1]

Nonpareil (Acq. 1865) Shand, Mason and Company, 450 gallons per minute (gpm)
Fire King (Acq. 1871) Merryweather and Sons, 600 gpm
Guardian (Acq. 1874) Shand, Mason and Company, 250 gpm

In addition there were two manual engines:

Tilley (Acq. 1871) seven-inch (17.78 cm) pump

Metropolitan Fire Brigade steamers in the parade celebrating the foundation of the Commonwealth of Australia, 1901

Express (Acq. 1872) four and three-quarter inch (12.07 cm) pump

To pull the engines the MFB purchased three horses, stabled at the rear of the Bathurst Street station, and utilised the physical power of the firemen who pulled the lighter manual by hand.

Because the newest appliance (the Guardian) was ten years old, the new Board immediately set about upgrading its firefighting equipment. On the recommendation of Superintendant W Bear, a number of single vertical steamers (350 gpm) and manuals were ordered from Shand, Mason and Company in England, the first steamer and manual arriving in 1885.

HORSE AND STEAM

The plant of the volunteer companies subsidised by the Board was even more rudimentary. None possessed steamers and many had only hose reels pulled by hand. As new steamers and manuals arrived from England the older plant of the MFB was transferred on loan to volunteer companies.

By 1888 seven volunteer companies (Alexandria, Ashfield, Burwood, Leichhardt, Manly, St Leonards and Waverley) held manuals owned by the MFB. By the same year the MFB owned six steam fire engines (held at the new MFB stations of Headquarters, George Street West and Marrickville) and eleven manuals (held at the above stations or on loan to the volunteer companies).

The completion of the new Headquarters Station in Castlereagh Street in 1888 allowed the

Many of the early volunteers still depended on manual pumpers such as this Tilley from No. 2 Volunteer Brigade (top). Even by 1905 the East Willoughby Volunteer Brigade in Laurel Street had only a manpowered hose reel (above)

utilisation of a telescopic fire ladder and van, built in the Brigades' workshop under the supervision of Superintendent Bear. The ladder, capable of being raised 50 feet (15.24 m) in height, was the first of a number of fire-escape ladders Bear proposed be deployed around the city. This plan followed a fire at Wentworth House on 25 December 1888 where two men died falling from the roof. By 1890 similar ladders were housed at each of the MFB stations.

In 1890 the Board ordered a new large steamer from Shand, Mason and Company, which arrived in January 1892. The Brigades were justifiably proud of their new five-ton engine bought at a cost of £1,328 ($2656) and described as 'the most powerful land steam fire engine that has yet been produced!' The following description emphasises the impressive performance statistics of the new steamer, christened *Big Ben*:[2]

> 100 lb [68.9 kPa] of steam were obtained from cold water in nine minutes fifty five seconds; and with a steam pressure of 110 to 120 lb [757.9–826.8 kPa] a one and three quarter inch [4.45 cm] jet of water was thrown horizontally to a distance of 318 feet [96.93 m]. This engine which is of the patent equilibrium type, is calculated to work at a steam pressure of 100 to 125 lb per square inch [689–61.25 kPa], but is capable of working much higher; it discharges 1000 gallons of water per minute [4550 L/m] and will project a one and three quarter inch jet to a height of 200 feet [60.96 m]. It is fitted with three steam cylinders, three double acting pumps, has a suction no less than seven and a half inches [19.05 cm] in diameter and five deliveries. Four of the latter are for two and three quarter inch [6.99 cm] hose, and one for three and a half inch [8.89 cm]. (MFBAR, 1891:2)

In August the following year the MFB acquired its first turntable (self-supporting) ladder; an 80-foot (24.38 m) extension ladder mounted on a horse-drawn chassis, designed and built by Shand, Mason and Company. The new ladder

The first turntable ladder acquired by the Metropolitan Fire Brigades. Purchased from Shand, Mason and Company in 1893 the horse-drawn chassis supported an 80-foot extension ladder

Cleaning of the Town Hall tower to celebrate the arrival of the large double-vertical steamer in 1899 (above left). Already in service at Balmain was this smaller Merryweather steamer (top right). The chemical hose carriages (above right) carried their own water supply

housed at Headquarters (No 1), was fitted in 1894 with a water-tower, which could be operated by men on the ground. In the same year the Board purchased a new light-weight, double vertical steamer from Shand, Mason and Company capable of pumping 260 gpm. This model proved particularly useful at suburban stations and was the forerunner of ten similar models purchased by the MFB from both Shand, Mason and Company and Merryweather and Sons between 1895 and 1906.

In January 1899 the MFB acquired its second large steamer, a 750 gpm, double vertical steamer, also from Shand, Mason and Company. On 28 February a public demonstration of the new steamer, along with *Big Ben*, took place at Town Hall. In a spectacular display watched by a large crowd of onlookers and special guests, both steamers 'threw water' more than twenty feet (6.10 cm) above the 198-foot (60.35 m) high Town Hall clock tower. As the crowd cheered, the firemen proceeded to give the Town Hall a much-needed wash. For Super-intendent Alfred Webb it was a fitting public introduction to his recent appointment as the head of the Brigades.

By the turn of the century, the MFB had substantially increased its plant beyond that obtained from the Insurance Brigade in 1884. The eleven permanently-manned brigades housed nine steamers, five manuals, an 80-foot (24.38 m) set of ladders, a 50-foot (15.24 m) curricle ladder (purchased from Shand, Mason and Company in 1898), six hose carriages, three hose reels, six carts, two buggies and more than 80 sets of scaling ladders. In addition the nineteen volunteer stations held a further fifteen manuals, fourteen hose reels, three hose carriages and some 70 scaling ladders, most of this plant belonging to the MFB.

Whilst most of the MFB equipment had been purchased from the English suppliers Shand, Mason and Company and Merryweather and Sons, many of the smaller appliances were locally made. The two main local suppliers were W Vial and Son[3], who built chemical hose

The first motorised fire appliance in Australia. Acquired in 1904 a 'petrol motorised' chemical hose carriage made by Merryweather and Sons. Metropolitan Fire Brigades Chairman, Charles Bown (driver's seat) poses proudly with his senior officers

carriages and R Bain of Ultimo, who built hose carriages, hose reels, curricle ladders and five-inch (12.70 cm) manuals. Earlier manuals had been built by T J Bown and Company in Bathurst Street.

The chemical hose carriages were an unusual innovation, first adopted in 1896. They proved ideal in containing small fires in situations where there was inadequate local water pressure. Carbonic acid held in a steel tube was released into a cylinder containing 60 gallons (273 L) of water until a pressure of about 75 lbs per square inch (516.75 kPa) was reached. This pressure had the effect of forcing out the water into 600 feet (182.88 m) of hose and projecting it through the nozzle to a distance of about 50 feet (15.24 m).

The turn of the century also signalled the first suggestion that the era of horse and steam might be coming to a close. In 1900 the Board noted that the demands of overseas war campaigns on horses was making it increasingly difficult to obtain suitable horses for the Brigades. The type of animal required by the Brigades to haul the steamers, manuals and ladders over the rough ground was one in excess of 16 hands, and powerful as well as speedy. The Board concluded: 'Under the circumstances inquiry is being made as to the practicability of auto-motor engines; and it may be that the substitution of motor for horsepower, for running steamers to fires, will be the solution of the difficulty' (MFBAR, 1900:3). The following year the Board reported:

> Steam and electricity are competing for supremacy, and the question of substituting liquid fuel for coal is also involved. If the report be true that the great American electrician, Mr Edison, has invented a vastly improved accumulator, by which he anticipates that locomotives and steamships will be cheaply driven, the question may be solved in favour of electricity; but at present the matter is involved in much uncertainty. (MFBAR, 1901:4)

Two years later Superintendent Alfred

Webb toured England and viewed a number of mechanised fire engines used by his old friend, London Fire Chief Eyre Massey Shaw. Impressed by their speed and ease of turn out, he introduced the first motorised appliance to Australian fire brigades in 1904. It was a 'petrol motorised' chemical hose carriage, purchased from Merryweather and Sons, and was stationed at No 2 station, George Street West. The Aster four-cylinder motor was chain driven, mounted on four artillery pattern rubber tyred wheels, with axles and springs. Carrying a five-man crew and driver the motor was capable of 24 mph (39 km/h).

Despite its speed advantage over horse-drawn appliances [which travelled at 5–10 mph (8–16 km/h)] the new motor was far from reliable:

> At last night's display by the fire brigades, great interest was taken in the motor fire engine, the latest in fire extinguishers.
>
> At the alarm the horses for the horse-drawn engines were harnessed with the speed of thought and clattered away into the night; but quicker than any horse-drawn engine the motor fire engine moved out of the station and the spectators imagined that at last the true key to fire-fighting efficiency had been found.
>
> Some time passed, and the engines returned—that is, the horse-drawn engines did. There was no sign of the motor. The horses were put in the stalls, the show wound up and the spectators moved for home.
>
> Passing round the block into George Street, one of the visitors saw the motor fire engine being shoved along by half-a-dozen firemen.
>
> 'I wouldn't take that thing to a fire' he said to one of the firemen.
>
> 'Why not?'
>
> 'Well, you might get it burnt before you could shift it.'
>
> The motor engine will not displace the horse engines just yet. (*Sydney Morning Herald*, 1904)

In 1903 the MFB acquired another 80-foot (24.38 m) high Bailey's extension ladder donated for services after the Anthony Hordern's fire of 1901 by Mr Samuel Hordern (Chapter 8). Despite its height it was well under the height of the largest city buildings. The Anthony Hordern's fire prompted other ladder acquisitions: a 70-foot (21.34 m) turntable ladder from Shand, Mason and Company in 1905 and fifteen 45-foot (13.72 m) curricle ladders between 1901 and 1906 (two having been purchased in 1898). Four of these were produced in the Board's workshops under the supervision of the MFB's first Principal Electrician, Edward Smith, and Principal Mechanic, Ephraim Stoneham.[4] Smith's appointment followed the introduction of electrical power to the Headquarters workshops in 1903.

Experimentation with motor power continued when a petrol motor pumping fire engine arrived from London on 6 September 1905. Purchased from Merryweather and Sons, the motor was the same as that for the motorised hose carriage. Mounted at the rear was a Hatfield pump capable of delivering 300 gpm. After modifications by the Sydney agents, Gibson, Battle and Company, the motor was placed into service in 1906. Whilst performing satisfactorily, the initial cost of £995 ($1990) and the high cost of maintenance made the new motor, at best, experimental. In 1907 a Merryweather 30 horsepower combined petrol motor chemical fire engine and salvage waggon was placed into service at Headquarters, and the following year another Merryweather motor pumping engine, capable of 25 mph (40.25 km/h) was also placed at Headquarters.[5] The earlier model was transferred to Darlinghurst. By 1909 the end of the steamer era was fast approaching. The last MFB steamer, a double vertical 450 gpm Merryweather, was purchased in 1906, and in 1909 T Green and Company exhibited a method of converting manual engines to petrol motor power.

It was also in the last throes of the MFB in November 1909 that the Board acquired its first motorised turntable ladder purchased from Henry Simonis and Company for £1,853 ($3706). Power was provided by an 80-cell battery under the bonnet which drove motors in the front wheel hubs. With a top speed of 18 mph (29 km/h) and a range of 25 miles (40.25 km), the 5 tons 7½ cwt (5.46 tonnes) Simonis could be operated by two men and raised to a height of 86 feet (26.21 m). On 7 December 1909 the ladders were formally named 'The Bown' (in honour of Mr Charles Bown) by the Governor of NSW, Lord Chelmsford. The ceremony on the steps of

A Halley turntable ladder (top) remounted on a motor-powered chassis and a motorised, chain-driven Merryweather fire engine (above)

NEDDIES AND COFFEE POTS
The Era of Horse and Steam

THROUGHOUT the MFB era individual stations were dependent on their faithful horses or 'neddies'. Horses such as 'Ginger' and 'Beauty' at Headquarters and 'Belfast', 'Shannon' and 'Limerick' at Redfern were known throughout the service for their speed, strength and hardiness. Their value was recognised in the scrupulous care of stables, the four feeds of chaff and one of greens each day and twice-daily exercise. If found ill or lame, the horses were spelled at the Brigades' 'convalescent' paddock at Mortdale.

Always at the ready in the stables, the horses were trained to trot out to the harnesses immediately the stable doors were opened on the ringing of the station bell. It was the duty of the watchroom staff to ring the bells, open the station doors (or if open, release the guide rope used to prevent horses bolting on to the roadway). The harnesses hung from the engine room roof and were of the American snap variety, taking less than 30 seconds to be snapped into position once dropped onto the backs of two horses.

The Brigades' steamers were known as 'coffee pots' because of their large boilers. The 'coffee pots', when free of horses, were shifted around the station by their centre harnessing

Neddies turn out the Big Ben steamer

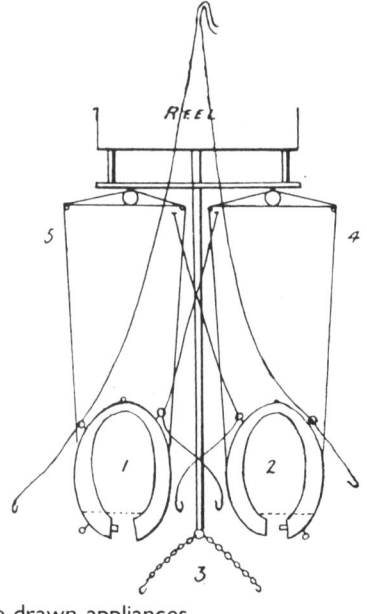

The American snap harness system drastically improved the turn-out of horse-drawn appliances

Headquarters' steamers immaculately presented both in the engine bay (top) and rear yard (above)

Big Ben with a good head of steam in the Paddington Fire Station yard

pole to prevent pistons and working parts setting. After each fire a kerosene-soaked tinder of wood and coal was left prepared in the fire box, situated beneath the engine's boiler.[6] After a turn-out an appliance was placed in its bay with this fire box positioned slightly behind the gas outlet which projected from the station's floor. A pilot light constantly burned at the head of this outlet and when actuated by lever control —in the manner of the familiar gas bath heaters—would cause a sudden blast of ignited gas to flash upwards. The lever which controlled the main gas flow could be operated by simply rolling one 'steamer' forward in its bay. This action would release the full blast of gas which, ignited, would penetrate the fire bars and set the tinder in the fire box ablaze.

In this ingenious way the steamer always had the benefit of an 'automatic' fire beneath its boiler at times of emergency. In three and a half minutes, 100 lbs (689 kPa) pressure of steam could be raised by this method.

When the bells sounded the coachman rapidly donned his tunic and gear, mounted the horseless engine and grabbed the reins. The stable doors were then opened while the horses, alerted by the ringing fire bells, would trot to their positions at the head of the appliance. Their bridles were hung on the stable doors, and their harness and tracing were suspended on a pole above the engine. This equipment was snapped into position.

The Station Officer and a fireman then mounted the appliance while another two firemen held the horses' heads from the front. The Station Officer and his counterpart on the other side of the appliance each controlled a handbrake which, upon mounting, they released after the officer had called to yet another man, usually the steam man: 'All right, kick away the chocks!'

The appliance would then roll forward a few inches, actuating the gas burner and igniting the fire in its fire grate. As 'neddies' and 'coffee pot' turned out, one of the watchroom staff halted traffic with a red flag or, at night, with a lantern.

the National Art Gallery concluded with a drive past and gallop past.

Despite the inroads of motorisation the Brigades were still heavily reliant on manuals, horse and steam in 1909. Equipment transferred to the new Board of Fire Commissioners (BFC) included 16 steam fire engines, 30 manuals, 29 coachmen, 137 horses and 30 horse-drawn ladders. It was the peak number of steamers and horses to be used by Sydney fire services.

MOTORISATION OF THE BRIGADES
Hatfields, Gwynnes and Garfords

The period 1910–27 witnessed the most dramatic changes in firefighting equipment in the history of Sydney Fire Brigades. Steam, manual and horsepower were replaced by petrol-driven motors. The changes went beyond a simple change in the mode of power—coachmen disappeared as did the farrier; workshop operators took on new skills; new workshops were added; the location and layout of stations changed; the speed of response was dramatically increased; and the daily station chores were altered. No longer did the stables have to be mucked out, the horses exercised or the steamers maintained.

One of the earliest changes after the formation of the Board of Fire Commissioners was the transfer of the Salvage Corps to the staff of the permanent Brigades. All equipment and monies were also transferred. Alteration of the manual pumps to petrol turbine pumps began in 1911 with the arrival of the first eight Gwynne petrol-driven turbine pumps.[7] Converted in the Brigades' workshops, the pumps cost £180 ($360) each, generated 16–20 horsepower and could deliver 150 gallons (682.5 L) of water a minute. Given the cost relativity of converting an existing manual (£180) to purchasing a new appliance [£250 ($500)] the Board proposed to convert all manual to petrol-driven motors 'as opportunity offers and means permit'. Between 1911 and 1919, more than 30 conversions were made in the Brigades' workshops.

At the same time the Board decided to continue experimentation with motor fire engines.[8] Two 350 gpm petrol motor Dennis Gwynne fire engines, with turbine pumps, arrived from London on 30 January 1912. The turbine pumps were manufactured by Gwynnes Ltd, while Dennis Bros provided the chassis and motor engine which drove the car and pump. One motor went to Newcastle whilst the other was installed at Headquarters.

Both sets of Shand, Mason and Company turntable ladders were converted in 1912 to motorised chassis. In both cases the ladders were remounted on 40 horsepower Halley chassis built by Dalgety and Company and 125-volt shunt generators were also installed providing power for elevation and extension. The only drawback with the alterations was that the safe working height of the 80-foot (24.39 m) extension was reduced to 65 feet (19.81 m).[9]

The years 1913 and 1914 were important in the transition to motor power. Three Merryweather 'Hatfields' and ten Dennis Gwynne motor fire engines, four rating 500–700 gpm and six 400–500 gpm were received by the NSWFB. Eight were installed in Sydney, along with a Simonis fire engine. This brought the number of self-driven motorised fire engines in the Sydney FD to fourteen. At the same time more of the converted manuals were installed at both Sydney and country stations.

The growing dominance of motor over horse was poignantly displayed in the death of the Board's paymaster, Mr A Hart, in 1913. Whilst delivering the pay to Balmain in a horse and buggy driven by Fireman James McNamara, the horse shied at a passing motor car. Hart was thrown to the ground and killed instantly. His widow received a gratuity from the Board of £200 ($400).

The onset of the war had a major impact on the Brigades: new appliances and parts became difficult to obtain from England and the Board was placed under severe cost restrictions. The Brigades became increasingly reliant on inhouse

One of the last turbine pumpers—withdrawn from Alstonville in 1931. The first horse-drawn appliance was placed into service in 1911. The turbines allowed manual pumpers to be converted to mechanical power

By 1918 Headquarters had been fully motorised for three years (left to right): the Halley ladders (partly obscured); the first salvage motor, a 1916 Garford; a 1913 Dennis Gwynne 75 hp; and a Dennis Gwynne 450

construction and modifications. In 1915 the workshops produced their first two motorised fire engines, a shaft-driven Dennis with Rees-Rotorbo pump installed at Ryde and the other, a chain driven Willys Gwynne, installed at Grafton. Several Willys were built and in turn were followed by Garford Model 64s. The four cylinder side-valve petrol engines were made in the USA. Chain-driven and with solid tyres, the Garford Model 64 chassis were fitted with a 200 gpm centrifugal pump. The body style, as in earlier fire engines, was a 'Braidwood' body—named after its designer, the first London Fire Chief, James Braidwood.[10] Firemen sat on both sides of the engine at right angles to the direction of the vehicle.

To cope with the increased workload, the Headquarters' workshops were reconstructed at a cost of £1,099 ($2198) and opened by the Governor of NSW, Gerald Strickland, on 24 September 1915. With the workshop alterations, Headquarters became a fully-motorised station, housing the electric Simonis ladders, two motor cars, two motor fire engines, a motorised salvage, the motor hose carriage and the steamer, *Big Ben* (now pulled by a truck). With the end of horses at Headquarters came the end of one of the Brigades' original old-timers. Farrier and former coachman Joseph Stanchell who had joined the MFB in its first intake of 1 July 1884 died in July 1916.

The war years saw a number of improved pumps with a pumping rate of 240 gpm fitted to Willys Garford chassis and installed in the Sydney FD. Produced by the Board workshops to a now 'standard' design the new motorised appliances were cheaper, more reliable, lightweight and ideally suited for suburban stations. They were the lynch-pin of the 1917 proposal to consolidate the Sydney FD. Whilst suitable for most stations the consolidation plan noted that Mascot and Lidcombe would have to persevere with horse-drawn appliances given the poor state of the roads.

Whilst the costs of motor replacement were still relatively high, each motor fire engine costing £750–800 ($1500–1600) and averaging £150 ($300) pa for maintenance, the savings were also substantial. Two horses cost about £106 ($212) per annum to feed; gear could be sold and two horses fetched £120 ($240); converted manuals could be reassigned to country areas and a saving could be made in the wages of coachmen. Local councils were enthusiastic about the motorisation program, but were less than enthusiastic about the plan for station closures. This opposition, along with that from the union, saw motorisation continue but very few closures in the 1920s.

By the end of 1921, 51 of the 65 Sydney fire stations were motorised and 22 motors were assigned to various country stations. The cheaper cost of the American chassis [£200–300 ($400–600)] had prompted the end of the manual conversion program two years earlier. Four 60 horsepower Dennis motor fire engines with a pumping capacity of 500–600 gpm arrived in 1921. Installed at Headquarters, George Street West, Newtown and Paddington, they became the main NSWFB first-response vehicles.

On 27 August 1922 a major disaster occurred at a fire at Adams' Cafe in George Street. With three men on its ladder sections the 86-foot (26.21 m) Simonis turntable ladder suddenly snapped. Third-Class Firemen William Brown was killed almost instantly whilst the two others, Firemen Chapple and Dwyer, were badly injured. The Coroner's inquiry returned a verdict of accidental death; however, there appears to have been three contributing factors: a strong wind gust, the weight of the water-laden hose, and the fact that the three firemen were grouped together on one section of the ladder, contrary to operating instructions that only one man should be on any section at one time.

The electric ladder, 'The Bown' had been remounted in 1918 by the Board workshop onto a special chassis propelled by a petrol engine manufactured by Hewitt-Ludlow Auto Company. Exhibited at the City Coroner's inquiry the ladders and chassis have not been seen by the Brigades since.

By the end of 1922 only two converted manuals (at Rozelle and Lidcombe) and three steamers (at Headquarters, Circular Quay and

Dennis Bros—the leading fire appliance manufacturer for the New South Wales Fire Brigades

Rozelle) remained in the Sydney FD. Nonetheless the equipment of some of the 'fringe' brigades was still rudimentary. Concord West, Freshwater, Gladesville, Northmead, Rhodes, Wentworthville and Willoughby were still dependent on hose reels whilst brigades such as Canterbury, Guildford, Matraville and Mortdale possessed only hose carriages. In a number of cases brigades lacked even a horse and relied solely on 'manpower' in turning out.

The loss of 'the Bown' ladders prompted the Board to order two 85-foot (25.91 m) Tilling-Stevens petrol electric turntable ladders. Arriving in 1923 one set replaced the Simonis at Headquarters and the other was placed at Newcastle. At the same time two 45 horsepower Dennis motors fitted with Tamini pumps (350 gpm) were installed at North Sydney and Randwick.

The year 1924 saw the end of 'neddies' in the Sydney FD. The last, 'Briton', was pensioned-off from Canterbury on 22 December. Three years later the last two horses in the NSWFB, 'Sandow' and 'Samoa' at Liverpool, were replaced by a motor fire engine. At twenty years of age, 'Samoa' was retired to the RSPCA home at Little Bay. With only two steamers left in the Sydney FD (*Big Ben* at Pyrmont and a smaller steamer at Circular Quay) the transition from horse and steam to petrol motor was virtually complete.

THE DENNIS ERA
Second-generation Motorisation

By 1927 many of the earlier motorised vehicles had themselves been replaced. In Sydney the replacements were large imported Dennis motors with a pumping capacity of 500–700 gpm, Dennis 350–400s or smaller Dennis 250–400s with a four-cylinder side valve engine. In country towns the replacements were mainly second-generation Garfords (model 15) with solid rubber tyres and a Hale rotary gear pump mounted under the seat.

The early hose carts and hose carriages were also being replaced by Essex and Dodge motorised hose carriages. Thirteen of these carriages were constructed within the Brigades' workshops on modified car chassis between 1925 and 1927.

Other specialised vehicles were also being replaced. In 1926 the old Headquarters' salvage (a 1916 Garford) was replaced by a new motor on a Garford Model 52 chassis, built by the workshops staff for £1,000 ($2000). With six gears (two reverse!) the massive motor had a top speed of 50 mph (80.5 km/h) and carried stretchers, first-aid equipment, electric cutters, welding gear, ladders, fire extinguishers, smoke helmets and more than 100 tarpaulins. A minor innovation was an 'electrical contrivance which throws on lights when the doors are opened' (*Guardian*, 28 January 1926).

In 1927 the NSWFB acquired an additional set of turntable ladders (now numbering four) for the Sydney FD: a Tilling-Stevens all-power electric set installed at Headquarters. A

Fire floats—a vital element of harbour fire protection—under the authority of the Harbour Trust

continuing 'bone of contention', argued by successive Chief Officers since 1884, was the absence of fire floats in the NSWFB firefighting fleet. Whilst Sydney possessed fire floats, they and the waterways were the preserve of the Harbour Trust authorities.[11] The Harbour Trust possessed three fire floats, the Hydra and Cecil Rhodes, capable of pumping 3500 gpm and the older Pluvius, 2500 gpm. Stationed at Goat Island, the floats were crewed by 26 part-time 'waterfiremen' under the command, since 1909, of Captain Carter. Whilst trained by NSWFB staff, there existed problems of coordination and delay—problems which the NSWFB have argued to the present day require a joint land-marine fire station manned by NSWFB staff.

Associated with the changeover to the two-platoon system in 1928 were a number of innovations in equipment. The establishment of a Flying Squad at Headquarters (Chapter 5) saw the introduction of a specially designed Flying Motor. The first 'Flyer' installed at the end of 1928 was a Dennis 500–700 gpm pumper with solid tyres and a 65 horsepower, four-cylinder engine. The Flyer was also the first appliance fitted with a siren, replacing the old rotary gongs with which other NSWFB vehicles were fitted. The following year other appliances were fitted with the new sirens, and a number of station entrances were fitted with similar sirens and lights to warn traffic of a station turn out.

In addition to the new Flyer, Headquarters also acquired a new 'No 10' motor car for the use of the Chief Officer. Nicknamed the *Red Terror*, the 1929 Hudson Super Six was the Brigades' pride and joy. Weighing two and a half tons, with a long and rakish red body and open butterfly exhaust, it was capable of 90 mph (145 km/h). With siren blaring and hood down the *Red Terror* left every other vehicle in its wake. The first 'No 10' was introduced by Superintendent Alfred Webb in 1910, housed in a garage in the southern corner of Headquarters yard, a garage which survives today. The *Red*

The first Headquarters' 'Flyer' (1928) a Dennis 500–700 gpm pumper, with solid tyres and rotary gongs

85-foot Morris Magirus ladders installed at Headquarters in 1929

Terror served for 28 years, before being sold in 1957 and subsequently discarded at a suburban tip.

There is little doubt that 1929 was the pinnacle year in the Board's acquisition of élite equipment. In addition to the Flyer and the *Red Terror*, the Brigades installed an 85-foot Morris Magirus turntable ladder at Headquarters and a new Ahrens Fox motor. The new ladders replaced the No 1 Halley set which was sold in 1930.[12] In 1931 an identical set of Morris Magirus ladders were acquired, the Brigades now having six turntable ladder sets, at Headquarters, Circular Quay, George Street West, Darlinghurst, Crows Nest and Newcastle.

Despite the Depression of the early 1930s, the Board's motor replacement program continued. All appliances were fitted with sirens in place of rotary gongs and pneumatic tyres replaced the original solid tyres. The magnitude of the replacement program is shown in the following figures. Between 1926 and 1934 the NSWFB acquired more than 70 Dennis 250–400 motors (fitted with ohv 40 bhp engines after 1930), 19 Dennis 300–400 motors (fitted with four cylinder side valve petrol engines of 60 bhp and two-stage turbine pumps), and 30 Dennis 500–700 motors (65 bhp, T-head engine). In all, almost £300,000 ($600 000) (40 per cent of the Board's assets) was tied up in fire appliances.

The association of Dennis Bros with the NSWFB was symbolised in the Dennis 250 Shield donated in 1932 for award to the leading team in the 'Dennis Motor Engine 250 gallons Suction Event' at the State Demonstration. The Shield was first won by Cronulla Brigade at the Wagga Demonstration of 1932. In 1934 Dennis Bros donated a similar shield for the large suction (400 gpm) event.

The last manuals had gone from Bega, Camden and Singleton by 1929 whilst the last horse-drawn turbines disappeared in 1933. In a number of cases, the engines' Gwynne pumps from these converted manuals were themselves converted into trailer pumps which could be towed by a motor car. By the end of 1934 all but three Sydney FD stations possessed motorised fire engines (Wentworthville had a motor hose carriage). The exceptions were Northmead and Malabar with hose carts and Matraville with a hose reel.

FLYING PIGS AND BIG 4s
Third-generation Motors

The second half of the 1930s witnessed a continuation of the motor replacement program which had such a dramatic effect on the Brigades' equipment in the previous five years. The last of the original Garfords, the first-generation standard motor, was 'retired' in 1935. Two years after the installation of a new salvage motor in 1933, Headquarters also obtained a new Morris Magirus turntable ladder. The first all-steel ladders commissioned by the Brigades, they were a vast improvement on the earlier wooden models, having an operational height of 100 feet (30.48 m), greater rigidity, automatic plumbing and wider operational scope. In 1938 an identical set of ladders was assembled on a Dennis chassis powered by a six-cylinder 100 bhp Meadows engine. Weighing nine tons, the ladders served the Brigades until 1973, with the 1933 set creating

The Headquarters' 'Flyer', 1930, fitted for the first time with sirens and pneumatic tyres

THE MOST POWERFUL OF THEM ALL!
The Ahrens 'Fox'

UNTIL the late 1920s, the Brigades' largest pumping appliance was the 1892 Shand, Mason steamer, *Big Ben*. On 8 March 1928 *Big Ben* fought its last blaze at the George Hudson timber yard fire (Chapter 8), although it was held in reserve at Pyrmont until 1938.[13] *Big Ben*'s replacement was the Ahrens Fox (Model PS.2) built by the firm of that name in Cincinnatti, Ohio.

The Ahrens Fox came with an imposing reputation as 'the most powerful and efficient fire engine in the world'. A New York model had achieved the incredible feat of pumping to the 58th floor of the Woolworth Building, 730 feet (222.50 m) above the ground.

The Ahrens Fox was powered by an 18 litre, six-cylinder petrol engine developing 130 bhp. Bright red, 22 feet (6.71 m) long, seven feet (2.13 m) high and weighing six tons, the Ahrens Fox was an awe-inspiring sight as it thundered through Sydney streets. Each cylinder possessed three spark plugs fired from three separate ignition circuits. The large sphere which adorned the piston pumps reduced pulsations of water pressure generated by a 1000 gpm pumping rate. The motor could be started by the electric starter or by manual cranking. However, only two men achieved the latter feat!—later Chief Officer H Pye and a fireman named Blackburn. Despite its pumping feats, the motor was described as a brute by those who tried to drive it.

In 1935 the 'Fox' proved its credentials at the huge Goldsbrough Mort wool store fire (Chapter 8), in the process creating an unparalleled pumping record. Draughting from a canvas dam fed by six hydrants, the Ahrens Fox delivered 4 320 000 gallons (19 656 kL) of water while pumping continuously, at half capacity.

One of the first NSWFB vehicles fitted with pneumatic tyres and four-wheel brakes, the Ahrens Fox was replaced in the 1940s by the Second World War Mack pumpers. Despite its imposing abilities the Ahrens Fox was rarely used at Sydney fires, with senior officers preferring the flexibility of two smaller motors. Today the *Fox* occupies pride-of-place alongside *Big Ben* at the Fire Service Museum.

Ahrens Fox—pride of Sydney fire brigades

Neddies, Coffee Pots & Flying Pigs / 175

PALACE
ARCADE
CRYSTAL PALACE
CRYSTAL ARCADE PALACE
MILK BAR

A Dennis Big 4 (above) and front view of the snub-nosed Dennis Ace (right)

a Brigades' aerial record of 48 years' service.

As with the earlier replacements the vehicles acquired between 1934 and 1939 were almost exclusively Dennis motors. The exceptions were three Leyland motors, the largest of which (the FT3A) had a pumping rate of 700 gpm from a Gwynne pump and was powered by a six-cylinder ohv petrol engine. The Leyland FT3A served at inner-city stations until the mid-1960s and as a back-up appliance until 1971.

The smaller Dennis motors acquired for use at suburban Sydney stations were Dennis Aces. Nick-named *Flying Pigs* (because of their set-back front axles designed for bus operations in narrow English streets), they were powered by a four-cylinder side valve engine of 55 bhp. One of the earliest Aces acquired by the Brigades was fitted out as a staff tender, capable of carrying twenty men and their equipment to major fires or bush fires. In all 35 Aces were acquired between 1934 and 1939. The other popular Dennis of the late 1930s was the 'Big 4', with a four-cylinder, 68 litre ohv motor and a 650 gpm centrifugal pump. Ten were acquired and stationed in high-

Firemen atop turntable ladders (left) battle a George Street blaze in 1939

risk metropolitan locations with each carrying a large tank of foam solution and a special foam-generating pump for oil fires. The largest Dennis, a one-off 'Big 6', was installed at Headquarters in 1935 as the new 'Flyer'. Powered by a six-cylinder 100 bhp Meadows engine, the 'Big 6' was capable of pumping over 800 gpm. Used at all major fires, the motor also served as a coffin carrier at official Brigades' funerals.

In 1939 Headquarters acquired a Dodge CO_2 tender to fight fires in underground electricity substations. As with the tender for transporting men to major fires, it was designed and built by workshop staff under the supervision of Principal Mechanic, Norm Lucas. The motorised equipment at Headquarters was now organised in much the same way as it is today: a first-response 'Flyer' (Dennis Big 6); a running motor (Dennis Light 6); Salvage motor; second-call motor; No 3 Morris Magirus ladders; and CO_2 tender. All inner-city calls involved an automatic turn out of the 'Flyer', Salvage and ladders. The running motor, as the name suggests, attended fires in 'A' District and backed up other city stations.

PENNY PINCHING
Post-war Replacement

The decade following the Second World War was a period of evaluation and re-equiping. Monetary constraints were such that the bulk of changes involved modifying and remounting existing equipment. This was particularly the case with equipment acquired during the War as part of the American lease-lend agreements.

At the direction of the Commonwealth Government 42 of the La France 1000 gpm pumpers, acquired during the War were transferred to the Forestry Commission of NSW in 1947. Four others were transferred to the South Australian Fire Brigades, one to the US Navy, another scrapped and two retained. The 25 Mack pumpers were absorbed into the NSWFB, with three of the Macks reconstructed in the Brigades' workshops as salvage tenders. Both sets of Morris Magirus wooden ladders were remounted onto Mack chassis, the first in 1952 and the second in 1968.[14] They followed the remounting of the Tilling-Stevens ladders (also onto a Mack chassis) in 1948.

The only one of its kind—a Dennis Big 6 installed as the Headquarters' 'Flyer' in 1935 and later used as the Brigade's coffin carrier

In 1938 Dennis Bros developed a new 'Light 4' fire engine to supersede the Ace model. Variations on the 'Light 4', with a pumping rate of 400 gpm were the main fire engine acquired by the NSWFB for use in suburban areas and country towns until the early 1950s. They were fitted with a variety of bodies (transverse and internal face-to-face) in experiments between 1948 and 1950 to evaluate a replacement for the 'Braidwood' style. When the face-to-face 'New World' style was adopted in 1950, the late model 'Light 4s' were fitted with this design.

In 1947 the Board acquired eight Chevrolet chassis bodies, which were rebuilt in the workshops for use as patrol waggons (Chapter 5). The following year three 'Blitz' bush fire tankers were also constructed with high-pressure pumps obtained from the Commonwealth Disposals Commission. One was stationed at Katoomba and the others at Kogarah and Hornsby. They were part of a major revamping of the Board's bush firefighting equipment in anticipation of changes to the Fire Brigades Act (1949) and the introduction of the Bush Fires Act (1949).

In 1950 the Board acquired its first-ever set of Merryweather turntable ladders. The 125-feet (38.10 m), all-steel ladders became the tallest in the Brigades, and were mounted on a Dennis chassis and powered by a Meadows six-cylinder motor. For the first time the turntable operator was carried on the turntable footplate, retaining the same relative position to the ladder. The following year all other ladders were modernised and fitted with pneumatic tyres.

A NEW ERA
Commers, Fords and Bedfords

The first major change in fire appliances since the beginnings of the Dennis dominance in 1927 occurred in 1951. The Board resolved that, rather than pursue the more expensive purpose-built chassis it would adopt the cheaper alternative of converting a standard commercial chassis. The first four of 16 Commer chassis acquired between 1951 and 1957 were received and fitted in the Brigades' workshops. The pumps fitted were in the main taken from 'retired' Dennis 250 engines and upgraded to 400 gpm. Following the successful introduction of a

An American Mack pumper, one of three, converted in the New South Wales Fire Brigades' workshops to a salvage tender

Morris Magirus wooden ladders remounted on a Mack chassis in 1952

The last Dennis models, acquired between 1952 and 1957, were six 800 gpm F2 pumpers. Powered by a straight eight-cylinder Rolls Royce motor they were used as first response motors at the large inner-city stations (including Headquarters). Whilst many of the pre-war Dennis models were being withdrawn from Sydney stations, they still formed the front line motor in many country towns: these and the 'Light 4s' provided the backbone of the country brigades until the 1960s.

In 1951 a motor vehicle maintenance section was established at Pyrmont Fire Station as part of a program of decentralising workshop activities from Headquarters. In the same year Matraville, the last Sydney fire station to be motorised, received its first motor to replace the existing hose reel.

Following the disastrous Blue Mountains bush fires in the summer of 1951–52, the Board acquired nine GMC trucks from the RAAF for use as bush fire tankers. These trucks were originally built in the USA and used as

prototype at Liverpool in 1955, other Commer chassis known as ME147 Commers were acquired in the second half of the 1950s. They were fitted with larger reclaimed Dennis pumps rated at over 500 gpm.

The Garford Hales served NSW country towns for a period of some 40 years

A GMC Bushfire Tanker acquired by the New South Wales Fire Brigades in 1952

THE RELIABLE GARFORD

DESPITE jokes about children on push-bikes passing Garfords travelling uphill, their ability as a reliable pumper was never in question. The following story about the No 90 Garford installed at Sawtell in May 1929 and replaced by a Bedford in November 1960 bears this out:

> During a severe water shortage at Sawtell from the 19th December, 1960 to 14th January, 1961, an approach was made by the Coff's Harbour Shire Council to Captain Hamey for the use of the Garford to pump water from Boambee Creek into the reservoir in order to provide sufficient water for firefighting and domestic use in Sawtell.
>
> After providing a special fitting for connection from the hose to the main, the Garford commenced pumping from Boambee Creek on Friday, 23rd December, 1960. A roster of volunteer workers, including all the Volunteer Firemen from Sawtell, provided the necessary labour to maintain the pump and other manual work. The Garford pumped continuously for twenty eight and a half hours and delivered approx. 85,000 gallons [386.75 kL] of water into the reservoir and raised the water above the serious danger level.
>
> The Garford commenced pumping again on Monday 26th December, and with intermittent stops pumped from the creek and water tankers until Friday, 13th January, 1961. On Sunday, 15th January, two inches [50.8 mm] of rain fell and the reservoir filled.
>
> During the pumping from Boambee Creek the motor and pump operated for fifty three and a half hours and pumped at the rate of 3000 gallons [13.65 kL] per hour and delivered an estimated 160 000 gallons [728 kL] of water into the reservoir, a distance of about four miles [6.44 km] from the creek, and a lift of approximately 170 ft [51.82 m]
>
> Motor and pump operated from tankers for 46 hours and pumped 235 000 [1069.25 kL] gallons of water at an average of 5000 gallons [22.75kL] per hour.
>
> Total pumping time 100 hours and 395,000 gallons [1797.25kL] of water pumped into the reservoir. (*Fire News*, 2(17), 1961:35)

Such was the contribution of the Garford Hales to the NSWFB, and to the people of NSW.

THE ELITE FIRE ENGINE
Dennis F44

THE Dennis F44/45, costing $20 000 was an elite fire engine, capturing the imagination of Brigades' personnel and also drawing the following whimsical review from a *Wheels* writer.

Claimed to be the world's latest, most modern fire engine—which is obviously a mistake, for it is certainly an ideal city-country car—it is distributed in Australia by Westeels Industries, a firm of solid worth, very proud of the fact that Dennis Brothers have been building these things since 1876, when they started supplying horse and cart units to the Fire Commissioners of the City of London. They have a more compact model, known as the D series, which sells for around $15 000 with 4.2 Jaguar engine and manual shift, and this might qualify as the near-ideal second car for the people of some substance. I will leave that to the reader's better judgment.

Handles Superbly

Fast (top speed 67 m.p.h., 0–50 in 29.8 sec, standing quarter-mile 33.0 sec) it also handles superbly, helped no end by the fact that it weighs a smidgin over eight tons on a 12 ft. 6 in. wheelbase. It also stops passably well, with 14 in. Dunlop discs, servo-assisted, on each wheel. Transmission is Allison automatic, and the steering is servo-assisted as well. The turning circle is ridiculously small—around 40 ft—but this unfortunately only bolsters Westeel's insinuations that the Dennis is built for fighting fires in narrow city streets and not for gentlemen.

It does, of course, have a three-year guarantee, which speaks highly for Messrs. Dennis and Royce and the quality of British workmanship. I was told by one Westeels chappie that he thought the transmission was American in origin, but I find that difficult to believe, as it works superbly well.

Description

But let's have a brief description of this interesting vehicle. First off, the chassis is very strong, being built of old Great Western Railway lines. The cab is framed in Iroko, and exterior panels are in fibreglass or aluminium sheeting.

It will seat six in lavish comfort, one each side of the interior engine housing, the front passenger having a floor button in front of him. Westeels assured me this is for a siren, but I am more of the opinion that it is an auxiliary dipswitch. The seating is best described as Fixed British Vertical, although the driver's seat does have a natty little worm-drive crank for height adjustment. The windows are lift-up type, a strange sign of spartan taste in such a well-furnished vehicle and a real throwback to the 1956 Vauxhall Velox. The floors are also a little utilitarian, being covered in patterned aluminium alloy sheeting where I think some good carpeting might be more tasteful. I also commented on the complete absence of ashtrays. 'Fire Brigades don't like any more smoke than is necessary', said the Westeels man, persisting in his charade.

Charming Style

The cabin is very well instrumented, most of the dials being grouped in the one nacelle around a big speedometer. Above the windscreen is an eight-day clock in charming 1914 baroque style, made by Dennis (in fact, almost everything in the unit is made by Dennis). The transmission selector is a big man-sized lever running north-south in a notched gate mounted on the dash. Labelled

1-2, 1-3, 1-4, N and R, the lever variously cuts out third and fourth gears. A hydraulic valve system senses engine torque and speed changes and alters the ratios accordingly. There are in effect two shifts for each ratio—one for speed and one for torque. This makes the F44 a little difficult to drive smoothly at first, as a kickdown on the detent produces two smart changes instead of one. However, this would only be a matter of familiarity. It is an excellent transmission; I hope it is British-made.

There are some nice tidy touches in the cockpit, like a hand-held spotlight, a big cover that lifts to reveal a murky Kokoda-green engine, quite unlike the polished alloy and brass one would expect from a Royce plant, and a big red button about five inches across which turns out to be the trafficator switch.

Pump Drive?

Between the driver's seat and the engine package is a very large lever like an outside handbrake. I asked the man what it was for ... ask a silly question ... he said it was to operate the pump drive and pointed to a sign on the dash which said 'When operating pump drive select 1-3 ratio in transmission'. He then took me around the back and showed me a great lump of cast metal with spigots and knurled wheels and a big pipe like a Bondi sewage outfall, and he said 'that's the pump drive'. Why the hell they want a fuel pump that size, I'll never know. Anyway, back to this lever; I tried it a few times and came to the conclusion that it operates a concealed spoiler for high-speed work ... very cunning.

Cocktail Cabinet

On the way back from examining the fuel pump I started idly flicking at some handles down the vast sides of this big red dear, and lo! Lockers for cocktail cabinet, refrigerator, camping bed, old shoes, unused bodies, grass clippings for the dump, places for keeping the children quiet ... really cunning design. There is a quick-fill racing cap over the petrol inlet, as well as a big sign saying PETROL, which is a very good idea, as some of these service station attendants are quite hopeless.

Illegal

It was then that I noticed the flashing red light on top of the driver's cabin.

This stumped me for a bit. After all, roof lights are illegal in Australia. Just ask the Marathon drivers and the West Australian police. However, I decided that it was put there temporarily as a publicity stunt, just to attract attention to what is already an unusual vehicle.

I then had occasion to give the big thing beggary around the bottom end of Warwick Farm, and I have to report that it is slightly sensational. The big (7.50-20 12-ply) Dunlops (dual wheels at rear) stuck like glue, and it was very difficult to make the unit slide.

Good Brakes

But it does go quite hard, albeit with a high level of engine noise, and it stops dramatically—just like a 'Formula' car. I went 100 yards deeper than Bartlett's last braking marker coming in to Creek—think about that! The steering is very good, calling for only light effort, although six turns lock to lock is a bit American for me. The ride is, as expected, very plush, and although rearward vision is a little restricted, there being no back window, only two outside mirrors, lane changing does in a sense become your province, as much smaller cars like Pontiacs and Phoenixes must give way to something about the size of the Queen Mary and painted red.

Family Crest

Which brings me to the most catastrophic point of the whole story. I was so pleased with this demonstration that I asked Westeels about delivery dates, whether I could trade in my Quintsvagen, and so on. And about the color: Perhaps a nice mid-blue or even a rich green, not that bloody awful red. And I don't want my family crest on the side, with my initials. Bad taste. The man who was getting the demonstrator had apparently asked for a sort of family coat of arms and his initials on each door. Still, he must have come from a very good sort of family, because he had a number of middle names. What was it now? ... N.S.W.F.B., I think! (*Wheels* August 1969)

decontamination sprayers during the war. To further bolster bush fire capability in the Blue Mountains, six Morris 'Composite' appliances were constructed in the Brigades' workshops. Capable of carrying 400 gallons (1820 L) of water, they also carried a demountable Coventry-Climax pump with a pump rate of 500 gpm.

By the end of 1955 the Board's fleet of motorised appliances stood at 280 fire engines, five salvage waggons, five hose carriages, one CO_2 appliance, seven turntable ladders, three tenders and fourteen bush fire units. After 1958 all body building and spraying operations were conducted at new workshops at Five Dock, removing the last of the motor workshops from Headquarters.

One of the more unusual appliances acquired by the NSWFB was an F12 pump-escape installed at Canberra for the Commonwealth Government in late 1957. The 800 gpm, centre-mounted Dennis pump had a forward control and a wheeled escape ladder.

By the late 1950s much of the Board's fleet in suburban areas of Sydney and in country towns was of pre-war vintage, more than twenty years' old. Many brigades in the smaller towns still operated pre-1930 Garford and Dennis 250 motors. Not since the earliest years of motorisation was the Brigades' vehicle fleet in such a poor state. The increasing obsolescence of these vehicles, difficulties in obtaining spare parts and mounting maintenance costs forced the Board to investigate a major program of replacement. Two avenues were taken.

In 1959 the Bedford chassis was chosen for use in small country towns. To save money they were constructed in the obsolete Braidwood body style and fitted with Dennis pumps of 350 or 450 gpm [at a total cost of £3,500 ($7000)]. In many cases these pumps were reclaimed from the old Dennis 250s they were replacing. As the 63 new Bedford motors were introduced between 1959 and 1966 the Garfords and Dennis 250s were withdrawn. The last Garford was withdrawn from Alstonville in 1969 whilst the last Dennis 250 left Yenda in 1970. In 1964 the Garford suction event was removed from the Volunteer Demonstration calendar, heralding the end of the Garford era.

The other Bedford acquisitions in the early 1960s were a number of Bedford 5–7 ton trucks, stationed at Pyrmont transport depot. Under

Morris 'Composite' (above), Bedford Water Tanker (above right) and Ford Thames CO_2 tender (right)

Transport Officer George Knight, the transport section (fourteen members) was responsible for the transport of Board members and the Brigades staff/stores of new fire engines to country towns.

The second major equipment decision was taken in 1961 when the Ford Thames was adopted as the standard chassis for the NSWFB. Between 1961 and 1966, 44 of the motors were purchased and fitted with Tamini 500 gpm pumps reclaimed from earlier Dennis pumpers. The Ford Thames were the first NSWFB fire engines to have a fully enclosed cabin for the crew. In 1966 two of the Ford Thames chassis were used for new Salvage motors, whilst a third was installed at Headquarters as a new CO_2 tender to replace the older Dodge.

Between 1966 and 1979 the Board acquired 24 bush fire tankers, designed and built by the Forestry Commission, to replace the older 'Blitz' and 'GMC' tankers in service since the end of the war. Mounted on a four-wheel drive Bedford truck chassis was a 850 gallon (3867.5 L) tank with most having a Day Holden 150 gpm centrifugal pump. The move to the Bedford water tankers in the Sydney FD was long overdue. Many of the fringe brigades possessed only a single on-road motor, almost entirely dependent on mains water, and unsuitable for fighting bush and scrub fires.[15]

In 1967 the Board adopted the newer Ford 'D' series chassis to replace the Thames and between 1967 and 1969, 57 were installed in the NSWFB. The largest were eight D750s fitted with upgraded 650 gpm pumps reclaimed from the Dennis 'Big 4s'. The smaller models were either of 500 gpm or 350 gpm rates, with many still in service in smaller country towns today.

A DENNIS REVIVAL

In 1969 the Board announced a reequipment program, with plans to purchase 51 new Dennis fire engines at a cost of more than $700 000. The final number was in fact 87 at a cost of $1.6 million. The front line units were Dennis F44s and 49s with Rolls Royce engines and a pumping capacity of 900–1000 gpm. Installed at Newcastle and all Sydney District Stations, they replaced the Dennis F2s acquired in the early 1950s. Nine are still in operation in the Sydney FD today, including the Headquarters 'Flyer' and 'Second Call' motor. The other Dennis acquisition was

The Dennis F45 'Flyer' leaves Headquarters within 15 seconds of the alarm

A NOSTALGIC TRIP
The Mack and La France Contribution

IN August 1949 the mid-north coast town of Kempsey was devastated by its worst ever flood. Six townfolk were drowned and 50 homes destroyed with an inestimable loss of stock and property. An SOS was sent out to the NSWFB and Forestry Commission for pumping assistance to restore the town's water supply and its sewerage system. A Newcastle Mack under Motor Officer Reub Hubbard and No 70 Sydney Mack with Ray Palmer, Lew Phillips and Rex Hopping joined seven Forestry La Frances.

The two Macks and a La France were put to work at an old quarry site pumping from the Macleay River. Eight lines of hose, each 300 feet (91.44 m), relayed to another La France at road level. From the La France two steel pipes were placed under the roadway to carry delivery lines to a town main. The delivery hoses were passed through the pipes by typical Brigades' ingenuity—a hose tied to a light, long line tied to the tail of a cat which in turn was sent through the pipe!

In all the motors pumped continuously for 75 hours, No 70 Mack using 16 gallons (72.8 L) of oil! With the three motors using a drum of oil in less than an hour, the Brigades' staff worked tirelessly day and night, catching a nap and meals when they could. Over the 75 hours the No 70 Mack clocked 2117 pump miles (3407 km) on the speedo. Based on a conservative rate of 750 gpm this adds up to pumping 3 375 000 gallons (15 356.25 kL).

The other La France motors and the Kempsey Dennis 500–700 were used to clear mud and water from the town's surviving business premises. After a week's work of pumping and cleaning-out, the local fire station [four feet (1.22 m) deep in silt], the Brigades' staff and motors returned home. Even the return home was a feat—neither the Mack nor the La France possessed a windscreen!

Two Macks and a La France pumper (centre) pump from the flooded Macleay River, 1949

the Jaguar-engineered D-series with a pumping rate of 600 gpm. With a five-speed gearbox the Jaguars were noted for their acceleration and manoeuvrability. They became the main motor at most Sydney suburban and larger country stations.

The introduction of the new Dennis motors coincided with the last throes of the pre-war Dennis. The last of the Dennis 250s, 300s, 500s and Big 4s were withdrawn from service between 1969 and 1971. The last to depart was the one-off Dennis Big 6 used at the training college and as a coffin carrier until 1974. In all, over 170 pre-war Dennis vehicles had served the NSWFB over 40 years. Through the Historic Fire Engine Association of Australia (formed in March 1969), a number of Dennis motors and other noteworthy engines have been restored and are currently held at the Fire Service Museum.

The late 1960s and early 1970s also saw an upgrading of the Brigades' aerial equipment. In 1969 a 118-foot (35.97 m) Merryweather turntable ladder was placed in service in the ACT and in 1971 a Magirus Deutz turntable ladder was installed at Headquarters. The 125-foot (38.10 m) Magirus ladder was a vast improvement on the earlier pre-war designs. Its major innovative feature was a travelling cage capable of carrying three people the full length of the ladder.

THE INTERNATIONAL ERA
Modernisation

In 1972 the Board announced a new vehicle program to replace the Dennis F2s and Commers acquired in the late 1950s. The motor selected was the International C1600, ordered through the Australian-owned firm Presha Engineering, Melbourne, then a division of Fire Fighting Enterprises. The International truck chassis was driven by a petrol V8, 212 bhp motor with automatic transmission and fitted with a Godiva pump rated at 500 gpm. A 400-gallon (1820 L) water 'first-aid' tank was also fitted [the largest previously fitted to a NSWFB vehicle being a 200-gallon (910 L) tank], allowing the vehicles to double in 'off-road' situations as bush fire tankers. Costing over $17 000 each, the first of fifteen new Internationals was installed at Mortdale on 31 October 1972. The others were progressively installed at Sydney stations throughout 1972–73.

In 1973 the Board announced a second International series (ACCO 1710) of fifteen units acquired through Fire Control Equipment of Rockdale. First installed at Mt Druitt, the new motors varied only slightly from the earlier model, providing a tilt cabin for ease of servicing. The year 1973 was an important one in the Brigades equipment history when, following observations in the United States and Melbourne by Chief Officer Vivian Lowther, the Board acquired two new aerial appliances: an International Simonitor and a Snorkel.

The International Simonitor, costing $61 000 with a rating of 1000 gpm, featured a 50-foot (15.24 m) water tower boom, capable of a 360 degree rotation. The first of its kind in Australia (having been released in the US in 1971), the mechanism incorporated an escape ladder for rescue work. In 1974 the Simonitor was installed at Parramatta along with a new International Salvage. The second acquisition was a $71 000 Snorkel unit. A giant appliance 37 feet (11.28 m) long and weighing 16 tons the Snorkel is especially designed for rescue work, and has an 85-foot (25.91 m) three-section boom and cage capable of carrying five adults. The boom also carries a monitor with a rating of 500 gpm. The two new aerial all-purpose appliances were the forerunners of a new era in fire brigade appliances. For the first time since the late 1920s, the NSWFB was on a par with overseas brigades in possessing the latest firefighting technology.

In 1975 the Board announced its third International program—fifteen motors to be stationed at country stations. It was the same year that the last Dennis Ace was withdrawn from service, from Orange in July. In all, 34 'Flying Pigs' had served the NSWFB since the first was installed at North Sydney in 1935. In 1975 the Brigades officially adopted a new Storz instantaneous coupling, removing the necessity for matching 'male' and 'female' brass thread couplings (in use since 1884).

To further upgrade its aerial fleet the Merryweather ladders originally acquired in 1950 were remounted by Presha Engineering of Melbourne on an International chassis and installed at Woollahra in 1975. The older (1935) Magirus ladders were also remounted on an International chassis in the Brigades' workshops. The following year a 15.7 metre 'Telesqurt' appliance, with a 15 metre articulated boom water rescue tower was placed at Wollongong.

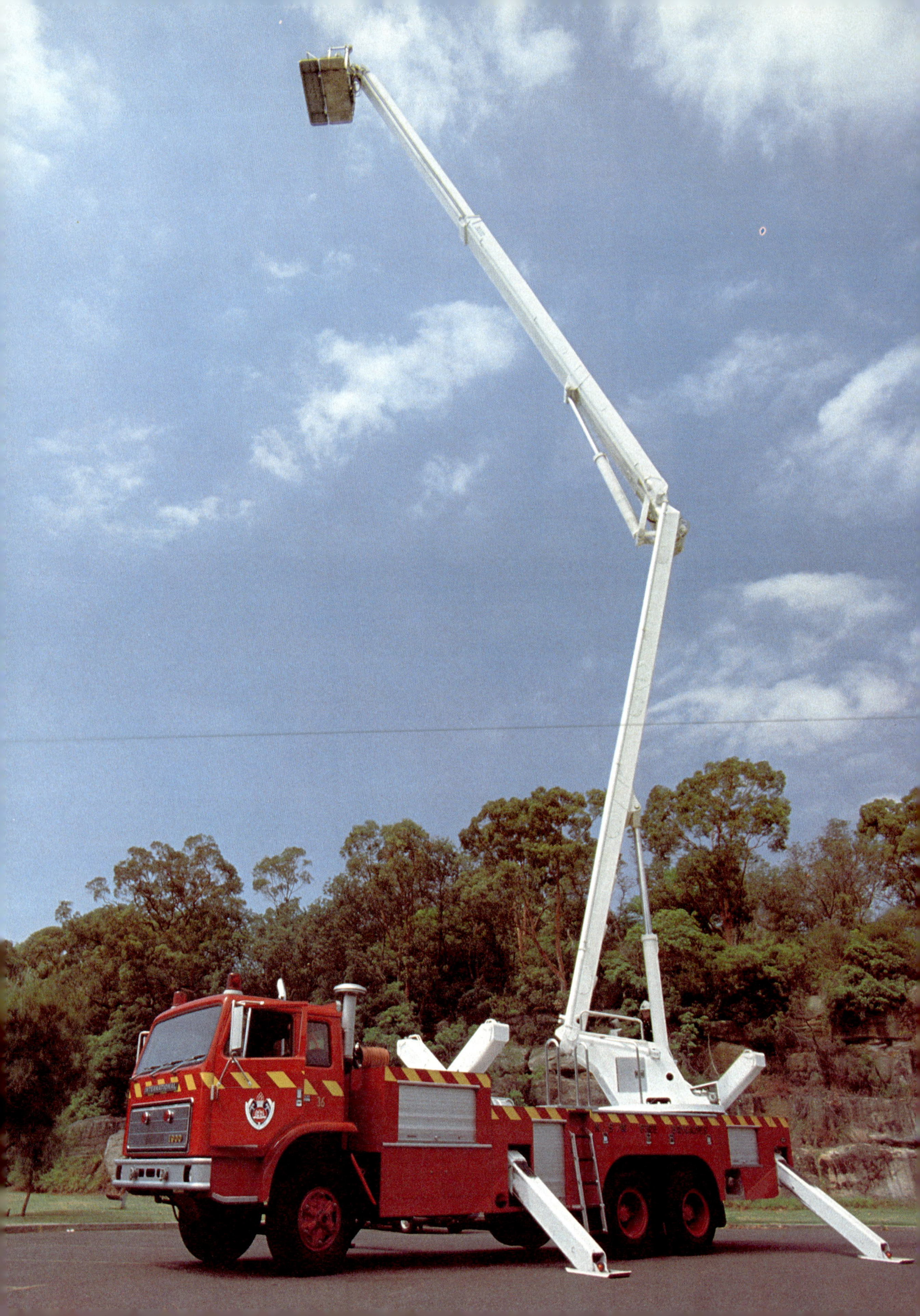
36

Capable of pumping at 1000 gpm the new Telesqurt also carried a tank of 400 gallons (1820 L) of water. Three other Telesqurts on International chassis were also procured later in the year. It was a far cry from the first ever 'Squirt' in Australia, T J Bown's original manual of 1850 (Chapter 1), capable of throwing water to a height of a single storey: from a single Squirt in 1850, to a fleet of 336 pumpers and 38 specialised appliances in 1984.

In 1977 the Board announced plans for a continuation of the International program (with a larger 750 gpm rate); a program involving country stations and also the replacement throughout the Sydney FD of the Dennis Jaguar D600 motors. It also announced future plans for the phasing-out of the Bedford and Ford Thames pumpers acquired in the 1960s. The dominance of the International is displayed in the most recent turntable ladder acquisition—a Magirus mounted in Australia by Wormald on an International chassis and installed at Manly in 1983.

The years 1978–79 saw the final phasing-out of a number of the Brigades' older vehicles. The last of the Dennis 'Light 4s' acquired in 1952 was retired, as were the 1956 Commers and the last three 1942 Mack Pumpers. In 1982 the three GMC bushfire tankers were also retired, severing the last link with the era of wartime reconditioning—an era in which the Brigades' workshops performed 'miracles' on a shoe-string budget.

As one era passed a new one blossomed. The Board expanded its aerial fleet with a new hydraulic platform (Snorkel) and two aerial rescue monitors (Skyjets) costing $120 000 each. The Skyjets are similar to the proven Telesqurts and were installed at Alexandria and Parramatta.

In recognition of the expanding nature and complexity of the Brigades' equipment, the Board appointed its first Technical Services Manager, Warwick O'Brien, in September 1979. He was made responsible for the mechanical, body repair, spray painting, electrical, and hose department operations, and for clothing and boot repair sections. The objective was to coordinate and integrate the various independent workshops. A critical element in this proposal is the Chullora workshop complex, the first stage of which was completed in 1982. With a second stage underway, the Brigades will shortly have, for the first time since 1884, a spacious and fully equipped service base.

Into the 1980s the NSWFB continued to acquire more specialised appliances: two breathing apparatus tenders (1980 and 1982); a lighting van (1982); an articulated all-terrain vehicle (1983); four 'Super pumpers' (1982–83), a Skymonitor hydraulic platform (1982) and a Command vehicle (1983).

Designed with the assistance of NSWFB staff and built by the Melbourne Company, Abbey Engineering of the Warman International Group, the Skymonitor is specifically designed for rescue and firefighting in narrow inner-city streets. Its capabilities indicate the amazing transformation in firefighting equipment in the last ten years: a 1000 gpm pumping rate monitor operated from the cage or from ground level; a sideways reach of 19.13 metres at 13 metres elevation; a maximum boom height of 31 metres; a cage which can be slewed to 45 degrees left or right of centre and which can be lowered 4.91 metres below ground level.

By the end of 1983 the complement of NSWFB firefighting vehicles was:

pumping appliances: 395
aerial appliances: 22
salvage motors: 13
bush fire tankers: 44
other: 7

In all the NSWFB fire appliances and equipment are valued at $12 776 209. Within the Sydney FD first-call motors are Internationals (with the exception of two Dennis Rolls Royce motors). Their station-by-station deployment is detailed in Appendix 4.1. They range from the smallest 500 gpm International 1600s acquired in 1972 to the four largest 1950C 'Superpumpers' rating 1200 gpm (the highest rating pumper in the history of the NSWFB). The Bedfords and Fords which proliferated in the 1960s are now principally second-call motors in Sydney and in the country, being progressively withdrawn from service since the late 1970s.

Neddies, Coffee Pots and Flying Pigs to Superpumpers—it has been a dramatic transformation.

Modern aerial appliances have transformed the Fire Brigades firefighting fleet. The Skymonitor hydraulic platform is capable of reaching 31 metres and has a 1000 gpm pumping rate monitor

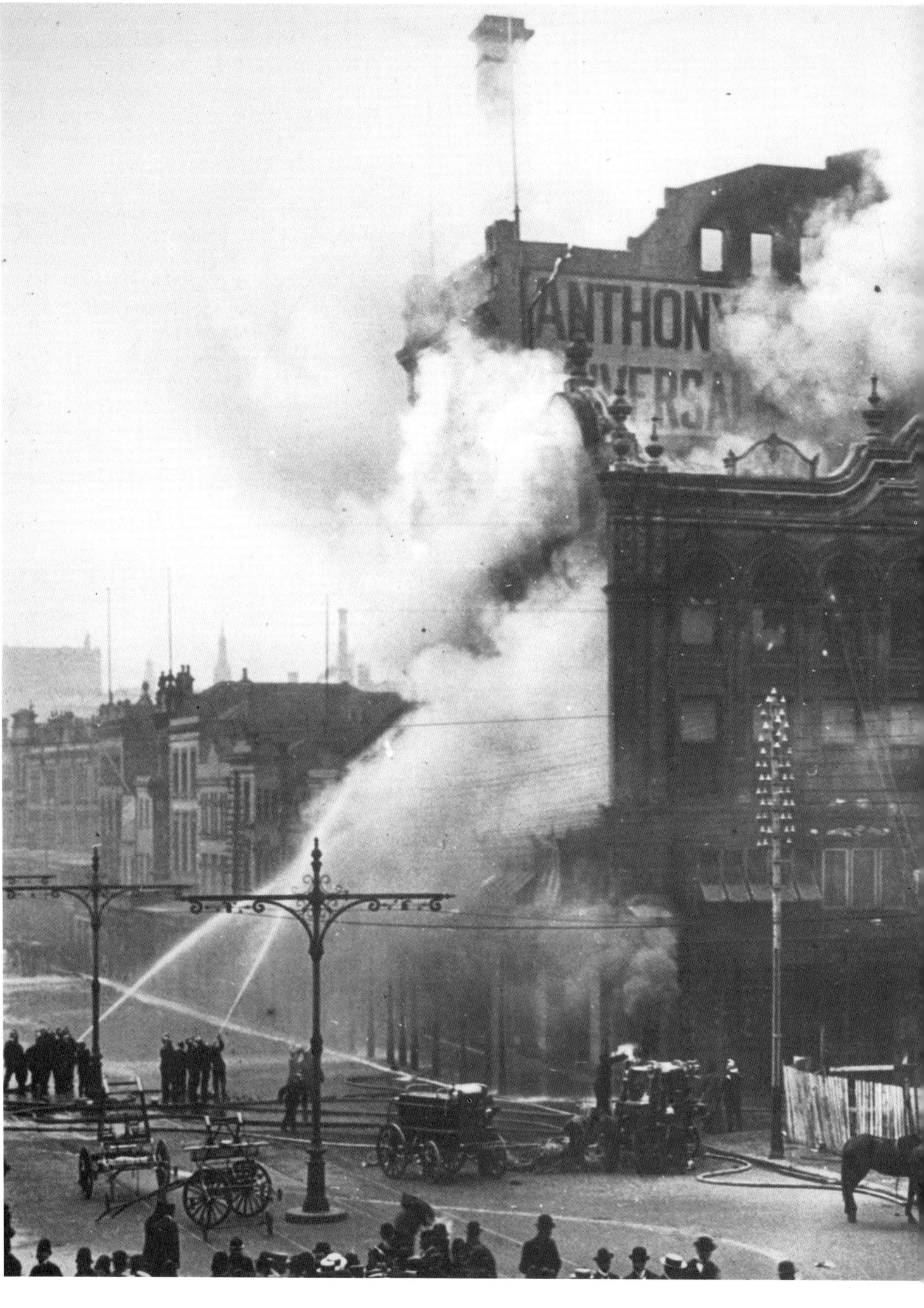
ANTHON
VERSA

8

RED ALERT

Fires and Rescues

THE GARDEN PALACE FIRE OF 1882 WAS described by observers at the time as the most spectacular blaze in Sydney's history. Little could they realise that the next century would see many fires of at least equal intensity, with greater loss of both life and property. The Great Fire of Sydney (1890), Anthony Horderns (1901), Goldsbrough Mort (1935), Pulpit Point (1964) and Australian Wool Stores (1969) are a few of the major conflagrations which live in the memories of firefighters.

It is not only the more spectacular fires which should be recalled. What the records describe as a 'typical' house fire may hide individual heroism, a lucky escape or tragedy. Any older firefighter can vividly recall a special

Anthony Hordern and Sons—Sydney's retailing giant of five shops in the Haymarket—destroyed by fire in 1901

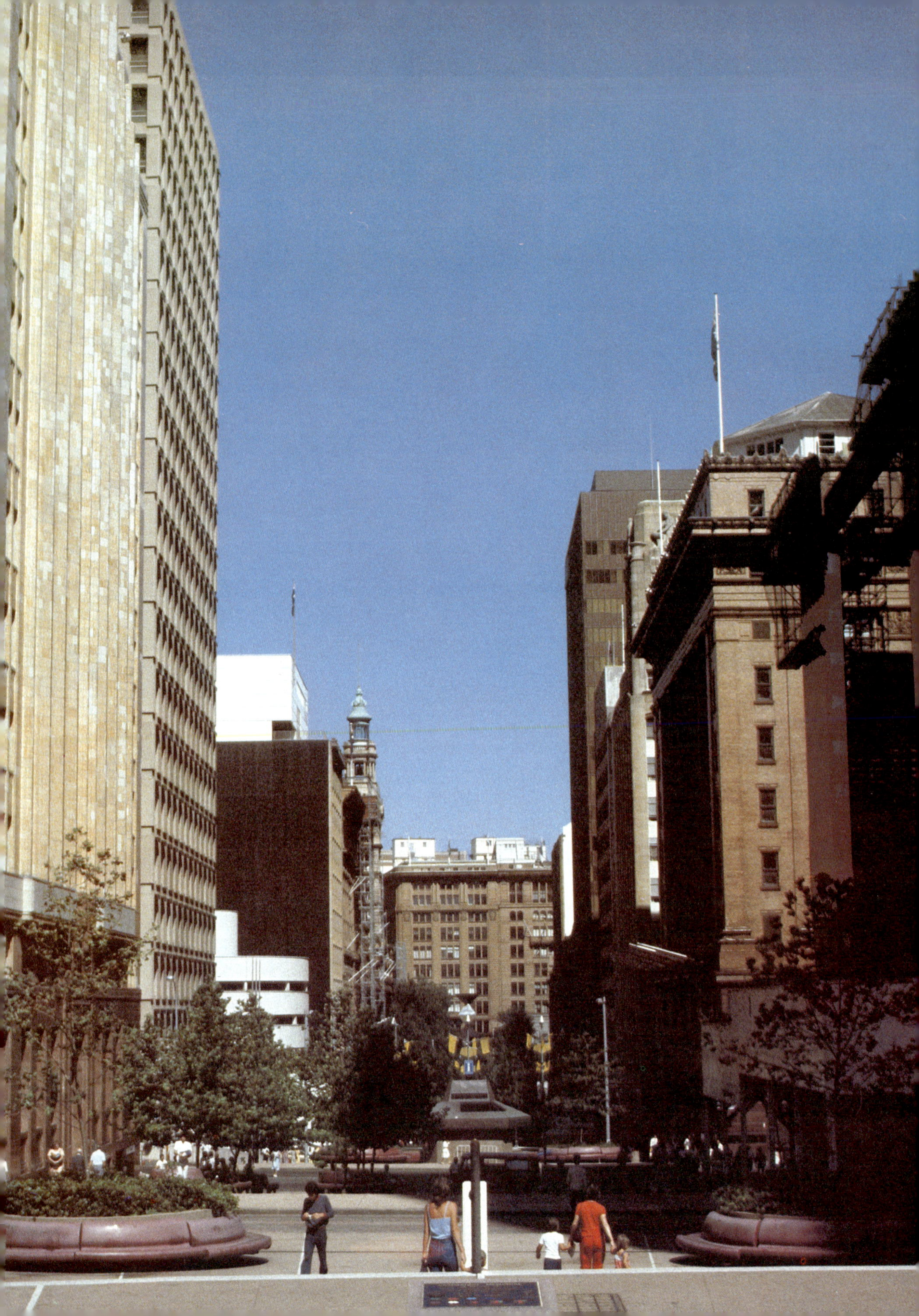

fire 'story' of a face-to-face encounter with death. The following accounts represent only a sample of the more than 700 000 alarms Sydney fire brigades have attended in the past 100 years.

After the official date of appointment of MFB firemen (1 July 1884) the first recorded fire occurred on Monday 14 July 1884. The *Evening News* gave the following account:

Fire in Little Bourke Street
Shortly before three this morning, a fire broke out in some stables belonging to Mr Wm Bourke in Little Bourke Street. It appears that the fire was first seen in the loft of the stable which is constructed of weatherboard and shingle roof, and the flames by means of a small window spread to the loft of an adjoining stable which was built of brick and slats. The upper floors of both buildings were consumed with the contents (consisting of a quantity of fodder, etc.) and the roofs of both buildings. The alarm having been given the Metropolitan Brigade, No 5 Volunteer Company, and the Surry Hills Brigade were soon in attendance with Mr Bear, Superintendent of Fire Brigades in command. There were about 18 horses, which were turned loose in the street and a number of vehicles on the premises none of which were injured [*sic*]. The buildings were insured in the Commercial Union, but for what amount is not known. The origin of the fire is unknown. (*Evening News*, 14 July 1884)

During the first year of the Brigades' operations, there were 225 fire calls (50 being false alarms).[1] Almost 70 per cent of calls were within the City of Sydney area, with the most fire-prone suburbs being Redfern (eleven calls), Balmain (six) and Waverley (six). Many of the fires were chimney alarms, whilst other common causes were 'candles', 'sparks', and 'children playing with matches'. Incendiarism was not uncommon: Messrs Gunther and Behn were charged with the arson of their restaurant at 529 George Street on 20 October 1884. A month later each was sentenced in Central Criminal Court to five years' hard labour. Unusual fire causes in 1884 included 'intoxication', 'overheating of still' and 'lime, slaked by rain'.

The year 1884 did not pass without two deaths. The first was Edward Hill, a lodger at the Coffee Palace in Pitt Street which was destroyed on 20 December and the second, Clara Rees, aged three, who died following a Petersham house fire caused by playing with matches.

In his first years in office Superintendent Bear warned prophetically that the growth in city buildings to some 100 feet (30.48 m), an inadequate water supply and the non-enforcement of building codes was creating a 'city fire risk' of unprecedented magnitude.

THE GREAT FIRE OF SYDNEY

At 2.30 am on the morning of 2 October 1890 a nightwatchman observed flames coming from the top floor of Gibbs, Shallard and Company, a printing and publishing firm situated between Hosking Place and Pitt Street. Within fifteen minutes and before the arrival of the MFB steamers and two ladders, the top floors were gutted and the four lower floors well alight. The narrow laneway of Hosking Place proved no barrier to the flames and by 3.00 am the whole block bounded by Pitt, Moore, Castlereagh and Hunter Streets was threatened.

By then volunteer brigades from throughout the city and suburbs had arrived and almost 200 firemen surrounded the block. Police and mounted troopers under Inspector-General

Martin Place today (left)—an outcome of the Great Fire of Sydney in 1890 (above)

A view from the General Post Office Tower on the western side of George Street shows the devastated heart of Sydney's business district in 1890 including the Central Bank (foreground)

Foobery were trying to control the thousands of spectators who had come to watch the spreading devastation. Many of the crowd had their pockets picked as they gazed in awe at the inferno.

Some time after 3.30 am the walls of Gibbs, Shallard and Company and the Southern Cross Club crashed to the ground, injuring ten firemen. An MFB fireman, Thomas Cutts, and an Ashfield Volunteer, William Rigney, had miraculous escapes after being totally buried by bricks and burning timber. Only the efforts of John Ford (Officer-in-Charge of George Street West) and Third-Class Fireman George Cobb, who pulled away the burning debris with their bare hands, saved the pair from almost certain death.

With the onset of a northerly wind, the flames attacked the buildings at the Moore Street end with renewed vigour. The four-storey warehouse of Messrs Lark and Sons was rapidly consumed, as was the City Bank.

It was not until 6.00 am when the winds had died and all fuel for the flames had been consumed, that the fire abated. Some twenty large buildings, affecting more than 100 tenants, were destroyed or severely damaged. The insurance bill ran to over £500,000 ($1 000 000) with the estimated real value closer to £1 million ($2 million).

Enquiries into the blaze continued for months. The scope of the inquest into the 'Great Fire' was widened to embrace the whole question of fire precautions within the City. Whilst an open verdict as to the cause was returned, a number of important recommendations were made concerning the inadequacies of building codes and City Council inspections, water supply and telegraph wires. As the Board's analysis of the blaze showed, the network of altered warehouses represented a gigantic flue linking Moore and Pitt Streets with Hosking Place. With no method of access, no fire shutters and insufficient water pressure, the firemen had little chance to isolate the blaze.

Within a year of the 'Great Fire' a section of the block was resumed by Legislative order and

Moore Street widened; one far-sighted observer suggested that Post Office Street (the extension of Moore Street) could one day be continued right through to Parliament House for the benefit of the city and its people. More than 90 years later the widened Moore Street is the pedestrian mall known as Martin Place.

New six-inch (15.24 cm) mains were also laid at a four-foot (1.22 m) depth in the heart of the City and within a few years the City's telegraph wires, which had obstructed the Brigades' ladders, were placed underground. In the protracted negotiations for a third City fire station, the Government had a sudden change of heart and in 1892 George Street North was opened.

These precautions were not able to prevent a continuing series of major conflagrations. In December 1890 over 80 000 cans of kerosene were destroyed at Gibbs, Bright and Company's Millers Point wharf and in June 1892 the 'second' Theatre Royal was lost. On 24 May 1893 the Harbour's fire protection shortcomings were displayed with the loss of the 2,000 ton (2032 tonnes) iron clipper, the *Port Jackson*, at Central Wharf.

In September 1894 John Lawler's George Street warehouse of three storeys was destroyed and ten adjacent buildings (including Central Police Station) were wrecked by falling walls. Senior fireman William Brown, Officer-in-Charge of Newtown and formerly of the Insurance Brigades, was killed in the wall collapse. The funeral procession along Castlereagh, Park and George Streets on 3 September 1894 was led by the Paddington Brewery Volunteer Fire Brigade Band. A crowd of more than 10 000 'sympathetic' onlookers, lined the streets and roadway 'baring their heads' in Brown's honour.

In October 1898 MFB firemen fought a long and exhausting battle for five days against a harbour fire in the SS *Buteshire*. Being outside the area covered by the Act, the Board sought compensation from the agents, Dalgety and Company, for the vessel. An offer of £100 ($200) was refused and the Board sued for £1,500 ($3000) salvage and expenses. In June 1899 Mr Justice Owen of the Vice-Admiralty Court delivered judgment in favour of the plaintiff. The decision created an unusual precedent, giving the Board salvage rights on any vessel in the Harbour saved from fire by Board staff.

A FIRE STATION ON FIRE!

An unusual fire during the MFB period was that which gutted the inside of George Street West fire station on 2 January 1901. As part of the carnival week to celebrate the formation of the Australian Commonwealth, all fire stations had been decorated with bunting, flags and steamers. The George Street West engine room had been decorated as a representation of Windsor Castle, with busts of Queen Victoria and Generals Roberts, Kitchener, Baden-Powell and Buller from the African campaigns. Chinese lanterns were hung near the engine bay doors and one of these was evidently knocked over, igniting the decorations. A strong wind fanned the flames, destroying much of the engine room, stables and fodder room. Two horses were suffocated by the smoke and the Brigades lost hose, coats, helmets and other equipment. As a result of the blaze, believed to be the first to occur in a fire station in Australia, the Board issued an order banning decorations in fire stations under its control.

CLEGG'S CHOICE—FLAMES OR DEATH LEAP?

Anthony Hordern's

No other fire in Sydney's history has evoked more publicity than the Anthony Hordern and Sons fire of Wednesday morning 10 July 1901. The growth of Sydney at the turn of the century was epitomised by the Anthony Hordern retailing giant, run principally by Sam Hordern. The Haymarket end of town, the retailing centre of Sydney, was dominated by five Hordern buildings in the block bounded by George, Gipps, Pitt and Hay Streets. Between the buildings ran the narrow Parker Street and Parker Lane.

At the time of the blaze Horderns' employed a staff of 1200, served more than 30 000 people a day and had an annual turnover of £1,500,000 ($3 000 000).

The fire started in the toy department of the central building on the corner of Gipps and Parker Street. By the time the first MFB steamers arrived, under the direction of Superintendent Webb, the adjacent haberdashery department was well alight. A strong south-westerly fanned the fire, which jumped Parker Street into the eight-storey furniture department building, where a number of employees were bravely directing water hoses from the upper floors

196 / *Fighting Fire!*

A view from Gipps Street of the smoldering Anthony Hordern buildings 1901 (above) including the furniture department (right) from which Harry Clegg jumped to his death. A street plan (below) shows the Anthony Hordern complex at the time of the blaze. The No. 1 Volunteer Fire Company had ceased operating by 1901, however, the building remains as the oldest fire station in Australia, built in 1857

across the street, oblivious of the threat below. A warning from Deputy Superintendent Sparks, who ordered all men out of the building, saved two lives but for three others, escape was blocked by a wall of flames. John Nicholls, a packer on the sixth floor, was roasted alive on the roof of a lift; Robert Malcolm and Harry Clegg managed to make their way to the roof. Malcolm fell back almost immediately into the flames, while Clegg tottered for over half an hour on the parapet. The Brigades' 80-foot (24.39 m) wooden ladders could not reach him and the peak-hour crowd of office workers and shoppers watched in horror as Clegg chose to jump, falling 120 feet (36.58 m) to his death on the Gipps Street roadway below.

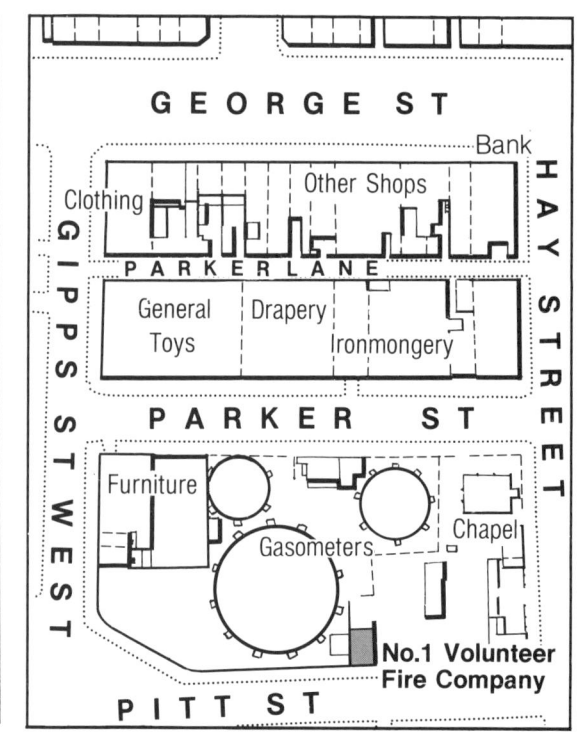

By now the fire had spread to the clothing department and to the ironmongery and threatened the three gasometers of the Australian Gas Light Company. As the wind dropped the 170 firemen, with ten steamers in action, started to get the upper hand and by 11.00 am, two and a half hours after the first alarm, the spread of fire had been stopped.

The blaze remained in the public spotlight for days to come. The morning after it was reported that in addition to Clegg, Malcolm and Nicholls, two other employees were missing. Walter Brett (brother of an MFB auxiliary fireman, Sidney Brett, who died a year later of acute pneumonia) and William Dashwood had been pumping water in the basement of the furnishing building. Evidently they were trapped by the barred basement windows and burnt to death. Thus five men had died in the fire. Two days later a further life was claimed when a City Council workman was killed by a falling beam during demolition of the dangerous walls. It was five days before the grisly remains of some of the dead were discovered amongst the ruins.

The inquest into the conflagration and the tragic loss of life dominated the press. The inadequacy of Brigade equipment, particularly the ladders, and the lack of fire escapes were given special focus. In its verdict of accidental death in the case of Harry Clegg, the jury stated:

> We are of the opinion that the said buildings owned and occupied by the firm of Anthony Hordern and Sons, should have been provided with some special means of escape in the case of fire, and that the employees should have been instructed in the use of appliances to extinguish fire. We intend these remarks to apply to all similar buildings in the city of Sydney. (MFBAR, 1901:2)

These conclusions, along with the public outcry, were to have a major impact on building codes in the years ahead (Chapter 3). In addition expenditure on equipment and manpower was expanded—led by the donation to the MFB of an 80-foot set of ladders by Sam Hordern.

Apart from the Anthony Hordern's fire in 1901, there were two other fires of note in the period before the demise of the MFB in 1909. On Sunday morning 24 March 1902 Her Majesty's Theatre (leased by J C Williamson) was destroyed, along with a number of surrounding shops. Also badly damaged was Duff's Hotel on the corner of Pitt and Market Streets (one of the occupants was a youngster, Leslie Edye Duff—later President of the Board, 1956–58). A woman, Bella Pye, was killed by falling walls at the height of the blaze after she had returned to

Firemen atop wheeled escapes attach hawsers to the tottering Anthony Hordern building walls

One of Sydney's numerous theatre fires—Her Majesty's Theatre, Pitt Street in 1902

search for her wedding ring, left in Gaffney's Bakery in Market Street.

On Saturday 20 November 1909 a huge blaze destroyed Saxton and Binn's Timber Yards at Pyrmont. Fourteen steamers and the fire floats *Pluvius* and *Powerful* from the Harbour Trust could do little to prevent the fire spreading. Property valued at over £80 000 ($160 000) covering about three acres (1.21 hectares) of land, went up in flames. In reporting on the blaze Superintendent Webb deplored the lack of an up-to-date float, commenting that the *Pluvius* could pump at the rate of only 2400 gpm (182 L/s) whereas a New York fire float pumped at 12 000 gpm (910 L/s).

By 1909 the number of alarms reported had risen from 225 in 1884 to 850. The number of chimney fires remained about the same, indicative of more stringent construction standards. Whilst the number of false alarms had doubled, it was the number of actual fires which had increased dramatically from 129 to 706. The common causes were foul flues, candles and 'lights thrown down', whilst the more bizarre were 'insanity', 'rats at matches' and 'tramps'.

The early years of the new Board of Fire Commissioners of NSW saw a number of major fires, including the spectacular explosion and fire at the Hotel Australia in 1915 which destroyed the top three storeys, but none were as sensational as the series of fires which led to the Industrial Workers of the World (IWW) trial in October 1916.

SYDNEY'S ARSON CASE OF THE CENTURY
The IWW Trial

On 10 October 1916 twelve members of the IWW organisation were charged with treason: 'That they feloniously and wickedly did conspire, consult, confederate, assemble, and meet together to raise, make, and levy insurrection and rebellion against the King ... to burn down and destroy buildings and shops in Sydney and elsewhere in New South Wales' (*Sun*, 10 October 1916). The charges followed a series of eighteen fires and attempted fires between June and September started by parcels containing cotton waste, phosphorous and other chemicals. The four largest of the fires occurred at Simpson's Bond Store, Winn's, James Stedman's and the Public Supply Co-operative Stores, with total damage of £250 000 ($500 000). The Co-operative Stores fire on 31 August coincided with Prime Minister Hughes' speech on patriotism, conscription and the fight for 'God, King and Country'.

Evidence produced at the trial showed that the IWW opposed the conscription of 'labour as cannon fodder' for the 'capitalists' war'. IWW members had a reputation for anti-war protests in the Domain and for propounding the use of sabotage through their paper, *Direct Action*. The Crown alleged that after the arrest of an IWW member, Tom Barker, a plot was hatched to terrorise the Government by incendiary acts. During the trial there were sensational accusations of conspiracy involving IWW members led by a Russian, Joseph Fagin, and a German escapee (named Georgi) from a concentration camp. Evidence linking the twelve IWW members to the fires was 'lamentably thin' (Turner, 1969:194) and consisted principally of guilt by association, for example, Crown evidence included a painting from the IWW offices in Castlereagh Street entitled 'Behold, I Bring you Freedom', which showed a woman with a torch looking down on factory buildings.

During the trial, on 28 October, three alleged attempts at incendiarism were made on Victoria Barracks. One man apprehended near the scene was a German, but charges against him were later dismissed. On 2 December 1916 the jury delivered its verdict on the three reduced charges of 'conspiracy to set fire to buildings, conspiracy to procure the release of Tom Barker by illegal means, and seditous conspiracy'. Relatives and IWW supporters in the courtroom and the hundreds waiting outside erupted in uproar when the twelve were found guilty on what the Judge admitted was largely circumstantial evidence. The seven found guilty on all three counts were sentenced to fifteen years' hard labour in Parramatta Gaol and the others received lesser sentences. When removed from the court and placed in the prison tram, a large burst of cheering echoed the crowd's sympathies, ending one of the most sensational criminal trials in the history of New South Wales. In the ensuing months union supporters of the twelve lobbied for their early release but it was not until a Labor victory at the polls in 1921 that the last, Charlie Reeve, was released. The release of Reeve in November 1921 preceded, by less than a month, a major fire described as the largest since the Anthony Hordern's fire of 1901.

WOOL STORE LIT UP
Pastoral Finances Association (PFA)

The PFA building opposite Circular Quay was a familiar sight to all Sydney Harbour travellers. With a large 'electric sign' on the roof the mammoth wool store covered five acres (2.02 hectares) of floor space, bounded by Campbell, Beulah and Carabella Streets, near Admiralty House on Sydney's North Shore.

On the morning of 13 December 1921 (the thirty-first anniversary of its construction) employees entering the building found a fierce fire burning in the wool. By 7.30 am the first brigade, North Sydney, had arrived, to be followed by the Harbour Trust fire floats *Hydra* and *Cecil Rhodes*. Despite their efforts, the building was alight from end to end by 8.00 am.

Without a bridge crossing the Harbour, there was the inevitable delay in despatching brigades from the City. The first to arrive was Circular Quay, which caught the Milson's Point punt. Chief Officer Sparks then commandeered two vehicle ferries and placed two of Headquarter's petrol motor engines aboard in order to pump from the Harbour.

At its height the fire threatened to engulf the whole densely settled neighbourhood and 300 naval ratings were called in to assist. Soon after 9.00 am a section of the front wall collapsed into the Harbour, followed by floor after floor giving way beneath the hugh weight of wool. The attention of the ratings and Brigades was turned to saving adjacent property and whilst many of the boarding houses and flats were scorched, all were saved, including the electric light plant and manager's residence within a few yards of the blazing inferno.

Not until 2.00 pm were the flames finally subdued; for days afterward a heavy pall of nauseating smoke hung overhead from the smouldering wool bales. Huge crowds and small craft dotted the Harbour near the fire, jostling for position with the Circular Quay passenger ferries, which were doing a 'roaring trade'.

With complete destruction of the PFA building and contents, the damage bill was a staggering £800,000 ($1 600 000). One of Sydney's notable landmarks had come to a sudden and devastating end.

Whilst no life was lost in the PFA blaze this was not the case in a fire which gutted the passenger ship *Canberra*, four years later. At the

The Pastoral Finances Wool Store ablaze in 1921

time the ship was the leader of the P & O fleet and a household name in Sydney. As such she attracted more than her share of press publicity. Soon after 2.30 am on 30 June 1925 the 7710 ton (7833.36 tonnes) *Canberra* caught fire whilst moored at Erskine Street wharf. The ship was laid up due to union trouble; luckily, few passengers and staff were aboard. It was only through the gallant efforts of a steward, Reginald Craythorne, that the passengers and crew escaped when suffocating smoke and flames spread rapidly through the vessel. Craythorne's heroism led to his own death. One of the women who was rescued said: 'If ever there was a hero, that man was one. It is too dreadful to think that he has succumbed to the effects of the gas and smoke. You could not stop him. He went in time and time again, until at last he was overcome.' Craythorne's body was later discovered in the music room, only two feet (0.61 m) from safety.

For the 40 Brigades firemen and the crews of the Harbour fire floats the *Canberra* fire represented, in the words of Chief Jackson, 'our hardest harbour task'. Smoke and fumes, and the intense heat forced the men to work in relays. As men collapsed they were replaced by new arrivals. By 4.30 am the sheer mass of water poured onto the fire had its effect and by 5.00 am the flames were under control.

The inquest into Craythorne's death and the fire recorded a finding of accidental death through carbon monoxide fumes. Despite numerous rumours of incendiarism and 'suspicious chemicals', the Coroner's finding was a 'fire of unknown origin'.

The next major Sydney fire was that on 2 January 1927 at the Metters six-storey building in Elizabeth Street. It proved to be one of the fastest spreading fires in Sydney's history. It began smouldering on Friday night, the whole building erupted at 4.30 pm on Saturday and within less than 30 minutes over £100,000 ($200 000) in property was consumed.

Although 1927 was a fairly quite year for fires (1966 fires, 44 chimney calls and 557 false alarms—a total of 2567), in less than twenty years Sydney's alarm rate had trebled. Whilst the City of Sydney area still dominated the number of calls (over 750), the rapid suburbanisation of Sydney during the 1920s boom saw suburban alarm rates increase appreciably (Chapter 4). In all there were 1816 suburban calls, with the most fire-prone suburbs being Randwick, North Sydney, Marrickville and Newtown. In the more 'distant' suburbs such as Rockdale, Hurstville, Bankstown and Ku-ring-gai, where brigades were only in their infancy, alarms were still few and generally only scrub or grass fires.

The 4476 calls in the Sydney FD in 1928 eclipsed the previous record of 1926 by 750. It was also a year for major fires. On the afternoon of 15 January, a spectacular blaze erupted in the eight storey Wynyard Building in Carrington Street. The building was totally destroyed and many of its neighbours damaged. The insurance bill was over £80,000 ($160 000). Two firemen, Dave O'Keefe and Jack McEachin, were rushed to hospital with serious facial burns.

Less than two months later George Hudson's large timber yard in Bridge Road, Glebe, was extensively damaged by fire. The combined efforts of more than 100 firemen from nine brigades, twelve Dennis motors, the *Big Ben* steamer and the fire-floats, *Hydra* and *Pluvius*, managed to restrict the blaze to only a section of the yard. Even so the loss of the log-mill, the ready-made houses' mill, saw-doctor's shop and several 50-foot (15.24 m) high timber stacks amounted to some £60,000 ($120 000).

TRAGEDY STRIKES
Vauxhall House

One of the most tragic fires in Sydney's history occurred in the five—storey Vauxhall House building, near the corner of Pitt and Bathurst Streets, during the afternoon peak hour of Monday, 30 June 1930. Whilst the cause of the fire was never found, it is believed that cigarette butts ignited celluloid film in fourth-floor offices. The flames spread rapidly to floors above, which included a caretaker's residence at the rear of the top floor.

Trapped in their four-room apartment were the caretaker's wife and his nineteen-year-old daughter, Rosabella Miller. As the flames and dense smoke entered their rooms they frantically sought escape in the bathroom. As flames burned their clothing, they screamed for help through the bathroom window.

The peak-hour crowds in the streets below watched in horror as the young woman collapsed and toppled through the window. A ghastly ball of fire, she fell to her death on the concrete below, missing by feet a jumping sheet firemen were desperately rigging in the street.

As the young girl was falling to her death, men under Flying Officer Shelley and SO Pickering of Salvage were making desperate attempts to reach the top floor. Pickering and Fireman J McCarthy were the heroes of the hour: brushing past other fireman overcome by fumes, they found a break at the head of the fourth-floor stairs. Whilst Pickering attacked the fire with a hose connected to the third-floor hydrant, McCarthy reached Mrs Miller, who had collapsed on the bathroom floor, then staggered back down the staircase. Assisted by other firemen, he carried her to the safety of the street.

George Hudson's timber yard Glebe, 1926 (above) and Metters store, Elizabeth Street 1927 (right), two of Sydney's larger fires in the 1920s

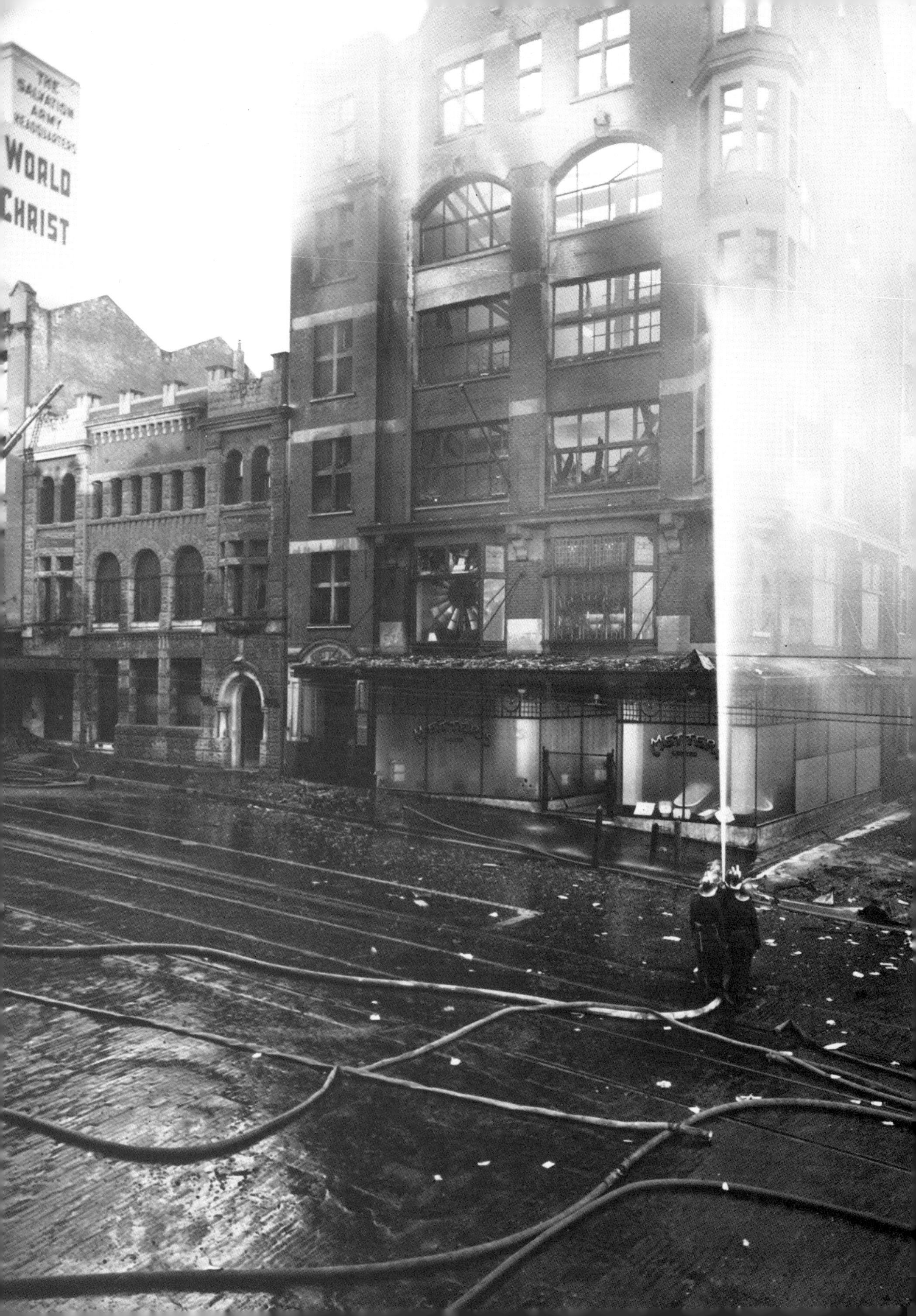
THE SALVATION ARMY HEADQUARTERS
WORLD
CHRIST

Tragically Mrs Miller also died, three days later, from the effects of severe burns and shock (although news of her daughter's death had been kept from her). Two other occupants of Vauxhall House were rescued from the fourth-floor parapet by the Headquarters ladders, which had battled a distance of less than 100 yards (91.44 m) through peak-hour crowds.

The lingering death of Mrs Miller, the grief-stricken father who arrived on the fire scene an hour after the fire, unaware of his loss, and the popularity of the young music teacher victim, Rosabella, all combined to arouse public sympathy. The funeral of Bella Miller attracted a crowd of over 6000 to Kinsela's Oxford Street funeral home, with a dozen firemen under Divisional Inspector Beare providing a guard of honour.

The inquest into the deaths revealed that the fire escape in Vauxhall House ended ten feet (3.05 m) below the bathroom from which the Millers sought escape. Because the building was less than 100 feet (30.48 m) in height, it did not come under the Height of Building Act. At the time there was no law to prevent smaller buildings of wood construction with three-ply partitions and without fire escapes in the city centre.

VOLUNTEER HEROS

F Braund and Co, Armidale

Whilst this book deals with the Centenary of Sydney fire brigades and fires within the Sydney FD, it would be incomplete without reference to the Armidale disaster of 18 May 1932. The following excerpt is taken from a report by Kevin Jeffcoat:

Armidale was asleep on that cool May morning in 1932 when it all began.

At least most were asleep. Brian Dunshea was wide awake. He'd been to see some friends off on an early train and it was just on 4.30 am when he arrived home.

As he was about to enter his front door the fire brigade siren suddenly throbbed into life, howling in mournful urgency through the still morning air across the sleepy town.

Dunshea was not a fireman. But he was interested, and dressed. So he got straight back in his car and drove down the street to find the fire. It wasn't hard to find. On the corner of Beardy and Dangar Streets, flames were leaping skyward from the storage yard of Braund's big produce store.

Dunshea parked his car and ran across to join about 20 others at a vantage point outside the low gates leading into the yard. The fire engine had already arrived and as he watched, three men—Sub Station Officer Fred Maizey, Volunteer Firemen Berry Jones and Bill Robinson—ran out a line of hose and got the motor to work.

Jones and Robinson took the branch up close and started putting water on the fire from a range of only a few yards. He could hear the hiss and crackle of it and thought 'my word they were quick'.

Meanwhile Fred Maizey, axe in hand, was heading for the loading dock to gain entry into the burning store through the big double doors.

Becoming aware of increasing activity, Dunshea noticed that other firemen had arrived and, in the midst of shouted orders, were running out another hose.

He looked back to where Maizey was trying to force the doors and suddenly there was a blinding flash and a tremendous bang. To Dunshea it felt like the end of the world. The whole of Armidale seemed to rock to its foundations and the air was full of hurtling debris and spearing glass in one terrible ear-shattering split second of time.

As if in a dream he saw the store-room blossom violently up and out. He saw Fireman Jones, like a broken doll, flung grotesquely through the air. Then the blast struck him with stunning force, hurling him to the ground and dislocating his knee.

What Dunshea didn't know, but the firemen did, was that Braund's were licensed to sell explosives. The blast that rocked all Armidale on that fateful morning came from 9000 detonators inside the store-room involved in fire.

But there was another grim complication, and the firemen were well aware of this too. Right next to the burning store-room, in fact almost completely surrounded by fire, stood the powder magazine—a small tin shed containing 400 sticks of gelignite, 10 lbs [4.54 kg] of dynamite and a box of cartridges!

Now gelignite on its own is not normally an explosive hazard in a fire. It needs

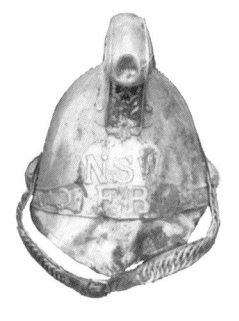

The remains of Braund's General Store, Armidale where two volunteer firefighters died as 9000 detonators exploded. The magnitude of the explosion is shown by their shrapnel-pierced brass helmets (right)

concussion, not heat, to set it off. But the box of cartridges in this case added the missing link. All it needed was for one shell to explode, or a roof beam to fall in, and bingo! Half Armidale shopping centre, and all the spectators, would have gone into orbit.

This is what Fred Maizey—and indeed all members of the brigade—knew when they ran into Braund's yard to come to grips with that deadly fire. It is to their everlasting credit that even after the shock and horror of the first blast, the surviving members pressed home the attack.

Another witness at the scene was Mr D J McCarthy, who was subsequently awarded the bronze medal and certificate of merit of the Royal Shipwreck Relief and Humane Society for his actions.

Several months after the event, McCarthy was interviewed by the Board of Fire Commissioners. His statement is simple fact, revealing little of the shock and fear which must have hit him—and every other man in the yard—after the first explosion. They could see the powder magazine still intact and they knew that another huge blast could come at any second. Read this between the lines of his story and you begin to see the meaning of courage.

'As soon as I heard the alarm,' said McCarthy, 'I rushed down. Just as I got there Mr Maizey and Firemen Jones and Robinson were there. They had taken the hose through the small gate, the other was locked. I could see they wanted that gate open, so I got hold of an axe. I jumped inside and just had the gate open when the explosion occurred. I threw the axe over and rushed up to where the fire was. I could see Fireman Jones a good way away, and Robinson was crawling about on hands and knees. I helped him away from the fire and put my overcoat under his head to keep it off the gravel.'

At this stage a policeman came running up and told McCarthy to get out as the magazine might blow at any minute. McCarthy refused. He could see that the fireman was badly injured and needed help. 'I told him (the policeman) that I would leave when Robinson was fixed up,' he said. 'I was very nervous,' he remembered, 'I knew that Fireman Jones was dead and that Mr Maizey had been taken out into the street. I asked Robinson where he was injured and he said he was shattered all over.'

In fact Fireman Robinson had a broken leg and forty puncture wounds all over his body. He died in hospital sixteen hours later.

Meanwhile, with S.S.O. Maizey unconscious and in a bad way, the brigade was without its officer and the fire still raged on.

The first line of hose had been ripped to pieces and flames were licking around the partly demolished magazine.

This was the moment of truth. This was the time when the whole brigade could have dropped their bundle and made a run for it. But they didn't.

During the subsequent inquiry Volunteer Fireman Thomas Snell, Snr., concluded his report with the factual masterpiece of understatement: 'On learning that the Officer in Charge was injured, it was my duty to take charge of the fire. I gave the order to replace a damaged length of hose and ordered the water to be turned on, also a second line of hose by breeching piece. By these two lines of hose the fire was extinguished.'

'It was my duty.' That could well have been the epitaph of the Armidale brigade. Instead, by a magnificent display of sheer guts they lived to add a new dimension to those simple words. They set the criterion of courage which succeeding generations of firemen will look to with admiration and respect.

The minutes that followed the explosion were charged with suspense. As the branchmen took water up to the fire they could plainly see the threat of violent death staring them in the face. The magazine door had been wrenched off its hinges, exposing the contents to the full heat of the fire. As they worked up to it, sweating and praying, desperately spraying water from shed to fire and back again, some of the loose gelignite suddenly burst into flames. Fear knotted their stomachs as they drenched the burning sticks. Could they put it out in time or would the whole lot go in one almighty blast?

As it happened, courage and determination won the day. Steadily the well-directed stream of water got the upper hand and soon, with a second line of hose at work from the rear, the fire was finally subdued and then knocked out completely.

The Armidale members made up their gear and went home. It had been a desperate and tragic job, one that every man would vividly remember for the rest of his life. But they were hardly prepared for the flood of public acclamation that followed hard upon the story of their feat to the outside world. Newspapers of the day carried such headings as: 'Police praise Firemen', 'Marvellous Save', 'Fire Board Filled With Admiration', 'Great Disaster Averted', and 'Heroic Fire Fighters'.

The Reverend Canon Best of Armidale summed it up this way: '... The community was stunned to learn of the tragic occurrence, which flung Beresford Jones from a full and active life into eternity and inflicted mortal wounds on Fireman Robinson,' said the Canon. 'All our sympathy goes out to the bereaved relatives in their sorrow, and we also pray that Fred Maizey may make a full recovery from his wounds. We are not only expressing our sympathy but our respect and admiration for those men who were tried in the balances, and were not found wanting.' (*Fire News*, 1(6) 1971)

For their actions all the members of the Armidale Brigade were the first recipients of the NSW Fire Brigades Medal for Conspicuous Bravery.

The year 1935 eclipsed 1928, with not only the largest number of fires but also the biggest. Of the 5065 calls the two largest fires were those in Hardwicke House, York Street, in February and the even bigger conflagration in the premises of Goldsbrough Mort on 25 September.

ONE THEY ALL REMEMBER
Goldsbrough Mort

The premises of Goldsbrough Mort consisted of two small wool stores and the main store, a brick and stone building of eight floors, having a frontage of 362 feet (110.05 m) to Pyrmont Street, Pyrmont, a depth of 106 feet (32.22 m) and containing over 40 000 bales of wool. The blaze, which was reported on the Reichel Alarm System at 7.15 am on Wednesday, was to be later described by senior officers as 'the largest yet seen in Sydney; greater in scale than even the PFA wool store inferno of 1921'.

Following the arrival of No 38 Pyrmont, other brigades were immediately dispatched and by 8.00 am the blazing central wool store was encircled by fifteen motors, three large ladders, 27 officers (under Chief Officer Grimmond) and 172 firemen. In all 28 powerful jets were directed on the fire from all sides.

The heat radiated from the fire reached

terrific intensity as the brigades battled to prevent the fire spreading to the smaller woolstores and the adjoining Pitt Son and Badgery's store. Many Brigade personnel had miraculous escapes as the wall of the main store collapsed. Pitt Son and Badgery's had been vacated for only seconds when the rear wall fell causing extensive damage to the adjacent buildings. Only minutes earlier the Tilling Stevens ladders were removed from the Fig Street frontage as it buckled and collapsed. Throughout the morning other sections of the wall were to collapse with further narrow escapes.

By 10.00 am, although the main blaze was under control, the Ahrens-Fox and two other engines continued pumping water on the ruins. In all, the pride of the service, the Ahrens-Fox, pumped continuously for 27 hours whilst two Dennis motors worked continuously for 4½ days. Over 10 800 000 gallons (49 140 kL) of water was pumped onto the fire, until its final

Firemen escape the immense radiant heat (above) from the Goldsbrough Mort wool store blaze 1928 (top)

extinction on 4 October. Seven firemen were injured fighting the fire, but only two—First-Class Fireman R Fawcett (No 2) with an injured knee and Fourth-Class Fireman A. Davies (No 7) with concussion—required hospitalisation.

Many of the men had worked beyond their 8.00 am shift and were not relieved until after 10.00 am when the fire had been contained. The Chief Officer's report recorded the dedication of all men at the fire stating 'that the officers and men lived up to the best traditions of the Fire Service', and had made miraculous saves of adjoining property.

AN 'OUT-OF-AREA' CALL WITH A DIFFERENCE
S S Ormonde, Twofold Bay

Whilst the Brigades often attend alarms out of designated fire districts, none rival that made to the Orient mail-liner, S S *Ormonde* in 1936. On 23 October 1936 the *Ormonde*, bound from London to Sydney with 320 passengers, put into Twofold Bay with her cargo of coir fibre on fire.

Called in by the Orient Company, Chief Officer Richardson arranged for a car crew with gas masks and oxygen containers to race to Twofold Bay from Headquarters. All ex-sailors, under SO (later Fire Commissioner) 'Mo' Campbell, the crew of George Fallon (driver), Senior Fireman Charles Milledge (later Chief Officer), Senior Fireman A Hunter, and First-Class Fireman J Craig, drove through the night.

On reaching the burning liner at 8.00 am, they donned smoke helmets and entered the No 4 hold. Despite appalling smoke and fumes that penetrated even the gas masks, they managed to create ventilation by smashing through the floors of the forward saloon. The firemen and crew then attacked the flames, pitchforking much of the smouldering coir fibre through the port holes into the sea. By 2.00 pm the fire had been subdued and at 3.25 pm the liner sailed for Sydney.

Only on arrival in Sydney was the full extent of the damage and danger realised. The decking had buckled, and on the port side the rivets had been started, forcing apart the ship's plates and making sinking imminent. Only the intervention of the Sydney 'experts' had averted a major tragedy.

Following repairs, the *Ormonde* returned to her trade, later serving as a troop carrier in the Second World War and finally being sent to the ship breakers in 1952.

The Brigades' ability to contain ship fires was put to further test within less than a month.

A SYDNEY FERRY EXPLODES
Bellubera

Without warning on Monday 16 November 1936 an explosion caused a blast of flame to burst through the 44-year-old, 499-ton Sydney Harbour ferry, *Bellubera*.

Trapped in the engine room by the raging fire, two men died and four others were injured and facing death when saved. Flames blazed around them for half an hour before they could be rescued, and for ten or more minutes the sides of their iron prison were red-hot and buckling.

On the arrival of the fire brigades it had been found that the *Bellubera*, moored to a wharf at Kurraba Point, was alight from end to end. The ferry, *Curl Curl*, lying alongside, was in danger of being destroyed and was already hidden behind the dense smoke. A police tug was immediately ordered, and the *Curl Curl* moved to safety.

As the fire raged along the *Bellubera*, fanned by a strong wind, Brigades officers and men went

Firemen load Proto gear in preparation for boarding the SS *Ormonde* at Twofold Bay

The Bellubera ferry well alight with one of her crew trapped below deck (arrowed). District Officer Griffiths donned an asbestos suit (right) during the rescue operation

into action. All rescue apparatus was transferred down a steep cliff from the salvage wagon to the wharf.

With the fire float, *Cecil Rhodes*, and a naval launch from Garden Island operating two jets onto the burning vessel an entry was attempted into the engine room. DO (later Chief Officer) Griffiths, in an asbestos suit with DO Currer, SSO Condon and Senior Fireman Milledge found four semiconscious men trapped in the flaming engine room.

Two of the men were carried out, but owing to the narrowness of the passageways from the engine-room and the size of the men concerned, two had to be hoisted by rope to the deck. Unfortunately, two of these men later died, bringing the death toll to four.

The *Bellubera* was at the time of the tragedy considered to be the most modern vessel of her type in Australia, and was the first Australian-owned ship to be equipped with full diesel-electric drive. She had been completely reconditioned and was to have continued with her trips on the same day as the fire which burned her to the waterline.

A RING OF FIRE
Black Sunday

One Black Sunday, 10 December 1938, Sydney recorded the greatest number of fire calls (individual alarms) in its history. The record of 348 alarms remains to the present day (despite the fact that the year 1938 recorded only 6150 alarms compared with 39 994 in 1983). With temperatures hovering on the century mark Sydney was hit by a devastating mid-morning wind storm: 'Struck by a fiery blast reaching hurricane force at 75 miles [120.75 km] an hour, Sydney today bore the aspect of a bombed city with havoc unparalleled on shore and on the harbour. Not one suburb escaped the dreadful fury of the wind, the velocity of which was the greatest ever recorded' (*Sun*, 10 December 1938:1). Wind gusts continued throughout the day as temperatures rose even further. Telephone communications were cut and trains on the Harbour Bridge were stopped. Fanned by the wind, bush fires broke out in unprecedented numbers ringing Sydney with fire. Throughout the afternoon and evening every Sydney brigade was out-on-call. Firemen's families manned the watchrooms, sending the exhausted firefighters on to a new fire scare each time they returned to the station. It was not until late evening that the winds died and firefighters gained respite from one of the most terrifying days in Sydney's history.

In the decade after the Second World War the most rapid suburbanisation in Sydney's history began. For example, the population of Sutherland more than doubled between 1947 and 1954, to 65 757. At the same time manufacturing was also moving from the traditional central city locale to Ashfield and Concord in the west, and Marrickville, St Peters and Mascot in the south.

By the mid-1950s the spatial distribution of

fire calls had changed significantly. Whilst the City of Sydney still dominated (with 768 actual fires in 1955), areas such as Bankstown (268 fires) and Sutherland now had much more frequent and serious calls. With the rapid growth in suburban fire calls the number of calls in the Sydney FD increased appreciably, and in 1951 for the first time exceeded 10 000.

EXPLOSION AND FIRE
HMAS Tarakan

On Wednesday 25 January 1950, HMAS *Tarakan*, berthed at Garden Island, was rocked by an explosion in her lower deck. An earlier explosion in 1947 had caused nine casualties aboard the vessel.

The 'Flyer', Running Motor and Salvage Unit were despatched from Headquarters along with motors from The Rocks, Paddington and Darlinghurst stations. A truck was also sent to the scene with additional Proto gear, gas masks and a 'smoke expeller'.

On the main deck Third Officer Edge, Sixth Officer McGrath (later Chief Officer) and firemen wearing breathing apparatus and gas masks endeavoured to locate the ship's complement who were in the mess room at the time of the explosion. Three injured sailors were found and removed from the shattered mess room. With the arrival of Chief Officer Griffiths further attempts were made to gain access below deck. The dense smoke and fumes made the work unbearable and a number of men, including the Chief, were overcome. After treatment at the wharf they were taken to St Vincent's Hospital. All recovered but, SO J L Nance was declared 'permanently unfit for firefighting', subsequently being appointed Instructor at Paddington Training College.

Eventually the smoke expeller, which had been put into action from the wharf through the companionway down to the main deck, dispersed the troublesome smoke. Rescue work continued in atrocious conditions; eight naval men died from extensive burns and shock.

The work of Brigades personnel in the *Tarakan* disaster, including the indomitable Chief, was in the finest tradition of courage and endurance. They proved beyond doubt that the fire brigades had an unmatched rescue capability. This rescue capability in a non-fire situation was put to the test four years later.

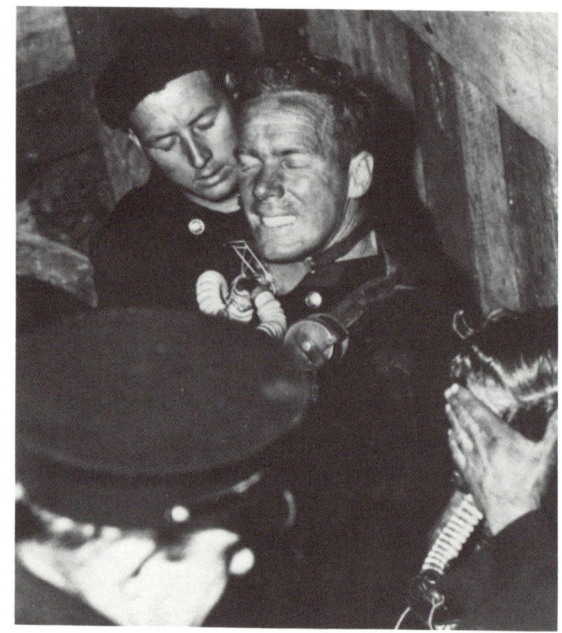

Fireman Don Knowles winces in pain after being dragged from a gas-filled water main at Rockdale, 1954

GALLANTRY AND COURAGE
Rockdale Rescue

On Tuesday 29 June 1954 Headquarters Control received a call that two Water Board employees were trapped in a water main under Prince's Highway, Rockdale. A rescue squad was immediately despatched under the direction of DO Featherstone.

Senior Firemen Norman Evans, Don Knowles and Colin McPhee entered the pipes with respirators and rope lines. McPhee had to be dragged out when his face piece slipped, and the others were forced back by poisonous air. They had inched their way along some 700 feet (213.36 m) of pipe on their stomachs through water up to a foot (0.31 m) deep. By now it was realised that both employees were dead, killed by carbon monoxide poisoning.

After thousands of gallons of water were pumped from the pipes, Evans donned Proto gear with two hours' supply of oxygen and reentered the pipe, lying face down on an electric trolley. In his own words Evans describes his experience:

> I was able to drive along the tunnel on the trolley. Water in the tunnel was up to a foot deep. Although air was being pumped into the tunnel there was still a lot of carbon

monoxide gas in it. I found one of the men overcome by fumes lying on his back 2000 feet [609.6 m] in. I was able to get him on to the mole and ride back to the mouth. I was in the pipe for three-quarters of an hour.

Both Knowles and Evans made attempts to extract the other body but were forced back by damaged gear, Knowles being in a state of collapse when he was dragged from the mouth of the pipe. At 2.30 pm, some nine and a half hours after the first call, Fireman Raymond Lewis recovered the body.

On 2 September 1955 Senior Firemen N S Evans, D Knowles, C H McPhee and R B Lewis and First-Class Firemen C W Knox, S C Hanslow and E R Bolton were each awarded the Royal Shipwreck and Humane Society's Certificate of Merit, in recognition of their gallantry and courage.

Late in December 1954 two spectacular blazes, later found to be the work of the same arsonist, destroyed the Variety Theatre, Pitt Street [causing damage in excess of £200,000 ($400 000)] and part of the top floor of the Royal Arcade on the opposite side of the street [damage £150,000 ($300 000)]. Eight firemen were injured, overcome by smoke and burnt by a shower of inflammable cleaning spirit.

On 10 December 1957 Third-Class Fireman D Cameron (Waterloo) became the ninth recipient of the NSW Fire Brigades Medal for Conspicuous Bravery (the first since the Armidale Brigade awards). His citation read: 'For conspicuous gallantry displayed on the occasion of a fire at premises, 124 Morehead Street, Redfern on 10th October 1957 in endeavouring to save the life of a child'. The tragedy typified the all-too-frequent occurrence of a young child playing with matches, causing his or her own death.

The Redfern tragedy occurred on the day which Chief Officer McGrath described as Sydney's worst day for fires in 35 years. Bush fires ringed Sydney for more than two weeks in unseasonally hot temperatures and dry westerly winds. Board brigades and bushfire units battled fires from Menai in the south and the Blue Mountains in the west to Berowra in the north. With over 200 calls in a single day within the Sydney FD alone, it is little wonder that 1957 was a record year for fires. The single-day figure had only been bettered once before, on 'Black Sunday', 10 December 1938.

A FUNNEL OF FIRE
Gibbs Chambers, Martin Place

One fireman at the scene described the Gibbs Chambers fire in the following terms: 'You could be in the job for 30 years and not get a job like Gibbs Chambers'. At 7.59 pm on Tuesday 24 March 1959 a number of calls were received at Control to a fire in Gibbs Chambers, 17 Martin Place (part of the main Commonwealth Bank premises).

Headquarters (with two motors, Salvage and turntable ladders), The Rocks (motor and turntable ladder), and Darlinghurst (one motor) immediately responded under the direction of Executive Officer Thompson. Gibbs Chambers, a building of seven floors, was well alight on its three top floors and threatening the adjacent buildings, the Hotel Australia and Somerset House. A red-alert was radio-telephoned to Headquarters, and motors from Crows Nest, Glebe and Redfern fire stations were ordered on.

Nos 2 and 8 Merryweather turntable ladders were fully extended in Martin Place and their hose monitors opened up a frontal attack on the blazing building. Two lines of delivery hose were taken into Gibbs Chambers as far as the fifth floor, and an additional pump was operated to supply two lines of delivery hose taken up to the sixth floor and roof of the adjoining Somerset House. So intense was the heat generated from the fire that a later inspection revealed that a brass dome of a soda and acid extinguisher, installed inside Gibbs Chambers, had melted. A heat somewhere between 1550°F and 1900°F (843.2°C–1037.7°C) would be necessary before this could happen.

It was not until 9.50 pm when the fire was brought under control that Acting Chief Officer Hawkins sent the 'Stop' message.

Damage from heat and water was extensive: Gibbs Chambers—fifth, sixth and seventh floors and their contents severely damaged by fire, all floors, the basement and contents severely damaged by water; Hotel Australia—western external walls and windows from seventh floor up damaged by heat; Somerset House—ground to seventh floors severely damaged by water, external eastern walls and windows from seventh floor up severely damaged by heat. In all, 154 694 gallons (703.86 kL) of water were used through 6000 feet (1828.8 m) of hose to extinguish the blaze.

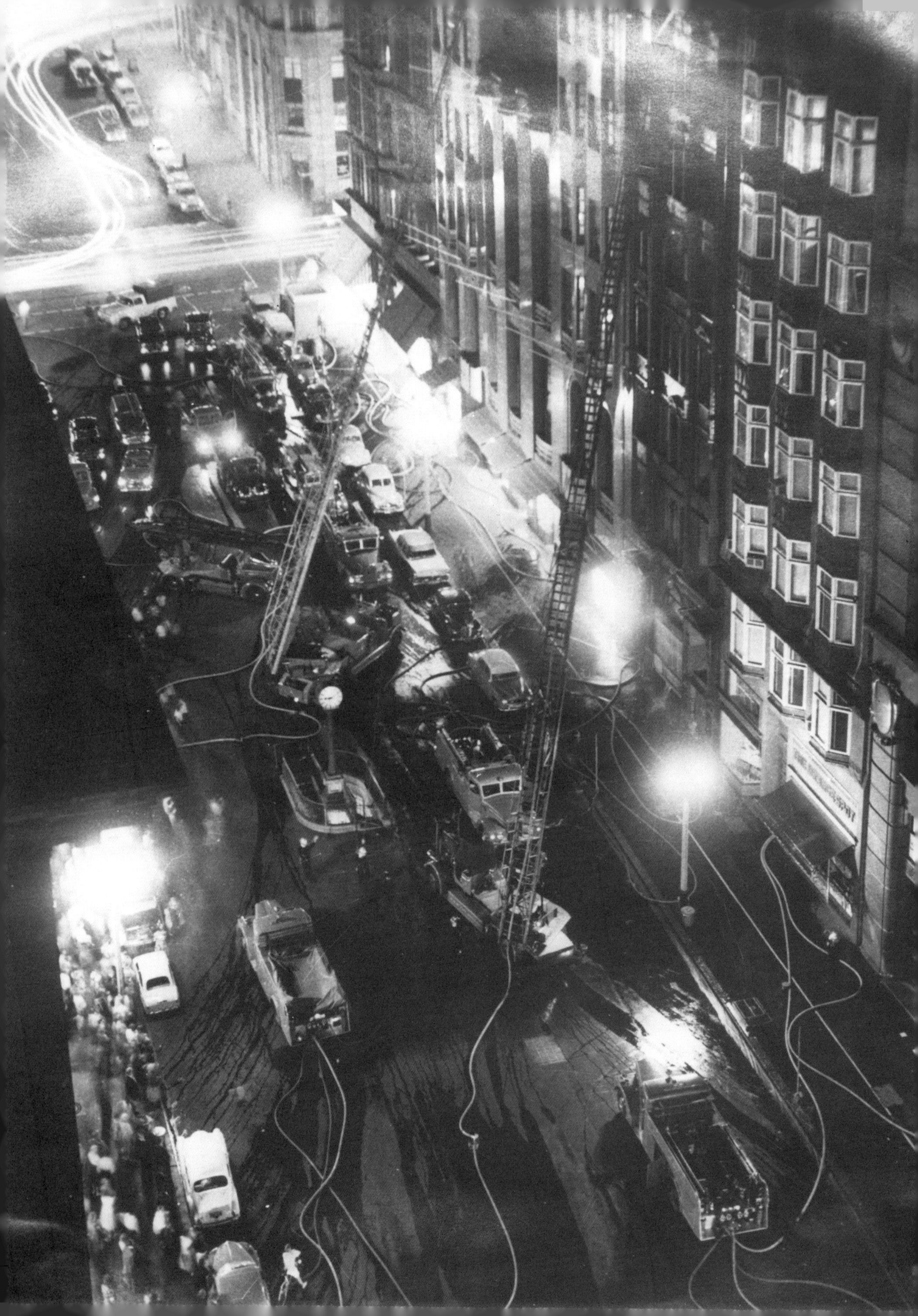

1961
Spectacular Fires and Rescues

The year 1961 will long be remembered for spectacular blazes and dramatic rescues. On 1 February 1961, Control received a call that two men had been overcome by fumes in the hold of the SS *Marine Discoverer* at No 1 Wharf Balmain. Following the arrival of Stanmore Brigade five Proto operators were ordered on from Headquarters.

Unable to don Protos because of the narrow opening into the ballast tank, Firemen A L Jacobson and J C Bennett discarded their equipment and climbed some 35 feet (10.69 m) to the bottom. After rescuing one man the pair were ordered out by DO Butcher. Overcome by fumes, they were hauled to the deck and resuscitated.

Firemen H G Pascoe, K J Albertson and E E Cribben then entered the tank and were lowered Proto sets by rescue slings. Three members of the crew found in the tank were then lifted to the deck where they were found to be dead.

On 20 October 1961 Sir John Northcott, President of the Royal Shipwreck Relief and Humane Society of NSW, awarded Jacobson and Bennett Bronze Medals, and Pascoe, Albertson and Cribben Certificates of Merit.

Three major blazes occurred in May, August and September 1961. The first, on 17 May, caused damage in excess of £350,000 ($700 000) at the Bankstown factory of Dunlopillo. Roaring like a blowtorch in a massive up-draught, the flames reached a height of 200 feet (60.96 m).

The blaze on 22 August was described 'as one of the largest and most spectacular fires seen in Sydney for many years'. For almost two hours 56 firemen under Chief Officer H W Pye and his Deputy, C A Welch, attempted to contain a blaze which destroyed Revlon Australia at Beaconsfield and the adjoining Australian Soaps building. Under DO J Ford the initial brigades on the scene, Waterloo, Mascot and Redfern, were unable to contain the blaze which had a good hold and was raging southward through the two-storey Revlon plant.

By 7.30 pm (22 minutes after the first call) the dividing partition between Revlon and Australian Soaps had collapsed, with the latter now seriously engulfed in fire. Strengthened by brigades from Headquarters, Newtown, Botany, Stanmore and Glebe the blaze was encircled, but it was not until 8.58 pm that the 'Stop' was sent to Headquarters Control.

A blaze of equal magnitude and causing in excess of £200,000 ($400 000) damage destroyed the Malleys building at 50 Mountain Street, Broadway, on 23 September 1961. The four- and two-storey premises was engulfed by fire before the arrival of the first brigades from Headquarters, Glebe and Pyrmont. Within seconds the roof of the two-storey section collapsed showering the surrounding area with sparks and burning embers. Fanned by a strong south-easterly wind, the blaze was in danger of becoming a major conflagration. However, frantic but disciplined efforts of 60 firemen from ten stations, with seven motors and four turntable ladders, contained the blaze to its original source.

HISTORIC THEATRE BURNS
Lyceum Theatre

Soon after 5.50 am on 25 February 1964, Control received a call that a large quantity of smoke was issuing from the historic Lyceum Theatre. Located in the Central Methodist Mission block, running from Castlereagh Street to Pitt Street, the theatre was one of the few survivors of Sydney's early theatre heritage. Two hours later, when Acting Chief Officer H R Barber sent the 'Stop' message, the Theatre and Lyceum Hall had been severely damaged by fire and the effects of a roof collapse. Surrounding offices were also severely damaged by fire and water.

Among the large crowd that had gathered to watch the blaze was the Reverend Alan Walker, then Superintendent of the Methodist Mission. During demolition, days later, a worker found an old poster attached to the wall at the rear of the theatre. It read:

SYDNEY VOLUNTEER FIRE COMPANY No 2
AN ADDRESS, Delivered on the Occasion
of a
BENEFIT IN AID OF THE FIRE ENGINE
FUND,
in the
LYCEUM THEATRE
ON TUESDAY, THE 16TH DECEMBER 1862.

The 'Address' extolled the virtues and bravery of a fireman rescuing a damsel in distress.

A congested fireground in Martin Place during the Gibbs Chambers' fire 1959

SYDNEY'S LARGEST OIL FIRE
Mobil Oil, Pulpit Point

On Tuesday afternoon, 27 October 1964, Hunters Hill was endangered when a fire broke out in oil and petrol drums at the main Sydney terminal of Mobil Oil. Covering 26 acres (10.52 ha), the depot contained 40 storage tanks, several large storage sheds and large, open drum storage areas.

The first brigade on the scene, Gladesville, found a large storage shed with a quantity of oil and petrol drums well alight and urgently radioed for further assistance. DCO Meeve on route to the fire from Headquarters, realising the potential danger, called for a 15-station alert and the support of the Maritime Services Board fire floats.

At the fire scene a lack of water from reticulated mains allowed only one line of hose, placing the firefighters in imminent danger. The strong north-easterly winds were fanning the blaze which threatened to spread to nearby tanks. With the arrival of the fire floats *Boray*, *Burrowaree*, *Bennelong* and *Endeavour*, further lines were laid ashore, allowing the fire to be attacked on all fronts and at the same time allowing screening and cooling sprays to be directed over the nearest tanks. During these operations, exploding drums were being hurled into the air, one landing 150 feet (45.72 m) south of the main fire which was now threatening the largest of the storage tanks.

Only after two hours of desperate fire-fighting was the blaze controlled and confined. The 75 officers and firemen who fought the fire had averted a disaster that would have been without parallel in Sydney's history. Texas City, USA, wasn't so lucky: in April 1947 an explosion at Monsanto Oil and Chemical Plant killed more than 500 people, including the entire volunteer fire company (pieces of steel from the explosion killed people five miles (8 km) from the centre of the blast).

A RECORD LOSS
Australian Wool Board Stores, Botany

Firemen debate for many hours as to which was Sydney's 'biggest' fire. The Great Fire of Sydney (1890), Goldsbrough Mort (1935), Fairfax Newsprint (1971), Ultimo Wool Stores (1978), all come into calculations. There is little doubt, however, that on a scale of property loss the Australian Wool Stores fire in 1969 must rank as Sydney's record fire.

Built in 1940, the Hale Street (Botany) warehouse complex covered an area of 32 acres (12.95 ha). The 26 timber and fibro sheds presented an open invitation for a fire disaster. With narrow separations, the buildings were tinder-dry. Floors were soaked with wool grease and piled high with combustible fuels. Bales of sheepskins, stacks of cardboard, stage scenery, motor tyres and rolls of paper provided ready fuel.

On Tuesday 30 September 1969 a truck unloading cardboard cartons at a warehouse dock suddenly burst into flames. Within seconds the flames spread through the loading bay into the warehouse complex. Shed after shed caught as the erupting inferno generated its own wind.

Within seconds of the arrival of the Botany Brigade a call was despatched to Control, that as much assistance as possible was required on the fireground. In all, eighteen stations, twenty motors and 150 men were turned out. Not the biggest ever in terms of deployment ... but certainly a major job! In the face of fierce heat,

Fire floats pump water from the Parramatta River (above and right) on the Pulpit Point fire 1964—Sydney's largest oil fire

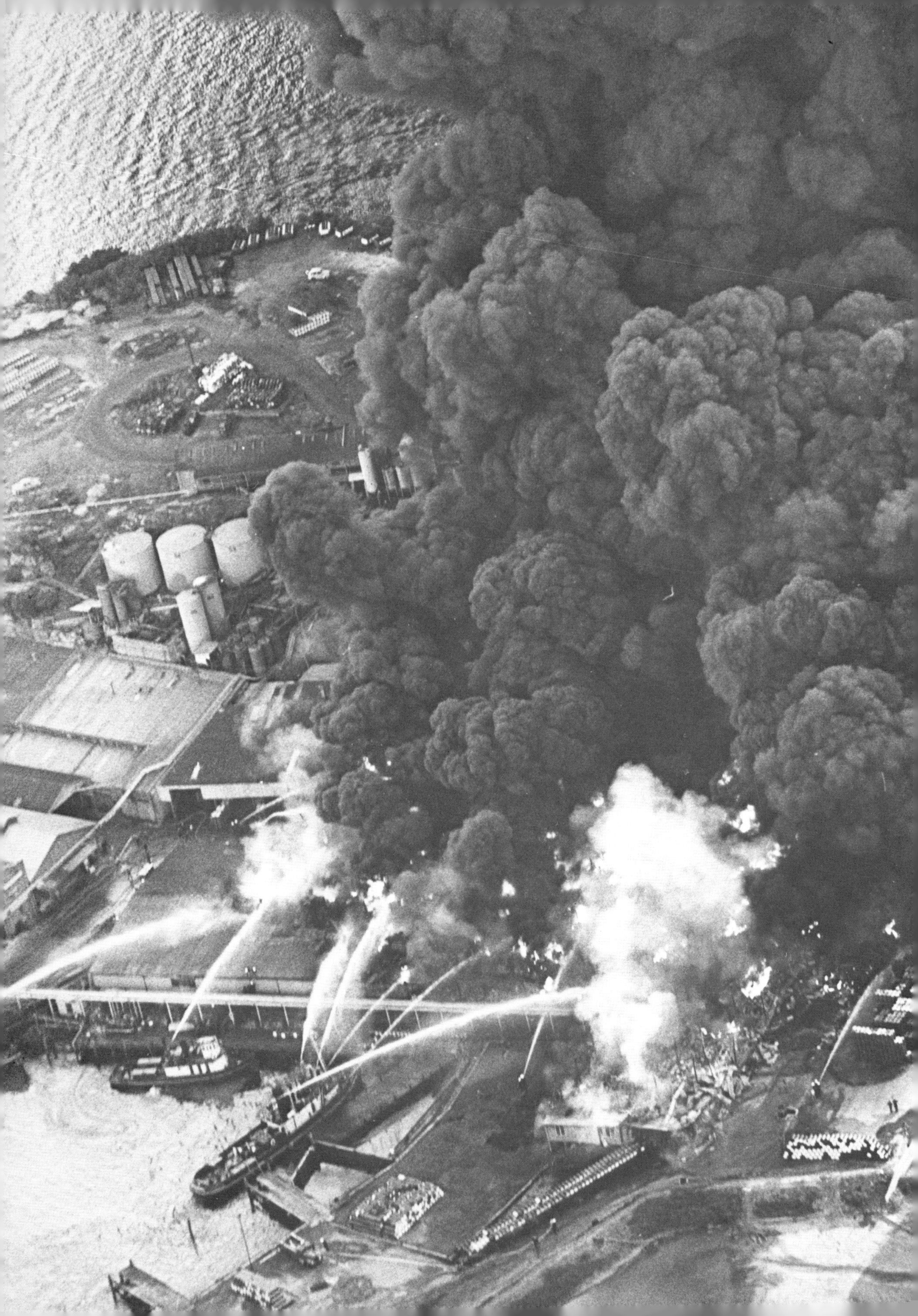

HEROISM
Senior Fireman W Doyle, Shore Motel Fire and Station Officer G Dowling, Enmore House Fire

THE following accounts of individual heroism give an insight into the personal qualities of two Sydney fire fighters, both of whom were awarded the Brigades' highest honour, the NSW Fire Brigades Medal for Conspicuous Bravery.

Returning home from night shift at Parramatta on 2 September 1967, Senior Fireman W Doyle came across the three-storey Shore Motel at Artarmon well alight. Realising people were trapped in the upper floors, he rigged an escape route consisting of a painter's ladder resting on a suspended plank. Climbing this precarious construction, he managed to help a number of people to safety. He then rigged scaling ladders to the second floor and occupants there were also rescued.

He was not yet done. Back on the ground he was told a woman was still trapped in one of the rooms. Re-entering the burning building, still without protective gear, he discovered the unconscious woman and carried her to safety.

In near-collapse from smoke and heat, he carried out cardiac massage until the arrival of a doctor. It was only then that Doyle allowed himself a respite. The effects of shock had set in and Doyle, along with seven motel guests, was taken to hospital. One guest subsequently died—but the others owed their lives to the resourcefulness, initiative and exceptional courage of Senior Fireman Doyle.

In the same spirit of tenacity and courage George Dowling (Stanmore) etched his name in the Brigades' history of gallantry. His citation reads:

At approximately 10.45am on Thursday, 6th June 1968 Station Officer Dowling with a crew of firemen from Stanmore Fire Station responded to a call of fire at 12 Pritchard Street, Enmore. On his arrival he found a

Sydney's most expensive fire—Hale Street, Botany warehouse complex 1969

Senior Fireman W Doyle earnt a place in the annals of heroic rescues at the Shore Motel fire in 1967

cottage, being one of a terrace of houses, heavily involved in fire and he was informed by members of the public that a baby was within the premises.

Without waiting for lines of hose to be got to work Station Officer Dowling endeavoured to enter the burning building by the front door but extreme heat drove him back.

He made a second attempt and was successful in entering the hall for a distance of six feet [1.83 m] but again flame, smoke and lack of oxygen made his position untenable and he had to withdraw.

Again he entered the building which was still burning fiercely and had a stream of water directed on to him and despite the severe heat and flame and live electric wiring hanging down from the ceiling, he recovered a basinette which contained the body of a three months old child, David Harper.

Station Officer Dowling by his actions suffered burns to both hands.

The Board of Fire Commissioners of N.S.W. considers that the extraordinary tenacity exhibited by George James Dowling and courageous actions shown by him in recovering the child from a building heavily involved by fire far exceeded the normal responsibilities placed on officers and firemen of a Fire Brigade.

firemen were continually forced to retreat as more and more of the sheds fell to the flames. Over a period of four hours firemen fought to contain the blaze. Eventually the fire was cut off on the one accessible flank and turned back.

In all, nine buildings and their contents were consumed—but seventeen were saved. The property loss was immense. The Australian Opera lost sets valued at over $250 000, the famous Tintookies puppets valued at $20 000; Phillipe Rives Company lost 600 bales of sheepskins, valued at $200 000. And so the list went on, reaching some $7 million; an unsurpassed insurance loss in the history of Sydney fires.

By 1970 Sydney's population exceeded two and a half million. The value of property risk within the city may be gauged by the estimate of Assessed Annual Value for the Sydney FD of $805 023 448. In 1969–70 claims under fire insurance policies cost the companies concerned over $20 million. Not surprisingly, the number of fire calls had also reached a record level: 31 626 in 1970. The sheer size of Sydney and its density of land use and habitation meant that major fires were inevitable.

Many of today's firefighters 'cut their teeth' at the big ones of the 1970s. Her Majesty's Theatre, City (1970); Fairfax Newsprint, Ultimo (1971); Woolworths, Liverpool (1972); Australian Chemical Refiners, Moorebank (1973); Warringah Mall (1973); Savoy Hotel, Kings Cross (1975); Strand Arcade, City (1976); Ultimo Wool Stores (1978); and Luna Park, North Sydney (1979). And who could forget the Granville train disaster (1977)?

The 1970s saw a continuation of the Brigades record of individual bravery. On 9 March 1971 SO Alfred John Robinson was presented with the NSW Fire Brigades Medal for Conspicuous Bravery. His citation read:

At 12.50 am on Sunday, 17 September 1970, the Liverpool Fire Brigade under the command of Station Officer Alfred John Robinson responded to a call of fire to a cottage alight at 29 McGirr Parade, Warwick Farm.

Upon arrival at the scene Station Officer Robinson was informed that two children were in the burning premises and he, without delay, secured a scaling ladder from the fire appliance, placed it against the wall of the cottage and broke a window of the front bedroom in order to gain entry. Mr Robinson entered the building through this window and in the process sustained severe lacerations to his left leg but this did not deter him and he found in the bedroom, which was heavily charged with hot smoke, a male child who was unconscious but still breathing. Station Officer Robinson passed the child through the window and then resumed his search for the other child.

At this point of time the whole of the cottage was heavily involved by fire, roofing tiles were collapsing into the main building but due to excessive heat and flame Station Officer Robinson could not pursue his endeavours to reach the rear of the premises where he believed the other child to be.

The Board of Fire Commissioners of New South Wales is of the opinion that the actions of Alfred John Robinson, a Station Officer of the New South Wales Fire Brigades, were in keeping with the highest traditions of the Fire Service and that such actions were beyond the normal call of his duties as a Fire Officer. In the circumstances as outlined above the Board believes he performed an act of exceptional courage and has accordingly awarded him the New South Wales Fire Brigades Medal for Conspicuous Bravery.

A FIRE STATION BURNS!
Hornsby

Not since the George Street West fire of 1901 had the Brigades suffered the embarrassment of a fire station fire. The year 1971 proved to have an even more dramatic fire in store. Opened in March 1925 Hornsby fire station was located on a bend in the busy Pacific Highway. Minutes before 5.00 pm on Tuesday, 5 January 1971, Control received a call from Hornsby's water tanker that a petrol tanker had overturned and the fire station was alight.

The first brigade on the scene, Gordon, found that the station was indeed well alight. A fully laden 6000-gallon (27 300 L) petrol tanker had overturned across the front of the engine bay. Petrol had gushed from the tanker into the station and ignited immediately. Added to this nightmare was a 300-yard (274.32 m) wall of flame along the blazing fuel which ran down the gutter of the main street, setting alight several shops and a service station.

Hornsby Brigade, thanks to their swift and dramatic eviction, already had two lines of hose at work from nearby hydrants and were operating hose reels from the Station's blocked-in water tanker. They had tried to get their Dennis Jaguar motor to work but were forced out by the quickly spreading flames. The Dennis was destroyed but the water tanker, parked in a lane next to the door, was saved.

Lucky escapes were the order of the day. The petrol tanker driver was pulled clear of the blazing wreckage unharmed. The fireman on Watchroom duty bounded out a side door only seconds before fire engulfed his office. Inspector Moss and his family, in residence upstairs, escaped with no time to save anything but their lives. Station Officer Brock, also in quarters above the Station, barely managed to get out one

The shell of Hornsby Fire Station with an overturned petrol tanker in the engine bay, 1971

jump ahead of the flames. Considering the speed and magnitude of the disaster, it is amazing that only one injury was reported—a civilian who cut his wrist while assisting the tanker driver to escape.

After the arrival of foam motors from Lane Cove and Drummoyne the situation was brought under control. However, Hornsby station was now just a gutted shell. Far more severe than the George Street West station fire of 1901, Sydney had for the first time completely lost a station to fire. Hornsby Brigade was housed temporarily in a vacant council factory and it was not until 1972 that the present Hornsby fire station was opened in Bridge Road.

HOT NEWS
John Fairfax & Sons Pyrmont Newsprint

In one of Sydney's largest ever blazes 34 000 rolls of newsprint, weighing 20 000 tons and valued at $4 million were destroyed on 7 February 1971. Within minutes of the first report of the alarm, the huge 134 000 square feet (12 449 m^2) warehouse, 45 feet (13.72 m) high, was completely ablaze, and within the following fifteen minutes the alarm had escalated to a 12-station response. Eventually the blaze was fought by eighteen motors, four turntable ladders, two fire boats, 21 officers and 70 firemen.

Fire floats Boray and Bennelong, eighteen motors and four turntables took nine hours to subdue this Fairfax Newsprint store blaze in 1971

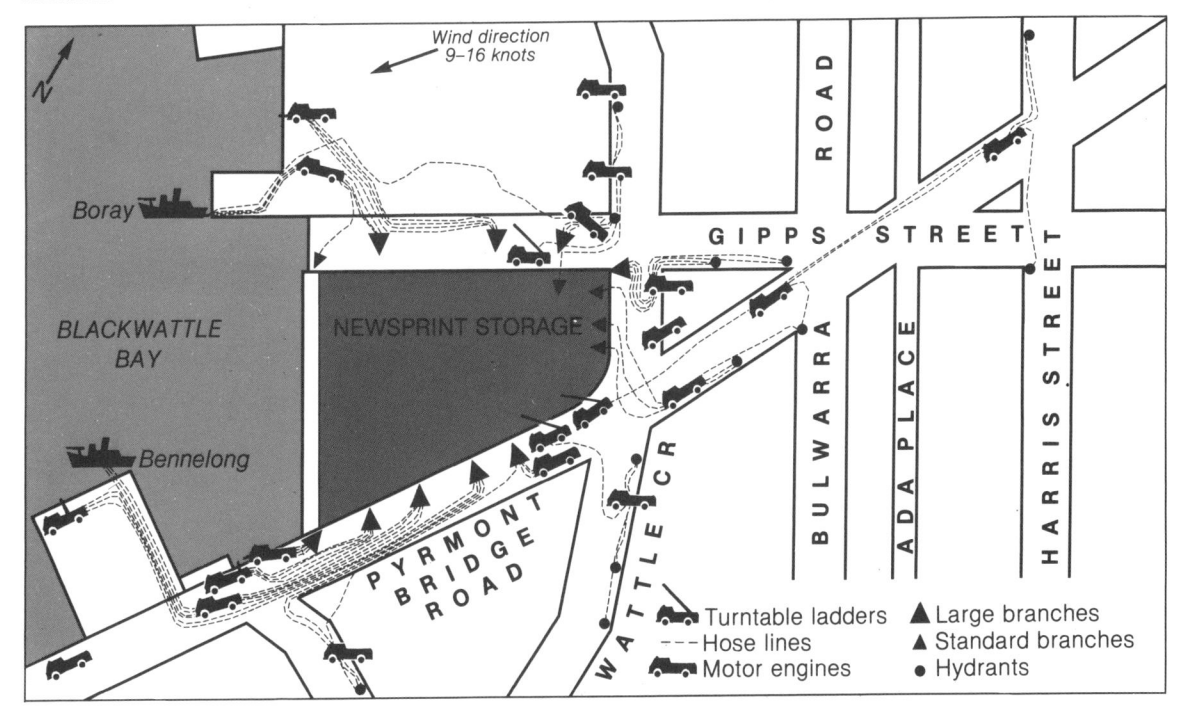

The rapid spread of the fire, attributed to layers of fine coal dust on the roof trusses and paper rolls, caused most of the northern wall [417 feet (127.1 m)] to collapse in the first fifteen minutes. Aided by a continuous supply of sea water from the firefloats *Boray* and *Bennelong*, water was pumped into the fire at a rate of 8500 gallons per minute (645 L/s).

It was exactly nine hours after the first call that a 'Stop' message was transmitted to control; and it was to be two weeks before fire duty at the scene was finally terminated.

A MULTIPLE BLAZE
Strand Arcade and 'Harpoon Harry's'

The greatest test of efficiency of any fire service is its ability to handle more than one blaze simultaneously. Sydney's test came on the morning of Wednesday, 26 May 1976. Two major fires were to break out within 400 metres and fifteen minutes of each other, in the heart of Sydney's central business district.

The first call at 3.23 am was to the historic Strand Arcade in George Street where one of the 'towers' was well alight. The narrow frontage, combined with the close abutment to the adjoining premises, made firefighting difficult. Crews from ten stations fought to contain the blaze to the Arcade, the fire by now having gripped the basement, ground and upper four floors of the George Street end of the Arcade.

At this point a further fire was observed, from the top of Headquarter's ladders. Only a few hundred metres down George Street 'Harpoon Harry's' restaurant, on the ground floor of a two and three floor building, was alight. Stanmore, on route to stand-by at Headquarters, was diverted by R/T and brigades from Balmain, Leichhardt, Crows Nest and Neutral Bay were despatched to the new threat. By 4.30 am both blazes were at their peak. When the glass roof of the Strand Arcade exploded, flames roared through, threatening the neighbouring Coles and Nicholson's Music Store. Only the quick action of firefighters in suppressing spot fires and the activation of internal sprinklers prevented further spread.

At 5.22 am a 'Stop' message was sent on the 'Harpoon Harry's' fire; at 5.36 am the fire in the Strand Arcade was contained. With both buildings badly gutted, the Brigades had again prevented a major conflagration. During the operations, normal 'back-up' procedures had been instituted with brigades from other districts brought in to protect the vacated station areas.

Today both buildings have been resurrected, and the Strand Arcade restored to its original 1891 appearance.

ULTIMO AGAIN
Two Blocks Destroyed

Only seven years after the Fairfax Newsprint fire, Ultimo was again the scene for another of Sydney's largest fires. At 3.15 am on Sunday 19 March 1978 Control received a '000' call that a large wool store was well alight. Less than one hour later fire fanned by wind gusts of up to 70 knots had completely devastated two blocks bounded by William Henry Street, Jones Street, Quarry Street and Bulwarra Road. Adjoining residences and warehouses were also extensively damaged by falling walls, fire and water.

Falling walls and the wind storm generated by a 20 knot southerly and the burning of highly inflammable plastics stored in the warehouses continually forced men and equipment to be redeployed. Men at the northern end of the fireground who took the full brunt of the radiated heat were forced to shield behind salvage sheets under a constant stream of water.

In all 26 brigades, 18 appliances, 36 officers and 103 firemen were deployed until the final 'Stop' message was issued by Chief Officer Fred Davies at 5.13 am.

MULTIPLE FATALITIES

Despite the far too frequent fire deaths in Sydney, until the mid-1970s the City had been relatively free of multiple fatality fires and other large-scale tragedies. The last eight years, however, have seen an unprecedented number of such disasters.

Early on the morning of Christmas Day 1975, Sydney's worst hotel fire occurred in the Savoy Private Hotel, Kings Cross. Fifteen of the sixty people on the premises at the time of the fire were to die from smoke inhalation and burns.

Built in 1925 under the provisions of the City of Sydney Improvement Act 1879, the Savoy had all the hallmarks of a fire disaster. Rather than acting as a means of escape the internal, non-fire isolated stairs acted as a flue, funnelling smoke and flames up the stairwells. Residents on

Two blocks of wool stores destroyed by fire in Ultimo 1978

the second and third floors had no avenue of escape. With no internal fire protection, they could do little but await rescue or death, whichever came first.

Over 30 people were rescued from the building by firemen from Darlinghurst and Headquarters under Inspector Stewart and DO Jacobson. Both turntable ladders and Snorkel were necessary to gain access to residents trapped in their smoke-filled second- and third-floor rooms.

Three months after the tragedy one of the occupants of the building at the time was convicted of arson and sentenced to fourteen years' imprisonment.

The worst train disaster in Australia's history occurred on 18 January 1977, when a Blue Mountains morning peak-hour commuter train crashed into an overhead road traffic bridge. The bridge broke in two and collapsed on to the train. Packed to capacity, 83 commuters were to die beneath the twisted wreckage.

Parramatta's Simonitor and Salvage, under DO Geoff Dudman, were the first emergency vehicles on the scene, with Senior Fireman A G Freeman the first under the giant concrete slab. With little thought for their own safety, Brigades personnel along with police, ambulance and other rescue workers set about the dangerous rescue task. With a lack of air and grave threat of explosion and fire, the rescuers were themselves at risk. Under the direction of Metropolitan Superintendent Neville O'Connel and later DCO J Moss, the full ambit of the Brigades' rescue gear was brought into use. Even the high expansion foam generator was utilised to extract stale air and propane gas, and allow an inflow of fresh air for victims and rescuers.

In all 26 Brigade members were awarded the Granville Rail Disaster Medal. On 1 November 1978, SO R K Ross, Senior Fireman A G Freeman and First-Class Fireman R G Carruthers were awarded the NSW Fire Brigades Medal for Conspicuous Bravery and in 1979 DO G Dudman

1 DEAD IN BED

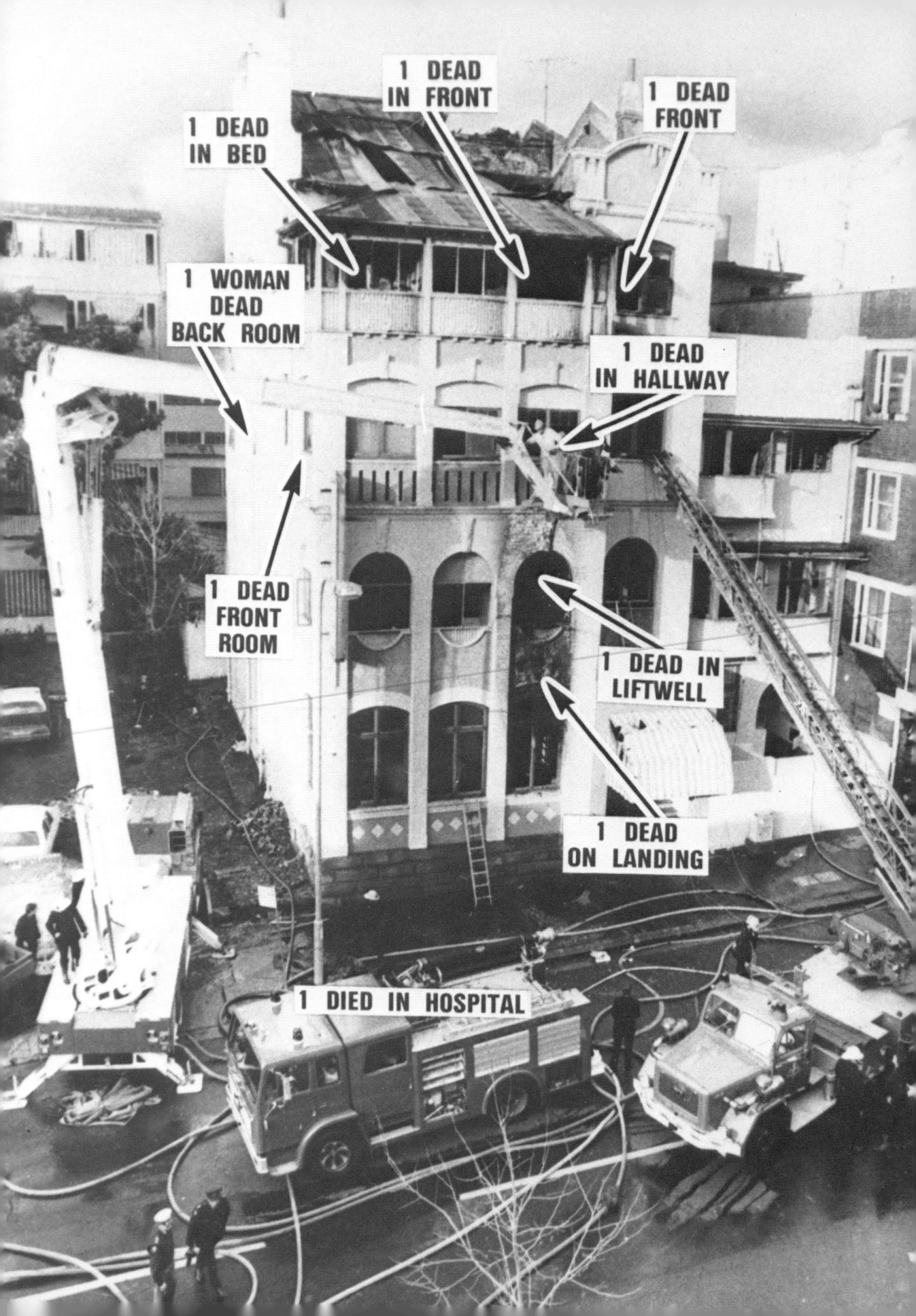

1 DEAD IN FRONT

1 DEAD FRONT

1 WOMAN DEAD BACK ROOM

1 DEAD IN HALLWAY

1 DEAD FRONT ROOM

1 DEAD IN LIFTWELL

1 DEAD ON LANDING

1 DIED IN HOSPITAL

was awarded the Queen's Fire Service Medal for leadership displayed at the train disaster.

Following the 'Ghost Train' fire at Luna Park in June 1979 in which seven died, two multiple fatality fires occurred in 1981. On 25 August nine people died in a fire at the Rembrandt Residential Apartments, Kings Cross. Senior Fireman Barry Garvin was later awarded the NSW Fire Brigades Medal for Conspicuous Bravery for his actions at the fire. His citation read in part:

> Reliant on breathing apparatus he risked his life by climbing from the cage of the Snorkel into the fourth level of the building and with difficulty assisted two people into the cage. Realising there was insufficient space in the cage to rescue another person trapped in the vicinity, he voluntarily gave up his position to remain in a room, which was becoming enveloped with fire, while the civilian was rescued.

Only months before, the highest death toll at a single fire in Sydney's history occurred at Sylvania Heights.

OUR MOST TRAGIC FIRE
Pacific Heights Nursing Home (Sylvania Heights)

Shortly before midnight on 29 April 1981, the single-storey Pacific Heights nursing home had 70 aged patients in residence, many bed-ridden. Later found to have been lit by one of the patients suffering senile dementia the fire spread rapidly from a linen closet to the ceiling. As the fire spread throughout the ceiling area, parts of the ceiling collapsed onto the sleeping patients. They were then overcome by the billowing smoke containing toxic gases from the polyurethane lining.

The first brigades on the scene, Miranda and Sutherland, were confronted with a situation of complete panic. Some civilians were removing patients from the unaffected eastern end of the building as others smashed windows in the smoke-logged front section. Without thought for their own safety and initially without breathing apparatus, firemen from both brigades (closely followed by Kogarah personnel) effected many rescues.

The combination of arson, deadly ceiling material, the time of occurrence and the frailness of the residents produced an horrific death toll within a matter of minutes. In all sixteen residents died in the blaze with another dying subsequently in hospital (although doubt remains as to the significance of the fire in this fatality).

In 1982 Sydney Fire Brigades attended a record 52 857 calls—29 180 fires/other emergencies and 23 677 false alarms. Whilst the busiest brigade remains Headquarters (over 1000 calls per annum in the Central City area), alarm rates on Sydney's fringe exemplify Sydney's remarkable post-war suburbanisation. Brigades such as Mt Druitt, Blacktown, Liverpool, Bankstown, Fairfield and Hornsby all have alarm rates exceeding 500 per annum and are now busier than many of their older, inner-area counterparts. The changing distribution of fire risk within Sydney *vis-à-vis* the age of many Sydney fire stations, raises important questions concerning station location, manning and equipment deployment (see Chapters 4, 5 and 9).

Whilst Sydney has thankfully lacked such devastating conflagrations as the Great Chicago Fire of 1871 and the San Francisco Fires of 1906, the examples illustrated show that Sydney has had its share of tragedy and property loss. During the span of one hundred years Brigade firefighters have daily risked their lives to save others. Individual acts of heroism abound—the examples cited merely serve as testimony to a 'Century of Service'.

Vehicles in attendance at the Pacific Heights Nursing Home fire, 1981. Sixteen residents died during this fire — the highest death toll from a single fire in Sydney's history

Fireman Barry Garvin earnt a Conspicuous Bravery Medal whilst working from the Snorkel cage (centre) during the Rembrandt Apartments' fire 1981 (left)

A.D. 1887
THIS FIRE STATION
was Erected by the Government for the Fire Br[igade]

CHARLES BOWN E*sq*   CHAIRMAN
MORDAUNT W. S. CLARKE E*sq* M.A.   VICE-C[HAIRMAN]
WALTER CHURCH E*sq* J.P.   SAM*l* E LEES E*sq*
RICHARD M*c* COY E*sq* J.P.   EDWARD J LO[...]

Superintendent of Fire Brigades
M*r* WILLIAM DOUGLAS BEAR

Colonial Architect
JAMES BARNET E*sq*   B[UILDER]
               JOH[N...]

9

A MILLION DOLLAR SERVICE

The Fire Service Today

THE MOST STRIKING FEATURE OF BOTH Sydney fire services and the institution responsible for fire service provision, the Board of Fire Commissioners of NSW, is their sheer scale. From modest beginnings in 1884 with one permanently manned station and twenty volunteer companies, Sydney's fire services now embrace 73 brigades with another twelve in outlying areas of the Sydney Basin. Expenditure on Sydney five services has grown from $36 000 to over $70 million and the number of firefighters from under 200 to almost 2000.

As a single authority, the Board of Fire Commissioners is the largest centrally administered fire service in the western world. With an annual State-wide budget now in excess of $100

New and old—Headquarters' engine bay 1984 with the marble opening tableau (despite the year shown, Headquarters was not occupied until 1888)

million the Board administers 318 brigades throughout NSW, has a full-time staff of 2414 (2234 firefighters and 259 administrative/technical services staff) and a volunteer firefighting force of 2981. Assets in property and equipment are in excess of $50 million. By way of contrast the Metropolitan Fire Brigades Board, Melbourne, administers only 48 brigades on a budget of $65 million.

A CENTURY OF SERVICE
Major Developments (1884–1984)

The growth in size of the NSWFB has been accompanied by major transformations within the service. Many mirror technological and societal changes in general whilst others are peculiar to the organisation itself.

Apart from the formation of a State-wide service in 1909, the institutional structure has been remarkably unchanged. Changes in the Act, constitution of the Board and funding have all been relatively minor modifications of a nineteenth-century institutional structure. Along with similar bodies, such as the MWSDB, the statutory authority constitution of the fire service has been remarkably resilient to change. As discussed later in this chapter it is doubtful if this structure has ever been under as much pressure for change as it is today.

In the area of fire prevention major changes have occurred over the past 100 years, despite strong resistance both within and outside the fire service against an expansion in the statutory fire prevention powers of the Board. Sophisticated thermal and sprinkler systems have been developed from earlier models, although the basic principles remain similar to those on which earlier models were designed (Marryatt, 1971). It is in the area of building codes, building design and construction standards that the most dramatic improvements in fire safety are noticeable. Since the appointment of Superintendent Bear as Kerosene Inspector and particularly since the late 1960s, the Board's Fire Prevention officers have been at the forefront of improvements in legislative regulations on fire safety.

Fire prevention is perhaps the most underrated Brigades' activity. Despite the wording of the Act: 'it shall be the duty of the board to take all practicable measures for preventing ... fires', fire prevention has played 'second fiddle' to fire extinguishing. The growing expertise of Brigades' staff in fire safety codes needs to be accelerated by special courses and specialist advice. The planned amalgamation of the Interim Fire Protection Code and Ordinance 70 creates an opportunity for the Fire Prevention Section to exert a prominent influence on the new legislation. The need for further legislation in such high risk areas as high rise buildings, hospitals and the transport of inflammable products requires new expertise and skills. If the Brigades are to be at the forefront of the new legislation and codes, fire prevention activities must be given an expanded and deserved status within the organisation.

Whilst many of today's operational fire stations were built in the station construction boom years of 1895–1927, their internal layout

Large warehouses (right) and skyscapers in narrow city streets (above) provide a major hazard to today's firefighters

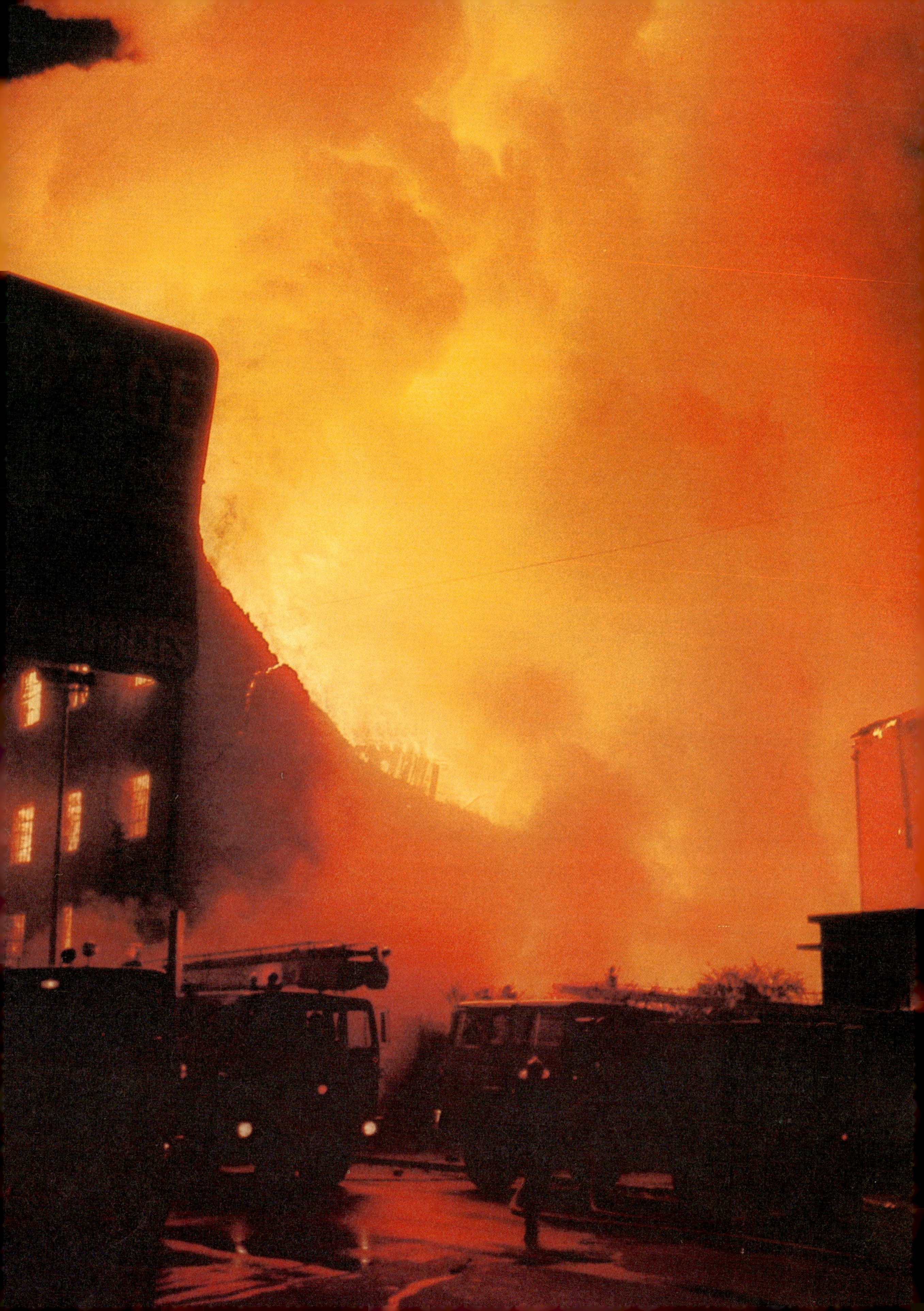

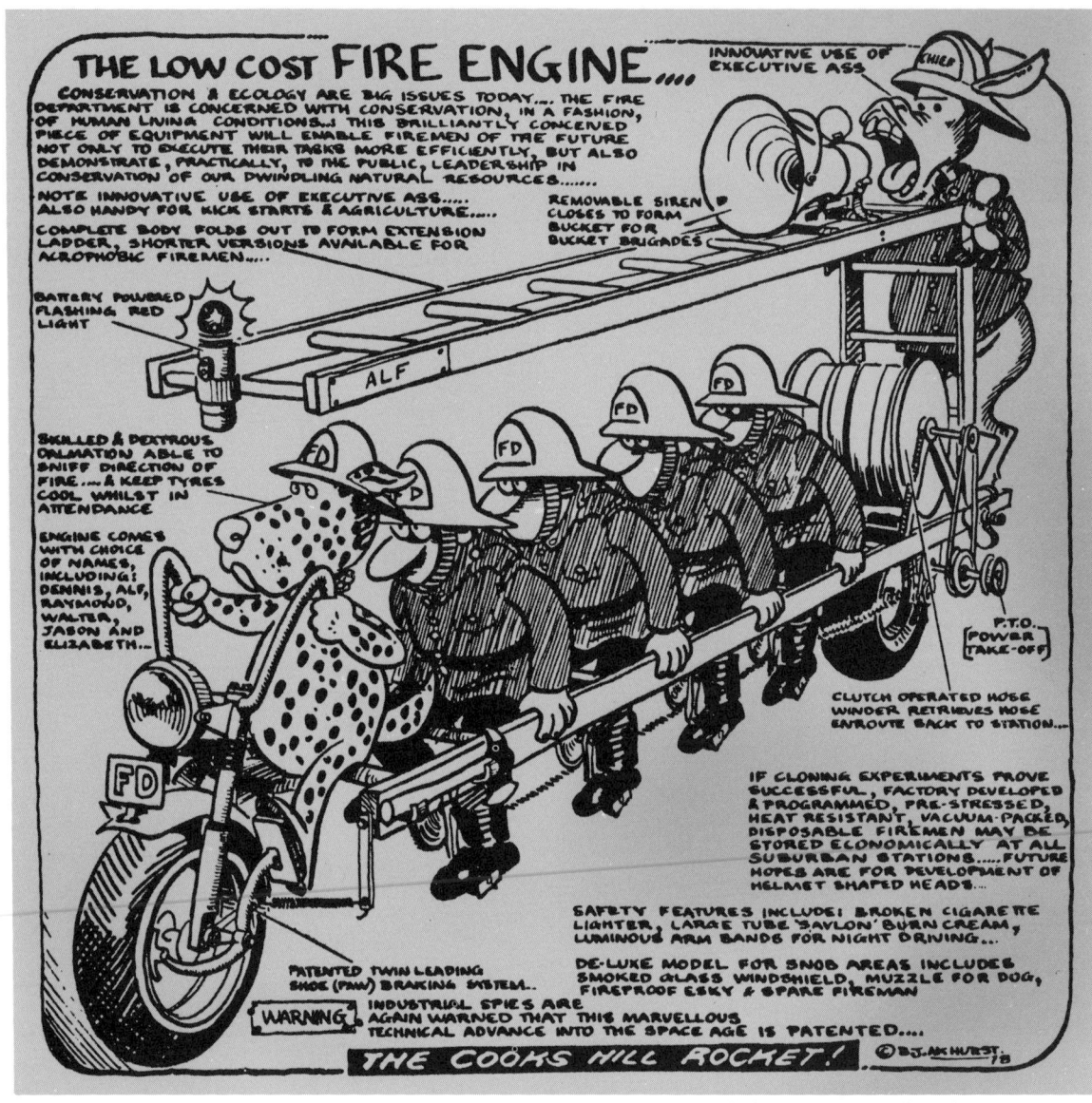

Firemen have never been backward in expressing their views on outmoded equipment and inadequate working conditions. The Board response has changed markedly for the better in recent years

has been dramatically altered. Gone are the large quarters and officer accommodation, stables, billiard rooms and fodder bins and in their stead are recreation rooms, change rooms and mess facilities. In many cases these changes have been slow to come about, cost economies and other priorities taking precedence. Today the Board is in the invidious position of having a number of 'key' stations on prime real estate which cannot be sold for redevelopment due to Heritage restrictions. At the same time the stations are unsuitable for housing modern fire appliances. In a large number of cases these stations are also no longer in the optimal location relative to the changed distribution of fire risk within Sydney.

The slowness of improvements in station housing, particularly as they affect the men who spend a significant part of their life within them, reflects the general trend of firemen's working conditions. Improvements in facilities, uniforms, pay, working hours and general conditions have all been 'hard won'. In very few cases, with the notable exception of the Weston era, have improvements in working conditions been initiated without resort to arbitration. Almost all have been gained from union submissions, delegations or strike action. In most cases the fire service has followed initiatives made in other

Volunteer Demonstrations (right) retain much of the camaraderie and their share of personalities — characteristics of the Brigades in earlier years (above)

sectors of the workforce, rather than being a leader in its own right.

Despite volunteer (since 1884) and permanent staff (since 1927) representation on the Board, the Board has principally seen its role as providing fire protection at minimal cost. Justifiable increases in expenditure have been seen by respective Boards in direct firefighting terms—equipment. It is perhaps somewhat ironic that despite this perception by the funding groups, expenditure on new stations and equipment has frequently been constrained because of wage gains (and staff increases) forced by union action. In the immediate post-war years and in the early 1970s the conflict between 'Board interests' and 'union interests' over the levels of expenditure were such that morale within the service was adversely affected.

Whilst many of the improvements in working conditions, such as shorter working hours, pay increases and leave entitlements, have postdated similar changes in the community as a whole, they have been no less significant. The 1884 continuous live-in system with six hours' leave once every ten days and a pension determined by the Board stands in stark contrast to the 1984, 42-hour working week, four weeks' annual leave and obligatory superannuation. Conditions today are certainly less harsh than in earlier decades, although it is perhaps food-for-thought that most 'old-timers' complain that something has been lost from the job. They argue the 'characters' have disappeared, along with their humour and seat-of-pants firefighting skills. The 'rough diamonds', 'smoke-chewers', and 'old sailors' are a thing of the past. So too are many of the fire brigade families—born and bred on fire stations with an affinity to both the fire service and the local communities of which they were a part.

Despite the changes many of the basic firefighting skills (and terminology) have remained the same. On the fireground in particular it is still the same attributes of speed, teamwork, courage and discipline which are required. Firemen are still required to run out hose, fix the standpipe, man the branches and perform rescues in the face of roaring flames and personal danger. Where the 1884 fireman would not recognise his 1984 counterpart (and vice versa) is in much of his equipment. No longer are appliances horse-drawn nor water pumped manually or by steam. Gone are the neddies, coffee pots, coachmen, boilermakers and farriers. Motorisation of fire appliances in the early years of this century dramatically altered two fundamental components of efficiency: response time and 'putting water on the fire'. The improvements in both cases have allowed the Brigades to surround and contain the largest conflagrations in minimal time and with maximum fire power. As a result Sydney has been relatively fortunate in the absence of widespread fire devastation (as it has from other disasters).

The impact of changing technology on the fire service has not been restricted to the fireground. Fire prevention has already been mentioned; on the administrative and technical services side dramatic changes have also taken place. Computerisation offers the Brigades a new era of data management; the opportunities in personnel records, accounting, inventory control, planning, fire report statistics—not to mention the computerised control system—are endless. Adapting to the new possibilities requires progressive and imaginative management.

The technical services branches—traditionally called the Workshops—have probably seen more dramatic changes than any other general

All-terrain vehicle acquired by the Brigades in 1983 for service in the Mt Kosciusko snowfields

A Million Dollar Service / 229

area of the fire service. The integration of new technology has had a high in-house component for cost-saving reasons. From appliance design and construction to station design and construction, Brigades' technical staff have supplied far more than a secondary support role. Throughout much of the Brigades' history they have provided everything from hose, salvage sheets, sirens, uniforms and furniture to motor parts. The degree of self-sufficiency achieved, particularly during the First World War and Depression, is a credit to the resourcefulness and ingenuity of the support staff during these 'shoe-string' budget eras. The new Chullora Workshops complex reflects a new era of modernisation within the NSWFB and the continuation of the contribution of the workshops' staff to the Brigades' operations.

The new Command Vehicle (top) and the Alexandria Control Centre (above) typify the dramatic improvement in Brigade communications in recent years

WHO RUNS THE SERVICE?
Recurring Issues

Despite the many notable changes in the nature and character of Sydney fire services the Board has been faced with many long-standing issues, none-the-least of which is its own future. Under ministerial control and direction since 1977 the Board (and its President) has lost much of the autonomy and power which characterised its existence in earlier decades. Today it is hard to conceive of Board President personalities with the political influence of Charles Bown and T J Smith.

Ministerial control in theory denotes leadership; however, in the words of retiring President Bill Weston, 'to date we have received a lot of control ... but very little direction' (*Fire News*, July 1983:16). Whilst many would argue that political control of such large public institutions as the Board of Fire Commissioners is necessary, the danger remains that the institution becomes a 'puppet' in the wider political context.

Despite the dangers of political control there is an increasing realisation that the current constitution and funding of the Board needs review. Since the first Brigades Bill was presented to Parliament in 1854, debate over the constitution of the Board has been unresolved. Despite the findings of Justice Street in 1968 that Board members should be above self-interest, the reality is that Board membership has been seen by 'interested' parties as a means to exert influence over the direction and level of expenditure of the Fire Brigades. As such the interested parties—fire insurance companies, local government, State government, volunteer firemen and permanent firemen—have lobbied strongly against/for changes to the Fire Brigades Act. In particular the groups have been most vocal when issues concerning Board representation and proportionate contributions have arisen. As the parliamentary debates outlined in Chapter 2 indicate, it is the link between contributions and Board representation which is central to the issue. Whilst the Board continues to be funded by insurance companies, local government and State government, it is clearly in each group's interest to 'maximise' its representation and influence on the level and direction of the Brigades' expenditure.

This is not the appropriate place to find the 'answers' to the questions of representation and funding; suffice to say that whilst the interlocking questions of funding and Board constitution have no 'optimum' solution, the present system is anachronistic. It is incongruous that a $100 million service should be administered by a part-time Board (with the exception of the President). The scale, complexity and financial requirements of the NSW Fire Service today are such that modern management and administrative skills necessarily require full-time members. At the same time the public nature of the service requires an emphasis on public input and public accountability. With the possible exception of the 1977 Committee of Inquiry, only very limited reviews of the Brigades procedures, planning and efficiency have been conducted.

The issues of funding and Board representation are not the only issues which have continued to surface over the past 100 years. Five other issues stand out:

(a) the powers of the Chief Officer (or his representative);
(b) links with other emergency services, in particular bush fire brigades;
(c) the areal extent of the Brigades' authority: the powers and responsibilities of the Brigades on Harbour waters and outside designated Fire Districts remains unclear;
(d) the tenuous and conflict-prone relationship between the Board (which traditionally has been dominated by 'funding' groups) and the Fire Brigade Employees' Union; and
(e) the role and powers of the Brigades in an unsung area of its responsibility—fire prevention.

Since the demise of Superintendent Douglas Bear in 1898 the Brigades' operational head has been appointed by the Government but is subject to the direction of the Board. Successive Presidents have ensured that the Chief Officer is in no doubt as to who controls the fire service. The growing size and complexity of the Brigades, the full-time devotion of his time to administration, his years of experience and the modern trend to relatively short-term 'outside' appointments to both Board and senior administrative positions would suggest that the Chief Officer (and his Deputies) will play an increasingly prominent role in the overall operation of the fire service. The Chief's attendance at Board meetings, and his experience

Off-road water tankers, deployed on Sydney fringes in an effort to combat an increasing bushfire threat

and status on key committees are indicative of this trend. This is not peculiar to the NSW fire service—indeed, South Australia has 'solved' the question of Board representation by appointing a fire officer as its Commissioner.

The question of rationalising emergency services and in particular, bringing bush fire and urban fire services under one central administration is currently under review by the Minister for Police and Emergency Services, Mr Peter Anderson. Serious bush fires in both Victoria and NSW in recent years, in which some twenty volunteer bush firefighters lost their lives, have again raised issues concerning their leadership, training, lack of equipment and administration. Continued disputation between Board brigades and council-operated bush fire units on the fringes of Sydney and elsewhere do little to encourage community confidence. In a similar vein, inter-organisational conflicts abound in the area of rescue operations.

Whilst the NSWFB have had an officially-authorised rescue role in non-fire situations since 1979 the realities are that its rescue capabilities are under-utilised because of inter-service jealousies. With police and ambulance services also having an authorised rescue role and each service vying for more funds and authority, there is an urgent need for direction, coordination and commonsense.

As early as 1884 Sydney fire authorities sought amendments to the Fire Brigades Act for powers to establish a joint 'land–marine' fire station and to control firefighting operations on Harbour waters. To the present day they have been unsuccessful (Sydney's fire floats remain under the jurisdiction of the Maritime Services Board). As with the questions of rescue jurisdiction and bush firefighting operations, successive governments have failed to resolve the issue, preferring to retain the status quo. The result is that Sydney Harbour—one of the largest in the world—with a yearly throughput of over 30 million tonnes and 3000 vessels, remains protected by a "part-time" firefighting force dependent on the NSWFB for its training and 'back-up'.

Since the formation of the NSW Fire Brigade Employees' Union in 1911 disputation has characterised relations between the union and the Board. There is little doubt that the dramatic improvements in the working conditions of firemen since 1911 have principally been the result of union action. In almost all cases the Board has religiously fought against worker improvements in the form of pay increases, shorter working hours, new uniforms and recreational activities. The opposition has continued in many cases (for example, the 40-hour week) long after a general acceptance of the improvement throughout the community as a whole. The reactionary role of the Board appears directly related to the prominence of funding groups in its constitution and the challenge which the union represents to the Board's statutory authority to set the terms, duties and working conditions of its employees. This has been particularly the case in the 'personal' confrontations between Board Presidents and union leaders. It is perhaps in this area, more than any other, where the Presidency of Bill Weston stands out. For perhaps the first time in the Board's history the focus has been on a positive attempt at conciliatory negotiation. With a change in the Board's attitude from cost cutting to increased expenditure on improvements in equipment, station living, training and Brigades activities, has come an increase in morale and pride in the service. Whilst disputation remains in certain areas (for example, promotion out-of-seniority) relations between the union and the Board are at their most constructive point since the formation of the BFC in 1910.

DEBATE AND CHANGE
Issues of the Day

In addition to those issues which have continued to be raised throughout the past 100 years, others of a more recent vintage are also being debated.

The 1980s has seen a sharp rise in the incidence of arson. There are some 100 school fires each year in the Sydney area alone. Current estimates suggest that the loss from arson is in excess of $200 million per year and perhaps as high as $800 million. Arson falls broadly into three categories: arson for profit (insurance fraud); arson to conceal some crime; and arson committed by vandals. During the economic recession of recent years, financial pressures on firms and individuals have seen a rash of suspected

A booby-trapped bookshop in Albury 1982—detonated by the Army—after firemen had a miraculous escape from death. Just one of the dangers faced daily by the State's firefighters

arson. Similarly, incidents of fires caused by vandals (most notably car fire-bombing) have also increased dramatically in number and severity. Plans for a Fire Investigation Team to support the Police Arson Squad are under review; however, the whole question of arson prevention and statistics needs investigation. At present no accurate figures on arson loss, types of arson, methods of arson nor culprits, are kept.

The second major 'issue of the day' is the question of equal employment opportunities. In his Review of NSW Government Administration Peter Wilenski commented:

> By-law 52 under the Fire Brigades Act requires that: 'An applicant shall be physically and mentally fit for employment as a fireman ... He shall be at least 168 centimetres in height, 915 millimetres natural chest measurement, and not under 18 years of age nor over 35 years of age. (Review of NSW Government Administration, 1977:109)

In November 1981 the legislation was repealed, setting the stage for the first intake of female firefighters into the NSWFB. Other obstacles to the total acceptance of women within the service still remain. However, the success of the Board's first female Deputy President in 'passing' the physical entrance test would suggest that female firefighters will feature in the protection of Sydney from fire in the NSWFB's second century.

The other major issue which requires comment is the question of management within the Brigades. The size and complexity of the NSWFB today is a far cry from that of the MFB in 1884 or the NSWFB in 1910. All three sections, fire fighting, technical services and administration have expanded. The requirements of senior officers and 'middle' management within these areas have similarly increased. In the past their duties have been strictly defined and supervised by superiors. As a statutory institution the Board has been loath to delegate authority and power, with most day-to-day decisions still requiring approval from the Board or one or two senior officers.

Current initiatives suggest that the second century of the Brigades will be markedly different. Within all sections of the service is the likelihood that far more decision-making will be delegated, to maximise the input of progressive

A humorous view of female firefighters joining the Fire Brigades

members of the service and to reduce pressures at the top. To facilitate the changes the present Board is looking at a variety of management courses, task forces, and committees, with many already in operation. As with any major organisational restructuring, resistance and conflict (for example, the issue of promotion out-of-seniority) arise. However, the success of the new management style lies in constructive collaboration among all members (and sections) of the service. It also requires direction, guidance and understanding from the Minister and the current Board, Chief Officer and Secretary, that is, from the traditional sources of power.

Whilst the Sydney fire brigades have had their share of conflict and controversy one should not lose sight of their contribution to the citizens of Sydney. For one hundred years firefighters have risked their lives to save the lives of others and to protect property. The fact that their bravery and dedication is taken for granted by the community belies the true significance of their role. It has truly been 'A Century of Service'—a period of service of which firefighters can be proud and Sydney's citizens thankful.

NOTES

Chapter 1
1. Whilst referred to as an engine it was most likely a small portable squirt.
2. These were called the 'Ordinance Engines'. The Barracks were behind today's Wynyard station.
3. Located on the site of the present Sydney Town Hall.
4. With Bown on the higher salary presumably, as he was an engine-maker.
5. Located between Central Lane and Wilmot Street.
6. The fire plugs were made of hardwood timber, 3 inches × 2¾ inches (76.2 × 69.85 mm) and were hammered by mallet into designed openings in the cast iron piping.
7. The title of this chapter, 'We Strive to Save', was the motto of the Victoria Volunteer Fire Company (No 1).
8. In 1871 Sydney city had a population of 74 400 with an additional 63 210 in the suburbs. Ten years later, 124 800 lived in the suburbs with 100 150 living in Sydney proper (Kelly and Crocker, 1978:31).
9. The 'Long Boom' refers to the sustained period of economic and urban growth from 1860 to 1890.

Chapter 2
1. McNamara had been sacked for refusing to be transferred from Vaulcuse to Auburn (having just purchased a residence near Vaucluse Fire Station).
2. The rationale was that despite a decrease from 25 to 12.5 per cent in their proportional share, section (2) allowed for an increasing rate of tax on UCV. With an increasing aggregate cost of fire brigade operations they could, in fact, be paying more.

Chapter 3
1. Webb appears to have been called on for all manner of duties. In 1900 he was approached by the Board of Public Health to supervise the cleansing of quarantined areas during the bubonic plague.
2. Designed by the firm of Spain, Cosh and Minnett and built by Robert Wall and Sons, the building has only recently been restored.
3. A former member of the MFB Board, Alderman Lindsay Thompson, an architect, had just returned from a tour of America.
4. In those days radios were banned from the track and many bookmakers took bets on interstate races for a number of minutes after they were actually run.
5. In contrast, citizens at station accounted for 756 and street alarms for 638 of the 6343 calls in 1939.
6. The representatives were: Chief Secretary's Department, Public Works Department, Department of Local Government, City Surveyor, Director of Civil Defence, traffic expert nominated by the Minister, Local Government Association, Board of Fire Commissioners, Royal Australian Institute of Architects, Institute of Engineers, Royal Australian Planning Institute.

Chapter 4
1. The site in 1884 contained cottages and Riley and Sons Upholsterers at the rear and, on Castlereagh Street, the Protestant Standard Office and the Royal Standard Hotel.
2. The Headquarters plaque lists the year of opening as 1887. The discrepancy occurs at a number of stations, where the opening plaque and/or a facade date differs from other official records (Appendix 4.1).
3. And has remained so to the present day with the Fire Brigades Act still not covering the 'Harbour', and fire floats still operated by the Maritime Services Board. Debate still continues concerning the establishment of a land-marine fire station.
4. In 1901 the volunteers disbanded to be replaced by seven permanent firemen and Balmain became No 12 on the MFB station list.
5. Dods replaced Minnett in the firm in 1914.
6. Spain and Cosh after the death of Dods in 1920.
7. G T Broadhurst was originally Captain of the Waverley Volunteer brigade (1890–1909) and joined the Brigades as Clerk of Works in 1909. His son Christopher J Broadhurst, joined as an auxiliary in August 1902 and rose to the position of Head Electrician, retiring in 1949. In turn his son, Arthur Broadhurst, joined in 1930, rose to be Head Mechanic, and retired in 1973. An enviable record of 83 years service to the Sydney Fire Brigades!
8. Many of the fine-line colour plans of the McNiven era were drawn by Fred Ross.
9. In fairness to the Board it should be pointed out that even the authority responsible for Sydney's planning, the Cumberland County Council had little realisation of the size of Sydney's growth. The 1954 Census showed that the rate of population growth in the County was about twice that forecast in 1948 (Harrison, 1972:74).
10. Again in fairness to the Board it should be pointed out that over the same period the AAV of the Sydney FD increased by only 120 per cent. The problem was not simply a lack of funds but more so the wage bill, which now absorbed almost 80 per cent of the Board's expenditure (and still does).
11. Architect Fred Ross retired in 1959.
12. The only higher call rates were: Headquarters (1355), The Rocks (1089), Darlinghurst (941), Crows Nest (862), Liverpool (764).
13. Followed by Penrith (9781) and Blacktown (8654).
14. Operating as John Roberts and Associates (1958–1971), John W Roberts and S A Baggs (1971–1977), Roberts and Hall (1977–).
15. The name of Vincent should be mentioned here. In 1981 Jack Vincent retired as Building Maintenance Officer after 44 years of service. His father had retired in 1957 after 32 years' service, reaching the position of Foreman Carpenter. Jack's son Alf who joined in 1964, is the Board's instrument maker.

16 Kurnell peninsula and its extensive industrial development remains to the present, outside the Board's fire districts and is protected by Kurnell bush fire brigade and a private industrial brigade.

Chapter 5

1 Including Henry Salter, who in March 1885 was appointed Superintendent of Fire Brigades, Adelaide, but died of typhoid fever in 1888. He was replaced as Superintendent by another Englishman, George A Booker, who had also been in the initial intake of MFB firemen and was to serve Adelaide as fire chief for some twenty years (Page and Bryant, 1983:170).
2 For more details of the Whaler Days see Giles, S, *Fire News*, 9(3), 1959:10–11.
3 Including Thomas Cutts (Acting District Officer) of St George District (Bexley, Hurstville, Kogarah, Rockdale, and part of Canterbury) created in 1909 with Kogarah the District Station.
4 Two at the Registrar-General's Office and two on Public Building Inspection.
5 At the end of 1983 there were still three: Rhodes, Mortdale and Merrylands.
6 Although the increase of 179 authorised positions in 1983 and a record intake of probationary firemen may, in the long term, prove of equal significance.
7 Another unusual death was that of First-Class Fireman Nicholas George Travers who died when he fell down the pole-hole at Circular Quay Fire Station, whilst sleep-walking, on 29 October 1922.
8 The Fire Brigade Employees Union of New South Wales adopted this new title in 1924.
9 It should be noted, however, that the rest of the community was now working a 44-hour week.
10 The youths were J F Ford, Jack K Mundey, Brian Smith, J Morris (son of SO Morris killed in 1926), Jim Ryng and George Eadie.
11 The 'Demonstration' consists of a series of events, covering a range of mock firefighting operations, in which teams of volunteer brigades throughout the State compete.
12 In fact it was a State government directive to all government agencies that sport be promoted to keep up morale during the Depression.
13 Who was also Professor of Trumpet at the Sydney Conservatorium. He took over as Bandmaster in 1922 following the death of the Brigades' first Bandmaster, Devlin, in 1920. Bandmaster J Pheloung was to serve in the position for 36 years.
14 In 1949 officers above the rank of Station Officer (led by later Chief Officer Charles Milledge) formed a union under the name of the New South Wales Fire Brigade Senior Officers Association.
15 'A' Division included the Fire Districts of Sydney, Avalon, Cronulla, Sutherland, Cabramatta and Liverpool.

Chapter 6

1 Much of this story comes from an article in *Fire News*, 5(4) 1983 by Ken Magor.
2 Constructed in the Board workshops on a Ford V8 truck chassis.

3 The Mack Type 75 pumpers were powered by 6 cylinder ohv petrol engines and fitted with 750 gpm pumps.

Chapter 7

1 Throughout the text pumping rates are given in gallons per minute (gpm) The metric (litres per second, L/s) equivalents are:

350 gpm = 26 L/s
450 gpm = 34 L/s
500 gpm = 38 L/s
600 gpm = 46 L/s
650 gpm = 57 L/s
1000 gpm = 76 L/s
1200 gpm = 91 L/s

2 This steamer is currently housed in the NSW Fire Service Museum.
3 This was the same William Vial who was originally a member of No 2 Volunteer Company and who saved the life of Prince Alfred in 1868 (Chapter 1).
4 The positions were officially introduced in 1904, although both Smith and Stoneham were in charge of the work at least four years earlier.
5 The Salvage motor was operated by a Salvage Corps of an officer and four men. This Corps operated from Headquarters as a separate organisation maintained at the sole expense of the insurance companies.
6 Steamers at Headquarters and a few of the larger stations were constantly supplied by 5-10lbs pressure (34.45–68.90 kPa) from a purpose-built heater.
7 The first of the converted manuals was installed at Kogarah (No 21).
8 These appliances travelled under their own power whereas the converted manuals still relied on horse traction.
9 The No 1 Halley (with the original Shand, Mason ladders) was installed at Circular Quay, No 2 ladders (the 'Bown') at Headquarters and No 3 ladders [70-foot (21.34 m) Shand, Mason ladders] at George Street West.
10 London Fire Chief from 1823 to 1861, James Braidwood revolutionised firefighting techniques and equipment until his death at the Tooley Street (London) fire.
11 And remain so to the present day under the Maritime Services Board.
12 These were the original Shand, Mason ladders acquired in 1893 and remounted in 1912.
13 Presented to the Museum of Applied Arts and Sciences in 1962 and subsequently acquired by the Fire Service Museum.
14 The ladder sections of this set were reconstructed in 1950–51 following their collapse.
15 Unfortunately this situation stills exists in the case of a number of brigades today.

Chapter 8

1 This includes the first six months of 1884 when the Brigades were still operated by the head of the Insurance Brigades, Charles Bown.

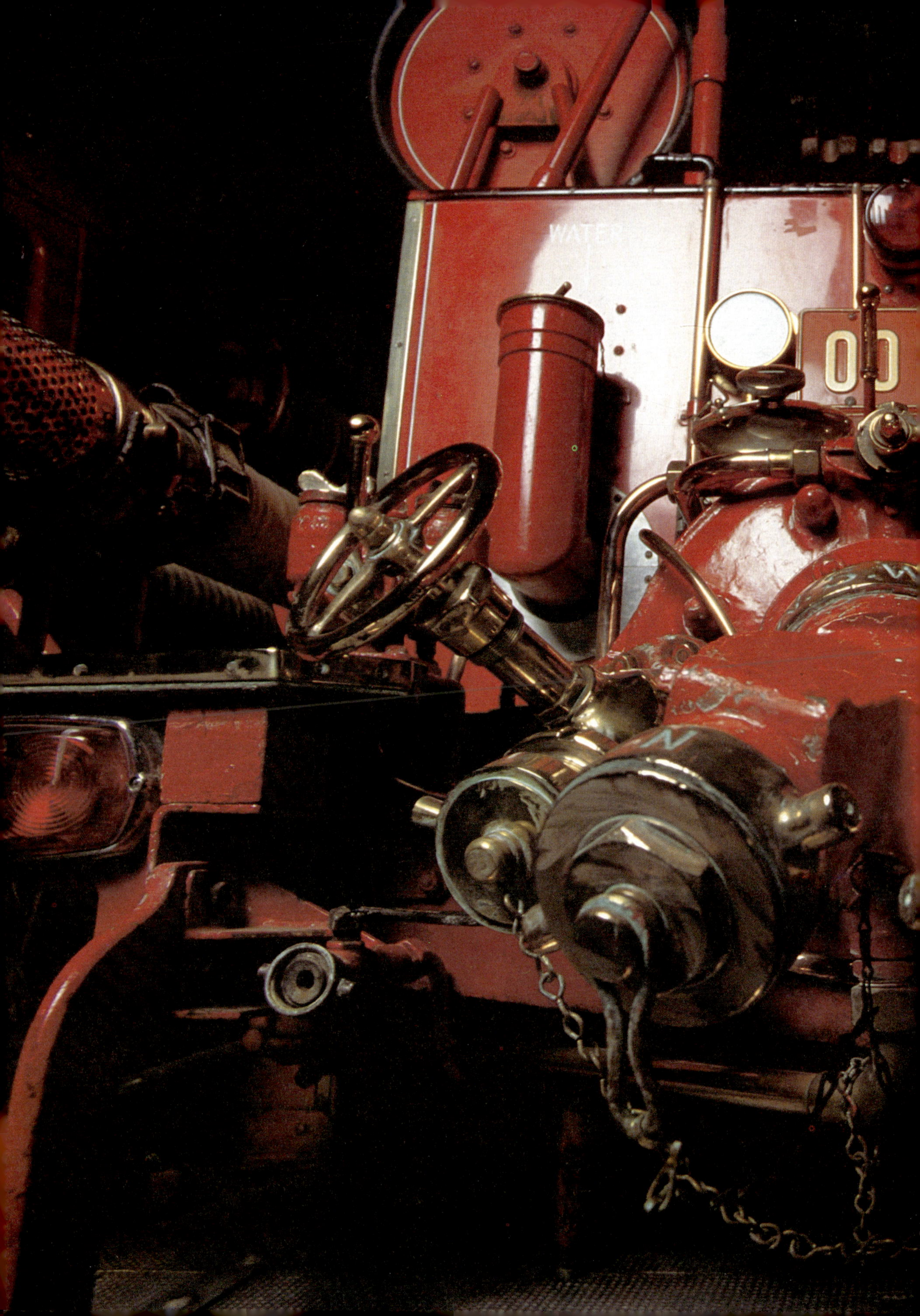
WATER
00

APPENDICES

APPENDIX 2.1
A Summary of Major Amendments to the Fire Brigades Act 238

APPENDIX 2.2
Metropolitan Fire Brigades and the Board of Fire Commissioners: Board Members, 1884—1984 238

APPENDIX 2.3
Presidents and Secretaries, 1884–1984 241

APPENDIX 2.4
Revenue and Expenditure 242

APPENDIX 4.1
Sydney Fire Brigades 244

APPENDIX 5.1
Chief Officers and Deputy Chief Officers 259

APPENDIX 5.2
Officers and Firemen Killed on Duty: Sydney Fire District 259

APPENDIX 5.3
Sydney Fire District: Number of Firefighters 261

APPENDIX 5.4
Recipients of the NSW Fire Brigades Medal for Conspicuous Bravery 262

APPENDIX 6.1
Reserves and Auxiliary Reserves (Second World War) 262

APPENDIX 7.1
Insurance Companies' Fire Brigade Plant (1883) 263

APPENDIX 8.1
Fire Statistics, Sydney Fire District 263

APPENDIX 8.2
Major Causes of Fire, Sydney Fire District 264

Rear view of Dennis Big 4 with multiple deliveries from a 650 gpm centrifugal pump

APPENDIX 2.1

A Summary of Major Amendments to the Fire Brigades Act

1884, 24 January (Act 47 Vic, No 3): Creation of Metropolitan Fire Brigades Board
1884, 4 July: Fire Brigades Board regulations passed
1885, 1 December: Fire Brigades Board further regulations
1902, 15 September: 1884 Act superseded by Fire Brigades Act, 1902 (Act No 80). Consolidation only, no major changes
1909, 1 December: 1902 Act suspeseded by Fire Brigades Act, 1909. Creation of the Board of Fire Commissioners of New South Wales
1910, 27 August: Fire Brigades Amendment Act, 1910 (Act No 15)
1919, 23 December: Fire Brigades Amendment Act, 1919 (Act No 40). Borrowing alteration
1927, 29 January: Fire Brigades Amendment Act, 1927 (Act No 4). Major changes in constitution and funding of the Board
1944, 19 April: Fire Brigades Amendment Act, 1944 (Act No 12). Introduction of 56-hour week
1949, 30 June: Fire Brigades Amendment Act, 1949 (Act No 16), Borrowing alteration
1955, 18 April: Fire Brigades Amendment Act, 1955 (Act No 17). Changes in working hours
1956, 7 September: Fire Brigades and Bush Fires Amendment Act, 1958 (Act No 4). Amendments made to financial arrangements with insurance companies
1965, 17 December: Bush Fires and Fire Brigades Amendment Act, 1965 (Act No 24)
1970, 26 March: Fire Brigades Amendment Act, 1970 (Act No 12). Reconstitution of Board and removal of limitation on borrowing powers
1974, 26 April: Fire Brigades Amendment Act, 1974 (Act No 10). Council funding and storage of inflammable matter
1977, 13 April: Fire Brigades Amendment Act, 1977, (Act No 28). Board of Fire Commissioners brought under the control and direction of the Minister
1979, 21 December: Fire Brigades Amendment Act, 1979, (Act No 153). Clarification of Board's powers and responsibilities; omission of insurance companies right to appeal
1981, 1 July: Fire Brigades Amendment Act, 1981, Act No 68). Changes to revenue procedures
1983, 4 May: Fire Brigades Amendment Act, 1983 (Act No 59). Changes of boundaries made to include National Parks and historic sites with provision to levy these services

APPENDIX 2.2

Metropolitan Fire Brigades and the Board of Fire Commissioners: Board Members

A number of Board representatives have served more than one period in office and in more than one capacity. Others served on successive Boards where the representative structure of the Board changed. Changes in structure are indicated by periods, e.g. 1910–1927, and are discussed more fully in Chapter 2.

Insurance Company Representatives

1884–1909 (two representatives)

Insurance Companies with Headquarters in NSW
Walter CHURCH (1884–1896) and (1898–1901) *Australian Mutual Fire Insurance Society.*
F. JACKSON (1896–1898)
Thomas TINLEY (1901–1902) and (1908–1909) *United Insurance Company*
Robert KERR (1902–1904)
George POPE (1904–1908) *Australian Mutual Fire Insurance Company*

Insurance Companies with Headquarters outside the Colony
Mordaunt CLARKE (1884–1888) and (1890–1892) *Liverpool and London and Globe Insurance Company*
W GIBB (1888–1890) *National Insurance Company of New Zealand*
William GODDARD (1892–1894) *Norwich Union Fire Insurance Society*
John WELCH (1894–1896) *Commercial Union Assurance*
Thomas TINLEY (1896–1898) *United Insurance Company*
S HAGUE SMITH (1898–1900) *New Zealand Insurance Company*
J MACADAM (1900–1902) *Atlas Insurance*
Charles ROYLE (1902–1904) *Standard and Sun Insurance*
John MINNETT (1904–1906) *New Zealand Insurance Company*
Henry FRANCIS (1906–1908) *Royal Insurance Company*
George ARTHUR (1908–1909) *North British and Mercantile Insurance Company*

1910–1927 (one representative)

George POPE (1910–1913) *Australian Mutual Fire Insurance Company*
Henry WANSEY (1913–1916) *Commercial Union Assurance Company*
Henry FRANCIS (1916–1922) *Royal Insurance Company*
Thomas DOUGLAS (1922–1927) *Indemnity Mutual Marine*

1927–1956 (three representatives)

Thomas DOUGLAS (1927–1946) *Indemnity Mutual Marine*
William CLARKE (1927–1934)
Edward HAYTHORPE (1927–1946) *Northern*
William BROWN (1934) *Australian Mutual Fire*

Board Members Walter Church (left) and William Brown (right)

Francis WALTON (1934–1949) *South British*
Walter CURREY (1946–1953) *Liverpool and London and Globe*
Leslie SKELTON (1946–1950) *Royal Exchange*
Stacy MORRISON (1949–1956) *Union Assurance*
Harold WATTS (1950–1956) *Sun Insurance Company*
Keith JENKINSON (1953–1956) *Insurance Office of Australia*

1956–1970 (one representative)
Clarence EDWARDS (1956–1966) *Employers Liability*
Kenneth TODD (1966–1967) *Queensland Insurance*
Charles KINGSLAND (1967–1970) *British Traders*

1970–to date (two representatives)
Owen BLOORE (1970–1975) *Carpenter Locke Insurance Services*
Charles KINGSLAND (1970–1975) *British Traders*
Roy DIXON (1975–1980) *Royal*
Wesley CLARK (1975–1980) *Commercial Union*
Reginald DOWN (1980–   ) *Phoenix*
Alexander ROGER (1980–   ) *QBE*

Council Representatives
1884–1909
City of Sydney
William KIPPAX (1884–1886)
S LEES (1886–1890)
J C BEARE (1890–1900)
George LANDERS (1900–1902)
Ernest LINDSAY-THOMPSON (1902–1908)
Andrew J KELLY (1908–1909)

Suburban Municipalities
Richard McCOY (1884–1890) *Marrickville*
Charles HELLMRICH (1890–1894) *Paddington*
William TAYLOR, MLA (1894–1909) *Rockdale*

1910–1927
Sydney and Suburban Councils
William TAYLOR, MLA (1910–1922) *Rockdale*
George BAKER (1922–1927) *Randwick*

Country Councils
Walter CRACKNELL (1910–1913) *West Maitland*
Hugh SHEDDEN (1913–1914) *Newcastle*
Richard SHEPHERD (1914–1921) *Berry*
Edward COLLINS (1921–1923) and (1925–1927) *Wagga Wagga*
Issac CULLEN (1923–1925) *Wagga Wagga*

1927–1956
Sydney and Suburban Councils
George BAKER (1927–1936) *Randwick*
Thomas MUTCH (1936–1946) *Randwick*
Leslie DUFF (1946–1956) *Woollahra*

Country Councils
Edward COLLINS (1927–1936) *Wagga Wagga*
Martin GRIFFIN (1936–1941) *Bathurst*
Hector MACKENZIE (1941–1956) *Orange*

1956–to date
Councils of the Municipalities and Shires of NSW
Albert SHAW (1956–1967) *Lane Cove*
John FORD (1967–1969) *Randwick*
Clive TREGEAR (1969–1980) *Campbelltown*
Barry LEWIS (1980–   ) *City of Sydney.*

Volunteer Firemen's Representatives[1]
1884–1909
Andrew TORNING (1884–1886) *No 1 Volunteer Brigade*
Volunteer brigades failed to elect a representative (1886)
Edward LOVE (1887–1909) *Parramatta Volunteer Brigade*

1910–1927
Edward LOVE (1910–1912) *Granville Volunteer Fire Brigade*
Andrew KELLY, MLA (1913)
Walter CRACKNELL (1913–1916)
John BESWICK[2] (1916–1927) *Permanent Fireman*

1927–1956
John BESWICK (1927–1949)
Frederick HARRISON (1949–1952) *Wentworthville Volunteer Fire Brigade*
Henry BROWN (1952–1953) *Permanent Fireman*
Albert CAMPBELL (1953–1956) *Permanent Fireman*

1956–1970
Ambrose MALLAM (1956–1966) *Permanent Fireman*
Vincent RILEY (1966–1970) *Tamworth Volunteer Fire Brigade*

1970–to date
Alexander McMURTRIE (1970–   ) *Wangi Wangi Volunteer Fire Brigade*

Notes
1 A 1970 Fire Brigade Amendment Act made it obligatory for the Volunteer Representative to be a registered volunteer fireman.
2 The longest ever serving Board Member.

Board of Fire Commissioners 1926: (left to right) H M Webb (Secretary), G J Baker, T J Smith (President), T S Douglas, J F Beswick (longest ever serving Board member) and E E Collins

Board of Fire Commissioners 1984: (left to right) B L Lewis, W B Rogers, R W Down, (Chief Officer) R Threlfo, K K Klugman, (Minister for Police and Emergency Services) P Anderson, (President) P Gallagher, (Secretary) J R Galbraith, A M Roger, A C McMurtrie

Permanent Firemen's Representative
1927–1956
James McNAMARA (1927–1937)
Maurice PIPER (1937–1943)
Sidney JORDAN (1943–1949)
Maurice STOLMACK (1949–1956)

1956–1970
Maurice STOLMACK (1956–1966)
John BENNETTS (1966–1970)

1970–to date
Maurice STOLMACK (1970–1975)
Warwick ROGERS (1975–   )

Deputy Presidents
1970–to date
Joseph O'DONNELL (1970–1972)
William McCAUGHAN (1972–1977)
John FORD (1977–1979)
Jack WATSON (1979–1982)
Kristine KLUGMAN (1982–   )

APPENDIX 2.3
Presidents and Secretaries

President		Secretary	
1884*	Charles BOWN	1884	Andrew BONE
1911	George PITT	1886	William AGER
1911	Frederick COGHLAN	1890	Zachary BARRY
1913	Frederick FLOWERS	1914	Henry WEBB
1915	Ernest FARRAR	1945	Albert STARK
1922	Edward HARKNESS	1953	Walter OSBORNE
1925	Thomas SMITH	1955	Lionel WATT
1956	Leslie DUFF	1956	William Orchard WIGGINS
1959	Benjamin ANDREWS		
1965	Leonard VERRILLS	1963	Derek WEBB
1977	William WESTON	1975	William BEARE
1983	Philip GALLAGHER	1982	John GALBRAITH

*Year refers to year of appointment

Former President Bill Weston

Former President Ben Andrews (left) and Secretary Bill Wiggins (right)

Former Board Secretaries William Ager (top) and Zachary Barry (above)

242 / *Fighting Fire!*

APPENDIX 2.4
Revenue and Expenditure

Year	Expenditure Aggregate[2]	Expenditure Sydney Fire District[3]	Revenue State Government Contribution[4]	Local Government Total Contribution	Local Government Sydney Fire District AAV[5]	Local Government Sydney Fire District Contribution Per £100 AAV[6]	Insurance Companies Contribution	Insurance Companies % of Premium[7]
	£	£	£	£	£	£	£	
1884		18 357	10 028	4 113	na	na	4 076	na
1885		27 613	3 000	2 882	3 291 905	na	2 949	na
1886		10 128	3 500	3 500	3 673 154	na	3 500	na
1887		16 500	3 000	3 000	3 945 291	na	3 000	na
1888		11 033	2 500	2 500	4 293 962	na	2 500	na
1889		11 280	3 500	3 500	4 419 293	na	3 500	na
1890		12 263	3 775	3 775	4 546 996	na	3 774	na
1891		12 058	3 800	3 800	4 694 207	na	3 797	na
1892		15 016	4 580	4 580	5 263 655	1s 9d	4 580	1.88
1893		17 215	5 500	5 456	5 416 778	2s 0d	5 408	2.10
1894		18 026	5 000	5 474	5 296 891	2s 1d	5 477	2.20
1895		19 408	6 000	5 846	5 226 072	2s 3d	6 006	2.40
1896		20 303	6 300	6 258	4 956 905	2s 6d	6 300	2.50
1897		21 032	6 700	6 356	4 719 961	2s 10d	6 700	2.68
1898		21 447	6 700	6 480	4 641 595	2s 10½d	6 690	2.66
1899		28 469	8 000	7 816	4 594 551	3s 6d	8 010	3.10
1900		30 439	8 500	8 322	4 615 852	3s 8d	8 500	3.20
1901		34 725	9 400	9 178	4 678 320	4s 0d	9 394	3.40
1902		39 031	10 200	10 281	4 777 703	4s 3d	10 235	3.50
1903		48 389	15 150	15 323	4 995 457	5s 0d	15 150	5.00
1904		45 235	14 000	13 943	5 183 033	5s 4d	14 000	4.60
1905		49 142	14 300	14 148	5 371 391	5s 4d	14 300	4.56
1906		51 505	14 700	15 146	5 492 281	5s 4d	14 700	4.52
1907		50 193	15 650	15 646	5 652 078	5s 6d	15 700	4.63
1908		59 356	17 400	17 567	5 933 847	5s 10d	17 400	4.82
1909		62 447	19 100	19 213	6 156 742	6s 2d	19 100	5.09
1910	84 549	64 872	28 183	28 183	6 291 988	6s 10d	28 183	7.05
1911	91 392	64 929	30 462	30 462	na	6s 8d	30 462	6.55
1912	108 860	60 300	30 288	30 288	na	5s 9d	30 288	5.62
1913	111 645	76 758	37 215	37 215	8 326 353	6s 10d	37 215	6.40
1914	124 686	87 600	41 562	41 562	9 916 075	7s 0d	41 562	6.66
1915	124 086	87 213	41 362	41 362	10 698 175	5s 10d	41 364	6.03
1916	124 740	87 213	41 580	41 580	11 202 005	5s 5d	41 580	5.81
1917	142 743	102 849	47 581	47 581	11 725 696	6s 1d	47 581	6.01
1918	142 734	102 693	47 581	47 581	12 236 426	5s 10d	47 581	5.56
1919	143 445	102 594	47 815	47 815	12 676 130	5s 7d	47 815	5.56
1920	193 424	143 424	64 416	64 416	13 936 912	7s 9d	64 416	6.20
1921	220 935	163 065	73 645	73 645	14 936 912	7s 9d	73 645	5.92
1922	220 935	161 937	73 645	73 645	15 933 780	6s 9d	73 645	5.54
1923	236 811	174 459	78 937	78 937	16 896 011	6s 10d	78 937	5.99
1924	247 914	182 304	82 648	82 648	19 666 371	6s 2d	82 648	5.92
1925	257 616	182 304	85 872	85 872	22 310 490	5s 5½d	85 872	5.51
1926	302 169	218 028	100 723	100 723	24 292 649	5s 11½d	100 723	6.58
1927	325 104	236 772	81 276	81 276	26 366 252	5s 11¾d	162 552	10.43
1928	389 880	295 616	97 476	97 476	28 952 813	5s 1d	194 933	12.71
1929	420 904	323 108	105 226	105 226	30 407 421	5s 4d	200 452	13.80
1930	441 548	335 252	110 387	110 387	32 950 401	5s 1d	220 774	14.11
1931	426 472	324 076	106 618	106 618	34 539 838	4s 8d	213 236	14.67
1932	387 596	294 272	96 899	96 899	34 775 138	4s 2¾d	193 798	14.92
1933	372 752	281 548	93 188	93 188	28 951 666	4s 10d	186 376	15.03
1934	366 172	274 064	91 543	91 543	27 671 732	4s 11d	183 086	15.09
1935	372 080	277 932	93 020	93 020	26 923 058	5s 2d	186 040	15.44

	Expenditure		Revenue					
		Sydney Fire District[3]	State Government Contribution[4]	Local Government			Insurance Companies	
Year	Aggregate[2]			Total Contribution	Sydney Fire District		Contribution	% of Premium[7]
					AAV[5]	Contribution Per £100 AAV[6]		
		£	£	£	£	£	£	
1936	371 228	276 024	92 807	92 807	26 876 113	5s 1½d	185 614	15.27
1937	385 280	285 816	96 320	96 320	27 119 788	5s 3d	192 640	15.27
1938	402 248	299 956	100 562	100 562	28 292 522	5s 3d	201 124	15.46
1939	474 708	365 108	118 677	118 677	29 422 601	6s 2d	237 358	18.20
1940	472 320	360 992	118 080	118 080	31 140 915	5s 9d	236 160	17.38
1941	506 136	391 584	126 534	126 534	33 652 070	5s 10d	253 063	18.09
1942	547 024	424 432	136 756	136 756	34 777 234	6s 1¼d	273 512	18.66
1943	571 668	447 148	142 917	142 917	36 297 960	6s 1¾d	285 834	18.69
1944	570 364	446 252	142 591	142 591	37 592 452	5s 11d	285 182	17.45
1945	563 724	439 880	140 931	140 931	38 637 143	5s 9¼d	281 862	16.76
1946	688 712	549 036	172 178	172 178	39 518 039	7s 1¼d	344 356	20.16
1947	740 192	588 936	185 048	185 048	39 989 137	7s 5½d	370 096	19.29
1948	816 992	647 292	204 248	204 248	41 533 620	8s 1d	408 496	18.80
1949	904 820	726 820	226 205	226 205	44 459 332	8s 9d	452 410	17.90
1950	1 075 208	879 080	134 401	134 401	46 967 557	4s 11½d	806 403	28.12
1951	1 258 488	1 027 888	157 311	157 311	50 719 021	5s 5¾d	943 866	28.60
1952	1 605 232	1 313 840	200 654	200 654	56 863 093	6s 5¾d	1 203 924	30.91
1953	1 840 072	1 451 392	230 009	230 009	68 260 506	6s 4¾d	1 380 054	27.03
1954	1 850 028	1 452 912	231 254	231 254	77 553 843	5s 4d	1 387 521	27.25
1955	1 824 792	1 443 496	228 099	228 099	86 631 616	4s 7¾d	1 368 594	26.32
1956	2 354 024	1 930 240	294 293	294 293	102 620 904	5s 6¾d	1 765 518	32.37
1957	2 409 040	1 959 696	301 130	301 130	117 119 599	4s 9¼d	1 806 780	31.86
1958	2 757 960	2 140 456	344 745	344 745	138 382 262	4s 6¼d	2 068 470	31.11
1959	2 843 052	2 673 872	355 381	355 381	153 906 264	4s 1d	2 132 289	17.22
1960	2 898 584	2 307 520	362 323	362 323	166 770 679	3s 9d	2 173 938	16.69
1961	3 475 184	2 831 808	434 398	434 398	181 014 678	4s 3d	2 576 805	18.89
1962	3 624 288	2 863 744	453 036	453 036	201 610 072	3s 11½d	2 717 819	18.41
1963	3 572 768	2 827 104	446 596	446 596	237 677 072	3s 6d	7 619 577	17.53
1964	3 735 360	2 917 664	466 920	466 920	260 249 127	3s 0¾d	2 801 520	16.99
1965	4 143 106	3 237 312	521 957	521 957	280 592 140	3s 1¼d	3 131 745	17.84
	$	$	$	$	$	$	$	$
1966	6 560 559	6 707 392	1 074 384	1 074 384	na	15c	6 446 304	17.22
1967	9 411 617	7 229 312	1 153 828	1 153 828	547 675 151	16.5c	6 922 968	17.22
1968	11 189 549	8 746 272	1 365 488	1 365 488	658 604 819	16.6c	8 192 928	18.56
1969	11 540 087	na	1 470 756	1 470 756	na	na	na	na
1970	13 277 263	9 338 272	1 511 132	1 511 132	805 023 448	14.5c	9 054 000	17.19
1971	15 001 399	12 317 184	1 947 009	1 947 009	869 366 460	17.7c	11 670 234	19.58
1972	16 383 700	14 108 608	2 172 040	2 172 040	936 080 679	18.8c	13 032 936	18.88
1973	19 822 851	14 287 584	2 254 736	2 254 736	1.07b	16.7c	13 528 416	17.64
1974	24 788 039	18 083 712	2 844 684	2 844 684	1.20b	18.9c	17 050 983	19.91
1975	30 798 438	23 897 728	3 710 941	3 710 941	13.34b	.0224c	22 277 243	22.87
1976	33 398 766	28 975 328	4 447 364	4 447 364	16.10b	.0225c	26 724 113	21.97
1977	40 219 436	32 446 624	4 902 520	4 902 520	16.69b	.0243c	29 414 160	19.21
1978	42 483 594	32 990 994	5 210 732	5 210 732	17.52b	.0268c	31 252 885	19.29
1979	50 489 500	37 557 140	6 192 204	6 192 204	na	.0268c	37 153 224	22.34
1980	60 647 318	48 704 928	7 881 340	7 881 340	na	.033c	47 128 099	27.57
1981	72 047 040	58 440 640	9 766 496	9 766 496	na	.0385c	58 598 976	32.00
1982	83 283 772	71 087 488	11 226 872	11 226 872	na	.0365c	67 361 232	32.62
1983	104 644 114	77 562 912	12 461 852	12 461 852	na	.0365c	74 667 264	30.44

Notes

1 Amounts are expressed in pounds, shillings and pence (£ s d) until 1966, after which the units are dollars and cents ($ ¢). £1 = $2.

2 Aggregate expenditure is expenditure for all fire districts belonging to the Board of Fire Commissioners of NSW formed in 1910. Before 1910 the expenditure

in the Sydney Fire District was equivalent to the aggregate expenditure.
3 State grants for land and stations are included in the expenditure for the period 1884–1909 only.
4 The State government contribution in 1884 included an establishment grant.
5 Assessed Annual Value (AAV) of property in the Sydney Fire District. From 1973 onwards the figure refers to billions of dollars. From 1975 the figures relate to Unimproved Capital Value (UCV).
6 The local government contribution is based on Assessed Annual Value (AAV) and is expressed as shillings and pence per £100 until 1965. From 1966–74 it is in cents per $100. From 1975 to the present it is cents per $100 of Unimproved Capital Value (UCV).
7 The contribution of the insurance companies has always been based on percentage of premium income. From 1892 until 1965 it is expressed in pence per £100, after which it is cents per $100. Figures are for Sydney Fire District only.

APPENDIX 4.1

Sydney Fire Brigades

An alphabetic list of all brigades and fire stations in Sydney. Whilst the list attempts to be comprehensive, dates of formation and the location of many of the pre-1884 brigades must be treated with caution. Unless otherwise stated brigades were formed with volunteer staff; the appointment of the first permanent staff at a later date is also given. In many cases brigades were formed a few months prior to the construction of their fire station, hence dates of 'opening' and 'formation' may vary. In these cases only one date–month–year is given. All abbreviations used may be found in the list of abbreviations. Current status is as at 31 December 1983.

Albion Volunteer Company Formed prior to 1884 in Buckland Street, Waterloo. Not registered with MFB. Disbanded 1885.

Alexandria (No 13) Also called Waterloo and Alexandria. Formed as Alexandria Volunteer Company in 1882 in Raglan Street. Registered with MFB in 1884. New company formed 1886 in Gerard Street. Volunteers resigned and permanent staff appointed 29 January 1897 (No 8 station). Government architect station 1907 cnr Mitchell Road and Ashmore Street. Additions 1910. Closed 1945. Sold to Sydney City Council 1972. Demolished late 1970s. New station (No 13) 1975 in Wyndham Street with staff transferred from Waterloo District Station. *Current Status:* District Station E District, 4 DO, 4 SO, 52 PF, Skyjet, International Salvage, command vehicle.

Annandale (No 63) Opened September 1916 in Annandale Street with permanent and volunteer staff. Closed 1945. Sold 1950.

Arncliffe (No 33) Opened 10 September 1909 cnr Forest Road and Gordon Street. Government architect

Arncliffe Brigade c. 1910

Auburn Fire Station, Harrow Road c. 1912

station [£1,596 ($3192)]. Closed 1945. Sold 1953.

Ashfield (No 14) Formed 1888 as Ashfield Volunteer Company in Liverpool Road and subsidised by MFB. New station 1 April 1901 cnr Victoria and Norton Streets [£1,900 ($3800)]. Numbered 14 in 1903. First permanent staff 1912. *Current Status:* D District, 4 SO, 8 PF, International 57 L/S.

Auburn (No 44) Opened May 1908 in Harrow Road. Government architect station. First permanent staff 1914. New station 1935. *Current Status:* G District, 4 SO, 12 PF, International 57 L/S.

Australian Volunteer Fire Company (*see* No 1 Volunteer Company)

Avalon (No 60) Formed in Warringah FD in 1940, incorporated into Sydney FD in 1950. New station and residence 1960 at 689 Barrenjoey Road. First permanent staff 1970. *Current Status:* B District, 4 SO, 8 PF, 12 VF, International 38 L/S.

Balmain (No 12) Formed as Balmain Volunteer Company 1875 in Booth Street. Branch station in Wise Street. Head station transferred to Montague Street in 1875 and Branch station to Darling Street between 1884 and 1888. Both stations registered with MFB in 1884. Both stations closed 1894. New station [£1,022 ($2044)] in Darling Street in 1894. First MFB-built volunteer station. Volunteers disbanded and first permanent staff appointed 1901. *Current Status:* A District, 4 SO, 20 PF, International 2 stage.

Bankstown (No 62) Volunteer Brigade formed 1916 in Chapel Road. Purchased property 1917 in Liverpool Road. First permanent staff 1919. Shed demolished in 1958; temporary premises in Claremont Avenue. New station 1975 in Liverpool Road. *Current status:* C District 4 SO, 12 PF, International foam.

Baulkham Hills (*see* Castle Hill)

Beecroft (No 58) Formed with permanent and volunteer staff December 1915 in Baulkham Hills Road (later called Beecroft Road). New station 1975. *Current Status:* D District, 4 SO, 8 PF, 6 VF, International 57 L/S.

Ben Boyd (*see* Neutral Bay)

Berowra (No 75) Formed 1962 in Berowra Waters Road. First permanent staff January 1971. *Current Status:* B District, 1 SO, 1 PF, 15 VF, International 57 L/S.

Bexley (No 34) Formed 1905 cnr Forest Road and Queen Victoria Street. Government architect station opened 7 March 1910 [£1,679 ($3358)]. First permanent staff 1915. Closed 1945. Currently used for storage of Demonstration equipment.

Blacktown (No 63) Formed 1927 in Flushcombe Road. Initially part of Blacktown FD, incorporated into Sydney FD in 1952. New station and first permanent staff 1961 in Austral Street. New station 1971 cnr Hereward Hwy and Kempsey Streets. *Current Status:* G District, 4 SO, 16 PF, 6 VF, International 57 L/S.

Bondi (No 76) Opened with permanent staff 1930 cnr Old South Head Road and Gilgandra Street. *Current Status:* A District, 4 SO, 16 PF, International 50 L/S.

246 / *Fighting Fire!*

Botany Brigade and Fire Station c. 1910

Cabramatta Fire Station c. 1928

Botany (No 35) Formed 1905 in Banksia Street. Government architect station. First permanent staff 1912. *Current Status:* E District, 4 SO, 24 PF, International foam.

Breathing Apparatus Section (No 9) Formed 1980 in Allen Street, Waterloo. *Current Status:* E District, 1 DO, 5 SO, 12 PF, two Ford F350s, one International Tender, one Lighting Vehicle.

Burwood (No 15) Formed prior to 1884 as Burwood Volunteer Company in Station Street. Registered with MFB in 1884. Moved cnr Burwood and Belmore Streets in 1888. New station 1900. Numbered 15 in 1903. First permanent staff 1912. New site and station December 1925 in Livingstone Street [£8,594 ($17 188)]. *Current Status:* D District, 4 SO, 12 PF, International 57 L/S.

Busby (No 31) Formed with permanent staff 1962 in Cartwright Avenue. *Current Status:* G District 4 SO, 8 PF, International 57 L/S.

Cabramatta (No 49) Also called Cabramatta-Canley Vale. Formed in 1928 in Railway Parade. Incorporated into Sydney FD in 1959. New station 1969 in West Cabramatta Road. First permanent staff 1955. *Current Status:* G District, 4 SO, 8 PF, International 57 L/S.

Campbelltown (No 42) Formed 1891 in Queen Street. Registered with MFB in 1907 when incorporated into the Sydney FD. Became part of the Campbelltown FD when established in 1910. New station built in 1961 in Broughton Street. New station 1976. *Still active.*

Campsie (No 52) Formed 1902 cnr Beamish and Claremont Streets. New station and first permanent staff August 1913. *Current Status:* C District, 4 SO, 12 PF, International 57 L/S.

Canterbury (No 45) Formed May 1908 cnr George and Church Street. Government architect station. First permanent staff 1915. Closed 1945. Sold 1952, used by Forestry Commission. Now demolished.

Caringbah (No 45) Formed 1953 in President Avenue

Campbelltown Fire Station c. 1908

Caringbah Fire Station c. 1965

in Cronulla FD. New station 1959 in Mansfield Avenue. Incorporated into Sydney FD in 1959 with permanent staff from Cronulla. Closed as fire station in 1974 when Miranda fire station was opened. Now used as State Emergency Services headquarters.

Castle Hill (No 71) Formed 1924 as Baulkham Hills in Baulkham Hills Road. Name changed to Castle Hill in 1945. New station 1948 cnr Old Northern and Brisbane Roads. First Permanent staff late 1950s. New station 1962. *Current Status:* G district, 4 SO, 8 PF, 10 VF, International 57 L/S.

Willoughby (later Chatswood) Fire Station c. 1912

George Street North (Circular Quay) fireman's pole c. 1938

Chatswood (No 32) Formed 14 January 1900 as Willoughby Brigade on Pacific Highway, Chatswood. First permanent staff 1912. Name changed to Chatswood in 1917. Closed 1945 and sold. Currently a billiards shop.

Circular Quay (No 3) Also called George Street North. Temporary station 1890. Government architect station opened 25 January 1893 [£1,069 ($2138)] cnr George and Queen Streets (later Barton Street). Extensions by government architect [£1,541 ($3082)] 1909. Closed 1947. Brigade transferred to The Rocks. Demolished late 1954–55.

City Fire Escape Volunteer Company Also called Hook and Ladder. Formed in 1880 in Queens Place (Dalley Street). Moved to rear of Town Hall in 1883; ordered out same year. Disbanded 1884.

City Volunteer Fire Company Formed 1879 as a breakaway from No 3 Volunteer Company at 312 Castlereagh Street. Moved to Park Street and later Druitt Street. Disbanded 1884.

Concord (No 16) Formed October 1901 at Mortlake. New station in Burwood Road, Concord, 1903. First permanent staff 1912. New station April 1929 cnr Concord Road and Wellbank Street [£4,149 ($8298)]. *Current Status:* D District, 4 SO, 12 PF, International 57 L/S.

Concord West (No 65) Formed 1921 with volunteers in Queen Street. Disbanded 1929 with opening of new Concord station and the formation of Rydalmere Brigade.

Cronulla (No 54) Formed 1930 in Gerala Street. First permanent staff 1931. Closed 1959. Permanent staff transferred to Caringbah. New station and Brigade 1976 cnr Kingsway and Franklin Road. Initially part of Cronulla FD, incorporated into Sydney FD in 1976. *Current Status:* C District, 4 SO, 8 PF, International foam.

Crows Nest (No 36) Formed with permanent staff on 30 November 1906 cnr Sinclair and Shirley Roads. Government architect station. Major additions 1912. *Current Status:* District Station B District, 4 DO, 4 SO, 56 PF, International 92 L/S, International Salvage, Hydraulic Platform.

Cumberland Street (*see* York Street North)

Darlinghurst (No 4) Formed with permanent staff 1896 at 250 Victoria Street. Government architect station opened 22 January 1912 cnr Darlinghurst Road and Victoria Street. *Current Status:* A District, 4 SO, 24 PF, International 50 L/S.

Darlington Volunteer Company Formed and subsidised 1887 from disbanded No 4 Volunteers. Not subsidised from 1890. Some members joined Newtown auxiliary corps in 1892.

Dee Why (No 69) Formed 1924 cnr Fischer Road and Hayes Street with permanent and volunteer staff. *Current Status:* B District, 4 SO, 8 PF, 6 VF, International 57 L/S.

Drummoyne (No 17) Formed as Drummoyne Volunteer Company 1892 in Lyons Road. New station [£500 ($1000)] owned by volunteers 1896. Government architect station [£3,043 ($6086)] and first permanent staff June 1910. Additional engine bay 1943. *Current Status:* D District, 4 SO, 24 PF, International foam.

East Sydney Volunteer Company (*see* No 5 Volunteer Company)

East Willoughby (*see* Willoughby No 40)

Eastwood (No 59) Formed 1914 in West Parade. New station and first permanent staff 1924 at 259 Rowe Street [£1,462 ($2924)]. *Current Status:* D District, 4 SO, 8 PF, International 57 L/S.

Enfield Fire Station c. 1915

Gordon Brigade parade their first motor 1922

Enfield (No 47) Formed 19 May 1911 cnr Liverpool Road and Edward Street. Government architect station. First permanent staff 1912. Closed 1945. Currently vacant (part used as residence).

Engadine (No 33) Formed 1966 with permanent and volunteer staff in Preston Avenue. *Current Status:* C District, 4 SO, 8 PF, 15 VF, International 2 stage.

Fairfield (No 73) Formed March 1920. New station [£1,328 ($2656)] January 1925 in William Street. Initially part of Fairfield FD, incorporated into Sydney FD in 1925. First permanent staff 1959. *Current Status:* G District, 4 SO, 8 PF, International 57 L/S.

Five Dock (No 51) Formed July 1909 cnr Garfield and West Streets. Government architect station [£1,700 ($3400)]. First permanent staff 1912. Control Centre during WWII. Closed 1945. Used for stores until 1970. Recently Five Dock police station.

Forestville (No 51) Formed 1962 in Cook Street. First permanent staff 1970. *Current Status:* B District, 4 SO, 16 PF, 15 VF, International 57 L/S, Bedford W/T.

Freshwater (*see* Harbord)

General Post Office Volunteer Brigade Formed 1862. Details unknown.

George Street North (*see* Circular Quay)

George Street West (No 2) Formed August 1886 as MFB permanent station at 57 Broadway. Sold to Government 1955. Demolished. Current site of Sydney Technical College.

Gladesville (No 23) Formed 1910 as Hunters Hill in Pittwater Road. Renamed Gladesville in 1915. New station and first permanent staff 1927. Old station sold 1934. *Current Status:* D District, 4 SO, 12 PF, International 57 L/S.

Glebe (No 18) Formed 1877 as Glebe Volunteer Company in Mitchell Street. Government architect station 13 June 1906. First permanent staff 1911. *Current Status:* A District, 4 SO, 16 PF, International 57 L/S, International Snorkel.

Gordon (No 37) Formed 1914 with permanent and volunteer staff cnr Pacific Highway and Bridge Street. New station 1936. *Current Status:* B District, 4 SO, 8 PF, International 38 L/S.

Granville (No 19) Registered 1891 as Granville Volunteers in Good Street. Temporary premises Sydney Road 1897–99. New station purchased by Government grant in Good Street occupied 7 January 1900. Additions 1909. First permanent staff 1913. Closed 1945.

Guildford (No 55) Opened 15 February 1915 at 287 Guildford Road. New station August 1928 in Guildford Road [£2,999 ($5998)]. First permanent staff 1925. *Current Status:* G District, 4 SO, 8 PF, International 57 L/S.

Harbord (No 54) Formed 1915 as Freshwater in temporary rented premises in Charles Street. Renamed Harbord 1924. New station [cost £1,430 ($2860)] in Lawrence Street. First permanent staff 1930. Closed 1945. Sold 1948. Now Baby Health Centre.

Headquarters (No 1) Opened 1884 with permanent staff in Bathurst Street (former Insurance Companies Brigade HQ). Closed when government architect station opened February 1888 in Castlereagh Street. 211 Castlereagh Street and 213–215 Castlereagh Street

Bill McNiven (left), the Board's first architect. His initial design was for a station at Dee Why. Fred Ross (right), McNiven's successor, whose designs include Gordon (1936)

250 / *Fighting Fire!*

leased 1902 and 1904 respectively. 213–215 purchased 1909 [£4,675 ($9350)]. Extensions to 'new station' completed 1913. New workshops 1915. 211 Castlereagh Street purchased 1923 [£20,000 ($40 000)]. Extensions 1929 — 'new station appliance bays'. Alterations 1956–57. Bathurst Street properties purchased 1962. *Current Status:* District Station A District, 1 CO, 2 DCO, 5 Insp, 8 DO, 2 SO, 163 PF, International 92 L/S, Dennis R/R 75 L/S, International Salvage, Magirus/D Ladder, Thames CO_2, Toyota Tender, Canteen vehicle.

Homebush (No 43) Formed July 1919 [cost £1,386 ($2772)] cnr Parramatta Road and Bridge Street with permanent and volunteer staff. Closed 1945. Sold 1960 and demolished.

Homebush Fire Station c. 1920

Headquarters—1909 (top), 1950 (above) and 1982 (left)

Hook and Ladder Company (*see* City Fire Escape)

Hornsby (No 50) Formed 1914 with permanent and volunteer staff on Pacific Highway at Waitara. New station on Pacific Highway, Hornsby, March 1925. Station destroyed by fire in 1971. Temporary accommodation in George Street. New station 1972 in Bridge Road. *Current Status:* B District, 4 SO, 28 PF, International 50 L/S, Bedford W/T.

Hudson's Volunteer Company (*see* Redfern).

Hunters Hill (No 46) *See also* Gladesville. Formed March 1919 cnr Church Street and Herberton Avenue [cost £1,332 ($2664)] with permanent and volunteer staff. Closed 1945. Sold to council for Baby Health Centre.

Hurstville (No 20) Formed 1897 in McMahon Street. New station 1911 [£1,776 ($3552)]. First permanent staff 1912. *Current Status:* C District, 4 SO, 12 PF, International 57 L/S.

Insurance Brigade Formed 1851 by T J Bown at 284–286 George Street, Brickfield Hill. Moved 1864 to 105 Bathurst Street. Ceased to operate with the formation of the MFB in 1884. (*See* Headquarters).

Kent Volunteer Company Formed 1880 by Tooth and Co. Located next to Volunteer Hotel. Not registered with MFB in 1884.

Kogarah (No 21) Formed 1895 as Kogarah Volunteer Company and subsidised by MFB. Name changed to Kogarah and numbered 21 in 1903. Government architect station 1907 cnr Kensington and Gray Streets. Old station transferred to Mortdale. First permanent staff 1912. *Current Status*: District station C District, 4 DO, 3 SO, 48 PF, Water Tanker; International Salvage, Rescue Monitor.

Lakemba (No 64) Formed 1921 with permanent and volunteer staff in Haldon Street [£6,975 ($13 950)]. *Current Status*: C District, 4 SO, 8 PF, International 57 L/S.

Lane Cove (No 6) Formed with permanent and volunteer staff in February 1916 cnr Longueville and Gordon Roads. *Current Status:* B District, 4 SO, 20 PF, International foam, Bedford W/T.

Leichhardt (No 22) Formed 21 April 1887 as Leichhardt Volunteer Company cnr Marion Street and Balmain Road. Subsidised 1888. Government architect station and first permanent staff 31 March 1906. Volunteers disbanded 1906. *Current Status:* D District, 4 SO, 16 PF, International 57 L/S.

Lidcombe (No 30) Formed 1892 as Rookwood Volunteer Company in Joseph Street. Subsidised 1893. Station owned by volunteers 1895. New station 1899 in Church Street. Numbered 30 in 1903. First permanent staff 1912. Renamed Lidcombe in 1913. *Current Status:* D District, 4 SO, 8 PF, International 57 L/S.

Liverpool (No 8) Formed 1898 as Liverpool Volunteer Company in Macquarie Street. Station owned by volunteers. Subsidised 1898. Numbered 23 in 1903. Government architect station opened March 1908 in Scott Street. Initially part of Sydney FD, incorporated into Liverpool FD in 1910 then returned to Sydney FD in 1959 as No. 8. First permanent staff soon after 1910. New station 1961 in Terminus Street. *Current Status*: G District, 4 SO, 24 PF, 6 VF, Dennis R/R 57 L/S, Bedford W/T.

Long Bay (*see* Malabar).

Malabar (No 75) Formed 1929 as Long Bay in Raglan Street. Name changed to Malabar in 1933. Closed 1950.

Leichhardt Brigade c. 1921

Rookwood (later Lidcombe) Brigade 1904/5

Manly (No 24) Formed June 1877 as Manly Volunteer Company in Market Square. Registered with MFB in 1886. New station owned by volunteers 1895. New MFB station in Sydney Road opened 25 February 1898. First permanent staff 1912. New station opened 17 August 1921 cnr Sydney Road and Thornton Street [£10,978 ($21 956)]. Old station sold [£5,343 ($10 686)]. *Current Status*: B District, 4 SO, 28 PF, International 57 L/S, Morris Magirus ladder.

Maroubra (No 70) Formed 1924 [£5,789 ($11 578)] with permanent staff cnr Maroubra Bay Road and Flower Street. Closed 1945. Reopened 1957. *Current Status*: E District, 4 SO, 12 PF, International 57 L/S.

Marrickville (No 28) Formed 12 June 1914 with permanent staff in Marrickville Road. *Current Status*: D District, 4 SO, 20 PF, International 50 L/S.

Mascot (No 26) Formed 1892 as North Botany Volunteer Company in Rickety Street. Station owned by volunteers 1895. Numbered 26 in 1903. Renamed Mascot and first permanent staff 1911. New station February 1913 in Coward Street [£1,798 ($3596)]. Closed 1945. Reopened 1960. *Current Status*: E District, 4 SO, 12 PF, International 57 L/S.

Matraville (No 56) Formed in 1909 cnr Beauchamp Street and Bunnerong Road. First permanent staff 1945. Fully volunteer brigade 1961–68. New station 1968. *Current Status*: E District, 4 SO, 8 PF, International foam.

Merrylands (No 72) Formed 1925 in Merrylands Road. New station on same site 1937. *Current Status*: G District, 16 VF, International 57 L/S.

Miranda (No 45) Formed 1974 cnr The Boulevarde and Pt Hacking Road with permanent and volunteer staff from Caringbah. *Current Status*: C District, 4 SO, 20 PF, 6 VF, Skyjet, Bedford W/T.

Mona Vale (No 6) Formed 1966 in Harkeith Street. First permanent staff 1969. *Current Status*: B District, 4 SO, 8 PF, International 57 L/S.

Mortdale (No 48) Formed February 1908 as Mortdale Volunteer Brigade in Morts Road. Old Kogarah Fire

Smoko (farewell) at Mortdale Fire Station 1931

Laying the foundation stone (above) of Paddington Fire Station 1899 (top)

Station used. New building 1915. Closed 1945. Reopened 1952 with volunteer staff. *Current Status*: C District, 15 VF, International 28 L/S.

Mosman (No 25) Formed 1901 in Myagah Road. First permanent staff 1915. New station April 1919 in Military Road [£3,319 ($6638)]. Old station sold to council [£750 ($1500)]. *Current Status*: B District, 4 SO, 8 PF, International 57 L/S.

Mt Lachlan (see Waterloo)

Mt Druitt (No 32) Formed 1971 with permanent staff cnr Belmore and Varian Streets. *Current Status*: G District, 4 SO, 8 PF, International 57 L/S.

Narrabeen (No 68) Formed 1 January 1920 as volunteer brigade cnr Devitt and Ocean Streets. Initially part of the Narrabeen FD, incorporated into the Sydney FD on 1 November 1923. New station September 1931 cnr Pittwater Road and Ocean Street [£3,399 ($6798)]. Old station sold to Ambulance Authority. First permanent staff 1931. *Current Status*: B District, 4 SO, 16 PF, International 57 L/S, Bedford W/T.

Neutral Bay (No 53) Formed 1909 with permanent staff as Ben Boyd (North Sydney) cnr Yeo and Barry Streets. Government architect station [£1,511 ($3022)]. Renamed Neutral Bay 1914. *Current Status*: B District, 4 SO, 8 PF, International 57 L/S.

Newtown (No 5) Formed 1874 as Newtown and Camperdown Volunteer Company in Railway Bridge, King Street. Registered with MFB in 1885. Moved to School of Arts 1876. Branch station established at Camperdown 1877. Head station moved to old Watchhouse, Newtown Bridge, 1890. New station 1891 in Australia Street [£648 ($1296)] numbered 5, the

Balmain (No. 12) steamer under G H Dadd visiting Parramatta Fire Station c. 1908

first MFB station to be manned by permanent and auxiliary staff. New station 1913 [£6,477 ($12 954)]. *Current Status*: E District, 4 SO, 16 PF, International 57 L/S.

North Botany (*see* Mascot)

North City Volunteer Company Formed 1880 in Cumberland Street. First subsidised by MFB in 1887. Last subsidised in 1893. Registration cancelled 1895.

North Sydney (No 6) Formed 5 June 1895 in Walker Street [£1,004 ($2008)] with permanent and volunteer staff from St Leonards Volunteer Company. Closed 1945. Now a restaurant.

Northmead (No 67) Formed 1922 in Windsor Road. New station 1973 in Hammers Road. First permanent staff 1979. *Current Status:* G District, 4 SO, 8 PF, 16 VF, International 57 L/S.

No 1 Volunteer Company Formed 19 October 1854 as Victoria Theatre Brigade, Pitt Street. New station in Pitt Street, Haymarket 1857 and name changed to Australian Volunteer Fire Company No 1. Name changed to Royal Alfred Volunteer Fire Company 1868. Unregistered with MFB. Last turn-out 1886. Property purchased by AGL 26 August 1901. Station still stands as oldest fire station in Australia (Heritage listing) and the site of Sydney's first volunteer fire company.

No 2 Volunteer Company Formed 1856 in Phillip Street adjacent to the Water Police Court. Branch station Wyatt's premises next to School of Arts in Pitt Street 1866. Later branch shifted to York Street Markets. Both registered with MFB in 1884. Not registered 1885. Last turn-out 1886.

No 3 Volunteer Company Formed 8 January 1875 in Barley Mow Hotel (Hotel Windsor). Branch station opened at 91 William Street in Rainford's Hotel 1876. Branch moved to cnr Oxford and Bourke Streets 1876. Head station moved 1887 to 312 Castlereagh Street and to Bathurst Street in 1879. Disbanded 1884.

No 4 Volunteer Company Also known as South Sydney Volunteer Company. Formed 1875 in Market Square cnr Pitt, Castlereagh and Campbell Streets. Moved to Hancock's Tower, George Street West. Registered with MFB in 1884. Disbanded 1886 (see Darlington).

No 5 Volunteer Company Formed 1875 in Campbell Street, Surry Hills. Registered with MFB in 1884. Disbanded 1886 (*see* Paddington Brewery).

No 6 Volunteer Company Formed 1875. Details unknown.

Paddington (No 11) Formed 11 April 1878 as Paddington Volunteer Fire Company in South Head Road (now Oxford Street). Registered with MFB in 1884. Disbanded 31 March 1899 when permanent staff appointed to new station at 257 Oxford Street. Brigade transferred to Woollahra in 1951 and station became the Board's training college in 1956. Closed 1978. Now commerical premises.

Paddington Brewery Volunteer Company Formed 1886 by members from No 5 Volunteers cnr Dowling and Oxford Streets. Registered with MFB. Renamed Paddington after 1898. Disbanded 1899–1900.

Parramatta (No 27) Formed October 1859 as

Randwick Volunteer Brigade 1891

Parramatta No 1 Volunteer Company in Church Street. Subsidised 1886. New station 1899 cnr Church and Fitzwilliam Streets. Numbered 27 in 1903. First permanent staff in 1913. *Current Status*: District station G District, 4 DO, 4 SO, 56 PF, Skyjet International Salvage.

Parramatta No 2 Volunteer Company Formed 1896 in Church Street and subsidised by MFB. Disbanded 1898.

Penrith (No 37) Formed 1905. Government architect station cnr Evans and High Streets 1908. New station 1908. Initially part of Sydney FD until 1910 when Penrith FD was created. New station on same site 1982. *Still active*.

Petersham Volunteer Company Formed prior to 1884 in Crystal Street. Registered with MFB in 1884. Disbanded 1885.

Pyrmont (No 38) Formed 18 December 1906 with permanent staff cnr Pyrmont and Gipps Streets. Government architect station. Closed 1945. Reopened 1960. *Current Status*: A District, 4 SO, 24 PF, International 57 L/S.

Pyrmont And Ultimo Volunteer Company Formed

Penrith Fire Station 1978

1881 in Union Street. Not registered with MFB. Disbanded 1885/6.

Randwick (No 39) Formed 1890 as Randwick Volunteer Company adjacent to Council Chambers. Registered with MFB in 1891 and 1893. First permanent staff in temporary station 20 November 1905 in Avoca Street. Government architect station 1908. *Current Status*: E District, 4 SO, 20 PF, International foam.

Redfern Brigade's Dennis Gwynne motor and crew c. 1926

Redfern (No 10) Formed 1870 as Hudsons Volunteer Company (later called Redfern Volunteer Company) in Regent Street. First registered with MFB in 1884. Not registered in 1889. Reformed late 1898 cnr George and Turner Streets. Station (converted from old courthouse and police station) opened on 29 June 1899 with permanent staff. New station 1972. *Current Status*: E District, 4 SO, 16 PF, International 50 L/S.

Revesby (No 47) Formed 1959 with permanent staff in River Road. *Current Status*: C District, 4 SO, 16 PF, International 57 L/S, Bedford W/T.

Rhodes (No 66) Formed April 1921 as volunteer brigade in Blaxland Street. *Current Status*: D District, 8 VF, Ford D200 29 L/S.

Richmond Volunteer Company (No 28) Formed and registered with MFB in 1898. Original station owned by volunteers. Subsidised 1898. Moved to new premises in March Street 1908. Initially part of Sydney FD until 1910 when Richmond FD was created. Still active in Windsor FD.

Riverwood (No 34) Formed 1962 with permanent staff cnr Jacques Avenue and Belmore Road. *Current Status*: C District, 4 SO, 8 PF, International 57 L/S.

Rockdale (No 29) Formed 1892 as Rockdale Volunteer Company on Princes Highway. First subsidised by MFB in 1894. New station 1897. First permanent staff 1912. New station 1938 in Bay Street. *Current Status*: C District, 4 SO, 8 PF, International 50 L/S.

Rookwood (see Lidcombe)

Royal Alfred Australian Volunteer Fire Company (see No 1 Volunteer Company)

Rozelle (No 49) Formed 1909 cnr Darling and Oxford Streets. Government architect station October 1909 [£1,785 ($3570)]. Closed 1945. Later used by Board's plumbers. Now Board's Bush Fire Organisation headquarters (No 99 Station).

Rydalmere (No 65) Formed 1929 in Victoria Street. First permanent staff late 1950s. New station 1961 cnr Park Road and Wattle Street. *Current Status*: G District, 4 SO, 8 PF, 6 VF, International 75 L/S.

Ryde (No 42) Formed with permanent and volunteer staff in 1914 in Blaxland Road. New station July 1915 [£914 ($1828)]. Closed 1945. Reopened 1960. *Current Status*: D District, 4 SO, 12 PF, International 57 L/S.

St Leonards Volunteer Company Formed June 1877 in Mount Street. Registered with MFB in 1884. Branch station 1885 in Milsons Point Road. Relocated in Alfred Street in 1888. Both stations disbanded 1895. Some members transferred to new North Sydney station.

St Peters (No 41) Formed 1907 cnr King Street and Canal Road. Government architect station. First permanent staff 1913. Sold to Railways 1921 [£1,050 ($2110)]. New station cnr King and Sutherland Streets 1921 [£6,975 ($13950)]. Closed 1945. Sold as Baby Health Centre 1949.

Silverwater (No 19) Formed 1966 with permanent staff in Adderley Street. *Current Status*: G District, 4 SO, 16 PF, International foam.

Smithfield (No 41) Formed 1975 with permanent staff in The Horsley Drive. *Current Status*: G District, 4 SO, 8 PF, International foam.

South Sydney Volunteer Company (see No 4 Volunteer Company)

Standard Brewery Volunteer Company Formed September 1884 in Foveaux Street. Registered with MFB in 1884. Disbanded 31 December 1896.

Stanmore (No 7) Formed May 1886 as Marrickville (No 3) with permanent staff in Stanmore Road. Renumbered 4 in 1892 and 7 in 1896. Renamed Stanmore in 1913 while new station (Marrickville No 28) was under construction. Oldest active fire station in Sydney. *Current Status:* District Station D District, 4 DO, 4 SO, 52 PF, International Salvage, Rescue monitor.

Strathfield (No 43) Formed 1906 cnr Homebush Road and The Avenue. No record of operations. Land sold to MWSDB February 1917 [£600 ($1200)].

Surry Hills Volunteer Company Formed prior to 1884 in Palmer Street. Registered with MFB in 1884. Disbanded 1886. Reformed 1886 as Her Majesty's Theatre Brigade in Market Street. Not registered with MFB.

Sutherland (No 46) Formed 1936 in Flora Street. Initially part of Sutherland FD, incorporated into Sydney FD in 1959. New station 1961 in Moore Street. First permanent staff 1970. *Current Status*: C District, 4 SO, 8 PF, 15 VF, International 57 L/S.

Sydney Fire Establishment (*see* Insurance Brigade)

Theatre Royal Volunteer Company Formed 1883 adjoining Theatre in Castlereagh Street. Registered with MFB in 1884. Last subsidised in 1886.

The Rocks (No 3) Formed 1947 at 166 Kent Street with permanent staff transferred from Circular Quay. New station 1962. *Current Status*: A District, 4 SO, 32 PF, International 92 L/S, Merryweather Ladder.

Toongabbie (No 74) Formed 1927 in Old Windsor

Woollahra Volunteers—replaced by permanent staff 1898

Road. New station 1967 in Cooyong Street. First permanent staff 1968. *Current Status*: G District, 4 SO, 8 PF, International 57 L/S.

Turramurra (No 57) Formed 1915 in Lane Cove Road. Disbanded 1920 when station sold.

Vaucluse (No 60) Formed 1913 as No 55. New station (No 66) 1915 [£2,564 ($3128)] in South Head Road. First permanent staff 1916. Closed 1945. Now a residence.

Victoria Theatre Volunteer Company (*see* No 1 Volunteer Company)

Waterloo (No 13) Also known as Mt Lachlan. Formed 1875 as Waterloo Volunteer Company in Kellick Street. Registered with MFB in 1885. Permanent staff 1902. Government architect station 26 February 1907 cnr Elizabeth and Bourke Streets. Another new station January 1918. Old station sold 1920 [£1,060 ($2120)]. Closed 1975. Brigade transferred to Alexandria.

Waterloo And Alexandria Volunteer Brigade (*see* Alexandria)

Waverley (No 31) Formed as Waverley Volunteer Fire Company in Carrington Road, Charing Cross. Listed in 1884. First registered with MFB 1887. Station rebuilt [£319 ($638)] 1895. First permanent staff 1914. Station rebuilt and opened May 1916. Closed 1945. Now Keiron Entertainment Centre.

Wentworthville (No 57) Formed 1920. New station 1934 cnr Garfield and Pritchard Streets. First permanent staff 1975. New station on same site 1983. *Current Status*: G District, 4 SO, 8 PF, International 57 L/S.

Willoughby (No 40) See also Chatswood. Formed as East Willoughby Volunteer Company 1905 in Laurel Street. First permanent staff 1914. New station December 1915 [£1,155 ($2310)]. Name changed to Willoughby in 1917. *Current Status*: B District, 4 SO, 8 PF, International 57 L/S.

Woollahra (No 11) Formed 6 September 1875 as Woollahra Volunteer Company in Moncur Street. New brigade 1885 in Tricket Street. Reformed 1886 in Moncur Street. Subsidised 1887. Volunteers disbanded. First permanent staff appointed (No 9) 28 February 1898. Government architect station 1905 in Forth Street. Closed 1945. Reopened 1951 with Brigade from Paddington (No 11) and renumbered 11. *Current Status*: A District, 4 SO, 28 PF, International 57 L/S. Merryweather Ladder.

Woollahra No 2 Volunteer Company Formed 1886 and subsidised by MFB. Disbanded 1887.

York St North (No 46) Formed 11 June 1906 with permanent staff as Cumberland Street at 147 Cumberland Street. Name changed in 1913 when new site identified in York Street North. Never occupied. Site being used for Harbour Bridge approaches. Closed 1917.

APPENDIX 5.1
Chief Officers and Deputy Chief Officers

Chief Officer
1884[1]	W D BEAR
1898	A WEBB
1913	N G SPARKS
1922	F JACKSON
1929	T P H NANCE
1934	G S GRIMMOND
1936	C D A RICHARDSON
1944	W H BEARE
1948	E J GRIFFITHS
1955	C A MILLEDGE
1957	J S McGRATH
1958	H W PYE
1964	H R BARBER
1967	V A LOWTHER
1975	F DAVIES
1980	R THRELFO

Deputy Chief Officer[2]
1884	J W DAWSON
1885	W BOUCH
1888	A WEBB
1898	N G SPARKS
1913	F JACKSON
1922	J GRAHAM[3]
1923	T P H NANCE
1928	G S GRIMMOND
1934	C D A RICHARDSON
1936	W H BEARE
1944	B L BARBER
1946	E J GRIFFITHS
1948	R J CURRER
	J A JOHNS (Acting)
	G P CONDON
1951	J EDGE
	G H GILMORE
1955	J S McGRATH
1956	H W PYE
1957	L W FISHER
1958	G M MCKINNON
	D R HAWKINS
1960	C A WELCH
1964	V A LOWTHER
	J MEEVE
1972	F C DAVIES
1975	J MOSS
1977	C F ROSE
1979	C F ROSE (Exec.)
	R C THRELFO (Services)
1980	R W AHERN (Exec.)
	R H NORTON (Services)

Chief Officers Charles Milledge (top) and Jim McGrath (above)

Notes
1. Year refers to year of appointment.
2. Between 1884 and 1909 the Chief Officer was known as Superintendent. His Deputy was known as Principal Foreman (1885–1892) and Deputy Superintendent (1893–1909). Between 1950 and 1952 the Deputy Chief became known as Assistant Chief Officer. In the periods 1956–1961, 1964–1967 and 1979–to date, there have been two Deputy Chief Officer appointments.
3. Deputy Chief Graham was later demoted to Station Officer, having been found guilty by the Board of being drunk at the Manning Chambers fire one night in March 1923.

APPENDIX 5.2
Officers and Firemen Killed on Duty Sydney Fire District*

25 May 1886	**Fisher** Frederick Patrick (Fireman 2nd Class), aged 33 years. Killed by falling walls at fire in Parramatta Road, Leichhardt.
22 February 1888	**Dalton** Richard (Fireman 2nd Class), aged 28 years. Killed accidentally falling down lift well in dense smoke at J Frazer and Co's premises at York Street, City.
10 July 1891	**Bowers** Charles William (Fireman 2nd Class), aged 38. Killed by falling off the sliding pole at No 2 Station, George Street West.
1 September 1894	**Brown** Edward Charles (Senior Fireman) aged 43 years. Killed by falling walls at Messrs John Lawler and Sons—the most notable fire of the year.
11 August 1895	**Lawton** George (Probationary Fireman) aged 31 years. Killed by falling off the ladder van while proceeding to a fire at the premises of Messrs J P Wright and

* This list includes only those firemen killed whilst actively involved on a fire call or from injuries sustained at a call.

Many onlookers were present at the blaze in Leichhardt (1901), which claimed the life of Assistant Officer Edward Roberts

11 February 1901	**Roberts** Edward J (Assistant Officer), aged 31 years. Killed when timber supporting the joists gave way at a fire at 401 Parramatta Road, Leichhardt. Father of Assistant Engineer Jack Roberts.
29 May 1912	**Wolfenden** George (Fireman 2nd Class) aged 43 years. Killed by a large brick chimney [100 feet (30.48m)] collapsing at the height of a fire at Dettman's timber yard.
25 January 1913	**Hancock** James (Fireman) aged 50 years. Died of injuries received in an accident when horses bolted while proceeding to a call of fire in Blues Point Road, North Sydney on 21.1.1913.
10 September 1920	**Gerard** Augustus J (Station Officer) aged 61 years. Died as a result of burns. He was returning from a fire at Elliott Brothers, Balmain when his clothes ignited whilst on the fire engine 3.6.1920.
27 August 1922	**Brown** William H (Fireman 3rd Class) aged 24 years. Killed as a result of the collapse of the 85-foot (25.9m) electric turntable ladder at a fire at Adams Co, Elizabeth Street. Lawton had been in the Service only a fortnight.
18 October 1926	**Morris** Frederick W (Station Officer) aged 56 years. Died as a result of burns received at a fire at Fowler's Tannery, Botany Road, Botany.
24 July 1936	**Hegarty** Samuel (Sub-Station Officer) aged 46 years. Died as a result of burns received at a fire at Standard Hosiery Ltd. Kippax Street. The fire was not extensive but oil falling from the floor above ignited.
25 March 1937	**Rust** John (Station Officer) aged 53 years. Killed by a wall collapsing at the concluding stages of fire extinguishing opera-

(Cafe, George Street, Sydney. He had served in The Great War with AIF.)

The funeral procession for Station Officer Morris

	tions at Hafoma Phonograph Company, Botany Street, Waterloo.
25 January 1940	**Plumbe** Wally M (Sub-Station Officer) aged 42 years. Died as a result of injuries received by the overturning of fire engine on which he was travelling whilst turning out.
11 June 1942	**Griffen** Michael L (Senior Fireman) aged 34 years. Killed by falling iron racks at R B Davies fire in Marrickville. Griffen had obtained distinction in fire-fighting, ARP work and in other fire brigade activities.
9 March 1945	**Mancy** Alexander V (Fireman 2nd Class) aged 28 years. Killed as a result of coming into contact with electric wires at a furniture factory at 85 Derwent Street, Glebe.
7 August 1947	**Knox** James McStranick (District Officer) aged 56 years. Died as a result of injuries received by falling from a motor fire engine responding to a call of fire at Woolloomooloo.
20 July 1963	**Jenkins** Ronald (Senior Fireman) aged 43 years. Died from carbon monoxide poisoning in Napolean Street sub-station.

APPENDIX 5.4

Recipients of the NSW Fire Brigades Medal for Conspicuous Bravery

In 1932 it was resolved:

> THAT the Board of Fire Commissioners of N.S.W. being desirous of recognising by some mark of distinction, deeds of conspicious bravery and gallantry performed on active service by members of the N.S.W. Fire Brigades by saving or endeavouring to save life and property, institutes and creates as a mark of its approbation of such heroic acts, a decoration styled the N.S.W. Fire Brigades Medal for Conspicuous Bravery, which decoration the Board is desirous should be highly prized. (Board Minutes, 13 September, 1932)

The official description of the award reads:

> The decoration consists of a bronze medal on the obverse of which, in relief, is the figure of a fireman in full uniform descending a ladder resting against a burning building, and bearing a rescued child on his arm, and on the reverse the inscription "For Conspicuous Bravery" surrounded by a laurel wreath, the name of the Service, N.S.W. Fire Brigades, being engraved around the outer edge; the rim being plain for the name of recipient and date of award. The riband is 1 3/8" in width and is of a cream ground with narrow red stripes at outer edges and wider one in centre.
>
> It is provided that a recipient of the decoration may, upon performance of a further act of conspicuous gallantry, be awarded a bar to be attached to the riband, and similarly for each such additional act.
>
> It is further provided that an award may be made posthumously, and the decoration presented to such person as, in the absolute discretion of the Board, is deemed most fit.

Medals Awarded

1932 Members of the Armidale Brigade: B JONES (posthumous), W ROBINSON (posthumous), T SNELL, F MAIZEY, T MUNSIE, R COLMER, R WICKS, T S SNELL, for bravery during a fire and subsequent explosion at a produce store known to contain a large quantity of explosives. May 1932.

1957 Third Class Fireman Donald CAMERON for the attempted rescue of a child at a fire at 124 Morehead Street, Redfern. On 10 October 1957, he ascended staircase well alight and was struck by portions of a falling ceiling. The body of the child was discovered under a bed.

1967 Senior Fireman W DOYLE for the rescue of three people and saving the life of an unconscious woman during a fire at the Shore Motel in Artarmon on 2 September 1967. Doyle was driving home when he spotted the fire and having ensured that the Brigade had been notified he organised nearby workers to assist him in an improvised rescue operation. Doyle later had to be treated for the effects of smoke and heat.

1968 Station Officer George DOWLING for

Fireman Donald Cameron

attempting to save the life of a baby in a burning terrace cottage at 12 Pritchard Street, Enmore on 6 June 1968. Upon arriving at the fire and learning that a baby was inside, he attempted to enter the house three times. The last time he had a hose directed upon him and despite the intense heat and dangling live wires he retrieved the basinette which contained the body.

1970 Station Officer Alfred ROBINSON for saving the life of one child and attempting to save the life of another in a cottage at 29 McGirr Parade, Warwick Farm on 27 September 1970. Arriving at the fire and learning that two children were inside the cottage he entered the cottage through a window lacerating his leg in the process. He found one child and continued to search for the second despite the fact that the whole cottage was well alight. Intense heat forced him to abandon his search.

1977 Station Officer Robert ROSS and First Class Fireman Anthony FREEMAN and First Class Fireman R CARRUTHERS for their actions in rescuing persons at the Granville railway disaster in January 1977. Each recipient's citation said 'without concern for his own well-being he performed many exceptional acts of courage'.

1980 Station Officer Michael GUIDER and Senior Fireman Peter SIMPSON for the rescue of a Fire Brigades Officer while fighting a major fire at Hy-Craft and Sheldon Buildings, Clarence Street on 15 November 1980. A section of the Sheldon Building wall crashed through the wooden roof of Hy-Craft House. Station Officer L Cooper was buried up to the waist in hot bricks and rubble, Guider and Simpson, with others, assisted him to safety despite the imminent danger of the wall collapsing further.

1981 Volunteer Fireman (Wallsend) Richard CURRIE for attempting to save the lives of two children in a burning house at Edgeworth on 13 March 1981. While off duty Currie entered the burning house three times. He located the bodies of the children but was forced back by smoke fumes and heat.

1981 Station Officer Barry GARVIN for assisting people to safety from a fire in the Rembrandt Residential Building, Darlinghurst on 25 August 1981. Relying on breathing apparatus, Garvin assisted two people on the fourth floor to the cage of the Snorkel and then gave up his position in the cage, and was for some minutes stranded in the burning building, for another person trapped nearby.

APPENDIX 5.3

Sydney Fire District: Number of Firefighters

Year	Brigades Permanent	Mixed[1]	Volunteer[2]	Personnel Permanent[3]	Auxiliaries	Volunteer[4]
1884	1	—	16	30	—	na
1894	5	—	24	51	5	394
1904	13	—	19	144	13	163
1914	30	18	7	291	—	144
1924	28	15	27	363	—	228
1934	31	21	24	608	—	252
1944	33	34	10	766	2 551	252

Year	Permanent	Mixed	Volunteer	Officers	Firefighters	Volunteer
1954	19	24	10	291	822	267
1974	54	14	4	205	1 228	182
1983[5]	55	15	3	313	1 247	60

Notes
1 Permanent and Volunteer.
2 For 1884 and 1894, includes only those Volunteer companies registered with the MFB.
3 Between 1884 and 1886 all personnel including the Secretary and Coachmen turned out for fires and were included in the brigade strength.
4 Between the years 1903 and 1912 volunteers were known as partially paid firemen.
5 These figures do not include an additional 172 officers and 82 permanent firemen employed in Sydney on 'Special Duties'.

APPENDIX 6.1

Reserves and Auxiliary Reserves (Second World War)

	Reserves	Auxiliary Reserves	Womens Fire Auxiliary		Reserves	Auxiliary Reserves	Womens Fire Auxiliary
1939	na	Established	na	1943	598	1526	527
1940	1	1453	na	1944	596	1526	429
1941	525	1540	Established	1945	442	Disbanded	Disbanded
1942	610	1540	250				

APPENDIX 7.1

Insurance Companies' Fire Brigade Plant (1883)

CONSISTING OF FIVE STEAM AND MANUAL Engines, and all Apparatus connected therewith.

One LARGE STEAM FIRE ENGINE (Shand, Mason and Company), Acq. 1865 *'Nonpareil'* with 9 inch Pump, Pole, Drag-handle, Swingle Trees, and five Lamps; four lengths Vulcanized India-rubber Suction Pipe (in all thirty-six feet); one Copper Rose, one Wicker Strainer, one Canvas Dam, eight lengths Copper Riveted Leather Hose (in all 320 feet), two lengths Vaucher's Patent Canvas Hose (in all 197 feet), four long, and one short Copper Branch pipes, fourteen Branch Pipe Jets (assorted from 1/2 to 1 2/8 inch), two Branch Staves, two Canvas Water Bags for wheels, three Brass Breech Pieces, four Canvas Buckets, one Rope, Hose and Suction Wrenches, Stoking Irons, Wrenches and Spanners, Engineers' Tools, and Sundries, etc.

One PATENT EQUILIBRIUM STEAM FIRE ENGINE (Merryweather and Sons Company), Acq. 1871 *'Fire King'*, with 3, 8 inch Pumps, Pole, Drag-handle, five Swingle Trees, four Lamps, three lengths, Vulcanized India-rubber Suction Pipes, (in all thirty foot), one large Copper Rose, and Wicker Basket, eight lengths Copper Riveted Leather Hose (in all 314 feet), one Rope, two Canvas Water Bags, four long and two short Copper Branch Pipes, eleven assorted Branch Pipe Jets, two Brass Breech Pieces, three Branch Pipe Staves, one Ratchet, one Crutch for Suction, one Hand-pump and Hose, two pairs Jet Tongs, one hexagon Spanner, set of spare Valves and Gauge Glasses, nine assorted Nut Wrenches, Four Hose and Suction Wrenches, Stoking Irons, Screw Wrench, Tube Brush, Oil and Tallow Cans, spare Ram and Bucket Leathers, Engineers' Tools, Sundries, etc, etc.

One SMALL VERTICAL STEAM FIRE ENGINE (Shand, Mason and Company), Acq. 1874 *'Guardian'*, with 8-inch pump, patent inclined water tube boiler and complete with the following apparatus, viz: Pole, drag-handle, three sway bars, three lamps, two lengths vulcanized India-rubber suction hose (in all 19½ feet), copper rose, seven lengths copper riveted leather delivery hose (in all 280 feet), one brass breech piece, two long and two short branch pipes, five assorted branch pipe jets, two branch pipe staves, two canvas water bags, canvas jumping sheet, canvas cistern, hand-pump with hose and jet ropes, stoking irons, oil and tallow cans, hose and suction wrenches, spanners, engineers' tools, etc.

One MANUAL POWER BRIGADE FIRE ENGINE, Acq. 1871 *'Tilley'*, improved pattern, seven-inch Pumps, eight-inch Stroke Pole, Swingle Trees, three Lamps, two Fire Ladders, four lengths Leather Suction Pipe (in all 27 feet), one length Canvas Hose, one Reel (67 feet), one Copper Rose, eight lengths Copper Riveted Leather Hose (in all 276 feet), one long and one short Branch Pipe, six assorted Branch Pipe Jets, one Breech-piece, Copper Goose Neck, one Double Stand Cock, one Canvas Jump Sheet, two Brass Connecting Screws, Canvas Dam, four Leather Buckets, one Rope, one double-ended Spanner, one Saw in Leather Case, Spoon, Crowbar, Wrenches, Spade, Falling Axe, Pick, Chimney Chain, etc.

One MANUAL POWER BRIGADE FIRE ENGINE, Acq. 1872: *'Express'*, (Small size) 4¾ inch Pumps, two Copper Side Lamps, one Officer's Lamp, two lengths Copper Riveted Leather Suction Pipes, one Copper Rose for same, three lengths Copper Riveted Leather Delivery Hose (in all 100 feet), two lengths Patent Canvas Hose (in all 120 feet), one Copper Branch Pipe, two Jets for same, Canvas Dam Board, Tarpaulin two Leather Fire Buckets, Hand Pump with Leather Hose and Jet, Copper stand Pipe for Hydrant, two Brass Connecting Screws, Screw Wrench, Drag Rope, Crowbar, Hose Keys, etc, Engine fitted with shafts for Cab-horse.

One BALANCE HANDLE HOSE REEL, with six lengths Patent Canvas Hose (in all 300 feet) six street Chains, one three-way Hydrant, one double Stand Cock, one Copper Branch Pipe.

Three LONG FIRE LADDERS, six short Fire Ladders, one Stand Cock, two Brigade Hand pumps, with Leather Hose complete, five Leather Fire Buckets, six Iron Buckets, Ropes, Chains, Picks, Crowbars, Fire Hooks, Saws, Augers, Canvas Sheets, Canvas Dams, Extra Boiler tubes, Valves, Pet Cocks, Leathers etc, for Steam Fire Engines, lot of Sundries, etc.

Fifteen LENGTHS THREE-INCH COPPER RIVETED LEATHER HOSE for Steam Fire Engines (in all 560 feet), with Brass Union Joints, complete, thirteen lengths 2½ inch Copper Riveted Leather Hose for Hydrant and Manual Power Engines (in all 535 feet) with Brass Union Joints complete)

Five DICK'S PATENT L'EXTINCTEURS, two No. 4, two No. 5, and one No. 6, complete one Pressure Gauge for Testing, extra charges, etc.

In addition the Brigades housed an Auxiliary Fire and Salvage Company. (Sydney Fire Establishment, *Annual Report*, 31 December, 1883)

APPENDIX 8.1

Fire Statistics, Sydney Fire District

Year	Fires/ Emergencies	Chimney Fires	False Alarms	Total Calls
1884	129	46	50	225
1885	196	64	42	302
1886	205	40	32	277
1887	207	60	14	281
1888	266	61	35	362
1889	215	45	33	303

264 / *Fighting Fire!*

Year	Fires/Emergencies	Chimney Fires	False Alarms	Total Calls	Year	Fires/Emergencies	Chimney Fires	False Alarms	Total Calls
1890	237	52	44	333	1939	4923	56	1364	6343
1891	263	33	52	348	1940	5857	58	1317	7232
1892	315	75	47	437	1941	3952	44	1270	5266
1893	258	75	68	401	1942	3932	34	1304	5270
1894	270	90	49	409	1943	3714	47	1366	5127
1895	369	82	82	533	1944	6315	72	1607	7994
1896	291	69	91	451	1945	4199	72	1679	5950
1897	449	76	86	611	1946	4988	141	1766	6889
1898	422	79	64	565	1947	3930	61	1558	5559
1899	520	106	67	693	1948	6122	102	2236	8460
1900	398	85	82	565	1949	4322	128	2216	6665
1901	477	86	94	667	1950	4573	52	2372	6997
1902	482	95	77	654	1951	8827	77	2611	11515
1903	458	69	89	616	1952	6521	103	3166	9790
1904	513	83	87	683	1953	7371	89	2931	10391
1905	517	79	79	675	1954	6478	70	3044	9592
1906	518	58	80	658	1955	6400	56	3556	10012
1907	636	70	108	814	1956	9173	75	4268	13516
1908	567	66	114	747	1957	12090	67	5026	17183
1909	706	53	91	850	1958	8362	50	4253	12665
1910	668	40	106	814	1959	6594	46	4239	10879
1911	888	49	155	1092	1960	12532	48	4745	17325
1912	1009	37	163	1209	1961	8811	37	4628	13476
1913	1390	28	170	1588	1962	9686	31	5038	14755
1914	1171	31	185	1387	1963	7511	30	5413	12954
1915	1366	41	178	1585					
1916	914	25	157	1096					
1917	893	38	159	1090	Year	All Fires Emergencies		False Alarms	Total Calls
1918	1560	29	203	1792					
1919	1458	31	231	1720	1964	14390		8500	22890
1920	1046	31	272	1350	1965	13573		9279	22852
1921	1105	24	256	1385	1966	9257		8808	18065
1922	1753	26	291	2070	1967	9852		9982	19834
1923	2231	43	337	2611	1968	17241		12278	29519
1924	1666	34	419	2119	1969	9631		11631	21262
1925	1722	35	415	2172	1970	16930		14696	31626
1926	3131	35	560	3726	1971	17004		15250	32254
1927	1966	44	557	2567	1972	14207		14935	29142
1928	3678	33	765	4476	1973	14140		15242	29382
1929	3160	44	941	4145	1974	14646		15108	29754
1930	2856	43	871	3770	1975	15473		15142	30615
1931	1777	28	844	2649	1976	14519		15697	30216
1932	2284	41	836	3161	1977	18730		16872	35602
1933	1965	42	704	2711	1978	13615		17452	31067
1934	2043	37	846	2966	1979	23274		12856	36130
1935	4023	57	985	5065	1980	23658		19536	43194
1936	3936	52	998	4986	1981	22519		16281	38800
1937	2829	40	1102	3971	1982	29180		23677	52857
1938	4626	42	1482	6150	1983	21056		18938	39994

APPENDIX 8.2

Major Causes of Fire, Sydney Fire District

	1	2	3	4
1884	Candles	Chimney Sparks	Gas explosions	Incendiaries
1909	Light thrown down	Foul flue	Candles	Sparks From Fire
1927	Light thrown down	Burning rubbish	Sparks From Fire	Vapour spirit
1939	Light thrown down	Electrical	Burning rubbish	Backfire
1955	Light thrown down	Electrical	Foul flue	Burning rubbish
1964	Matches	Rubbish bins	Bush, scrub fires	Fireworks
1970	Matches	Electrical	Burning rubbish	Fats, cooking oils

BIBLIOGRAPHY

A century of progress: Rockdale 1871-1971. St George Historical Society, 1971.

Adrian, C, 1982. Evaluating the provision of an impure public good: fire services in the Sydney region. Unpublished PhD thesis, University of New South Wales, Faculty of Military Studies.

America burning. National Commission on Fire Prevention and Control, Washington, DC, 1973.

An illustrated guide to Sydney 1882—Gibbs, Shallard and Co. (facsimile ed.) Angus and Robertson, Sydney, 1981.

Auditor-General's Report, 1918. Respecting Aspects of Administration of the Board of Fire Commissioners of NSW, *NSWPP* 1918 (6).

Bank of New South Wales, 1908. *Views of premises.* Bank of New South Wales, Sydney.

Birch, A and Macmillan, D S, 1982. *The Sydney scene 1788-1960.* Hale and Iremonger, Sydney.

Board of Fire Commissioners of NSW. *Annual Reports 1910-83.*

Boyd, R, 1960. *The Australian ugliness.* Melbourne.

Bryce, F, 1982. Address to the National Command Course, Fiskville by the Secretary, NSW Fire Brigade Employees' Union. September. (unpublished).

Carroll, J, 1963. *The settlement and growth of Mosman.* Mosman Historical Society.

_____ 1949. *The Mosman that was, 1789-1900.* Mosman Historical Society.

Chubb, W, 1912. *The jubilee souvenir of the Municipality of Newtown, 1861-1912.* Newtown Municipal Council.

Clark, D, 1978. 'Worse than physic': Sydney's water supply 1788-1888. *In* Kelly, M (ed.), 1978.

Committee of Inquiry into the NSW Fire Brigades 1977. Recommendations.

Dowd, B T, 1959. *History of the Waverley Municipal district 1859-1959.* Waverley Municipal Council.

Dunlop, E, 1974. *Harvest of the years: the story of Burwood 1794-1974.* Municipality of Burwood.

Gibbs, Shallard and Company, 1885. *Map of Sydney and suburbs.* Sydney.

Gordon, G, 1978. *Harbord, Queenscliff and South Curl Curl 1788-1978.* Begg Printers, Sydney.

Groom, B and Wickman, W, 1982. *Sydney—the 1850s, the lost collections.* The Macleay Museum/Southwood Press, Sydney.

Harrison, P, 1972. Planning the metropolis—a case study. *In* Parker, R S and Troy, P N (eds), 1972.

Hawker, G N, 1971. *The Parliament of New South Wales: 1856-1965.* Government Printer, Sydney.

Howard Tanner and Associates, 1983. *Report on Sydney's oldest fire station,* North Sydney.

Hughes, A, 1981. Conservation and restoration program, Headquarters Fire Station, 213 Castlereagh St., Sydney. Unpublished BArch thesis, University of Sydney.

Hughes, C and Graham, B D, 1968. *Australian Government and Politics: 1890-1964.* ANU Press, Canberra.

Hurstville Council, 1937. *The jubilee history of the Municipality of Hurstville.* Municipality of Hurstville.

Jervis, J, (1952). 'Notes and Queries', *Royal Australian Historical Society Journal* 39(3): 151.

Kelly, M (ed.), 1978. *Nineteenth-century Sydney.* Sydney University Press, Sydney.

_____ and Crocker, R, 1978. *Sydney takes shape.* Doak Press, Sydney.

Larcombe, F A, 1970. *The history of Botany 1788-1970.* Council of the Municipality of Botany.

Lynch, W B and Larcombe, F A, 1959. *Randwick 1859-1959.* Municipality of Randwick.

Marrickville Municipal Council, 1956. *A history of the Municipality of Marrickville to commemorate the 75th anniversary, 1861-1936.* Marrickville Municipal Council.

Marryatt, H W, 1971. *Fire-automatic sprinkler performance in Australia and New Zealand 1886-1968.* Australian Fire Protection Association, Melbourne.

Mayfield, H, 1978. *Servant of a century—first 100 years of the Mercantile Mutual Insurance Company.* Mercantile Mutual Insurance Company.

Metropolitan Fire Brigade. *Annual Reports 1884-1909.*

Neutze, M, 1977. *Urban development in Australia.* George Allen & Unwin, Sydney.

Page, M and Bryant, M, 1983. *Muscle and pluck forever: the South Australian Fire Service 1840-1982.* South Australian Metropolitan Fire Service, Adelaide.

Parker, R S and Troy, P N (eds), 1972. *The politics of urban growth.* Australian National University Press, Canberra.

Poulsen, M and Spearritt, P, 1981. *Sydney: a social and political atlas.* George Allen & Unwin, Sydney.

Report from the Board Appointed to Enquire into the Best Means of Affording a Supply of Pure Water to the City of Sydney. *NSWVP* 1852 (1).

Royal Commission of Inquiry, 1911. *Report* (of inquiry) into certain matters in connection with the administration of the Fire Brigades Act. *NSWPP.*

Russell, E, 1966. *Willoughby: a centenary history, 1865-1965.* Municipality of Willoughby.

Select Committee, 1854. *Report.* On Fire Brigade Bill. *NSWPP* 1854.

_____ 1876. *Report.* To make better provision for the extinction of fires. *NSWPP* 1876 (26).

_____ 1908. *Report.* To inquire as to the dangers to which Sydney and its suburbs are liable from fire, and as to what means of control or prevention would be practicable for the future. *NSWPP* 1908.

_____ 1939. *Report.* Working Conditions of the Employees of the Board of Fire Commissioners. *NSWPP* 1939.

Sparks, N G, 1907. *Firemen's manual.* Metropolitan Fire Brigades Board, Sydney.

Spearritt, P, 1978. *Sydney since the twenties.* Hale and Iremonger, Sydney.

Sub-committee, 1905. *Report.* Theatre fire safety.

Superintendent's Report to Board, 1905, *contained in* BFC Correspondence Files, held at the State

Archives.
Sydney Fire Establishment (Insurance Brigade), 1872. *Annual Report* Sydney.
The first century: the United Insurance Company Ltd. 1862–1962. United Insurance Company.
'The future of Australian architecture—III: a review of the work of architects Spain, Cosh and Minnett, of Sydney'—editorial. *Building* 12 March 1910: 38–43.
Tuck, F A, 1895. Diary of probationary fireman, Headquarters. Unpublished. Family collection (supplied by F Johnson).
Turner, I, 1969. *Sydney's burning: an Australian political conspiracy.* Alpha, Sydney.
Weirick, J, 1976. 'Editorial', *Building Ideas* 6(1).
Wilenski, P, 1977. *Direction for change: interim report of the review of New South Wales Government Administration.* Government Printer, Sydney.
Woollahra Municipal Council, 1960. *The history of Woollahra: a record of events from 1978 to 1966 and a centenary of local government.* Woollahra Municipal Council.
Wotherspoon, G (ed.), 1983. *Sydney's transport: studies in urban history.* Hale and Iremonger, Sydney.

OTHER SOURCES
Archival Material
Blacktown Council *Minutes*.
Board of Fire Commissioners of NSW. Newspaper Clipping Service 1866–1960. State Archives.
____ Records, Minutes and Correspondence. Records Branch and State Archives.
____ *Manuals of Instruction*. 1962, 1975 and 1981.
City of Sydney Archives, 1842–43. Book 21:576.
Metropolitan Fire Brigades Board, 1909. List of stations, appliances, fire alarms, permanent men and volunteers.
Sutherland Council *Minutes*.
Upton, W., 1983. Correspondence, 6 October. Public Buildings Research Section, Government Architects Office.

Government Publications
New South Wales Parliament Debates (NSWPD).
New South Wales Parliament Papers (NSWPP).
New South Wales Votes and Proceedings (NSWVP).

Legislation
Acts of the New South Wales Parliament (as amended).
Architects Act 1923.
Bush and Rural Fire Prevention Orders 1944.
Bush Fires Act 1930.
Careless Use of Fires Act 1912.
Child Welfare Act 1939.
City of Sydney Building Act 1837. An Act for regulating Buildings and Party-walls and for preventing mischiefs by Fire in the Town of Sydney.
City of Sydney Improvement Act 1879.
Explosives Act 1905.
Factories, Shops and Industries Act 1962.
Fire Brigade Bill 1854. For the Formation and Regulation of a Fire Brigade and to authorise the destruction of buildings with a view to preventing the extension of fires within the City of Sydney.
____ 1855.
Fire Brigades Bill 1872.
____ 1876.
____ 1881.
____ 1883.
Fire Brigades Act 1884. An Act to make better provision for the protection of Life and Property from Fire and for other purposes. [24 January 1884], NSW Public Statutes, Government Printer, 1886.
____ 1909 (and By-laws as amended).
Gunpowder and Explosives Act 1876.
Height of Buildings Act 1912.
Inflammable Liquids Act 1915.
Kerosene Act 1871.
Liquefied Petroleum Gas Act 1961.
Local Government Act 1919.
Maritime Services Act 1935.
Private Hospitals Act 1908.
Public Hospitals Act 1929.
Real Property Act 1925.
Shop and Factories Act 1896.
Sydney Harbour Trust Act 1901.
Theatres and Public Halls Act 1908. Act No 13. Statutes of NSW, Government Printer, 1909.

Serial Publications
Australian Insurance and Banking Record
Australian Town and Country Journal
Daily Telegraph
Direct Action
Empire
Evening News
Fire News. Official Journal of the New South Wales Fire Brigades, 1955–1983. Also named *Fire Service*, 1955–56, and *Fire*, 1957–67.
Firefighter. Official Journal of the New South Wales Fire Brigade Employees' Union.
Guardian
Illustrated Sydney News
Melbourne Punch
North Shore Times
Sands Sydney Directories
Sun
Sunday Guardian
Sunday Times
Sydney Gazette
Sydney Mail
Sydney Morning Herald
Sydney Punch
Wentworth Courier
Wheels

ACKNOWLEDGEMENTS
Board of Fire Commissioners of NSW
President: P Gallagher
Deputy-President: K Klugman
Insurance Company Representatives: R Down, A Roger
Local Government Representative: B Lewis

Volunteer Firemen Representative: A McMurtrie
Permanent Firemen Representative: W Rogers

Staff

Secretary: J Galbraith
Chief Officer: R Threlfo

R Ahern, G Arrowsmith, R Atkinson, H Bailey, A Baker, B Baker, O Barton, V Bayliss, J Boath, K Bowman, K Bradey, R Bradley, W Brownjohn, G Buchtman, J Cadger, K Collett, J Collins, J Cooper, R Cooper, T Dawes, M Des Fosses, S Desilva, R Dobson, D Dostine, M Driscoll, S Dubrovich, P Dunstan, D Eadie, S Edwards, W Edwards, A Fien, G Fisher, R Fox, R Freeman, A Gallego, T Gavan, M Gibson, E Goodman, G Gosch, R Goudie, G Haines, T Hamon, G Hilder, C Holcroft, S/O Johnson, E Johnstone, P Kennedy, A Lewis, A Liddiard, P Lau, G Louis, J Lynne, J Lyras, C McCombe, R MacDonald, A McGrath, R Manser, N Martin, W Meehan, J Morris, T Mlynarz, A Newton, R Norton, W O'Brien, D Pendergast, R Rabbidge, N Ransom, W Richardson, S O Roberts, W Rogers, W Rowlings, B Roy, A Schwer, E Shenton, R Stein, L Sutton, N Sweatman, R Templeman, D Thomas, K Tyrrell, K Valentine, A Voysey, R Weir, B Winch, B Winters, S Woods

Former Staff

S Archer, J Ball, A Barnes, W Beare, A Broadhurst, P Bullock, P Couch, B Davies, J Ford, S Giles, K Griffiths, B Harcus, G Hinton, R Hopping, M Hunt, A Jacobson, S Johnson, B Jones, V Lowther, J McNamara, K Magor, C Milledge, J Morris, J Nance, L Pickering, J Poupart, W Rodney, C Rose, W Seghers, M Stolmack, J Telford, J Vincent, D A Webb, W Weston, W Wiggins, N Winter

Urban Research Unit, ANU

S Craig, P Denoon, W Dziubinski, P Troy, J Wells

George Allen & Unwin

R Black, J Iremonger, J Vago

NSW Fire Brigade Employees Union

F Bryce, D Ford

NSW Fire Service Museum

B Blunt, B Dalton, S Feirson, A Hughes

Archives/Organisations

Art Gallery of New South Wales, Australia Post, Australian Broadcasting Commission, Australian Gas Light (R Broomham), Blacktown Historical Society, Bushfire Council of NSW, City of Sydney Council (J Howse), Department for Police and Emergency Services, Department of Tourism, Government Architects Office (W Upton), Government Printing Office (A Clifford), Howard Tanner and Associates, Insurance Council of Australia, Insurance Institute of New South Wales (R McPherson), Josef Leboric Gallery, Macleay Museum, University of Sydney (C Snowdon), Maritime Services Board, Mercantile Mutual Insurance Company, Metropolitan Water, Sewerage and Drainage Board, Mitchell Library, National Trust Centre, Roberts and Hall, St Marys Historical Society, St George Historical Society, Spain, Stewart and Lind, Stanton Library, State Archives Office, State Library, State Rail Authority, Sydney City Library, Westpac (L Milton)

Photography

R Berg, B Chandler, R Cooper, L Danieli, P Dunstan, D Eastwood, T Gavan, V Giles, G Hall, C Holcroft, D Horne, Jadon, K Jeffcoat, Kerry collection, R Orrell, J Park, WSF Pascoe, W Rowlings, Studio Commercial (R Freer, M Thorpe, S Stafford)

Councils

Blacktown, Burwood, City of Sydney, Fairfield, Hurstville, Marrickville, Mosman, North Sydney, Penrith, Randwick, Sutherland, Warringah, Waverley, Willoughby, Woollahra

Individuals

G Adams, Mr Boland, D Brown, P Burke, W Chapman, A Evans, D Flack, C H Franks, H Gerard, P Grattan-Smith, G Griese, Mr Johns, F Johnson, M Newman, Mrs Old, Mr and Mrs C Redknap, K Richards, Mr Roberts, M Simpson, W Spratt, R Trevan, P Ulrichsen, M Webster

Picture Credits

Albury Border Morning Mail, 232; W Beare, 52; R Bradley, 255; J Cadger and Gibbs family, 20, 74; Consolidated Press, front jacket, end papers, 199, 208, 212, 214 (bottom), 216, 217 (top), 224, 259 (bottom); Council of the City of Sydney, 92; Dixson Galleries, 29, 32 (top); Fairfax Press, 13, 67, 133, 136 (bottom), 144, 152, 154, 164 (top), 172, 176, 193, 207 (left), 215, 219, 220, 221, 231, 247 (right), 251 (top); Fire Museum, 15, 25, 44, 113; D Flack, 63; J Ford, 54, 130; Foster Collection (Mitchell Library), 200, 201; C H Franks, 116, 145; Mr Gerard, 121; A Goodsell, 246 (bottom); Government Printer, 78 (top), 84, 144, 156; K Griffiths, 68; Hall and Company, 149; R Hopping, 186; F Johnson, 114, 163 (top); M Lamb, 123 (bottom), 227 (top); Macleay Museum, 88, 244, 252; K Magor, 136 (top), 146 (bottom), 150, 170 (bottom), 226; C Milledge, 206; Mitchell and State Libraries, 17, 24, 30, 31, 42, 65 (right), 160, 190, 194, 196, 251 (top); R Newton, 119; M Newman, 19, 32 (bottom left), 33; D Pendergast, 122; Penrith City Council, 256 (bottom); Randwick Municipal Council, 256 (top); W Rodney, 99 (top), 253 (bottom), 257; Sands Directory, 27, 36; W Seghers, 249 (top); Stanton Library, 111; M H Streeton, 6; Tyrell family, 169, 171, 178; Webb family, 51, 78 (top), 81, 90, 92 (bottom), 117, 120, 160, 165 (top), 248, 250 (bottom); Westpac, 76 (top); D Williams–McKenzie, 217 (bottom); Willoughby Library, 158 (above), 247 (bottom left)

All remaining illustrations are the copyright of the Board of Fire Commissioners of NSW.

INDEX

aerial appliances 140, 187-9, 219, 221, *see also* ladders, *140, 188*
Ager W 37, *242*
air raid precautions 66, 147-9, 155
Albertson K 211
Albion Brigade 111
Alexandria Brigade 87, 96, 101, 106, 111, 152, 154, 158
Alexandria Training College 139-41, *139*
Andrews B 50, 104, *242*
Annandale Brigade 95, 101, 154
architects 92, 95-100, 105-6, 234; *see also* Government architect; *64, 249*
Armidale Brigade 126, 202-4, *203*
Arncliffe Brigade 89, 100, 101, 154, *244*
arson 12, 16, 30, 193, 198-9, 209, 219, 221, 232-3
Arthur G S *39*
asbestos suits 130, 207
Ashfield Brigade 87, 92, 100, 158, 194
Auburn Brigade 97, 234, *245*
Australian Capital Territory 50, 184
automatic fire alarms 62, 65, 67-9, 71, 77, 204, 224, *see also* telephone fire alarms
Avalon Brigade 105-6, *103*

Baber A 122
Bain R 161
Baker G J 240
Balmain Brigade 83, 86, 96, 111, 121, 218, *255*
band 49, 55, 126, 134-5, 139, 146-7, 155 195, 235, *135, 146*
Bankstown Brigade 95, 105, 221
Barber B L 132
Barber H R 136-7, 211, *136*
Barnaby J W 132
Barry Z 38, 41, 43, 51, *242*
Baulkham Hills Brigade 98
Bear W 37, 58, 81, 85, 112-5, 120, 158, 193, 230, *115*
Beare J C 52-3, *52*
Beare W H 51, 53, 102, 115, 132, 151, 153, 202, *52*
Beare W R 52-3, *52*
Beecroft Brigade 95, 148
Bennett J 211
Bennetts J 50
Berowra Brigade 104-5, 137
Beswick J F 42, *240*
Bexley Brigade 89, 100-1, 152, 154
Blacktown Brigade 103-4, 107, 221, 234
Blanchard R 50
Board; borrowing 40, 43-6, 51;

Chairman/President 37, 39-41, 241; expenditure 38, 45, 55, 101, 105, 126, 223, 242-4; funding 36, 38, 40, 43-6, 49, 55, 86, 105, 131, 230, 242-4; representation 33, 36-7, 39-45, 47, 49, 50-1, 54, 85, 104, 112, 131, 153, 227, 230, 238-41, Secretary 37-8, 40, 43, 241; *34, 35, 39, 47*
Board of Fire Commissioners of NSW 39-55, 118, 238-41
Bolton E 209
Bondi Brigade 100
Bone A 37
Booker G A 235
Botany Brigade 211, *246*
Bourke W 50
Bown C 22, 27, 33, 36-7, 41-2, 161-2, 230, 235, *39, 87, 161*
Bown T J 16-8, 22, 26-7, 37, 39, 118, 161, 189, 234, *27*
bravery awards 54, 126, 204, 209, 214-5, 219, 221, 261-2, *see also* medals
breathing apparatus 55, 65-7, 69, 72, 73, 147, 170, 189, 206, 208, 211, 221, *see also* smoke helmets, *67*
Brett S 197
Brewer E W 50
Broadhurst family 96, 234
Brock 216
Brown E 169, 195, *6*
Brown W 239
Bryce F 54
building codes 14, 16, 18, 36, 58, 59, 63, 71, 73, 113, 141, 193-4, 197, 218, *65, 224*
Bundeena Brigade 105
Burwood Brigade 87, 96, 97, 111, 158, *108*
Busby Brigade 104
Bush Fire Committee/Council 50, 67, 70-1, 103, 136, 153
bush fires 11, 55, 67, 94, 104, 136, 179-80, 184, 207, 209, 230-1, *231*
Butcher C 211, *42*
Butler G M 50
Button N 70
by-laws 44, 46, 62-3, 66

Cabramatta Brigade 103, *246*
Caller G 99
Camb W 28, 33, *20*
Camden Brigade 105, 173
Cameron D 209, *262*
Campbell A H 47, 206
Campbelltown Brigade 38, 87, 103, 105, *246*
Campsie Brigade 92, 96, 100
Canterbury Brigade 96, 100-1, 154,

169-70
Caringbah Brigade 101-2, *247*
Carruthers A G 219
Castle Hill Brigade 101
Challis G 122
Chapple 169
Chatswood Brigade 87, 100-1, 138, 150, 154, *247*
Cheal H 122
chemicals *72-3*
Chief Officers 259
Chief Secretary *see* Colonial Secretary
Church W 37, 239
Circular Quay Brigade 81, 83-4, 91, 116, 169, 172, 195, 199, 235, *84, 247*
City Brigade 28, 111
Clarke M 37
Clarke W 45
Clay H 133
Cobb G 194
Coghlan F 41, 96
Coghlan H 122-3
Collins E *240*
Colonial Architect *see* Government Architect
Colonial Secretary 37-8, 40, 112, 114, 132, 134, 147, 152, 155, *47*
Commissions/Committee of Inquiry 41-2, 52-3, 55, 60, 71, 96, 131, 139, 147-8, 230
communications 55, 61-2, 68-71, 77, 98, 104, 110-1, 148, 151, 228-9, *58, 61, 62, 68, 229*
Concord Brigade 97
Concord West Brigade 169
concourse duty 68, 134
Condon 207
Cooper W 122
country fire boards 38-40
Craig J 206
Cranney J 131
Cribben E 211
Cronulla Brigade 102-3, 106-7, 173, *107*
Crows Nest Brigade 89, 96, 138, 148, 172, 209, 218, 234
Cruise W J 153
Cruse R 155
Crum V 141
Cummings J/R 150-1, *150*
Cunningham A 50, 104
Currer 132, 207
Cutts T G 119, 122, 194, 235

Dadd G 116, 119, *255*
Dakin Captain 42
Darling J 150
Darlinghurst Brigade 86, 89-91, 172,

208-9, 219, 234, *91*
Davies D 206
Davies F 137-9, 218

Dawes H T 98-9
Dawson J 114
deaths 191-221, 259-61
Dee Why Brigade 97
Deputy Chief Officers 259
Devenport H *95*
Devlin J 146-7, 235, *146*
Digby C *119*
Douglas T S 124, *240*
Dowling G 214-5
Down R *240*
Doyle W 214-5, *215*
drill 78, 116-7, 155, *117*
Drummoyne Brigade 89, 148, 152, 217, *85*
Dudman G 219
Duff L E 49-50, 102, 134-5, 197
Dwyer 169

Eadie G 235
East Willoughby Brigade *158*
Eastwood Brigade 95, 148
Edge J 132, 208
Edwards C *49*
electrician 38, 62-3, 68, 70, 131, 162, 234
Enfield Brigade 89, 101, 154, *248*
Engadine Brigade 104, 106, 137, 139
Equal Employment Opportunities Legislation 151, 233
Eustace C 129
Evans H 47, 134, 141
Evans N 208-9
explosives 37, 126

Fairfield Brigade 98, 123, 221
Fallon G 206
false alarms 65, 71, 193, 198
Farrer E H 41, 43-4, 95, *44*
Fawcett R 206
Featherstone 208
Fire Brigade Employees Conciliation Committee 124, 130
Fire Brigades 244-58, *31*: country 38-40, 50, 67, 118, 121, 126, 151, 172-3, 180, 184, 186-7, 202-4, 206, *see also* Individual Names
Fire Brigades Association *see* Fire Brigades Employees Union
Fire Brigades Employees Union 42-9, 54, 71, 96, 100, 103-4, 119, 123-5, 129-34, 137-9, 141, 144, 148, 153, 155, 226-7, 230-2, 235, *42, 129*
fire engines 43, 89, 94-5, 98-9, 106, 120, 126, 148, 151-2, 156-89, 199-200, 204-5, 235-6, *156-89;* manual 4, 13, 16, 17, 18-9, 26, 34, 78, 110, 113, 117, 157-8, 161, 167, 169, 173, 189, 234, 263, *4, 17, 19, 158;* steam 10, 22-3, 26-7, 78, 83, 98-9, 110, 115, 118, 156-74, 193, 195-96, 198, 200, 228, 235, 255, 263, *10, 34, 156-74*

fire escapes 66, 197
firefighters 51, 53, 115, 118, 148, 151, 197; deaths 259-61, *6, 260;* hours 45, 47, 98-101, 108-41, 148, 153-4, 227, 232, 235; pay 53, 115, 119, 123-4, 130-1, 134-5, 137, 141, 148-9; ranks 47-8, 53-4, 96, 108-41, 147; reserve 68, 134, 147-8, 150-2, 155, 262, *152;* staffing 45, 52, 75-107, 108-41, 148, 154, 262; training 55, 101, 108-41, 232, *139, 140;* working conditions 46-9, 53, 75-107, 108-41, 144, 147, 148, 226-7
fire floats 38, 81, 148, 170-1, 198-200, 207, 217-8, 234, *170, 212, 217*
firemarks 18, *15*
Fire Museum 63, 174, 187, 235
fire pole 77, 235, *247*
fire prevention 12, 44, 57-73, 114, 120-1, 136-7, 141, 194, 224, 228, 230
fires 191-221, 263-4; Adams Cafe 169; *Ann Jamison* 13; Anthony Horderns 60, 162, 191, 195-8, *190-1, 196, 197;* Australian Wool Stores 191, 212, *214; Bellubera* ferry 130, 206-7; Blackwell Wool Stores *24;* Braund's Produce Store (Armidale) 126, 202-4, *203;* Buckinghams *cover, end pages; Canberra* 199; Castlemaine Brewery 28; *HMS Dromedary* 13; Dunlopillo 211; Fairfax Newsprint 215, 217-8, *217;* Gibbs Bright & Co. 195; Garden Palace Fire 191, *29;* George Hudson Timber Yard 174, *200;* George St West Fire Station 195; Gibbs Chambers 209-10, *210;* Goldsbrough Mort 174, 191, 204-6, *205;* Great Fire of Sydney 59, 191-5, *192, 193, 194;* Hardwicke House 204; Harpoon Harrys 218; Her Majesty's Theatre 30, 61, 215, *197;* Hornsby Fire Station 72, 216-7, *216;* IWW 198; John Lawlers 195; Jones Kerosene Bond 58; Luna Park 221; Lyceum Theatre 211; *SS Marine Discoverer* 211; Metters 200-1, *201;* Mobil Oil, Pulpit Point 191, *212; SS Ormonde* 206; Pacific Heights Nursing Home 221; Pastoral Finances Association 204, *199; Port Jackson* clipper 195; Prince of Wales Theatre 22, 30; Rembrandt 221, *220;* Revlon Australia 211; Savoy Hotel 218; Saxton and Binns 198; St Mary's Cathedral *22;* St Phillips Church 12; Strand Arcade 218; *Tarakan* HMAS 130, 208; Theatre Royal & Hotel 16, 19, 30, 118, 195; Tooth & Company Brewery 18; Ultimo 218, *219;* Variety Theatre 209; Vauxhall House 202; Victoria Theatre *30;* Wentworth House 159; Wiltshire (Parramatta) Wheatfields 12; Wynyard Building 200

fire stations 45, 75-107, 154, 224-6, *21*
Fisher P 58, *113*
Five Dock Brigade 89, 101, 134, 151, 154
Flyer 208, *125, 171, 178, 185*
Ford J F Jnr 50, 54, 70, 129, 133, 211, 235
Ford J F Snr 54, 116, 121-2, 194
Ford L 126
Franks C D 122, *145*
Freeman A G 219
Freshwater Brigade 94-5, 169

Galbraith J *240*
Gallagher P 55, *240*
Garvin B 221
General Post Office Brigade 4
George Street West Brigade 81, 92, 96, 101, 116, 148, 158, 169, 172, 194-5, 217, 235, *80*
Gerard A *121*
Gibbs A *74*
Giles S 133, 235
Gilmour G M 67, 132, 136
Gladesville Brigade 89, 169, 212
Glebe Brigade 26, 28, 89, 111, 209, 211
Gordon Brigade 95, 216, *249*
Gorman T 116
Gosling R T 50
Government Architect 76, 83, 86, 88-9, 91
Graham J 119
Granville Brigade 85, 87, 101, 154, *86*
Granville Disaster 219
Green T 162
Griffen M L 155
Griffiths E 102, 115, 130-3, 207-8, *130*
Griffiths K 70, 131
Grimmond G 96, 129, 204
Guildford Brigade 95, 169

Hanslow S 209
Harbord Brigade 94-5, 101, 148, 154, *94, 95*
Harkness E 43, 94
Harper G 122
Harris 16, 17
Hart A 167
Hawkins 209
Headquarters Brigade 40-1, 59, 61, 66, 70, 75-9, 81, 88-9, 92, 96, 98, 102, 116, 118, 125-6, 128, 130-2, 137, 145, 148, 151, 155, 158, 160, 162, 167-73, 178, 180, 184-5, 187, 193, 199, 202, 208-9, 211-2, 218-9, 221-2, 234-5, *1, 76, 77, 78, 79, 165, 168, 172, 173, 222, 250-1*
Hellmrich C 79, 83, 86
helmets 137, 155, *2, 136, 142, 203*
Hinchcliffe N G 50
Hinchy W 26
Hodgson C 127
Holdom C 50

270 / *Fighting Fire!*

Homebush Brigade 97, 101, 154, *250*
Hook & Ladder Brigade 28, 33, 37, 111
Hopping R 133, 186
Horan J 37
Hornsby Brigade 72, 96, 148, 216-7, 221, *216*
horses 78, 79, 92, 98-9, 158-70, 173, 228, *108*
hose 78-9, 85, 96, 110, 117-8, 147, 152, 158, 160-1, 169-70, 173, 180, 184 *74, 158, 160, 161*
Hubbard R 186
Hulbert F 133
Hunter A 206
Hunters Hill Brigade 89, 95, 101, 154
Hurstville Brigade 86, 92, 98, 100
Hudson's Volunteer Brigade 28
hydrants 59, 66, 69, 132, *see also* water supply

In-orders 120
Institute of Fire Engineers 54, 133-4
Insurance Companies 14, 16-8, 20, 26, 28-9, 36-8, 43-4, 50-2, 58, 100, 118, 126, *see also* Board representation, Board funding; *36*
Insurance Companies Brigade 17, 22-30, 33, 36, 39, 59, 115, 118, 156, 160, 195, 263, *76*
Interstate Fire Brigade Conference 38

Jackson F 45, 116, 119, 122-3, 125, 128, 199, *43, 123*
Jacobson A 211, 219
James C 50
Jeffcoat K 202
Jenkins R 69
Jones B 126, 202-4
Jones W 122
Jordan S 47, 153

Kelly A *39*
Kelly W S 33, 36
King G 145
Kinnear J 133
Kippax W 37
Klugman K *240*
Knight G 185
Knowles D 208-9, *208*
Knox C 209
Kogarah Brigade 86, 96, 100, 128, 148, 235

ladders 78, 83, 98, 104, 117, 126, 155, 159-63, 167-72, 178-80, 184, 187-9, 193, 195-7, 202, 204-5, 209, 211, 217-9, 235, *159, 163, 168, 172, 176, 180*
Lakemba Brigade 96
Lambert J 47, 153

Lambourne J 96, 122
Lane Cove Brigade 95, 138, 217
Lang G 116
lease-lend agreement 152, 178, *142*
legislation 24, 28, 29, 31, 34, 36, 38, 40, 46, 48, 50-2, 87, 100, 118, 131, 134, 153, 224, 230, 238; building 16, 19, 37, 60, 63, 65, 67, 69, 71, 109, 137, 202 *see also* building codes; bush fires 67, 71, 153, 179, 231; fire prevention 55-73, 109; harbour waters 38, 81, 148, 230-1, 234; theatres 30, 61, 65, 71, 120
Leichhardt Brigade 88-9, 158, 218, 252, *88*
Lewis B *240*
Lewis R 209
Lidcombe Brigade 87, 97, 168-9, *253*
Lister 96
Liverpool Brigade 87, 103, 106-7, 170, 180, 221, 234, *74*
Local Councils *see* Board
Love E 37, 41, 85, *39*
Lowther V 133, 136-8, 187
Lucas N 178

McCarthy J 200
McCoy R 37
McEachin J 200
McGrath J S 134-5, 208-9, *259*
Mackenzie M 47
McMahon B 17
McMurtrie A *240*
McNamara J 44-5, 124, 131, 167, 234, *45*
McNiven W 96-8, 234, *249*
McPhee C 208-9
Macquarie Fields Brigade *105*
Magor K 131, 235
Maizey F 126, 202-4
Malabar Brigade 173
Mallam A *49*
Manly Brigade 86, 94, 96-7, 111, 148, 158, 189, *97*
Maroubra Brigade 96, 101, 154
Marrickville Brigade 100, 116, 158, *81*
Mascot Brigade 86, 92, 101, 103, 154, 168, 211
Matraville Brigade 96, 152, 169, 173, 180
medals 54, 63, 119, 121, 126, 128, 131, 137-9, 203-4, 211, 214-5, 219, 221, 261-2, *see also* bravery awards, *52*
Meeve J 54, 69, 133, 136-7, 141, 212
Menzies J 146-7, *146*
Merrylands Brigade 137-9, 235
Metropolitan Associated Fire Brigades 28-9, 37
Metropolitan Fire Brigades 30, 34-40, 57, 168, 193-4, 196-7, 238-40, *see also* Board
Military Barracks 234, *13*
Milledge C 54, 124, 128, 132-4, 206-7, 235, *259*
Ministerial Control 52, 54, 139, 230, 233

Miranda Brigade 106-7, 221
Morris F 235, *260*
Mortdale Brigade 95, 100-1, 137, 139, 152, 154, 164, 169, 187, 235, *253*
Mosman Brigade 96, *87*
Moss J 219
Mount Lachlan Brigade 28, 112
Mt Druitt Brigade 104-5, 187, 221
Mundey J 133, 235

Nance J 128, 133, 208
Nance T P H 96, 100, 125-6, *128*
Narrabeen Brigade 123
Neill T 150
Neutral Bay Brigade 89, 96, 100, 218
Neville J J 132, 147
Newtown Brigade 26, 28, 82-3, 113, 131, 169, 195, 211, *82*
No 1 Fire Company 20-1, 23, 28, 33, 37, 111-3, *196*
No 2 Fire Company 20-1, 23, 28, 33, 37, 110-1, 211, 235, *20*
No 3 Fire Company 26, 28, 111
No 4 Fire Company 26, 111
No 5 Fire Company 26, 111, 193
No 6 Fire Company 26
Northmead Brigade 100, 106, 137, 139, 169, 173
North City Brigade 28, 37, 111-2
North Sydney Brigade 96, 101, 154, 169, 187, 199, *86*

O'Brien W 189
O'Connel N 219
O'Keefe D 200
Oliver J 94-5, *94*
Oram E 28

Paddington Brewery Brigade 195
Paddington Brigade 28, 92, 101, 111-2, 116, 132, 148, 169, 208, *87, 112, 166, 254*
Paddington Training College 101-2, 132-4, 208, *132*
Palmer R 186
Parker H 135
Parkinson K 53
Parks G H 132
Parks T 133
Parramatta Brigade 37, 41, 87, 97, 148, 187, 214, *255*
Pascoe H 211
patrol cars 68, 132, 179
Penrith Brigade 38, 87, 105, 234, *256*
Peters J E 38
Petersham Brigade 111
Pheloung J 126, 135, 235
Phillips L 186
Pickering O 200
Piper M J 131, 153
Pitt G H 41
Plumbe D 151
Plumbe W 138, 150-1, *125, 150*
Pye H 69, 102, 134-6, 174, 211, *47*

Pyrmont Brigade 101, 103, 111, 121, 146-7, 151, 154, 174, 180, 204, *146*

Randwick Brigade 87, 89, 169, *256*
Reay M 139
Refern Brigade 87, 98-9, 106, 111, 164, 209, 211, *99, 257*
rescue role 55, 72-3, 191-221, 231, *57, 73*
Rhodes Brigade 137, 169, 235
Richardson C 66, 115, 129, 131, 153, 155, 206
Richmond Brigade 38, 87
Rigney W 194
Riverstone Brigade 105
Riley V A 50
Robinson A 215-6
Robinson W 126, 202-4
Rockdale Brigade 86, 100
Rodney B 132
Roger A *240*
Rogers W B *240*
Rookwood Brigade 87, 97, *253*
Rose C F 139
Ross F A 50, 98, 101, 104, 151, 234, *249*
Ross R K 219
Royal Alfred Australian Volunteer Fire Co. *see* No 1 Fire Co.
Rozelle Brigade 89, 96, 101, 118, 121, 154, 169
Rudd W 150
Rydalmere Brigade 103
Ryde Brigade 95, 101, 103, 154
Ryng J 235

Salter H 235
salvage 162, 167-8, 170, 173, 178-9, 184-5, 187, 189, 200, 207-9, 219, 235, *57, 168, 179*
Satchell A 139
Senior Officers Association 137-8, 147, 155, 235
Shaw A *49*
Sheddon H 42
Shelley 200, *125*
Smith B 235
Smith E 62-3, 162, 235, *63*
Smith T J 43-8, 66, 68, 134, 153, 230, *43, 45, 151, 240*
Smithfield Brigade 106
smoke helmets 59-61, 65-6, 120, 170, 206, *60, 61*
Snell T 204
South W 27, 38, *118*
Sparks N 61, 95, 115, 117, 119, 122-3, 196, 199, *39, 122, 123*
sports 54, 117, 122, 126-8, 130, 139, 145, 147, 155, 235, *117, 122, 127*
St Leonards Brigade 28, 158, *111*
St Peters Brigade 101, 154
Stanchell J 168
Standard Brewery Brigade 111-3
Stanmore Brigade 81, 148, 211, 214, *81*

State Government *see* Board
Stewart 219
Stolmack M 46, 48, 49, 141, *49*
Stoneham E 147, 162, 235
strikes 134, 153-4, *129, 154*
Superintendent 24, 34, 36-7, 259, *see also* Chief Officer
Surry Hills Brigade 28, 37, 111, 193
Suters G 150
Sutherland Brigade 102-3, 221
Sydney Fire Establishment *see* Insurance Companies Brigade

Taylor W 41, 86, *39*
telephone fire alarms 58-60, 65, 67-70, 89, 115, 149, 155, *55*
The Rocks Brigade 208-9, 234
Theatre Royal Brigade 110-1, 147, *110*
theatres 20-3, 30, 121, *see also* Fires and Legislation, theatres
Thompson L 209, 234
Threlfo R 55, 139, *141, 240*
Tinley T M *39*
Toongabbie Brigade 100, 104
Torning A 19-21, 28, 32-3, 37, 112, *19, 32, 33*
Travers G 235
Tuck F A 79, 122, 147
Tuck S A 115, 147
turncocks 17, *59*
Turramurra Brigade 96

United Volunteer Fire Brigade Association 28, 33, 37

Vaucluse Brigade 95, 154, 234, *101*
Verrills L G 50, 70
Vial W 23, 160, 235
Victoria Theatre 16, 19-20, 30, 33
Victoria Theatre Fire Co. 19-20, 33, 234, *18*
Vincent Family 234
Volunteer brigades 19-21, 23-8, 30, 33-7, 41, 59, 81, 83, 85-6, 89, 95, 103-6, 110, 115-6, 118-20, 134-5, 137-8, 158, 160, 193, 212, 223, *see also* individual brigade names
Volunteer Demonstrations 29, 53, 121, 126, 147, 173, 184, 235, *47, 227*

Walsh J 132
wars 40, 143-55, *143, 144, 145, 152*
water supply 13, 17, 22, 24, 26, 28, 30, 59, 61, 193-4, 208
water tankers 106, 179-81, 184-5, 187, 189, 216, *181, 184, 231*
Waterloo and Alexandria Brigade 28, 211
Watson H 68
Watson S 116, 119
Watt L 122
Waverley Brigade 95, 101, 111, 134, 154, 158, 234

Webb A 51, 59-60, 65, 87, 89, 95, 115, 119-21, 126, 160, 162, 171, 195, 198, 234, *39, 78*
Webb D A 50-1, 120-1, *47*
Webb H M 38, 51, 115, 120-1, 124, *43, 240*
Welsh C A 136, 211
Wentworthville Brigade 98, 100, 169, 173, *106*
Weston W 54-5, 71, 139, 141, 226, 230, 232, *242*
White W 126-7
Wiggins W O 50-1, *47, 242*
Willis J 44
Willoughby Brigade 87, 95, 169, *247*
Wilson F 122
Windsor Brigade 105
Winter A 122
Womens Fire Auxiliary 142, 148-9, 151-2, 155, *142, 149*
Woollahra Brigade 26, 28, 87-9, 100-1, 111, 132, 154, 187, *258*
Workshops 53, 68, 70-1, 78-9, 92, 96, 101, 106, 113, 128, 144, 147, 151, 159, 162, 167-8, 170, 178-9, 184, 187, 189, 228-9, 235, *116*
Wright W 150, *138*